The Morning Chronicle's

LABOUR AND THE POOR

Volume X

LIVERPOOL

The Morning Chronicle's

LABOUR AND THE POOR

VOLUME X

LIVERPOOL

CHARLES MACKAY

Edited By
Rebecca Watts & Kevin Booth

Ditto Books
www.dittobooks.co.uk

First Published by Ditto Books 2020
© Ditto Books 2020

A catalogue record for this book is available
from the British Library

ISBN 978-1-913515-10-2 (hardback)
ISBN 978-1-913515-20-1 (paperback)

Cover Image:
View of Liverpool, from the Mersey
From "The Traveller's Album and Hotel Guide"
Published 1862
Image courtesy of The British Library

"Last week I had three days' work. It was the best week I have had for six months, and I was able to get my boots out of pawn. I have got them on now, but I expect I shall have to send them back to the pawn-shop next week, if I don't get a job or two."

Contents

List of Illustrations

Preface

This work attempts to be a faithful reproduction of the "Labour and the Poor" letters as printed in *The Morning Chronicle*. Only obvious typographical errors and omissions have been corrected. Variations in the spelling and hyphenation of words have largely been retained. We hope any such inconsistencies prove to be of some historical interest to the reader.

As much as possible we have tried to recreate the original layout and styling of the text and all factual tables have been reproduced as closely to the originals as possible with only minimal alterations made where necessary to improve readability.

Not all letters were titled. Where missing we have added titles to the Table of Contents to assist navigation and explanation of content. The letters themselves are as per the originals.

A handful of illustrations have been added to each volume. These did not appear in the original text but hopefully provide added interest.

R. W.
K. B.

Introduction

In 1849 a leading London-based newspaper, *The Morning Chronicle*, undertook an investigation into the working and living conditions of the poor throughout England and Wales in the hope that their findings might lead to much needed change.

The reputed catalyst for their "Labour and the Poor" series was an article written by Henry Mayhew recording a journey into Bermondsey, one of the most deprived districts of London, which was printed in September 1849. Following this it was proposed that an in-depth investigation be carried out and "Special Correspondents", the investigators, were selected and distributed around the country. The first article or "Letter" appeared on the 18th of October 1849 and the series would run for almost 2 years and 222 letters.

The well-known and respected writers and journalists recruited for the task included Henry Mayhew who was assigned to the Metropolitan districts, Angus Bethune Reach to the Manufacturing districts, Alexander Mackay and Shirley Brooks to the Rural districts and Charles Mackay to investigate the cities of Birmingham and Liverpool. The author of the letters from Wales is as yet unknown.

The "Labour and the Poor" letters were extremely popular at the time, being widely read throughout the nation and even abroad. The revelations in them caused quite a stir amongst the middle and upper classes of Victorian society. *Letters to the Editor* poured in with donations for specific cases of distress that appeared in the letters and also for the general alleviation of the suffering of the poor. A special fund was set up by *The Morning Chronicle* to collect and distribute these donations.

These *Letters to the Editor* have been included in this series, predominantly in the Metropolitan district volumes whose letters elicited the majority of responses. They provide a unique window into the thoughts and sentiments of the Victorian readership as they react to the incredible accounts of misery and desperation being unveiled.

The Morning Chronicle's extraordinary and unsurpassed "Labour and the Poor" investigation provides an unparalleled insight into the people of the period, their living and working conditions, their feelings, their language, their sufferings and their struggles for survival amidst the poverty and destitution of 19th century Britain. An investigation of such magnitude had never before been attempted and the undertaking was truly of epic proportions. Its impact at the time was profound. Its historical importance today is without question.

LABOUR AND THE POOR.

LIVERPOOL.

[FROM OUR SPECIAL CORRESPONDENT.]

THE BURDENS UPON TOWNS.—IRISH PAUPERISM.

LETTER I.

Next to the metropolis, Liverpool is perhaps the most important town in the kingdom, whether as regards its past and present state or its future prospects. Its rapid and almost unparalleled rise from obscurity and poverty to renown and splendour, makes its past history highly interesting. Its future prospects offer quite as much to rivet attention. The undeveloped wealth of the United States and Canada—to say nothing of Mexico, Brazil, and the southern and south-western Republics—which only awaits the hand of man to call it into being and distribute it over the world, must flow, in large proportion, into Liverpool, as the great, and almost the only port by which the New World carries on its intercourse with Great Britain. So that, whether we regard Liverpool in the past, or in the present, or endeavour to portray its future state to our imagination, it is equally interesting as an object of study and speculation. In the latter point of view, there are many who consider that, great and powerful as Liverpool now is, it is destined to be yet greater and more powerful at a future time, and to rival, if not to eclipse, the grandeur of the "modern Babylon."

Liverpool, which some of the inhabitants call the "modern Tyre," was an insignificant town in the reign of Queen Elizabeth, and prayed at that time for the remission of a small tax, on the plea of its extreme poverty. It was "her Majestie's poor and decayed town of Lyverpoole," and could not pay it. Local history does not state whether the prayer was granted, and the general history of that day almost ignores the existence of such a place. In the year 1636, Liverpool had not greatly increased in wealth, if its condition may be estimated by comparison of the assessments of some other cities and towns of the kingdom in that year, towards the navy of forty ships raised for the service of King Charles I. London had to provide 7 ships, 1,560 men, and 5 months' pay for them. Bristol, 1 ship, 40 men, and £1,000 pay. Preston had to make a money payment of £40, Lancaster of £30, and Liverpool of £25 only. In 1699, Liverpool was first made a parish, and separated from the parochial jurisdiction of its small neighbour Walton, with which it had formerly been conjoined. In the following year its population was estimated at 5,714. It then possessed one dock, in process of construction. The number of ships or small vessels that traded with the port was 60, with an aggregate burthen of about 4,000 tons. From that time to the present, the history of Liverpool is a record of increasing population and prosperity. Its population at the census of 1841, amounted to 286,483. In the year 1846, when a new water act was applied for, the population, according to a careful estimate then made, was 361,128. It is now estimated at nearly 400,000, of whom it is supposed that at least 100,000 are Irish. By some it is estimated that the number of Irish is much larger than this, and that if the persons born in Liverpool of Irish parents were added, one-half of the whole population would either be Irish, or of Irish extraction.

Liverpool now possesses 22 large and commodious docks, exclusive of half-tide and graving docks, covering altogether an area of nearly 173 acres, constructed at a cost of about thirteen millions sterling, and paying for town dues an annual sum of upwards of £100,000. The net amount of town dues for the year 1849 was £101,016 14s. 6d. The total revenues of the town from all sources, for the same year, was £152,258 14s. 3d. This sum is altogether exclusive of the revenues of the Dock Trust.

The docks of Liverpool are by far the most extensive and remarkable constructions in the town. From Sandon Dock and Basin on the north, to the Brunswick Dock on the south, they extend along the Mersey for a distance of nearly four miles. The following are their names and order, from the north or entrance direction of the Mersey, southwards:—Sandon Dock and Basin, Wellington Dock and half-tide Dock, Bramley Moore Dock, Nelson Dock, Stanley Dock, Collingwood Dock, Salisbury Dock, Clarence Dock and Basin, Trafalgar Dock, Victoria Dock, Waterloo Dock and Basin, Prince's Dock and Basin, George's Dock, Canning Dock and half-tide Dock, Salthouse Dock, Albert Dock, King's Dock, Queen's Dock, Union Dock, Coburg Dock, and Brunswick Dock. Another dock has been planned, and is now in process of construction. The total revenues of the dock estate, of which a statement is annually laid before the public, amounted from the 24th of June, 1848, to the 24th of June,

1849, to £748,594 3s. 2d. The vessels that cleared inwards in the same year were 20,733, and their tonnage was 3,639,146 tons.

The national revenue, in the shape of Customs Duties, levied at Liverpool, amounted in the year ending on the 31st of December, 1849, to £3,474,224, exclusive of £300,000 levied in Manchester on goods imported into Liverpool. These extensive docks, and this vast trade, in addition to the direct and indirect employment given to a multitude of persons in almost every department of manual and intellectual labour, give direct occupation to large bodies of men in the loading and discharging of ships, and in the porterage of their cargoes from the quays to the lofty bonded and free warehouses that line the shore, or to the private warehouses of the merchants and consignees in various parts of the town. The number of "dock labourers" and operative porters who gain their subsistence either by loading and discharging vessels or by working on the quays is—as nearly as can be ascertained, for no record is kept of them in any of the public offices of the town, and no license is required for their business—from 14,000 to 18,000. In the year 1846, when tickets were issued, the numbers were ascertained to exceed 14,000. It is calculated that the almost daily arrival of Irish labourers, fit for strong work, if for nothing else, has added since that time at least 3,000, and probably 4,000, men to their number. The present condition of these 18,000 men—representing, with their families (calculating on an average each household at four persons), no less than 72,000 individuals—the misery in which they live, the keen struggle for employment in which they are daily engaged, the competition of the unskilled against the skilled porters, and the grievances of which the older and better members of the body complain, between the "lumpers" and "master porters" on the one hand and the "Grecians" or unskilled Irish on the other, will form the subject of future letters.

The stranger in Liverpool cannot but be strongly impressed by its activity, bustle and opulence. A walk along the extensive line of its magnificent docks, impeded now and then, as it is sure to be, by the raising of the drawbridges for the entrance and departure of ships, many of them of 1,000 and 1,200 tons burden, will fill the mind of any ordinary spectator with genuine admiration of the industry, energy, and successful enterprise of which the tangible results surround him wherever he casts his eyes. The Mersey swarms with ships, and the immense line of docks is so closely packed with vessels as to appear at some little distance to form a compact mass, dense as a forest of tall pines in an untrodden wilderness. The imagination is confused by their number and complexity, and endeavours in vain to place an intelligible and calculable money-value upon such aggregations of riches. The quays and streets are even busier than the docks, and are filled with innumerable carts and waggons, passing to and fro in all directions. Some of them, and by far the greater proportion, are laden with huge bales of cotton, destined to feed the hungry mills of Yorkshire and Lancashire; others with sacks of grain from the fertile valleys of the western world; others, again, with barrels of pork and provisions from New York; others, but in smaller numbers, with rum casks and sugar hogsheads from the West Indies; and large numbers of carts, with immense wheels of eight or nine feet in diameter, with enormous logs of timber from the forests of Canada and New Brunswick. The quays, in addition to these moving vehicles, are lined with carts and "lorries" waiting to be hired. They may be counted at times by hundreds in a string, each with its couple of strong horses and strong men. At every corner sturdy fellows are to be seen employed at porter's work; and also at every corner are men waiting for porterage, which they are not always fortunate enough to procure, though they may wait for a month in daily succession. The splendid bonded and free warehouses along the line of the river, behind and around the docks—many of them seven or eight stories in height—complete the effect of the busy scene. Some of these are silent enough, like boa-constrictors that have eaten their dinners. It is the silence of repletion, and their doors and windows are only closed because they are "choke-full" of merchandise, and can contain no more under the penalty of bursting. Others show signs of activity. They are in the process of being gorged, and keep the pulleys busily at work, whilst up to the second, third, fourth, or fifth stories, or to 80 or a 100 feet above the head of the passenger, the operative porters and other labourers haul up the plethoric cotton-bales, or barrels of provisions and stores, to their temporary destination. If the stranger turns from the docks and walks into the town, the signs of its flourishing condition are equally apparent. It is not so much the beauty and wealth of the shops, or the crowds in the streets, but the new and splendid public and private buildings in course of erection in almost every part of the town, which prove, without necessity of further evidence, that Liverpool is highly prosperous and well inclined to expend its superabundant wealth in luxury and adornment.

This is but one side of the medal. This rich, enterprising, and increasing town is oppressed with pauperism, and contains moreover a large population of working men but little removed above pauperism, in daily danger of sinking into it—discontented with their lot—living precariously at most times—dependent upon the wind for the chance of procuring a subsistence; and forming a class which, though naturally laborious, honest, and well-inclined, needs but little provocation, of ill treatment on the one hand, or of severe distress on the other, to become dangerous. Liverpool is furthermore oppressed by a grievous, if not intolerable, burden, which bears with almost fatal weight upon the middle classes, who form the great majority of the ratepayers, and with much severity even upon the richer class of inhabitants. Though not the nearest, it is the most convenient, and by far the richest, port towards Ireland. The consequence is that the wretched people of that country, to whom a shilling a day is high wages, swarm into England by way of Liverpool, and inflict the injury of their presence upon that town in the first instance. They stay as long as they can in search of work or charity, thence spread themselves through England when work fails, and ultimately return to Liverpool to be maintained as paupers, or to be reconveyed, at the expense of that town, to their own country. A great deal has been said lately of the burdens upon LAND. Without entering upon that question at all, I shall endeavour to show, in the sequel of this letter, a few of the burdens upon this town consequent upon its proximity to Ireland, to say nothing of any other burdens of which it may reasonably or unreasonably complain. Liverpool in this respect is peculiarly unfortunate, and shares with Glasgow the distinction of possessing a larger Irish population than any Irish town—Dublin, Cork, and Belfast excepted—and with Bristol as well as Glasgow, the unenviable distinction of being compelled to maintain an amount of Irish pauperism, or to pay charges on account of Irish paupers, almost equal in amount to the sums which it is called upon to expend on its own poor.

In my inquiries into the state of "Labour and the Poor" in Liverpool, the Irish question must be the first in importance. The town of Liverpool feels, through the sensitive medium of the pocket, that it has to pay a large price for the privilege of being the greatest port in the west, and that its advantages in being the outlet to America are nearly counterbalanced by its disadvantages in being the inlet from Ireland. The "Irish difficulty" may puzzle statesmen, and increase the National Debt; but the people of Liverpool, in addition to being as much, if not more, puzzled than statesmen, and in addition to paying their share of the general taxation which provides for the interest on the National Debt, have their own peculiar burden in bearing a larger share of the support of Irish pauperism than any town in England. I shall pass no opinion upon the matter, but confine myself to the bare statement of the facts of the case—facts collected and verified with the utmost possible care, and with the most earnest desire to state the simple truth, and no more.

The subject has many ramifications. *First*, there is the cost in the workhouse of the Irish poor, who may be considered to have a real industrial settlement; *secondly*, there is the cost of out-door relief to the Irish poor; *thirdly*, there is the cost of sanitary arrangements—no inconsiderable item—which the pressure of vast numbers of Irish living in the extreme of dirt, disease, and misery, entails upon the town; *fourthly*, there is the expense of Irish vagrants, tramps, and casual poor; *fifthly*, there is the distress caused among the steady labourers of the town, many of them householders and ratepayers, by the overwhelming numbers of utterly superfluous Irishmen that compete with them for bread, and sometimes force them upon the parish; *sixthly*, there is the largely increased amount of expenditure for the police force and the criminal judicature consequent upon the crime that is the result of the extreme poverty and degradation of this mass of unemployed men and women; *seventhly*, there is the expense of annually passing over to the nearest port in Ireland vast numbers of Irish, who congregate in Liverpool from all parts of the kingdom for the express purpose of being sent home again at the public expense. I have no means of arriving at a strictly accurate estimate under all these various heads. As regards some of them, no estimate is possible; but as regards two or three of them, the statistics are precise enough, and will be precisely stated. Whenever a speculative approximation is made in default of sufficient data, I will state that it is an approximation only and leave the reader to decide upon its probable correctness.

Upon the first head, I am enabled to speak exactly, having been favoured with extracts from the parochial books and with other authentic information. I should premise that these figures relate to the parish of Liverpool only, and not to the entire borough, within the boundaries of which are included the large and populous parish of Toxteth-park. The population of the parish of Liverpool, in 1841, was 223,054, and at present is calculated at 270,000. The net cost of the indoor pauperism of this large parish for the six months ending the 24th of March, 1849, was £6,451 5s. 6¾d.; and for the six months ending on the 22d of September, in the same year, £5,405 12s. 8¼d.; making a total for the year of £11,856 18s. 3d. From the quarterly summaries, drawn up by the governor, I learn the proportion of Irish paupers in the workhouse at four different periods of the year. Of 2,370 paupers in the house at the end of the first, or Lady-day, quarter, 1,066 are entered as Irish, Scotch, and foreigners. Of 2,308 in the house at the end of the Midsummer quarter, 1,052 were Irish, Scotch, and foreigners. Of 2,194 admitted between Midsummer and Michaelmas 1849, the number of Irish, Scotch, and foreigners was 878. In the last quarter of the year, out of 1,798 paupers, 742 were Irish, Scotch, and foreigners. These figures give a total for the year of 8,670 admissions, of which 3,738 were Irish, Scotch, and foreigners. The Irish, therefore, form a fraction more than 43 per cent. of the whole number. The number of Scotch and foreign paupers was very small, not amounting to 3 per cent.; but calculating it at 3 per cent., it will leave 40 per cent. composed entirely of Irish. It will follow, therefore, from these figures, that two-fifths of the expense of the indoor poor of Liverpool is incurred for the support of Irish people—born in Ireland. If the calculation were extended a little further, it would be found that, out of the remaining three-fifths, a large proportion consisted of children born in Liverpool of Irish parents, and that, on the most moderate calculation, it might be estimated that fully one-half of the cost of the Liverpool workhouse is rendered necessary by the constant influx of a distressed Irish population.

Some time ago it was found that there was not room in the workhouse for the large number of children thrown upon the parish, and it was determined to erect an industrial school for their maintenance and instruction at another part of the town. I paid a visit to this establishment—a very handsome pile of building at Kirkdale—and found that it contained 1,150 children, of whom 377 were girls, and 773 boys. This building cost £32,000, and the expense of maintaining it was last year £10,483 1s. 9d. The children in this establishment are instructed in reading, writing, and arithmetic, and in the trades of the tailor, shoemaker, carpenter, and sailor, as well as in some kinds of agricultural work. The girls are taught knitting and plain needlework, and instructed in household work of all kinds. The great majority of the boys have a predilection for the sea, and a ship has been erected on the grounds, in which, under the direction of an "ancient mariner," they go through a kind of *dry* apprenticeship to the business of a sailor. Altogether the establishment is a highly interesting one, and seems admirably conducted; but I only allude to it here as an item in the burdens of Liverpool. No classification of these children, into English and Irish, has been made; but the parish officials seem to consider that about as large a proportion of them are Irish, as exists among the inmates of the workhouse; so that forty per cent. of the charge incurred for this establishment may be set down amongst the Irish burdens upon the town of Liverpool.

The proximity of this town to Ireland has led to a system which, in its operation, forms a very peculiar burden upon its patience as well as its resources. It has of late years become a regular practice amongst a portion of the poorer orders of Irish women, resident in Ireland, married as well as unmarried, to come to Liverpool in the last month of their pregnancy, for the purpose of being confined and attended to during and for some weeks after this delicate period, at the expense of the generous and charitable English of Liverpool. The deck fares from Dublin, by some of the steam-boats, are often as low as sixpence a head. Provided with that sum, and a crust of bread, the pregnant Irish pauper woman of the class who have learned this secret, leaves her native land to try her fortune in Liverpool. Immediately on her arrival, she applies at the gate of the workhouse for relief. It is in vain for the authorities to attempt to get rid of the infliction by the payment of another sixpence to send her back in the way she came. The medical officers of the parish must first certify whether she is in a fit state to be removed. I cast no imputation upon the character or motives of the medical men on whom this duty devolves, but I state the fact, as told by the parochial authorities—that it is a very rare case indeed for a medical man to certify that such a pauper is in a fit state to be sent back again before her *accouchement*. The medical officers of the parish derive no inconsiderable portion of their professional incomes from the fees payable for this service—ten shillings for an ordinary, and as much as two guineas for a difficult, case. Under such a system the result stated is not at all surprising. The Irish women who come to Liverpool upon this errand, ignorant as they may be in other respects, have sense enough to comprehend very clearly that, once in the streets of that town in an advanced stage of pregnancy, there is no difficulty before them. They are sure of subsistence, shelter, and medical attendance until two or three weeks or a month after their *accouchement*, and then the parish gets rid of them as fast as it can, and is only too happy to pay their passage to the place from whence they came. Many of them spread themselves over England as tramps and beggars, and some return to Ireland at the parish expense, to favour Liverpool with another visit whenever they find themselves in the same situation. In the first quarter of the year 1849, the number of women confined in the workhouse was 61, of whom 26 said they were married; in the second quarter the number confined was 65, of whom 30 declared they were married; in the third quarter of the year the number was 42, of whom 12 declared they were married; and in the last quarter of the year the number was 58, of whom 22 claimed to be married. It is not asserted that all these women were Irish, nor have I been able to ascertain what proportion the immigrants of the class alluded to bore to the whole number. To state it at two-fifths, or even one-half, would not in all probability be an exaggeration.

The second ramification of the Irish burden is the cost of the out-door relief afforded to the poor. During the year ending on the 28th of February, 1850, it amounted, in money and food, to £34,429 6s. 6d., of which £26,132 9s. 2d. was given in money, and £8,296 17s. 4d. in kind. The cases of settled poor relieved during the year were 147,941, including 302,034 individuals; but as many of these are several times entered in the books, and appear again and again whenever necessity compels them, the numbers are not to be taken as the numbers of habitual and professional paupers. The number of strictly Irish cases relieved with money during the year, was 57,832, including 165,379 individuals of all ages. In addition to these, 35,648 cases, including 94,621 individuals having no settlement, received out-door relief, of whom at least one-half were estimated to be Irish. The sum of £8,296 17s. 4d., administered to the poor in food, was divided between the Irish and all other applicants. I leave out of the calculation the cost of the vagrant sheds, which will form the fourth head, under which the subject will be treated. The proportions of this total sum of £34,492 6s. 6d. for the out-door relief of the poor, classified under these various items, would be, for the Irish alone, as follows:—

For the Irish poor claiming to have a settlement ...	£5,464
One-half of the total cost of relieving with money the poor having no settlement	1,697
One-half of the relief administered in kind	4,148
	£11,309

I believe that these figures are under the mark, and that much more than one-half of the casual cases, and of the poor without set-tlement, are Irish. I do not take into the account the voluntary charity of the people of Liverpool to the Irish beggars that swarm about the streets, whose importunity it would be difficult to resist, even if their squalor and wretchedness, and the number of their miserable and half-starved children, did not plead for them more loudly than their own vociferations. Had I had access to the documents to prove the burdens upon the whole borough of Liverpool, including the Park parish, with the townships of West Derby, Everton, and Kirkdale, the Irish burden would appear even more oppressive. The Park parish and townships contained a population estimated at 112,839 in the year 1846, of whom a large proportion, as in the rest of the borough of Liverpool, were Irish of the most distressed class. This calculation, however, I have not gone into, having confined myself in these pauper statistics to the parish of Liverpool alone.

Under the *third* head of the expense devolving upon Liverpool by the presence of so many permanent poor Irish, and by the fluctuating visitations of the wandering poor of the same country, it will be impossible to state with precision what portion of the total expense of carrying out the provisions of the local sanitary act is caused by their wretchedness and dirt—both of habitation and of person. During the year when fever and cholera swept so many thousands of the poor people into their graves, more than one-half of the extraordinary expense of sanitary regulations and of fever hospitals was incurred for the Irish. The expense of the sanitary operations of the borough—not the parish—for the year ending the 31st March, 1849, to which time the last published accounts are made up, was £149,696 10s. 9½d. The total receipts for sanitary purposes derived from rates on the inhabitants, and from a few other sources of revenue, was £149,766 18s. 11½d. The filthy cellars and courts, inhabited by the Irish, that abound in the poorer districts of the town, with the lodging-houses of mendicants and thieves, and of all the distressed labourers who are burdensome to the parish but who are not yet driven into the workhouse, are a continual source of expense, on account of the periodical visitation to which it is necessary to subject them in order to preserve the town from the constant scourge of a desolating fever. Upon this head, I shall enter more fully in a subsequent letter, when I shall give a full detail of the sanitary state of the borough. At present, and considering it merely as an Irish burden, it may be estimated, without exaggeration, that fully one-third of the whole expense is rendered necessary by the enormous number of the lowest class of Irish. This would make the burden under this head no less than £49,898 16s. 11d. Many gentlemen in the town to whom I have submitted the estimate, consider that two-thirds—rather than one-third—would be the proper calculation.

The *fourth* sub-division of expense is the evil of the "Vagrant Sheds," or Refuge for the Destitute. This is a considerable item in the annual charges of the town of Liverpool. For the week in which I visited the establishment, the total number of persons who had been accommodated with beds, and with a piece of bread at night and in the morning, was—men, 681; women, 541; children, 284; total, 1,506. The night when I visited the sheds was considered a "slack" one, there being a great fair at Halifax, in Yorkshire, to which large numbers of the regular tramps and vagrants had gone, begging and plundering on their way. This was on the 26th of February, and the intelligent master of the establishment gave me the following extract from his books, showing the number and character of the vagrants that had taken refuge within its walls on the previous evening and on the corresponding evening of the previous year. On the 25th of February, 1849, the numbers were 97. On the 25th of February, 1850, they amounted to 204, being an increase of 107. Of these 204, the English tramps and vagrants numbered 100; the Scotch, 7; the Irish 81; and aliens, including negroes and other foreign sailors, 16. Thirteen of the number were well-known thieves, and 40 of the females well-known prostitutes. Sixty persons of both sexes were professional tramps and vagrants, leaving 91 persons as real strangers and wayfarers, not known to be tramps, though possibly belonging to that fraternity. Taking the week as a fair average one, and multiplying the number by 52, there would result an annual visitation to the vagrant-sheds of Liverpool of 78,312 persons. By a return from the vestry-clerk's office, with which I have been furnished, the number of admissions appear to be 77,167. But many of these are constant visitors, so that the actual number of cases must be less, and, according to the vestry-clerk's return, is 33,314. One boy, who begged during the day about the streets, had made his appearance in the shed for 26 nights in succession, and had been duly relieved with two slices of bread, and his bed upon the boards. Others had made their appearances with as great regularity, and effected periodical descents upon the hospitality of Liverpool—hospitality of a very questionable prudence, when it is considered how much it must tend to the increase of crime and pauperism, and to the encouragement of habits of vagrancy amongst a class of the people already unsettled enough, who use these pauper-sheds as rich men use hotels, namely, as halting-places on their travels. It is sometimes, both in Liverpool and elsewhere, impossible to preserve decency or order amongst the inmates. The girls take a frantic freak in their heads at times, and dance about the sheds in an indecent manner, singing obscene songs, and otherwise misconducting themselves; and the male vagrants, though generally more manageable, are at times as bad as those of the other sex. I took down the story of one of the best conducted of the inmates of the Liverpool shed, and present it in the words of the narrator—a good-looking and intelligent young man, with a tolerably good suit of clothes on his back, such as might be worn every day by a working man in regular employ.

"My name is John L———. I am 27 years of age, and unmarried. I was born in the county of Meath, and have been in England about ten years. I never learned any trade. I worked in Ireland as a ostler for Mr. Peter Purcell, the great coach contractor. I was discharged because I was not wanted any longer. I might have got employment in Dublin, if I had stayed there, but I wanted to try my fortune in England, and see what the country was like. I came to Liverpool for 2s. 6d., which I paid out of my savings. From Liverpool I went to Prescot, Wigan, and Manchester. I paid my way as I went. I did not know what tramping was then; I was too rich and too proud to be a beggar. I don't remember how much money I had, but I had some. When I got to Manchester I thought myself in luck. I fell in with a man (an Irishman), who gave me work at drawing sand out of the 'old river'—the Irwell. The sand is used for building purposes. He was a good master. I stayed with him for five years, and had regular wages of 18s. a week all that time. It was very hard work, and lasted for twelve and often for fifteen hours a day. I might have lived comfortably on 12s. a week, and saved 6s.; but somehow or other I spent it all. I can't tell how much 6s. a week would have run up to in five years, but I can count it if you will give a little time. (A piece of paper and a pencil were handed to him, and he readily calculated the amount, stating it to be £78.) I am certain £78 is the sum. I wish I had saved it. I can read and write pretty well, and cypher also. I could once extract the square and the cube roots. I don't think I could manage the cube root now, or the square root either. I know vulgar fractions, but I do not quite understand the decimals. It was not because I drank that I did not save my earnings. I did not get drunk. I used to drink beer. My work required it. I got very wet and cold, having to stand in the water, and the beer was a comfort to me. I was discharged because my master had no further occasion for me. There were no floods in the 'Old river' to bring down the sand, and he could not afford to keep me on. I could get no other work in Manchester, though I tried very hard for it. I stayed for ten weeks without work. A woman who kept a huckster's shop gave me credit. I had dealt with her for five years, and she did not like to see me want while I was out of work. I ran up a score of £2 with her. I never could pay her. I fell very low at last, and had to go to the Night Asylum, where I got six ounces of bread and a pint of coffee at night, and six ounces of bread in the morning. I fell in with tramps there, and heard all their conversation about the different towns where they had been. I got the first thoughts of tramping from them. I went to Bolton, ten miles from Manchester, to try my luck at it. The police gave me an order for half a pound of bread. I did not beg on the road, and did not at all like the tramping business, from what I saw of it. I then went back to Manchester, to the Night Asylum, and tried for work during the day. I could not find any one to employ me, so I thought I'd give the tramping another trial. I then went to Stockport. I was all alone, and not up to begging. I didn't like it. At that time I felt savage, and would much sooner have robbed than begged. I didn't rob, I hadn't a chance. You must not ask me too particularly about everything. I never was in prison for stealing, and never stole that I remember. I came to Manchester the second time, and stopped there a few days. I met a man in the Night Asylum who had been a painter. He was on the tramp, and knew all about it. He brought me into the way of it. I went with him to Stockport and Macclesfield. I first began to beg in Macclesfield, and got bits of bread and broken victuals, but little money, scarcely any. I had a working dress on, and continued begging in the neighbourhood, but not in the town, for fear of the police. I then went regularly on the tramp for three months. This was in 1846. I was put into gaol at Shrewsbury for begging. I was in for fourteen days. Found it very indifferent. My friend the painter was 'nabbed' along with me. They made us pick oakum, and did not feed us well, at least not so well as I liked. When we got out we went to Bridgnorth and Kidderminster, tramping all the way. At Gloucester the painter left me, and I made up my mind to go to the old place, I mean Manchester, and try for work. It was all of no use. There seemed to be a spite against me. No, not a spite of men, they did not know me; but a spite of everything. Nothing went right with me. For two years after this I did not get above a fortnight's work at different times, though I was able and willing. I visited different parts of England in this time, and found my way to London. I was put into Tothill-fields prison for 21 days for begging. When I got out I could do nothing but tramp. Nobody would employ a gaol-bird with his head cropped. I went to Barnett, St. Albans, and a lot of places that I can't recollect the names of, until I got to South Wales. I was five months on this journey. I was in no hurry. I began to like tramping. Some of the tramps are clever fellows. We have a good deal of fun at night. We tell stories. The best liar is the best man among the tramps. We sing songs—some of them very good songs—sentimental ones; some of them are very bad, and some of them are worse than bad. We always tell each other the best unions to go to. I mean by the best unions those where we got the best bed and the most to eat. Tramps are not drunkards. They very seldom drink. When I arrived in South Wales the railway was being made. I got work upon it as a 'navvy,' for about six months, at 15s. a week. I then lived in Bridgend. Provisions were dear in the place, and it cost me 11s. a week to live. When discharged from the railway I got a job in a foundry at 12s. a week. My work was to feed a 'blast tenter' for 'moulders.' I was there six months, for I preferred work, however hard, to tramping. At last the manager found a man who offered to do my work for 10s. I would not stand that. I would not work for 10s., and tried several furnaces in Wales in hopes of work. A good many furnaces were stopped at this time. The end was that I went on the tramp again. The people of South Wales are good people. They are very kind and charitable. They gave me plenty of food when I begged; but they never gave me any money. I was seldom refused when I called at a farmhouse. I used to sleep in barns, and always got a good breakfast in the morning, and very often a supper of 'cowal.' Cowal is very good stuff. It is made of cabbage, beef, 'taturs, and all kinds of vegetables. I often got a breakfast as well as a supper of 'cowal.' I remained in South Wales until April, 1849, and then came on to London, on the regular tramp. I lodged in several unions on the way, and was in the casual ward at St. Pancras parish, where I got four ounces of bread night and morning. After being in London for a few days, I started for Liverpool, with 2½d. During all the time I begged, I never received more than 2s. 6d. from one person, and that was from a clergyman. Once I got 6d. from a woman; she was rather a poor looking woman, with a kind face. I have got no work since I came to Liverpool. Though I can read pretty well, I don't read much. I have read some of the Bible, and some of the

National School books in Ireland. I have never read a novel—I know what a novel means. I never read a history. I look at the newspapers sometimes. I never look at the politics. I read the 'police' first, and the murders, and the robberies. I read the fires and the accidents, or anything wonderful. I like to read the Irish news—about repeal. I was once a Repealer, but I don't care about it now. I hope this summer to get a chance somewhere or other. I would like to get out of England. I would go to America, or anywhere else, where I could live. I would have enlisted long ago, but I am not of the right height; and, besides, I have hurt my right leg. I never tried any of the vagrant 'lurks.' I passed as a labouring man, which I am. There are several classes of tramps and vagrants. The worst dressed are always the worst off. The well-dressed ones, like broken-down tradesmen, are the best. A 'broken-down parson' is a capital 'lurk,' as I have been told, but I never tried it. If a man can't tell lies, it's of no use going on the tramp. Tramps are generally very good to each other, and share their food with those who are in want. I shall leave Liverpool to-morrow and try my luck once more."

The annual expense of the vagrant sheds at Liverpool amounted, for the year ending on the 28th of February, 1850, to £4,274 2s. 3d. Two fifths of this sum, or £1,709 12s. 11d., is the proportion fairly chargeable by Liverpool to the accident of her position as the nearest large port to Ireland.

The *fifth* branch of the subject is one which it is utterly impossible to bring to the test of figures, but the evil comprised in it is keenly felt by vast numbers of the labouring population—many of them Irish themselves—who might do tolerably well, were it not for the daily influx of raw and unskilled labourers, called 'Grecians,' who think a shilling a day high wages, and who will often labour for 6d. or 9d. a day rather than not get a job. In fact, the labour market of Liverpool is cruelly overstocked; yet every week, and every day, the sixpenny deck passengers from Dublin and elsewhere pour in their multitudes, at the imminent risk of pauperizing of thousands of men who have hitherto managed to earn a decent subsistence. Upon this subject I shall enter into fuller particulars when I come to treat of the dock labourers and the operative porters—a very important branch of my inquiry.

The *sixth* diversity of the Irish burden is the increased police force and other expenditure for the prevention or punishment of crime, which is rendered necessary by a population into which has been infused so large an element of Hibernian misery. Upon such a point it is impossible to speak with accuracy. There are no sufficient data upon which to form an estimate. I will, however, show as nearly as I can the total expenditure of the borough under the various items into which its criminal charges are resolveable; leaving the candid reader to estimate the amount chargeable to the Irish population, at such per centage as may seem fairly due, considering their numbers on the one hand, and their poverty and demoralization on the other.

The net expense to the borough of Liverpool for the constabulary force, after deduction of watch-rates, and other receipts for the year ending the 31st of August, 1849, was £22,670 11 8
For maintaining bridewells and police-stations   2,205 7 10
Stipendiary magistrate 1,600 0 0
The Borough-gaol 13,208 13 1
Prosecutions at the assize and sessions 5,838 0 11
On account of the new Assize Courts 12,588 6 1
____
£58,110 19 7

Under the *seventh* head—the expense of the Pass-office, for passing Irish paupers to their own country and maintaining them in the interval between the granting of the pass and the departure of the vessel which is to convey them—I am enabled to speak with more precision. A weekly record of the arrival of Irish paupers and emigrants in Liverpool was kept by the police from the 1st of January, 1847, to the 19th of July, 1848, when for some reason or other it was discontinued. On the 3d of November, 1848, finding a large and unusual number of Irish paupers in the town, the vestry requested that the head-constable would resume the account, through the police, of the daily arrivals of deck passengers from Ireland, and, as far as the officers could judge, of their business in Liverpool, under the two heads of emigrants and jobbers and of paupers. By jobbers are meant pig-drivers, and men and boys in charge of oxen, sheep, or horses. The results of both inquiries appear in the following table:—

Return of the passengers who arrived in Liverpool from Ireland "weekly," from January, 19, 1847, to January 12, 1850, inclusive. At least 99 per cent. of these were deck passengers, and were either emigrants and cattle jobbers, or paupers:—

Date. 1847.	No.	Date. 1848.	No.	Date. 1849.	No.
Jan. 19...	5,827	Jan. 5...	1,195	Mar. 10...	5,516
26...	5,221	12...	2,079	17...	4,629
Feb. 3...	7,668	19...	1,816	24...	4,797
10...	7,526	26...	2,281	31...	5,272
17...	4,457	Feb. 2...	2,774	April 7...	6,135
24...	8,278	9...	2,646	14...	6,521
Mar. 3...	10,029	16...	3,158	21...	6,686
10...	10,630	23...	3,373	28...	6,148
18...	11,522	Mar. 1...	3,818	May 5...	5,589
25...	11,045	8...	5,341	12...	6,117
April 2...	15,291	15...	3,598	19...	6,989
9...	12,814	22...	3,138	26...	6,435
17...	17,517	29...	5,752	June 2...	6,364
26...	12,389	April 5...	4,718	9...	5,751
May 3...	8,194	12...	4,850	16...	7,431
11...	7,930	19...	4,878	23...	9,409
19...	8,535	26...	3,711	30...	7,994
26...	6,848	May 3...	5,763	July 7...	5,469
June 2...	7,561	10...	5,980	14...	4,038
9...	5,850	17...	4,248	21...	3,763
16...	6,827	24...	6,782	28...	4,696
23...	7,394	31...	4,291	Aug. 4...	8,287
30...	7,983	June 7...	7,308	11...	4,978
July 7...	7,096	14...	4,104	18...	4,896
14...	5,507	21...	8,698	25...	2,974
21...	4,477	28...	7,146	Sept. 1...	2,909
28...	4,612	July 5...	7,164	8...	2,076
Aug. 4...	9,025	12...	4,583	15...	2,828
11...	5,195	19...	3,506	22...	3,217
18...	3,664	Discontinued until		29...	3,591
25...	2,987	Nov. 11.		Oct. 6...	3,485
Sept. 1...	3,054	Nov. 11...	5,341	13...	3,711
8...	2,050	18...	3,675	20...	4,348
15...	2,847	25...	3,323	27...	3,706
22...	1,562	Dec. 2...	3,610	Nov. 3...	3,973
29...	3,379	9...	2,355	10...	3,722
Oct. 6...	3,148	16...	2,572	17...	3,507
13...	3,799	23...	1,797	24...	3,244
20...	2,955	30...	1,239	Dec. 1...	3,280
27...	3,425	1849.		8...	2,101
Nov. 3...	3,012	Jan. 6...	2,381	15...	3,361
10...	2,785	13...	2,026	22...	2,172
17...	2,430	20...	3,327	29...	1,920
24...	3,011	27...	3,427	1850.	
Dec. 1...	2,258	Feb. 3...	4,178	Jan. 5...	2,413
8...	1,742	10...	3,854	12...	2,718
15...	1,807	17...	6,234		
22...	2,091	24...	5,287	Total ...	694,293
29...	1,154	Mar. 3...	5,394		

A portion of these pig-jobbers and others might fairly be classed
amongst the paupers. It is not an uncommon thing amongst this class

to hire a boy of twelve or fourteen years of age to come over to Liverpool and look after the animals on deck, under the superintendence and orders of the regular driver or jobber. The fee for this service is sixpence, to be paid as soon as the animals set foot on the quays of Liverpool. The sixpence, of course, is soon spent, the boys are utterly destitute, and either linger about the town to beg or steal, taking refuge at night in the vagrant sheds, or disperse themselves through the country in search of work, or go as regular tramps and vagrants. Many of them soon make their re-appearance in Liverpool, and are passed over to Ireland at the expense of the parish.

During the dreadful year 1847, the number of Irish paupers removed from Liverpool was:—

To Ireland	15,020
To Scotland	531
To the Isle of Man	20
Total	15,571

The cost of their removal, including food after application, their passage money, their food during the voyage, and 6d. each in money, was £4,633 16s. 6d.

In 1848 the numbers were not so large, being 7,600 only. The cost was £2,214 15s. 6d. In 1849 the numbers were:—

To Ireland	9,509
To Scotland	543
To the Isle of Man	19
Total	10,071

The cost to the parish was £2,600 8s. Previous to the 8th of August, 1845, or 8th and 9th of Victoria, cap. 117, this expense was borne by the county. The most frequent of these cases appear to be of women who have come to England in search of their husbands, and of men and boys attracted by the chance of porterage and harvest work. The passage money, as I have already mentioned, is very low at present, which is scarcely a gain to the parish, as the cheaper the fare, the greater the multitudes that swarm over and ultimately burden the town as beggars or thieves, or have to be sent back to Ireland at its expense. I saw, and took down the statements of, several of these people, and select a few from the number. The first specimen of a class was a woman of between 40 and 50 years of age. She said:

"I am without family; my husband brought me from Thurles, county Tipperary, to Dublin, last Thursday fortnight. We walked all the way. My husband deserted me in Dublin, and went off with a 'boy' (a word applied very generally by the lower Irish to express a man) to get work in England. He left me no money. I pawned my clothes for four shillings, and paid my passage to Liverpool. I thought I should find my husband there. I found out the lodging where my husband stopped, and the 'boy' who came over with him. He told me my husband had gone to Shrewsbury to try for work. I followed him. I walked to Wem, fifteen miles away. I had no money—not a '*fardin* at all.' I begged for a 'bit' along the road. I then went to Shrewsbury, and after that to Wellington—getting a bit as I could. I did not hear of my husband at all. I quite lost him. I then came back to Liverpool, as I was minded to go back to Thurles. On Sunday an Irishman gave me 2½d. I have nowhere to go to in Ireland, but the union."

The next was a young man of five-and-twenty, who looked at least double the age. He said:—"I am married, and have one child. I belong to the County Armagh. I have been married two years. I left my wife and child at Dundalk six weeks ago, and came to this country to get work—any kind of 'labouring work.' I sailed from Belfast to Ardrossan, and paid two shillings to come across. I stayed a few days. I could get nothing to do. I had an uncle at Dumfries, and I walked from Ardrossan to Dumfries to find him. I thought he would be a *frind* to me. I found him sure enough, but he was 'beat up' (*i.e.* ruined). I then went on to Carlisle. I had no money. I begged on the way, and slept at the unions. At Wigton I slept in a house where an Irishman took pity on me, and gave me lodgings. I cannot remember all the towns I came to. I remember Keswick, where I stayed near a week. The farmers were kind thereabouts, and gave me a 'bit.' The farm-mistresses were kinder than the farmers, and gave me bread and meat, but seldom a copper. I stayed about Lancaster for near upon a week, and slept in barns and outhouses—sometimes by leave of the masters and servants, and sometimes 'unbeknownt' to them. I was two days walking between Lancaster and Liverpool. I never got a turn of work all the time, either in England or Scotland. I slept at the vagrant sheds here, and got a bit of bread at night, and another bit in the morning. I want to go back to Ireland. If I can only get 3d. a day and my meat, it will be better than driving about in this way. I was never in the union in Ireland, but if I can't get a turn at work, I must go there with the wife and child."

The next was an unfavourable opinion of the Irish labourer, but whether it were vice or misery that had set so harsh a seal upon his countenance I cannot say. His hair was closely cropped, showing that he had recently been in prison. "My name," said he, "is Patrick C——, I am 28 years of age. I left Galway two months ago to come here to earn something at farmer's work. I had four shillings when I left. Some 'boys' gathered the money for me to give me a lift. I paid a shilling for my passage. I had been out of health for some time in Galway, and had been three months out of work. I did not stay in Liverpool, but went to Warrington with a 'boy' I met in the packet. I don't know why we went to Warrington. Neither of us knew anybody there. The 'boy' had more money than me, and often gave me a 'bit' when I needed it, which sure, as God knows, was often enough. I stayed with him three weeks at Warrington, without work. The 'boy' got work among the farmers, but I could get none of it. I was laid *hould* of by the police at Warrington for begging, and sent to Kirkdale prison for fourteen days. I came out on Saturday evening, and got 6d. I went to a lodging in Liverpool, and paid 3d. for a bed in a cellar. I had a bed to myself, but there was a power of other 'boys' in the cellar. I paid 2d. for my bed the night after. I walked out among the people begging, but I only got a penny. I came here to the Pass-house to be passed to Ireland, and then I got a 'bit.' When I get back to Ireland I shall have to go to the union."

The last case I shall cite was that of a little dirty but bright-eyed and rather intelligent boy, of 14 years of age. He said: "My name is James B——. I am near about 14—somewhere thereabouts—it may be 15. I came over here a week ago. I belong to the county Down. I have no father and no mother, no brothers or sisters, only an aunt. My aunt lives with a 'boy' in Belfast. The 'boy' isn't my uncle, but I call him my uncle. He isn't married to my aunt. I *stowed* over from Belfast to Liverpool [*i.e.*, hid himself about the ship till it was out at sea]. I covered myself over with hay, among the horses, when the captain came. I never told my aunt. She does not know where I am. The sailors soon found me out, and one of them gave me a kick. I didn't care. He made it up with me, and never told the captain. All the sailors were alike. They let me cover myself with hay when the captain and the mate came. I had nothing to eat, and did not want anything. I was sore sick. I don't know the name of the ship. It was a steamer. I couldn't spell the name. I have been to school, and know my letters, but I can't read. I stayed in Liverpool only half a day, and went out into the country towards Ormskirk. I had no money. I saw a 'boy' in a cellar, eating his breakfast. He was an Irish 'boy,' and gave me half of his loaf and a drop of coffee. At Ormskirk I slept in the relieving-office. I could get no work. I begged on the road, and a farmer one night gave me a good supper, a good bed, and my breakfast. I stayed about Ormskirk for a week, and then came back to Liverpool. I didn't like begging. I can't get a good bed by begging. I have to sleep upon boards. I should like to work for a good bed and plenty of meat. I shall go back to my aunt. The 'boy' that lives with her is a sailor, and goes fishing. I hope he will take me with him."

I have now detailed, with as much accuracy as possible, the nature and amount of the burdens borne by the parish and borough of Liverpool, on account of the Irish poor. These burdens are not so severe at present as they were in the year of the great potato famine, when, as will be seen by the tabular statement given above, Irish paupers arrived in the town at the rate of 10,000 or 15,000 per week for many weeks in succession. If such a state of things had continued until now, Liverpool, rich as it is, and supported by £100,000 of town dues levied upon the general commerce of the country, must have been made bankrupt by the infliction. But though happily the evil has much diminished, the number of Irish paupers that pass into or out of the town and become a charge upon it, or that stay within its bounds as a permanent residuum of misery, is a curious feature in the modern history of the poor, and one that merits the attention of all who are interested in the social welfare of the great masses of the people.

LABOUR AND THE POOR.

LIVERPOOL.

[FROM OUR SPECIAL CORRESPONDENT.]

THE LIVERPOOL DOCKS—THEIR MANAGEMENT AND MISMANAGEMENT, AND THEIR INFLUENCE UPON THE SOCIAL AND MORAL CONDITION OF THE POOR.

LETTER II.

The Docks of Liverpool are alike the glory and the shame of the town. The principal inhabitants seem to be split up into the two great parties of defenders and opponents of the management of the Dock Trust. A constant squabbling goes forward—one party attacking, and another praising, the acts of the "Dock Committee"; one party insinuating, and the other denying, jobbing and corruption; one clamouring for and the other resisting reform, retrenchment, and diminution of rates; and both carrying on, in a thousand different forms, the acrimonious war of local politics. Notwithstanding all this, the people of Liverpool are justly proud of their Docks, and point to them as striking examples of the energy, perseverance, and success of Englishmen—which, favoured by circumstances, have, in a little more than a century, called the whole of these harbours into existence, and raised an insignificant provincial town to be the second, if not the first, commercial port in the world.

The Docks of Liverpool, as stated generally in my first Letter, extend from south to north, on the right bank of the noble estuary of the Mersey, for a distance of nearly four miles. They will afford, when the North Docks are opened, fourteen miles and one hundred and nineteen yards of quay room. Their total area will be 195 acres 524 yards. Seen from the opposite shore of Birkenhead and Woodside, or from the deck of a vessel in the middle of the river, they are well calculated to fill the mind of the beholder with lofty ideas of the wealth of Great Britain, and of the ceaseless commercial activity of her children. On a fine day the scene is highly beautiful and animated. In the offing the white sails of numerous inward and outward bound ships gleam in the sunshine. In the roadstead there may probably be seen at anchor one or two American liners deep in the water, outward bound, with living freights of some hundreds of Irish emigrants, and large cargoes of iron rails and English manufactured goods. Scores of smaller craft enter or leave the docks, and wave to the breeze, or flaunt to the sunlight, the flags of every civilized nation in Europe or America. First-class steam-ships laden with emigrants and cattle from Ireland, or with cattle only from Scotland, cleave their way leisurely through the narrow channels of the deep water, and approach the docks set apart for steam commerce; while numbers of smaller steamboats, filled with passengers, dart to and fro between the George's landing pier and Birkenhead, Monksferry, Woodside, Seacombe, Egremont, Rockferry, New Brighton, and the other towns and villages which have arisen on the opposite side of the Mersey, to afford breathing-places to the jaded and pent-up citizens of Liverpool.

But beautiful as is the scene upon the river, that from the northern to the southern extremity of the docks, as beheld from its bosom, is more impressive. The one scene is busy and animated—the other is completely silent. A dense accumulation of tall masts rises, with occasional breaks, for fully two-thirds of the whole line, behind stone walls and embankments, or intermingled with dwelling-houses and huge warehouses eight stories in height, amid which an occasional spire, or tower, and the domes of the Custom-house and Town-hall stand prominent. The wind playing among the rigging and cordage of this vast assemblage of ships, finds here and there a flag or a pennant to put in gentle motion; a few gulls occasionally sail by with graceful and leisurely motion, displaying their snow-white bosoms against the dark back-ground of the town; and here and there the smoke from the funnel of a steam-ship passes over the tops of the masts on its way to the clouds; but otherwise the picture is one of utter quietude and repose. The ships lie motionless in the Docks; and their spars and rigging, in all their simple, but apparently complicated tracery, are as fixed as in a painting or a photograph. The multitudinous and noisy life of the quays and thoroughfares of the town finds no reverberation in the mid-stream. Nothing is to be seen or heard there of the busy crowd of sailors, porters, policemen, emigrants, carters, warehousemen, clerks, and merchants, that are congregated in and around these numerous docks, and their loading or discharging argosies. But if the passenger lands and takes a stroll upon the quays, a very different scene presents itself. He has no longer the telescopic and quiet view of distance—he sees as through a microscope into that which is near. Hundreds of porters are busily engaged at their work; hundreds of others, equally strong and equally ready, look on with hungry eyes, from the corners of neighbouring streets, unable to obtain a job, and envious of those who have got one; carters, carmen, and "lorriemen," rattle through the streets, driving their fat heavy-footed horses, and conveying bales of cotton and bags of corn or Indian meal to the near or the remote warehouses of the town, to the imminent danger of all unwary pedestrians; busy officials rush to and fro; emigrants, care-worn and sallow—the women barefooted and squalid, and encumbered with children—the men with long antiquated swallow-tailed coats, with knee-breeches unbuttoned, with black stockings and heavy shoes, and redolent in their whole persons of Skibbereen or of Connemara—saunter lazily by, with short pipes in their projecting jaws, and their hands in their pockets; multitudes of ragged children, who ought to be at school, learning to become cleanly, honest, and self-respecting members of society, prowl about looking for plunder amid the cotton-bales; sailors roll by with a motion, even when they are sober, which suggests either intoxication or the pitching of a ship at sea—while every now and then may be seen a man-catcher lurking at a corner, and "seeking, whom he may devour."

The docks of Liverpool may be divided into three classes—first, those which are enclosed with walls; second, those which are unenclosed; and third, those which are enclosed with walls and warehouses. The first comprise the Sandon and Wellington Docks, not yet completed at the extreme north of the line; the Bramley-Moore, the Nelson, the Stanley, the Collingwood, the Salisbury, the Clarence, the Trafalgar, the Victoria, the Waterloo, and the Prince's Docks. The second class runs from the Prince's Dock southward, and comprises the older docks of the town—namely, George's, Canning, Salthouse, King's, Queen's, Union, Coburg, and Brunswick Docks. The third class of docks numbers as yet but one specimen. The Albert Dock, situated in the district between the Salthouse and King's Dock, is the sole dock in the port, constructed upon the model of those in London—surrounded by its own warehouses, worked by its own porters, and denying access within its gate to ragged children, beggars, thieves, and all who can give no account of their business. Upon this system and its advantages, and the consequences to Liverpool of the existence of so many docks governed upon a different principle, and depending upon policemen and acts of Parliament for their protection from plunder—not upon their own bolts and bars—I shall have occasion to dwell at some length in a subsequent part of this Letter.

At the south end of the town three new docks have been constructed without warehouses. These are the Toxteth, the Harrington, and the Herculaneum Docks. The Harrington and Herculaneum Docks were originally the property of a private company, but now form part of the Dock Estate. In the heart of the town, amid the unenclosed docks, are also the private docks constructed by the late Duke of Bridgewater, now the property of the Earl of Ellesmere, and called the "Duke's Docks." There are also two small docks, called "Corporation" Docks—one the Manchester dock, and the other the River-craft dock.

The docks of Liverpool are estimated in round numbers to have cost £9,067,000 sterling, exclusive of interest upon borrowed money, of which upwards of £4,000,000 is still owing. With interest paid, the cost of the docks to the present time would amount to £13,637,000. The accommodation is still insufficient for the increasing trade of the town, and the consent of Parliament has been obtained for the construction of another dock, which is to be called the Wapping Dock. The site chosen is in the older or southern part of the town, in the neighbourhood of the Union and Coburg Docks, where at the present time the demolition of valuable property is rapidly proceeding to clear space for it. One hundred and nineteen warehouses have already been partially or totally demolished.

The first, or original dock of Liverpool, which was also the first dock constructed in Great Britain, occupied the space upon which now stand the Custom-house and Post-office. It is thought by many that a great mistake was committed when that dock was filled up, and that the proper site for the construction of the Liverpool Docks was the course of the ancient Pool, which gave a name to the town, and which has been totally filled up and built over. It is alleged that the true policy would have been to have occupied all the low-lying land for the commercial purposes of the town, and to have formed a line of docks upon the level of the Pool, proceeding into the heart of the lower town, in a north-easterly direction, to Paradise-street and Whitechapel, and so onwards to Byrom-street and Scotland-road, for a distance of 2,000 yards: that the line should then have curved to the north-west for another space of about 2,000 yards, till it joined the Mersey, north of the Clarence Dock—the docks thus forming a triangle, of which the Mersey, from north to south, would have been the base for the distance of 3,500 or 4,000 yards. By this plan, the area of this triangular island might all have been cut up into docks and dock warehouses, and the town itself might have been forced upon the higher ground, to the great improvement of the salubrity as well as of the beauty of modern Liverpool. The town, however, did not foresee its own greatness. The docks were constructed as they were wanted—not before; and it is more than probable that if any far-seeing and daring man of genius had at an early period of the history of Liverpool suggested a scheme so magnificent, he would have been laughed at as a fool, or avoided as a lunatic.

The following figures will show not only the immense extent of the commerce of Liverpool, but how nearly in some respects it is equal, while in others it is superior, to that of London itself. The amount of Customs revenue collected at the port in the year 1849 was £3,774,202. From a Parliamentary Return, moved for by Mr. Cardwell on the 25th of February, 1847, and ordered by the House of Commons to be printed on the 31st of June in the same year, the comparative commerce of London and Liverpool, in 1846, stood as follows:—

LONDON.

British ships clearing inwards	... 5,123 ...	1,109,387 tons.
Ditto outwards	... 3,326 ...	825,744 „
Foreign ships clearing inwards	... 2,439 ...	393,104 „
Ditto outwards	.. 2,262 ...	360,622 „

Total tonnage .... 2,688,857 tons.

LIVERPOOL.

British ships clearing inwards	... 2,810 ...	914,352 tons.
Ditto outwards	... 2,919 ...	924,097 „
Foreign ships clearing inwards	... 1,235 ...	492,189 „
Ditto outwards	.. 1,278 ...	488,376 „

Total tonnage .... 2,819,014 tons.

It will be seen from these figures that the total tonnage of Liverpool, inwards and outwards, was 2,819,014; and of London only 2,688,857, making a difference of 130,157 tons in favour of Liverpool; although the number of ships entering and leaving the port of London was much the greater of the two. This is explained by the superior magnitude and tonnage of the Liverpool traders, and by the fact that a large proportion of the London tonnage was that of colliers, for the domestic supply of the metropolis—a supply which Liverpool receives by railway from her immediate neighbourhood. In the year 1848, the number of British vessels that cleared outwards from Liverpool was 2,885, and the tonnage, 943,388. The number of foreign and colonial ships that cleared inwards in the same year was 2,228, and their tonnage, 813,395; and the total tonnage, inwards and outwards, was about 3,113,566. In 1849, the total tonnage inwards was 1,639,146, and the tonnage outwards very nearly the same, or a total of 3,278,292 tons.

The first dock, or Old Dock of Liverpool, was commenced in the year 1699. It was not until nine years afterwards that the sanction of Parliament was obtained for its completion. In this Act, 8 Anne, chap. 12, the national purposes of the dock were clearly stated. "The entries into the harbour or port," says the preamble, "having been found so dangerous and so difficult that great numbers of strangers and others have frequently lost their lives, as well as ships and goods, for want of proper landmarks, buoys, and other directions into the said harbour; and when such ships have entered the said port, have been exposed to great dangers for want of a convenient wet dock or basin; and whereas it is conceived to be highly necessary for the preservation, not only of merchants' ships, but of her Majesty's ships of war, that a convenient wet-dock or basin should be made, &c. &c.—all which will be a means greatly to encourage trade, advance her Majesty's revenues, and the public good, not only of the said town and port, and the counties adjacent in particular, *but of the nation in general*—be it enacted," &c. In the year 1717 additional powers were obtained from Parliament for the construction of a second dock, also for national as well as local purposes. This was called the Dry Dock, and is the same as that which is now called the Canning Dock; and which is, in point of fact, the oldest dock in Great Britain, its immediate predecessor having been filled up and built over. The population of Liverpool at this time was only 10,446. Every successive act of Parliament, from the time of Queen Anne's act to that of 1848, asserts the national right as well as the local control. The third dock, now called the Salthouse Dock, was commenced in 1733, and finished in twenty years afterwards. The fourth was the George's Dock, for which the act was obtained in 1743; the works were not completed until 1771. The fifth dock was the King's, for which the act was obtained in 1784; this dock was completed in 1788. The sixth was the Queen's, authorized by the same act, but not completed until 1796. The seventh was the Union, and next in succession followed the Coburg and the Brunswick.

With the exception of the Prince's Dock, the act for which was obtained in 1799, all the other docks of Liverpool are the creations of the present century. Within the last six years the work of dock-making has proceeded at a rapid rate—too rapid, as many believe, and constantly assert—and not only too rapid, but ill-judged. At the end of the year 1843 the debt of the Dock Estates was estimated in round numbers at £1,000,000. It now amounts to £4,300,000, and when the works actually in progress are completed, it will reach within a trifle of the sum of £6,000,000.

This vast estate, though it must be considered far more of a national than of a local trust, is governed wholly by local agency. The members of the Liverpool Town Council form two separate and distinct corporations—the one elected under the provisions of the Municipal Reform Act, by the title of the mayor, aldermen, and burgesses of Liverpool; and the other, constituted under the various Dock Acts, by the title and style of "The Trustees of the Liverpool Docks." Although the individuals forming these two corporations are the same, their powers and authorities are entirely distinct. The corporation of Liverpool are the legal depositaries of the property of the trust; but the entire management and control of that property, and of all dock affairs, are vested in a body called the Dock Committee, composed of thirteen members, elected by the Town Council out of their own body, and of eight members elected by the merchants and shipowners of the town, being payers of dock rates. This arrangement was made by the Act of 6 George IV., cap. 187, under the advice and sanction of Mr. Huskisson. Before the passing of that Act the docks were wholly managed by the Town Council of Liverpool, but as that body was elected by a large majority of shopkeepers, warehousekeepers, and poor ratepayers in the town, having no peculiar interest in and not understanding the wants of the commerce of the port, the merchants expressed much dissatisfaction; and the new arrangement was made with a view of giving a voice in the control of the docks to those who contributed so largely to their prosperity—the merchants and shipowners. Virtually, however, the Town Council, having the majority of the Committee, is the governing power, and the representatives of the local interests of men who are not merchants regulate the commerce of Great Britain with America.

The Dock Estate is strictly a public and national trust. The docks are national harbours of refuge, and as such were sanctioned by Parliament. Manchester and the whole of the manufacturing districts are as much interested in their good government as Liverpool; and Liverpool, wealthy and independent as she may consider herself, is but the immediate port of Lancashire, and the general port of Great Britain, for the American trade. No beneficial interest in the Liverpool Docks is vested in an individual or body of individuals; and the surplus dues beyond the amount necessary for maintaining and paying their working expenses are periodically applied, and are ordered by Parliament to be applied, to the increase of dock accommodation and to the reduction of the dock rates. Since the year 1836 the rates have been reduced to the extent of about 38½ per cent. It was evidently the intention of the Legislature that Liverpool should ultimately become a free port— a consummation devoutly to be wished, not only by the merchants of Liverpool, and those interested in the trade and manufactures of the north of England, but by the whole empire.

The rate-payers of Liverpool generally do not seem to be at all aware of the national nature of the Dock Trust. For nearly half a century a contest has raged, with more or less virulence, in the town and in the town council, as to the propriety of rating the docks for the support of the poor. A bill was some time since introduced into Parliament by the parish of Liverpool to rate the docks for all local purposes, parochial and sanitary—although the town and parish of Liverpool receive, in the shape of town dues upon the shipping entering the port, no less a sum than £100,000 per annum, which goes to the diminution of local burdens, and which during the present year will enable Liverpool, notwithstanding the pressure of Irish and other pauperism, to pay all pauper and sanitary charges with a rate no larger than 2s. in the pound. This sum of £100,000 is, in point of fact, a tax upon the general commerce of the country for the benefit of the rate-payers of Liverpool. They are not, however, contented with this sum, and they do not reflect that by the act which established the docks in the reign of Queen Anne, the corporation were made trustees of the docks, and of the revenues derivable from the dock rates, upon condition that they would appropriate those rates and revenues to the repairs and maintenance of the dock, to the extension of accommodation to the commerce of the port, *and to no other purpose whatsoever.* For nearly a century the docks were managed under this constitution, and though the administration of the trust, as already stated, has been in some degree modified by the admission of eight members not of the Town Council, its objects and liabilities remain the same. About twenty-five years ago the overseers of the parish, forgetting the interests of the great commerce which made the town rich, and which enabled shopkeepers to live, resolved to try this question, by rating the docks to the relief of the poor. The dock committee appealed against the rate. The appeal was ably argued, and ultimately decided in full court in the King's Bench—the judges being unanimously of opinion that the rate was bad, and that the docks were exempt, not only because there was no beneficial interest, but because their revenues were all appropriated by act of Parliament to other and to national purposes. Recently this question of rating has been revived; the rate-payers and parochial party, as it may be termed, insisting that the docks should contribute to the support of the poor; the commercial party insisting, on the contrary, that the docks are national and not local—that they are administered by Liverpool people for the general purposes of the country—that the original law expressly exempts them from rating—and that to rate the Liverpool Docks to the poor would be to rate Manchester, Rochdale, Bury, Oldham, Stockport, all Yorkshire and Lancashire, and in fact all England, to the support of the pauperism of Liverpool. They further allege that, even if the law were in their favour, it would be the height of impolicy to rate the docks, as the charges upon commerce being thereby increased, commerce would flow into other channels, and Liverpool, as a parish, would suffer more from the rating than she could possibly gain by it. With a poor-rate upon the docks, Liverpool could never become—what the act intended, and what the interests of the town as well as of the whole of the north of England require it to be—a free port, and its trade would probably flow to the other side of the Mersey. For some of these reasons, when the parish brought a bill into Parliament for rating the docks to the poor, the merchants and manufacturers of Manchester, Bury, Rochdale, and other towns of Lancashire, united with those of Liverpool in protesting against and opposing it; and, after much local bickering and animosity, the bill was ultimately withdrawn in 1849.

It will be seen from this statement that the shopkeepers and householders of Liverpool, who have the power in their own hands of returning the town council of the borough, have manifested a desire at variance with the true interests of the port. There is still a danger that the question is likely to be revived at the periodical election of town councillors, unless the shopkeepers of Liverpool can be once for all convinced that law and policy are alike against them, and that the Liverpool Docks, although situated in the town, do not exclusively belong to it.

I now proceed to show how this local control over the docks and their construction imposes charges upon the commerce of the district, which are prejudicial to our manufacturing system generally, and which, in addition to this evil, encourage and perpetuate crime in Liverpool. As I have already said, there is but one dock in the town which is thoroughly enclosed and protected, and in which the cargoes can be at once lifted from the ship's hold into proper warehouses, without the expense of cartage to distant parts of the town, and without the risk of fire. That is the Albert Dock, erected on the earnest remonstrances of the merchants, as an experimental one to test the principle, and which was opened by Prince Albert with the usual solemnities of such occasions on the 15th of March, 1845. The Northern Docks are all walled in, but they have no warehouses within the enclosure. Their gates are open all day, and any one may walk in—with business or without business—man, woman, or child. It is true that the police are stationed inside and at the gates to protect property, but, as will hereafter appear, they are not able to prevent frequent if not daily robberies to an enormous amount. The Southern Docks have not even the protection of walls. They are as open as the streets to all comers, although the quays are absolutely incumbered with valuable property, as if to tempt the superabundant and starving population to help themselves. Cotton bales lie in immense heaps upon the quays, where, in defiance of the utmost vigilance of the police, swarms of children prowl about during the day and the night to abstract it by handfuls, and conceal it amid their rags until they can transfer it to a depraved mother or father, who watches in a dark alley or in the shade of a large warehouse to receive it from them. Sacks of meal, corn, beans, rice, and coffee—all equally tempting to dishonest poverty— invite young thieves to learn their unhappy trade at the expense of the merchants of Liverpool and Manchester. The Southern Graving Docks belonging to the corporation are equally open. When ships have been placed upon the stocks to be re-coppered, the young thieves drive a profitable business in picking up the copper nails and the old copper sheathings that are scattered about, with no protection but the eyes of a policeman. Cotton picking is, however, the principal source of plunder for the juvenile criminals of Liverpool, and this, together with copper nails and sheathing, old ropes, and other ship-stores, supplies the marine store-dealers with a great amount of property. The evils of this state of things are well-known to, and keenly felt by, the merchants of Liverpool—not simply as regards the losses sustained by robbery, but as regards the charges imposed upon commerce under a deficient and erroneous warehousing system. Hitherto local influence has been all-powerful in preventing a change. The existing warehouse-men would suffer if the system were reformed; and being a numerous body, capable of returning a majority of the Town Council, by the judicious use of their votes they have succeeded in maintaining the docks upon their present footing of inefficiency, extravagance, and insecurity.

I shall first of all consider the system with reference to its encouragement of crime, and then proceed to show its injurious effects upon the town in other respects, as well as upon the general trade and manufactures of the north of England.

The number of marine store-keepers (the receivers of all the stolen goods of the docks) whose names appear in the books of the Town Council, amounts at present to 437. Mr. Rushton is particularly severe in dealing with these encouragers of crime when brought before him on charges of receiving stolen property; and, during the years 1848 and 1849, he deprived of their licences, and punished by imprisonment, no less than 68 of them. At one time during the last year there were a dozen of them, males and females, in gaol at one time. But there seems to be something wrong in a system which has permittcd such a number of these people to be licensed in the town. In the first place, the licensing fee, five shillings, is too small; and in the second, there does not appear to be sufficient discretion left to the magistrates to refuse licences. If the applicant produces a proper certificate from two householders, and nothing is known to the impeachment of his character, the licence is granted him. Of course it must be presumed that among these 437 marine store-dealers, there are some who carry on a fair and honest business; but it is generally supposed, by those who have the best means of judging, that few of the whole number could come with clean hands into a court of justice—or of honour. In addition to the marine store-dealers there is a numerous class who purchase cotton only, for which purpose they require no licence. These act as middlemen between the thieves and the marine store-dealers. Their numbers are estimated at upwards of five hundred. Some years ago Mr. M. M. G. Dowling, the present head-constable and commissioner of police, adopted the following plan to ascertain, if possible, the amount in one year of cotton robberies from the dock quays, and from carts, lorries, and warehouses. Two notorious marine store-dealers having been convicted of receiving stolen cotton, Mr. Dowling placed two trustworthy police constables, properly disguised for the purpose, in these two shops, in order to ascertain the secrets of their traffic. The constables played their part extremely well. They were not at all suspected by the thieves, and they carried on the business prudently and successfully for a fortnight. The cotton was brought in small quantities by people of all ages, and of both sexes. Women and children were the most frequent customers; but porters and labourers occasionally made their appearance laden with plunder. The cotton was of all qualities, and included small portions that had probably been picked out of the streets by children; but the larger portion had been pulled out of the bales, and then trodden in the dirt, so as to make it pass for a damaged article. It also included "samples," purloined from offices and warehouses. The policemen kept their books with great regularity and method; and it appeared that each establishment bought, during the fortnight, about 800 lbs. of cotton, or 400 lbs. per week, at a price varying from 1d. to 1¾d. per lb. The ordinary price of cotton in the market was at that time about 8d. per lb. It was known that there were upwards of forty marine store-dealers in the town, who did a similarly extensive business; from whence it would follow that these "forty thieves" received 16,000 lbs. of stolen cotton per week, or 832,000 lbs. per annum. Calculating its value at only 6d. per lb., it would amount to £20,800. No calculation was made at the time of the amount of corn, coffee, sugar, or other produce, or of ship's stores, that was brought to these shops in the same way; but it was doubtless not much inferior to the cotton robberies. These "forty" were, as already stated, the most noted receivers of stolen goods in the town; but if the 437 marine store-dealers carried on, upon an average, a trade only a fifth-part as extensive, the merchants of Liverpool would have to add another sum of £40,000 per annum to the £20,800 already mentioned, in order to arrive at an estimate of their losses upon the article of cotton alone, by the combined agency of thieves and receivers. Since that period, cotton-stealing has by no means diminished. There is a larger trade in the port, and a larger number of starving people in the town; and it is thought by those who have devoted attention to the subject, that the depredations of cotton and other articles from the quays amount at present to little short of £100,000 per annum. In the year 1848, the extent of cotton-stealing is represented as having been unprecedented. The starving Irish that landed by thousands in a week on the quays of Liverpool could not resist the temptation thrust before them by the open and exposed state of the docks, and by the transit through the streets of countless waggons loaded with unprotected property. The evil somewhat diminished in 1849, in consequence of the general revival of business, and the relaxation of the severity of the Irish invasion; but at the present time the cotton plunder affords a means of living to great numbers of people, and trains up multitudes of children to be the pests and the disgrace of society.

Although the Prince's, the Waterloo, and the Victoria Docks are enclosed, they are free of access to all comers. Women are often seen to follow the lorries or carts laden with bags of Indian corn or bales of cotton, to rob them on their way to the warehouses. It is their practice to make a hole, either with a knife or a pair of scissors, in one of the bags of Indian corn, and hold up their aprons to catch the contents as they are jolted out by the movement of the vehicle. When their aprons are full, they squat down under the vehicle just as it approaches the dock gate on its way out, and, creeping under the feet of the horses, get clear off, although the police may be standing at the gate. Ragged children, from 8 to 14 years of age, both boys and girls, drag the cotton from the bales in the docks; the boys stuffing it into their pockets, and the girls into the bosoms of their frocks. The women stuff cotton into their bosoms and under their clothes, until they look quite corpulent—dragging it out of the bales in large handfuls. This plunder is not only made in the docks, but during the progress of the lorries through the town. Sometimes a dozen lorries, filled with cotton bales, may be seen standing at one time at a warehouse door; and the confusion that ensues is a rich harvest for the cotton-pickers. The driver is unable to prevent these robberies. He has quite enough to do to mind his horses. The women sometimes go in gangs; and when one picks the cotton out of a bale, she passes it on to another, so as not to be found with it in her possession, if she should be captured by a policeman. They also steal corn, coffee, and other articles in the same way; but cotton seems to be preferred; and they wear dresses made on purpose for this kind of robbery, with large receptacles or inner flounces, which they stuff with cotton. The captain of a coaster informed me that he once captured a boy in the act. There was no policeman near, and he begged hard to be let go. The following dialogue took place between the two:—"Can you read?"—"A little." "Do you go to school?"—"Not now." "Do you know the ten commandments?"—"Some of them." "Do you know that one of them says, 'Thou shalt not steal?' "—"Yes." "Then why do you steal?"—"I am obliged." "Who obliges you to steal?"—"My father and mother." "Do you always steal in the docks?"—"There is no good chance anywhere else." "Have you any brothers and sisters?"—"Yes." "Do they steal?"—"Yes, sometimes, and sometimes beg." "Does your father steal?"—"Yes, when he gets a chance."

The Prince's Dock

I was once present in the police court, when my attention was strongly directed to a similar case. A little boy, ten years of age, whose head was scarcely visible above the rails of the dock, was charged by the police with an attempt to commit a robbery in a shop. His face was like that of an old man; and was care-worn, intelligent, and cunning. It appeared in evidence that he walked boldly into the shop, and made for the till, when he was seized by the shopkeeper and given into custody. The boy told his story to the magistrate, to the following effect:—He thought he was ten years of age, but was not sure. His father and mother kept a lodging-house, and were in the receipt of relief from the parish. He had an elder brother now in prison for a robbery in the docks. His father turned all his children into the streets to beg and steal, and they loitered about the docks and warehouses both by day and night, to pick up what they could. His father always beat him severely when he came home without money. On the previous night his father beat him with an iron bar over the back, then turned him out of doors, saying that he was not half so good a boy as his brother in prison, who always brought home either money or cotton. Dreading to return to his father's roof, he attempted to rob the shopkeeper's till, with the hope that he might be taken and sent to prison, and that Mr. Rushton, if he behaved well in prison, would afterwards get him into the Industrial School. Such was the tale told by this miserable but clever child, and which, as far as regarded the father's character, was corroborated by the police, who added that the lodging-house which the man kept was of the lowest kind, inhabited by the filthiest and poorest class of prostitutes. It is such people as these who are the principal agents in dock robberies.

Copper-nail stealing used formerly to be a profitable business, but it has been greatly diminished by the efforts of Mr. Dowling to prevent the swarming of thieves and vagrants into the graving docks. Formerly the corporation paid a contractor a considerable sum to clear the graving docks every time the tide went out. The contractor, unaware of the value that might be concealed in the mud and slush, had it laid up in heaps on the sides of the docks. The starving people, who had free access to the place, soon discovered that there was something in the mud which made it worth their while to carry it away. It was a very animated scene at the graving docks after every tide—where, first of all, scores, and afterwards hundreds, of men, women, and children daily made their appearance with baskets, cans, and all sorts of utensils to carry away the mud. The attention of Mr. Dowling, at that time chief of the dock police, was directed to this subject, and he discovered that considerable quantities of copper nails and pieces of copper were mixed with this mud and slush. A man was stationed in the dock at a salary of 15s. a week to collect the mud and refuse, to dry it, and afterwards to riddle and burn it. The result in one week was a quantity of copper by which this man by his own labour netted for the benefit of the dock the sum of £2 over and above his wages. A large furnace was immediately built by the dock surveyor; the mud was properly collected, several regular hands were employed to dry, to riddle, and to burn it—and the sum of about £1,600 in one year found its way into the coffers of the corporation, derived from this source alone.

The following document shows the number of prisoners charged with felony in the docks and town during the year 1849:—

A RETURN SHOWING THE NUMBER OF PRISONERS BROUGHT BEFORE THE MAGISTRATES FOR FELONY, DISTINGUISHING DOCK AND TOWN OFFENCES, FOR THE YEAR 1849.

	Males.			Females.			Total.		
	Dock.	Town.	Total.	Dock.	Town.	Total.	Dock.	Town.	Total.
January	102	362	464	15	210	225	117	572	689
February	63	277	340	13	210	223	76	487	563
March	90	318	408	16	243	259	106	561	667
April	84	248	332	11	218	229	95	466	561
May	74	272	346	13	240	253	87	512	599
June	59	262	321	4	200	204	63	462	525
July	64	263	327	7	189	196	71	452	523
August	46	243	289	5	192	197	51	435	486
September ..	34	258	292	2	194	196	36	452	488
October	46	250	296	2	242	244	48	492	540
November ...	54	273	327	4	224	228	58	497	555
December ...	46	265	311	3	192	195	49	457	506
Total	762	3291	4053	95	2554	2649	857	5845	6702

This table, however, does not give the whole number of felonies which are traceable to the unprotected nature of the docks—as robberies committed from carts and lorries after they have left the dock-quays, and when they are either on their way to or standing at the doors of warehouses in distant parts of the town, are classed as "town offences." Cases of robbery in warehouses are likewise town offences, as also are the cases of marine store-dealers, who have been convicted of receiving stolen goods. When these facts are borne in mind, and when it is stated in addition that out of the 6,702 felonies above referred to, only one was a burglary in a dwelling-house, it will be evident that a much larger proportion than 857 out of 6,702 may be set down as dock-quay, cart, or warehouse robberies. In the year 1848—that year of universal distress and suffering—the number of dock and town offences was almost double what it was in 1845, a year of great commercial activity and prosperity, as will be seen from the following table:—

A RETURN SHOWING THE NUMBER OF PRISONERS COMMITTED FOR TRIAL, SUMMARILY CONVICTED AND DISCHARGED, IN THE TOWN AND ON THE DOCK-QUAYS, DURING THE YEARS 1845, 1846, 1847, 1848, and 1849.

Years.	Number of Prisoners.
1845	3,889
1846	4,740
1847	6,510
1848	7,714
1849	6,702

It appears from the above that there has been a steady and very alarming increase of crime in Liverpool since 1845; and that, although the return for the last year shows a diminution as compared with 1848, it is far above the returns for 1845 and 1846, and nearly 200 above that of 1847. Besides the expense of prosecuting and maintaining these criminals in prison, which falls upon the borough, the Dock Estate paid from the 25th of June, 1848, to the 25th of June, 1849 (which is their last published statement), the sum of £16,017 14s. for the salaries of police constables for watching the docks and quays—in addition to the sum of £321 7s. 4d. for watching the graving docks, and to that of £4,242 10s., their proportion of the cost of clothing, printing, stationery, and the general expenses of the force, an item which appears in the annual accounts of the corporation. The total expense in round numbers is about £20,000—a sum which, if properly expended every year in walling in the docks and building warehouses within the inclosures, would seriously diminish crime in Liverpool. What the undiscovered depredations committed by poor porters, lumpers, and others engaged in the docks may amount to, there is no possible means of ascertaining.

With reference to the general question of the burdens upon the commerce of the country, caused not only by these constant robberies, committed by the starving poor, and by warehousemen in situations of trust, but by the expense of cartage to distant parts of the town, the additional rent demanded by private warehousemen, who are uncontrolled in their charges by the trustees of the docks—and also by the additional premium of fire insurance—I find the following statements in a document prepared for parliamentary purposes, and entitled "The case of the merchants of Liverpool, seeking the extension of warehouses on the quays of the docks thereof:"—

"The Liverpool docks," say the merchants alluded to, "are, with one exception, open docks, unfurnished with warehouses, exposed to storms, to theft and robbery, to the commission of which crimes the youthful poor of both sexes, with the porters, lumpers, and others engaged in discharging ships, in weighing, and loading off merchandise from the open quays are thus almost irresistibly allured. All this, however, is merely initiative to crime on a more extended scale, and of a deeper dye. The valuable merchandise which should find its safe receptacle on the quays at which it is landed, in warehouses of superior fireproof construction, has to be loaded off, frequently in the twilight of winter evenings, to warehouses scattered throughout the town, many at great distances, and in the most inconvenient situations for their business. In these dispersed warehouses, owned, rented, or variously managed by private individuals, there is no perfect or general system to regulate or restrain the porters or others employed; and any superintendence which these people are occasionally subjected to is that of warehousemen, who almost always have been taken from the ranks of the porters themselves. The result of thus entrusting the countless amount of valuable portable property, deposited in situations most convenient for being purloined, has been severely felt by numbers of merchants in the dishonesty of their warehousemen, in treble premiums of fire insurance, and by the fire insurance offices themselves, who have paid millions of money for warehouse conflagrations in this town, for the origin of which there has been frequently no probable means of accounting but that of the recklessness of porters in smoking their pipes, or for the purpose of concealing robberies which would otherwise be detected. Of the vast extent of crime produced by the exposure of valuable merchandise on open quays, and by the present vicious system of private warehousing, the stipendiary magistrate has more than once given evidence before parliamentary committees, and the head of the Liverpool police can testify as strongly to the same fact. Other evils attending the present defective system may be enumerated as follows:—

"1. The practical utility of dock warehouses is unquestioned; their location on the best possible site, their superior construction, their systematic disciplined management by those whose salaries depend upon the conservation of their trust insure every attainable advantage, the proof of which is that while private warehouses are empty the Albert Dock warehouses continue full.

"2. Dock warehouses can work much longer hours, for the Customs revenue being therein secure, cargoes are permitted to be landed with all possible despatch and placed at once, without the delay of weighing, safe from weather or dishonesty. Ships are thus relieved of their cargoes in little more than as many hours as the open dock and distant-warehouse system required days; they are thus so much sooner ready to undertake other voyages, and frequently to sail in time for countries and climes, as Canada, the Baltic, the West Indies,

&c., which the approach of winter, the hurricane seasons, or certain monsoons would, at a later date, forbid. By despatch, the shipowner promptly obtains his freight, the merchant his cargo, which he so much sooner realises in money, to be again invested in trade; fewer ships, less capital are therefore required to do the same amount of business. Interest of money, expense of ship's detention, cartages, and porterage, double or treble fire insurance, damage from exposure to weather, loss by pilferage, altogether forming a monstrous per centage on business, a consequent augmentation of the cost and price of goods to the consumer and exporter, with a reduction of, or retardation to the increase of, business at the port where such unnecessary burdens are suffered.

"3. Dock warehouses under public management offer security, as already shown, not only from theft, robbery, and fire, but from the insolvency of warehouse owners, which sometimes has exposed goods to seizure for head rents, and at other times caused heavy expense in removing merchandise out of suspected quarters. Dock warehouses, giving permanent accommodation and unvarying rates of storage, save merchants from the grievous wrong of having the rent of their warerooms raised—sometimes doubled—after the deposit of their merchandise; and this extortion practised in private warehouses is generally without remedy, on account of the expense of removing bulky goods of uncertain sale or retention. This grievance, which usually accompanies a heavy influx of foreign produce, is the more galling upon glutted and losing markets. Dock warehouses under public management are not only security for merchandise, but by a well-organised system of warrants they impart an exchangeable faculty to property there deposited, which, although undisturbed, is transferable in value, without delay, expense, or difficulty, from one party to another. Warehouses, it is obvious, must be the greatest security to dock bondholders. Of open docks there will probably soon be too many; their redundance will be a source of loss in interest, maintenance, repairs, &c.; while dock warehouses, which admit of no rivalry, being far within the requirements of trade, must always yield income to cover their own interest and charges, with a large surplus in aid of the dock rates. They will also rescue the trade of this country from the cost and maintenance of hundreds of horses, which, with their carts, are now employed in dragging heavy loads of merchandise to distant up-town warehouses, whence they are frequently to be carted down again to the dock side, in all cases causing wasteful expenditure and unnecessary transit of heavy vehicles throughout the town, to the injury of the streets and great inconvenience of foot passengers, who are obliged, in thoroughfares upon which warehouses are very much placed, to relinquish the footways, or incur the risk, which has been fatal to several persons, of packages, in process of being hoisted or lowered into or from warehouses, falling upon their heads."

The warehouse owners and the carters form a numerous body in the town; the carters alone are supposed to amount to 3,000. All the warehouse owners have votes in the election of the town council, as have also a number of the carters. The whole of their influence is used to prevent the erection of warehouses connected with the docks. The question has been mooted, in the town council and dock committee, at various times from 1807 to 1837—when, and in subsequent years, the then Dock Committee brought forward plans for dock warehouses, which the town council, under the paramount influence of the warehouse-owners, rejected—until 1841, when the Albert Dock Act was passed. In this Act, which provided for a new dock, to be surrounded with warehouses, the warehouse-owners succeeded in imposing restrictions against building the north and east sections of the Albert Warehouses until two years from the opening of the warehouses on the west and south side of that dock; and clause 58 enacted that "it should not be lawful for said trustees to erect or build, or to adopt any proceedings for enabling them to erect or build, any warehouses (other than those authorised by this act) on any of the present dock quays belonging to them, until the expiration of four years from the completion of the warehouses by this act authorised to be erected or built."

"When, however, the warehouse interest, by successful electioneering in the wards, acquired," says the document already quoted from, "an ascendancy in the dock committee and town council, this construction of the clause was disregarded; and although several acts of Parliament were, since 1841, obtained for making ten new open docks, no provision whatever was suffered to be inserted for furnishing any of these new docks with warehouses. The trustees, with the chairman of the docks at their head, refused to take even a discretional power for the purpose. Thus, the old warehouse ownery was permitted to appropriate to itself, not only the whole existing trade, but that which was then, and has since been, so rapidly increasing as to require new docks, and, of course, additional warehouses for its accommodation. These continued injurious restrictions against the trade of Liverpool roused the interference of merchants, at whose instance a clause was obtained in the Dock Act of 1846, obliging the trustees of the docks to come to Parliament, within two years, for powers to build warehouses on all the docks of Liverpool; and although another Dock Act was sought for and obtained in the year 1847, the whole two years have been allowed to expire, and the power now sought for, in obedience to Parliament, has been rendered nugatory by the unwillingness of the influential portion of the dock committee to act upon them."

As regards the frequency of fires in warehouses, above alluded to, many of which were suspected to be the work of incendiaries, originating in their desire to conceal, by this means, some enormous plunder of which they had been previously guilty—the following have occurred since 1833. On the 14th of January in this year, 14 warehouses and 9 dwelling-houses were burnt down in Lancelot's Hey; the value of the warehouses was £28,000, of the dwelling-houses, £2,000; and of the merchandise in the warehouses, £168,000. On the 31st of May, in the same year, a warehouse in Gibraltar-row, near Prince's Dock, was entirely destroyed by fire; the estimated loss was £40,000. In October, 1834, a warehouse in Lancelot's Hey was burnt down, containing 1,600 bales of cotton, 37 hogsheads of sugar, 150 casks of molasses, and other articles. From this time to 1842, several extensive fires are annually mentioned; but as they are not stated to have been warehouses in the chronological table from which the facts are drawn, I shall not enumerate them. On the 23d of September, 1842, there was a fire in Compton-street, Formby-street, and Neptune-street— the block of buildings formed by which cover from six to seven acres of ground. Almost every building within this space was destroyed, including nine large warehouses. The amount of property destroyed was valued at £500,000, and part of it was insured for £370,000. In December of the same year two large warehouses were destroyed, containing cotton and other produce estimated at £50,000. A fire took place in the Bridgewater warehouses, in the Duke's Dock, on the 4th of May, 1843, and a second fire in the same place on the 27th of the same month; the value of the property destroyed was from £15,000 to £20,000. A reward of £500 was offered for the apprehension of the incendiaries. On the 17th of February, 1846, two warehouses in the Goree-piazza were burned down; the loss was estimated at £65,000. Various other fires, some of very large extent, in workshops, sheds, and mills, are not included. It should be noted that warehouse incendiarism in Liverpool has greatly diminished since the water at Green Lanes, in a reservoir higher than the top of the highest warehouse in the town, has been brought into requisition for the extinction of fires. So constant a supply at high-pressure can be immediately brought to play upon a fire, that the object of the incendiary is defeated, and the fire is got under before it has answered his purpose of concealing the amount of his depredations.

"What a fruitful source of evils," says the letter of a "Liverpool Merchant," "has been our vicious warehouse system! preventing ample returns from our docks, by limiting to the least advantage the space on their quays for accommodation to the public, whether regard be had to the ships or their cargoes—the fruitful parent of two per cent. charge for fire insurance, unnecessary portage and cartage, dear warehouse rent, and constant pilferage. A neighbour of mine, a most respectable East India merchant, informs me, that although he preferred this market to any other in the United Kingdom for the sale of his silk, he had yet been induced, by the consideration of high charges alone, to send his goods up to London! And I myself have witnessed hundreds of bales of the bulkiest and most valuable staple imported here, having been forwarded from the ship's side forty miles into the interior in order to avoid our exorbitant and insupportable rates."

Under the act of 1848, by which they borrowed £500,000, the trustees have the power, and are required, to construct warehouses and enclose all new docks; or, in case of their neglect or refusal to do so, it is competent for the merchants or others to apply for a *mandamus* to the Court of Queen's Bench to compel them. It will be some time, however, before the new dock is completed, even without the warehouses. What is really wanted is an Act to compel them gradually, but effectually, to enclose all the docks, both old and new, and to construct warehouses in all new docks. Nothing less than this will make the docks of Liverpool a paying concern with such an enormous debt upon them; for docks without warehouses can give at best but little dividend. Nothing less than this will serve the exigencies of an increasing commerce, and meet the incipient but growing rivalry of the magnificent and infinitely cheaper docks of Birkenhead; and nothing less will effectually remove from a starving and over-numerous population a temptation to which no government, whether local or national, has a right to subject them. A line of railway now in course of construction from end to end of the docks will somewhat diminish the evils of the cartage system; but it will only be a diminution, not an entire removal, of the mischief. Carts must still be employed to convey the property to the remoter warehouses, or to all that are ever so short a distance off the line.

It is not only crime but pauperism which is increased by the un-protected state of the docks. It is scarcely too much to assert that Liverpool might maintain *all* its poor, without a poor-rate, from the proceeds of the town dues, if it did not itself encourage, by its present warehousing system, a daily influx of destitute and unskilled labourers and their families, from the densely-peopled shores of Ireland. Liverpool and her docks attract swarms of wholly superfluous labourers. They come not only from Ireland, whence they are brought over like cattle, at 6d. or 1s. a head, but from all parts of the country where men are unfortunate, and have courage enough to hope that Liverpool, without asking their character or previous pursuits, will employ them in porterage. Failing in obtaining employment in a market already ru-inously overstocked with labour, they offer their services at reduced rates to "middlemen" who make a profit out of them, and they thus help to pauperize the whole class of porters and dock labourers. They do not always succeed even to this extent in procuring employment; and they either spread themselves over England, begging on the way, or apply to be passed back to Ireland at the expense of the parishes of Liverpool. If they remain in the town, they can but steal on the quays, beg in the streets, or be a burden to the parish. They make their choice of the three. In the first case the merchants are the principal sufferers; but the town endures the infliction of heavier prison rates than would otherwise be required. In the last case, merchants, traders, manufacturers, shop-keepers, and professional men—the whole body of ratepayers in the town—suffer in common. The introduction of a proper warehousing system—opposed by the very parties who wish to rate the docks to the poor, because they consider the poor-rates burdensome—would greatly abate this nuisance. The enclosed docks would employ their own regular and permanent hands—men without character and experience would have no chance of employment, and would cease to apply for it—and the possibility of plunder would be so greatly diminished, that these swarming paupers, and the young children whom they train to steal, would have no reason to select Liverpool as the scene of their operations. Thus the burden both of crime and pauperism would be lessened, and the town and the docks would be alike benefited.

In my next Letter I shall enter into the consideration of another important branch of the subject, and show how certain regulations of the Dock Committee, which have been in operation for nearly half a century, have tended to demoralize the sailor, and to fasten upon

Liverpool the character of being perhaps the most depraved sea-port, not only in Great Britain, but in the world.

LABOUR AND THE POOR.

—◆—

LIVERPOOL.

[FROM OUR SPECIAL CORRESPONDENT.]

THE PROHIBITION OF FIRE AND LIGHT IN THE LIVERPOOL DOCKS.

LETTER III.

The exact number of ships in the Liverpool Docks on any particular day may be known by reference to a small commercial publication, called the *Liverpool Telegraph and Shipping Gazette,* which is published every morning. When I consulted its columns I found that on the previous day the number of ships in the river, outward bound, was 5; that the day's arrivals of ships were 21; and the day's departures 31. The total number of ships in the Docks, exclusive altogether of steam vessels, was 849. I ascertained, upon inquiry, that this may be considered about the average number of vessels in the docks on any day of the year; that there are seldom above 1,000, and sometimes not above 700. Taking the average number of men forming the crews of all vessels, small and large, to be ten, which it appears is a moderate and fair calculation, it will result that there are at all times 8,490 sailors in the port of Liverpool, exclusive of the crews of steam-vessels. What with the large American steam packets arriving and departing weekly, and the mail steamers to Ireland, Scotland, and other parts, it may be estimated that about 500 additional sailors are employed, so that in round numbers it may be computed that nearly 9,000 British and foreign sailors, employed or unemployed, are daily to be found in the streets, docks, and lodging-houses of Liverpool.

The vessels that arrive in this or any other British port may be divided into three classes—foreign vessels, British ships in the foreign and colonial trade, and coasters. Foreign vessels maintain their crews all the time they are in port; coasters do so likewise; British ships in the foreign and colonial trade discharge their men on arrival. For the benefit of the last-mentioned, and to protect them against crimps, sharpers, mancatchers, and the multifarious varieties of the genus "rogue" who consider the sailor fair game, benevolent men in Liverpool have erected a "Sailors' Home." I shall have occasion to enter upon that subject in a subsequent letter. At present I shall confine myself to the condition of the sailors in port who are not discharged from their ships, but depend upon the owners for board and lodging during their stay. It will be seen that the inquiry is an important as well as an interesting one. It will be found to affect not only the comfort, the health, the morals, and the efficiency of a large proportion of the British and foreign sailors who are daily in port, but the character of the population of Liverpool, the humanity of the members of the dock committee, and the general interests of commerce.

It was stated in the second letter of this series that fires in warehouses were formerly of much more frequent occurrence in Liverpool than they are now. In the year 1802 a fire took place in the Goree warehouses, a large and valuable pile of buildings, filled with an immense quantity of property, the whole of which was destroyed. The damage was estimated at £330,000. This fire created very great alarm in Liverpool, and the smouldering ruins emitted smoke and occasional flame for a period of nearly three months. The value of the warehouses destroyed was £44,500; and of the articles consumed, the grain was estimated at £120,000; the sugar at £60,000; the coffee at £8,500; the cotton at £30,000; and sundries at £60,000. Before the alarm caused by this conflagration had died away, a flat or lighter from Northwich, in Cheshire, took fire in the docks. The fire was speedily extinguished, but, although it did no mischief, it acted upon the minds of the Liverpool people, upon the merchants, upon the fire-insurance offices, and upon the warehouse owners in such a manner, combined with the still prevalent fear created by the Goree conflagration, as to make all parties yield their assent to a provision introduced into a subsequent Dock Act, that neither fire nor light should be allowed on board of any vessel in the docks of Liverpool. This law has now been in operation for nearly half a century, and must necessarily have affected for good or for evil a very large number of men. Whatever may be the daily number of sailors in the port, it may be presumed that it is wholly or partially changed, from time to time. Perhaps it would not be far wide of the mark if it were admitted that the maritime population is changed fifteen times in a year, which would allow a period of three weeks and a half for every vessel to arrive, discharge her cargo, transact her business, take in a fresh cargo, and depart. This would make 135,000 as the total amount of the maritime population periodically entering and leaving Liverpool in the course of a twelvemonth. As many of these appear in the town several times in a year, no possible estimate can be formed of the exact number of individuals. We may safely infer, however, that the number, whatever it may be, is very considerable, and that about one-half are engaged in the coasting trade, or belong to foreign ships frequenting the port. It was in the interest of this large body of men, who cannot cook on board of their ships for want of fire, nor remain in them in the evening for want of light, and who will not sleep on board, without fire and light, while they have money to pay for a lodging, reputable or disreputable, on shore, that, in consequence of representations made to me by aggrieved parties, I instituted an inquiry into the practical operation of the law prohibiting fire and light. The regulation is, it seems, peculiar to Liverpool. Fires and lights are permitted on board of vessels in the docks in London, up to a certain hour of the evening, when it is time for the men to go to their berths. Fire and light are also permitted in every other British, and in every European and American port, as far as I could learn. It is only at Liverpool that the sailor is driven on shore to save himself from the discomfort and hardship of cold and darkness. The society into which he is led will appear from the evidence collected.

Any breach of the law which prohibits fire and light is punishable by a fine of £10, but at the discretion of the magistrate it is reducible to 10s., and 4s. 6d. costs. The friends of the law allege in its behalf, that if Liverpool be singular in this respect, it is only a proof that the docks of Liverpool are better regulated than any other docks in the world; and that the danger of fire is really so great, that it is much better to inflict a little temporary hardship upon the sailors and officers than relax the law, and by relaxing endanger the safety of millions worth of property. Those who differ from this view of the case allege, on the other hand, that the prohibition is so cruel and oppressive that it cannot be enforced; that, as it is impossible to stow a large ship without lights, the lumpers secretly use them, in defiance of the dock regulation; and as they do so at their peril and risk, the chances of accidents by fire are greatly increased. They furthermore assert, that the expense of boarding the captains, officers, and men on shore amounts, in reality, to a heavy and unjustifiable tax upon foreign and coasting vessels, and the commerce which they carry on; and that—worse than all— the regulation has the direct effect of sending the sailors into public-houses, beershops, low dancing-shops, and brothels, in search of the common comforts of light and fire; that they are thereby demoralized, and rendered unfit for their business; that their health, character, and worldly prospects are alike injured; and that very often valuable ships, on leaving Liverpool, are lost on account of the inability of the men to perform their duty after two or three weeks revelling among the debaucheries and depravities of the town.

The supporters of the dock regulations only reply to one of these allegations, which is, that as large ships cannot be properly stowed without the use of lights, the dock committee are willing to grant permission that they shall be used, provided a policeman be stationed on board, to watch that there be no danger, and that this policeman be paid 7s. for a day's and 7s. for a night's attendance. To this answer it is again objected by the friends of fire and light, that a tax of 14s. for twenty-four hours use of a light is an unfair and injurious tax upon commerce; and, moreover, that it is in reality no reply to the case, inasmuch as it does not touch the question of fire on board, by means of which the men might be enabled to cook and sleep in their ships. I find, upon reference to the published accounts of the dock committee for the year ending the 23d of June, 1849, that the sum of £884 0s. 3d. was paid to the police during the year for permission to use lights on board ships in the docks. I should add to this general resumé of the case, that in the Duke's Dock, which is the private property of the Earl of Ellesmere, in no wise under the control of the Dock Committee, and which is frequented by great numbers of "flats" or "lighters," there is no such prohibition. The lightermen in that dock, in which large quantities of gunpowder are shipped and unshipped, live entirely on board of their vessels, with their wives and families.

Entrance to Duke's Dock

With this preface the reader will be enabled to understand the following evidence, which was collected from the parties having most experience of the grievance complained of. Among those who made statements were several American captains engaged in the American trade; the captains and mariners of coasting vessels; and many flatmen or lightermen from Wales, Cheshire, and the inland counties who frequent the port.

The first, an American captain, sailing with American and partially with British crews, gave the results of his experience, as an apprentice, a mate, and a commander, in the following terms:—

"I have been in the trade between Liverpool and Philadelphia for twenty-two years; for nearly twenty of which I have commanded a vessel. I have regularly made six passages per annum across the Atlantic, ever since the year 1828. I have only missed one voyage during all that time. Previous to coming as a master, I came as a boy and mate for two years. As a boy, I was compelled to live on board in Liverpool, and sleep in the forecastle without fire or light, exposed to damp and wet. In the winter time, about six o'clock in the evening, myself and the other apprentices left the ship to get our tea or supper at a boarding-house. After tea, as we had no place to stay at, and as we did not choose to return on board to the dark and cold forecastle, we sallied out in search of adventures, and often found ourselves in very disreputable places, that I do not at present care to think of. They were as bad as bad could be. If I had been addicted to liquor, which fortunately I was not, I should have been ruined as a seaman before I became a mate. As it was, I did myself no good; and whatever harm I then imbibed, I can attribute to nothing else than to the denial by the Liverpool dock authorities of those absolutely essential articles to the comfort both of boy and man—I mean fire and light. On my return to Philadelphia I was enabled to sleep on board ship if I pleased, or go home. I had no inducement to go into any kind of bad company. As a mate, I frequented Liverpool for about eighteen months. My experience was of the same kind as when a boy—or, if anything, worse; for, having a little more money to spend, I was led to spend it in public-houses, and still more improper places. I don't think I would have done so if I could have had light and warmth on board ship. I have often preferred to remain on shore till two or half-past two in the morning, even when the ship had to sail the next day, such a dread had I of going into a cold, damp berth without a light. Out of all the mates that I knew at that time—and they were a good many—only two ever became captains of ships in the Liverpool trade. They were all spoiled by the temptations and dissipations into which they were led on shore. They were positively ruined in health, character, and prospects. I do not know what became of them. I soon lost sight of them out of the trade. I used to be quite unfit for my duty on board after leaving Liverpool—until I had been a few days at sea, so utterly was I knocked up by the results of a few weeks' stay in the town. As captain I cannot speak in any degree more favourably of the results of the Liverpool dock regulations. I have lived on shore, at hotels or lodging-houses at very considerable expense, an expense which is wholly caused by the prohibition of fire and light. I should mostly live on board of my ship, if I could sit by a fire, and read, and have my victuals cooked. I have had about twenty boys as apprentices since I commanded a ship; all promising young lads, who might have risen to be captains, if they could have taken care of themselves, or if I could have induced or compelled them to remain on board at night. Out of that twenty, only one was ever promoted to be an officer of a ship; he was only a second mate, and after going a voyage or two, he was discharged. He soon died a confirmed drunkard. The greater portion of the boys get into such bad and dissipated habits as to become quite useless. They are soon 'used up;' and either run away, or are discharged as fit for nothing. When a man or a boy fairly gets into this bad track, two or three years are sufficient to knock him up. If we were allowed to have fires and lights on board, we might save a great portion of these boys. I do not mean to say that we could save them all, because there are some young men who are naturally so predisposed to evil courses, and so easily led astray, that they would go wrong in spite of any effort to preserve them; but I am quite certain that we could rescue two-thirds of them from destruction if we could retain them on board ship and make them comfortable. I speak from long experience and study of this matter. Two years ago I knew a man who served as mate in one of the New York liners. He had just come into the trade, from the East India trade, and had never been in the port of Liverpool. He bore the highest character for sobriety, industry, and honesty. Any captain would have been glad to have had him in his ship. I am quite sure that I would; as I set a high value upon him in every respect, both as a sailor and a man. His own captain paid him extra wages out of his own pocket as a superior man. But even this man could not bear up against the discomfort of the Liverpool docks. After coming into the Liverpool trade he was driven on shore, like others, from his cold berth and dark cabin, and compelled to seek for that warmth, light, and comfort out of his ship, which he could not find in it. He soon went wrong. Liverpool is notorious for the depravity of the population, male and female, that make it their business to prey upon the sailor; and he by degrees grew fond of the company that he met in public-houses, or worse places, and was quite ruined. I saw him lately in New York, wandering about the streets unable to obtain employment. When he came into the trade he was quite competent to take the command of a ship, and was rec-ommended by myself and others to a house in New York as the best man they could give a ship to on the occasion of a vacancy. This is not a solitary case. I could name scores of others equally strong, and all clearly traceable, in my opinion, to the depravity of Liverpool, into which men are forced by the denial of that comfort to which they are entitled on board of their ships. The seamen themselves go still fur-ther wrong than their officers, although that is needless. It used to be, and I believe is still, the practice in Liverpool, to 'skin' the sailors—that is for prostitutes to rob them of their clothes, and send them out into the streets in a state of nudity. The sailors often come on board in the morning, after having been out all night, with nothing on but their drawers and shirts. I have known cases where they have been left without even their drawers, having been robbed of all their money and every article of clothing but their shirts. In one instance I saw a man who was robbed of everything—shirt and all—and who on finding out his deplorable plight in the morning, seized hold of a sheet, tied the ends round his neck, wrapped it round his limbs in the fashion, as I should suppose, of an ancient Roman toga, and in this trim ran through the streets to the docks. A mob followed at his heels, shout-ing and hooting, and pelting him with mud and filth all the way to his ship. As he ran the gauntlet down the street the sheet was of very little use to cover him—he might almost as well have been without it. There were hundreds of people after him, men and women, boys and girls, shouting and yelling in the most fearful manner. A similar case occurred not long ago, but not to one of my sailors. The man was robbed of all his money and clothes, and had to run down the streets of Liverpool to the Waterloo Dock, in a cold and, fortunately, dark winter morning, with not a stitch of clothing, but a woman's apron, which the mistress of a disreputable house, somewhat more tender hearted than her lodger, had bestowed upon him. My second mate was once served in a similar way in Liverpool, and made his appearance on board one morning without a single article of clothing, except an old ragged red coat, which he would never tell me how he had procured. It was the only thing on him, and as you may easily imagine, it was of little use to him as a decent covering. I could relate hundreds of such instances in Liverpool; but I never heard of any cases so bad in New York, Philadelphia, New Orleans, or London, or any other port in the world. The captains in the London trade have no such trouble with their men as we have in Liverpool. The New York ships bound for London can always get better men than we can get if we are bound for Liverpool. The really good sailors on our side dread coming to Liverpool, and prefer the London trade on account of the comfort and conveniences of the docks. The sailors in Liverpool are so demoralized, that they continually pawn all their clothes after a voyage to provide means for their debaucheries on shore. Out of the usual crew that I bring over at least two-thirds generally desert the ship before she is ready to sail again. I have made passages without being able to retain even one of them for the ordinary business of the ship in port. It is the general complaint of the captains in our trade. The wages from New York to Liverpool are $15 or rather more than £3 per month. If the men remained with the ship, which they would do if there were comfort and convenience in the docks to keep them from the temptations on shore, they would get their advance money at the same rate of wages a day or two before the ship sailed on her return. But they are so eager for money to spend on shore that they will offer themselves to another ship at £2 5s. a month, in order to get an immediate advance of £1, which they no sooner get than they waste it in drink and dissipation—all the mischief being, as I think, traceable to the regulations of the docks, which condemn them to cold and darkness as long as they remain in Liverpool. The 'Sailors' Home' may be all very well for sailors who are not attached to any ship, and who are waiting to be shipped, but to foreign and coasting vessels it will be of no use. We captains consider the members of the Liverpool dock committee, though they may not know it themselves, to be the greatest encouragers of vice and immorality in the port, and the means not only of demoralizing and ruining the sailors, but of sending many of them to premature graves. We have already appealed to the humanity of the dock committee, but they have not acceded to our request to allow us fire and light. They may think themselves the friends of the port, but they are not so in reality, and they are anything but friends to the sailor. They are his worst foes, and their regulations are alike stupid and cruel, unjust and impolitic—mischievous both as regards seamen and the general interests of the commerce of the port."

The next evidence is that of a captain of a New York liner, delivered in presence of five other captains, four of them American and one English, who severally agreed in the general truth of his statements, and confirmed it in all essential particulars by the result of their own experience. This gentleman, I should add, has taken an active part in urging upon the dock committee the justice as well as expediency of a change. He said—"I am the captain of a ship trading between New York and Liverpool, and have been in the trade, more or less, for twenty years, and regularly for the last three years. All the captains that I know dread coming to Liverpool, and would never come if they could help it. I commanded a packet from New York to London for four years. In London there is no law forbidding the use of fire and lights on board ships in the docks. The consequence is, that the captains and crews of foreign ships live on board, with all the comforts about them to which they are accustomed at sea, and which they can procure at almost every port in the world except Liverpool. In London, by this system, the captain has the complete control of his crew: they pass the night on board, and are not led away into drinking shops, and low lodging houses, and dancing shops, with prostitutes and other bad characters. The captain of a New York packet, on arriving with a crew at London, can keep the whole of his men till he sails again, and can save from £10 to £15 a week by the difference of price between feeding and lodging them on board and feeding and lodging them on shore. I wonder what the Liverpool dock committee would say if we captains of ships had the power to get an act of Parliament, preventing them from having fires and lights in their houses, on the plea of danger to public and private property? I should think they would cry out lustily against the hardship and injustice; and, I conceive, we could show a better reason for the prohibition against them, than they can show against us. In the first place, if a ship is on fire in a dock, it can be moved out of the way of other ships. In the second place, there is always plenty of water to be procured to extinguish the fire; and, in the third place, if the danger to other ships be very imminent, the ship can be scuttled. But if the house of a member of the dock committee were to take fire, it could not be moved, like a ship, out of harm's way from its neighbours. There might not always be a sufficiency of water to play upon it, and it could by no manner of means, as I guess, be scuttled. I should very much like to deprive the whole dock committee of fire and light in their houses for a month, just to give them a taste of the miseries they inflict upon us. I calculate they would see the justice of our demands before the month was up, or a week either. On arriving at Liverpool we generally lose two-thirds of our crew before we have been three days in port. I find it utterly impossible to attempt to keep the men on board at night without either fire or light. It is also an evil to be compelled to send them to and fro between the ship and their boarding-houses, two or three times a day. To get to the boarding-houses they are obliged to pass through the most profligate and disreputable parts of the town. Both in going and coming to their vessels they are waylaid by gangs of prostitutes and other bad characters; and sailors are not very well able to resist such temptation. No scheme that human ingenuity could devise for the encouragement of vice and immorality among seamen could be more successful than the regulations of the Liverpool Docks, which prohibit fire and light. The evil, great as it is, does not end here; for the dissolute habits in which the sailors have been tempted to indulge by the discomfort of their ships, and the gaiety and cheerfulness that surround them on shore, up to the last moment of their stay in Liverpool, totally unfit them for their duty. It is not until they have been a week or two at sea, that they return to anything like the regular habits which are essential to the due performance of duty and the safety of the ship. They are in fact debilitated and dispirited, and quite unfit for their work. In many instances they have not only spent all their money in gin-shops and brothels, or been robbed, but they have pawned the last article of clothing they possessed to provide funds. Every captain knows that a sailor at sea without proper clothes, is of very little use. Indeed, I can't say that he is of any use at all. He goes about the decks half dead, and is fit for nothing. Not unfrequently there is but one pea-jacket and a pair of mittens among a watch of fifteen or twenty men, which passes from one to the other as the wheel is relieved. It is astonishing that the underwriters do not see that the frequent losses occurring immediately after ships leave the port of Liverpool, are principally, if not entirely, owing to the cause I have just mentioned. If they would only calculate the losses of ships leaving Liverpool, and of those leaving London, they would see at a glance that there must be something wrong in Liverpool of which they have previously taken no account. The navigation of the port of Liverpool is not more dangerous than that of London; I cannot say that it is even as dangerous. The losses almost invariably occur of ships leaving Liverpool, and not of ships entering it. The fact is quite notorious among seamen, and yet the underwriters do not seem to be aware of it. I hope this statement will enlighten them. I can enumerate nine New York packets that have been lost since I have been in the Liverpool trade, eight of which were outward bound from Liverpool, and only one inward bound. The names of the eight were—the Pennsylvania, the St. Andrew, the England, the United States, the Ocean Monarch, the Caleb Grimshaw, the Hottinguer, and the John R. Skiddy. The inward bound ship was the Stephen Whitney. Another bad effect of this Liverpool system is, that whereas in London the captains and their officers (I speak principally of the American trade) are men who have been in it from boys upwards, and who have gone through all the gradations, it is rare to find in Liverpool a captain who has been regularly brought up in the trade of the port. The dissolute habits they acquire either knock them up in health, or so damage their characters that they cannot procure any situation of trust. They either die off, or are kicked from forecastle to forecastle as common sailors. It seems very strange that the Liverpool people should imagine that there is any peculiar danger to their town in having lights and fires on board ships in the docks. In London and Bristol, and even at Birkenhead, on the other side of the Mersey, and in the Duke's Dock in this port, there is no such prohibition; and I never heard that any fires had occurred, or that the people of London, Bristol, or Birkenhead had any fear on the subject, or that the people of Liverpool were in any particular alarm about the Duke's Dock. In the Liverpool docks, where they are so preposterously severe and stringent about fire and light, I remember at least three fires within as many years. The truth is, that the very precautions taken by the authorities defeat their own object. We must have lights on board, and we do have them in spite of the dock committee and their regulations; and, using them secretly, and at the hazard of a fine of 10s. and costs if detected, we cannot take such precautions against danger as if the lights were openly carried. As it is utterly impossible to stow our ships without lights, the stevedores carry candles in their pocket and boxes of lucifer matches; and a sufficient number of candles are lighted to enable the men to carry on their work. They could not get on at all without them. One of their party, who is perfectly acquainted with the person of every one about the dock, whether of the regular or the detective police force, is stationed on the deck to look out. Each officer of the police is cunningly and strictly watched. We have 'cute fellows on board; and if an officer makes any movement to come on board, a peculiar whistle is given as a signal, and all the lights are instantly put out. He would be a sharp officer who could swear to seeing one on board. When the danger is over, and the policeman is out of sight, another signal is given; the candles are again lighted, and the lucifer matches are thrown down in the hold. The captains are obliged to wink at this manœuvre, or they would never get their ships stowed. This doubtless is a dangerous practice, as the lucifer matches sometimes get scattered about, and if accidentally trodden on they ignite and do mischief. If we were allowed to carry masked lanterns, which are always used at sea without the slightest evil consequence, there would be no possibility of danger; but working in the way we are obliged to work in the docks, from the foolish regulation of the dock committee, I conceive there is a very great and very constant danger of fire. It is generally thought among seamen that the loss of the Ocean Monarch was solely owing to this unhappy regulation, and it is almost certain that the Caleb Grimshaw took fire in this way, as her hatches were all caulked down before she left the Waterloo Dock, and were not opened until the fire was discovered at sea, after she had been several days out. There is no means of accounting for the loss of that ship, but on the supposition that some of the lucifer matches used by the stevedores in stowing the cargo were dislodged from a shelf or ledge where they had been placed, that they fell between the boxes of goods composing her cargo, and were ignited by the friction caused by the rolling of the ship. The people of Liverpool think themselves very wise and very secure, but the security of many of their most valuable ships rests, I am certain, at the mercy of a box of lucifer matches. Lucifer matches are very cheap. That is a fortunate thing for us while we are in dock; but they are as dangerous as they are cheap, which is an unfortunate thing for the underwriters. Let us have masked lanterns in a regular and comfortable way, and there will be no danger whatever."

The next evidence was that of an English captain engaged in the foreign trade, who gave another illustration of the hardships inflicted by the regulations, as regarded apprentices:—"When an apprentice myself, in the midst of the long winter nights, when it began to grow dark at four in the afternoon, I and the other apprentices had no place to go to but the cold forecastle, as the master and owners would not pay for our accommodation ashore. The cold was extreme, and as the only means of passing the time, we were obliged to go to bed about five or six in the afternoon, where we remained till eight in the morning. On the first night this was not so bad, but from the absence of fires the ship and berths soon grew damp and uncomfortable, and were enough to give us our death. When we struck a light in defiance of the regulations, and shut the forecastle scuttle, we were in constant terror of being surprised. If we heard a footstep on deck our lights were immediately put out, for fear it should be that of a policeman, and the lights were not always extinguished in a safe way. There was not time to think of safety; out went the lights anyhow. We had to thrust them under the bed, or under the clothes—anywhere to prevent the smell betraying us. It is impossible for me to state at this distance of time the miseries we endured; but remembering my own sufferings, I feel for the apprentices who are now confided to my charge, and am obliged to wink at their having lights on board. I know they have them, but I pretend not to know it. They can't have fires, although they have lights. They, therefore, take every opportunity to leave the ship, and they no sooner set foot on shore than the blaze of the public-house and cheap concert shop salutes them on every side. They are soon led away in this manner, and I am convinced that many a well-meaning lad, who has been afterwards ruined, may attribute his ruin to this very circumstance."

An English captain, who had formerly commanded a ship in the coasting trade, and who is now engaged in connection with the Bethel Union, a society established for the spiritual instruction of seamen, made the following statement as the result of his experience, both as boy and man:—

"About seventeen years ago, when I was an apprentice on board a ship coming to the port of Liverpool, we generally arrived in the depth of winter. It was so uncomfortable in the ship's forecastle that we generally made up our minds to have lights, although we well knew that we should get into trouble if we were found out. None of the crew slept on board, except the apprentices. The lights were of very little use without fires, but they were better than total darkness. If we heard any one on deck we put our candles into buckets of water. Frequently on account of the cold and the dampness of our beds, we determined to go ashore, although by the captain's orders we were forbidden to do so. It was a treat to get sight of a fire, at a dancing shop or public-house. Then the lads would go from the public-house to worse places, where they were frequently robbed of all they possessed by prostitutes. I have known cases where they have returned, not only without a farthing of money, but without their coat, waistcoat, trowsers, shoes, or hat—with nothing, in fact, but their shirt and drawers. On two occasions the mate of our ship came on board in this state. The first time he lost, besides his money and a great portion of his clothes, a valuable watch, and the second time he had literally nothing whatever left him but his shirt. I am convinced that such things would not have occurred half so frequently if we could have had fires and lights on board; but the men were driven into such places for warmth. Our beds were damp—I may say, they were not merely damp, but wet. Instances occurred, when we were on shore in the evening, just to cheer our eyes with a sight of a fire, and to avoid being chilled to death, of the forecastle having been broken open, and our clothes stolen. The thieves also robbed the ship of pieces of rope, and everything they could lay hold of. I remember that a vessel from the Mediterranean, which had just arrived in dock, was abandoned for a few hours in the evening by all the boys who were left in charge, and in their absence almost every article that was worth taking away, or was light enough to be carried, was stolen. I have discharged and loaded in the St. Katharine's Dock, London, and in the London Dock, and have remained there for a month at a time, without ever having been out of my ship to sleep, nor the sailors and apprentices either. We were allowed to have lights and fires on board till eight or nine in the evening, which made us very comfortable. The boys could then read and improve themselves in the study of navigation. One boy would read aloud while the others mended their clothes. Nothing of this kind can take place at Liverpool; but instead of that it is the grog-shop and the brothel. It was in the port of London, when a boy, that I studied mathematics and obtained a knowledge of navigation, and I am quite certain that if I had always traded to Liverpool I should have had no such opportunity, and should not have become a captain, or what I am now. My education in London fitted me for my business; my education in Liverpool would have ruined me body and soul. I have known several captains of coasting vessels, who before they frequented the port of Liverpool were considered sober moral characters and good seamen; but who as soon as they arrived in Liverpool and were driven out of their ships in the cold winter nights, by the denial of fire and light, took to the public-house, and ruined themselves. I could name half a dozen captains of coasting vessels who have been utterly lost by the contamination to which they were thus subjected. As for sailors, I cannot even guess at the number who might otherwise have remained sober and virtuous men, who have been rendered useless in their business, and a curse to society, by the habits of intemperance and brutality acquired in this manner. I met the captain of a small coaster, who in the winter time makes two voyages to Spain for nuts, who stated to me a few days ago, that while in any Spanish port, or in any port of Great Britain, except Liverpool, he could manage without difficulty to keep his men on board. They did not seem to want to go ashore, except to take a stroll in the day-time or on the Sunday; but as soon as he arrived in Liverpool he could scarcely keep a man on board at night. The cold and darkness were too much for them—they would not stay, and went off to singing-shops, to beer-shops, and to brothels. He found it quite impossible to restrain them. He had no such trouble anywhere else. My own experience as a captain is exactly the same as regards the vice and immorality caused by what I cannot but consider the cruelty or stupidity of the dock regulations of Liverpool. It is forbidden even to smoke a cigar in the docks, for fear of setting the ships on fire—another deprivation which, of itself, is quite sufficient to force those sailors who like a pipe or a cigar into public houses ashore. They manage to smoke, however, and that pretty often, and no regulation or act of Parliament will prevent them. The dock committee may strive to prevent fires and light, and may succeed to a certain extent; but they cannot always do so. The captains often have lights, and fires too, in spite of the regulations. The 'flatmen' or captains of the 'lighters' or 'flats,' while they are in the Mersey bound for one of the docks, make up a large fire, and feed it till it burns red, and gives out little or no smoke. They enter the dock with this fire burning, and as there is no smoke by this time, the dock authorities are not aware of it, and it burns itself out, giving the flatmen the advantage of a few hours' warmth, which they would not otherwise have enjoyed. At night, in the George's Dock, and in the northern and unenclosed docks generally, fires of coke and charcoal are often lighted, as I learn from the flatmen, and they escape detection 99 times out of a hundred. Indeed, I may say they are never detected, for, often as I have heard of men being fined by Mr. Rushton for using lights on board, I never heard of any one being discovered and fined for lighting a fire. The berths are often so excessively damp, that captains and others, who are compelled to sleep in them, resort to various expedients to dry and warm them. I do not know whether they take their bedding to public-houses on shore to dry, but I was told the other day of the following mode adopted for the purpose. I called to see a captain whom I knew. He told me that in the morning he had been drying his berth by means of burning brandy; and that I would be astonished at the heat it caused, and how speedily it dried his damp berth. 'In order,' said he, 'to convince you of its effect, I'll show you how I do it.' With that he took a brandy bottle from the locker, and poured a considerable quantity into a flat brass candlestick, and set fire to it with a lucifer match. He put the candlestick on the cabin table, and it burned for several minutes, making the cabin exceedingly warm and comfortable. I have been told by several people, who know the docks and the practices carried on in them, that it is a customary thing to have small portable stoves on board of the larger ships, in which the captain and officers burn spirits of wine and boil water, so as to make themselves a cup of tea or coffee. I have seen one or two of them myself. Labouring, as I do now, for the benefit and improvement— physical, moral, and religious—of the sailors, I constantly hear of the evil effects of this system of driving the men out of their ships, which are as bad as dungeons to them. The worst of criminals could not be put in a worse place than a cold, dark, damp ship. The drunkenness which it causes is incalculable. Fights are of constant occurrence in the low streets adjoining the dock; and I should think that Mr. Rushton, if asked how much of his time was occupied in hearing such cases, would confess that it amounted to a very severe tax upon him. It was formerly a frequent occurrence for sailors to fall into the docks in re- turning to their ships at night, after having been out on the spree, and regaling themselves in the warm public-houses; and I remember within the last twelvemonths that several fatal cases of drowning have occurred, from this cause alone. I cannot state the number of cases, but there were a good many. They shut the dock gates against them now—at least, such docks as have got gates. In short, I think that if the dock committee were fully aware of the countless evils caused by this regulation—the injuries to health, to morals, and to discipline which it causes, as well as the danger of fire arising from the secresy with which lights are carried—that they would, as Christians and hu- mane men, see the necessity of putting an end to it. I am sure its abo- lition could do no harm, while it would effect an immensity of good, and improve not only the condition of the sailor, but the character of the town of Liverpool."

In consequence of the fatal accidents alluded to in this captain's statement, the dock committee, some months ago, issued a regula- tion, by which drunken sailors returning to their ships at night are not allowed to pass the dock gates. This regulation, of course, can only apply to the Northern Docks, because the Southern Docks are wholly unenclosed. The drunken sailor, if he have sufficient sense left to be aware of this regulation, does not attempt to return to his ship, and becomes all the more readily the prey of the abandoned women, who are always on the look-out for such as he. If he be determined to resist this peril, and cannot procure admission into a respectable lodging-house, his sole resource is a miserable place, popularly called the "Sailors' Home" (not to be confounded with the public institution of the same name)—which affords lodgings to all comers who can pay threepence or fourpence for a share of a dirty bed, in a small room, where there may be half a dozen other sailors in a similar state. This establishment is as well-known as the splendid building whose name it usurps. An inscription, scrawled with a piece of chalk on the wall between the window and the door, points it out to the notice of sailors.

The following statement was made by an intelligent young man, who came up from his work on board a flat, to aid what he called the good cause. He spoke with great propriety and feeling, and seemed in every respect a very favourable specimen of the "flatmen." He said:—"I am the master of a flat, trading between Manchester and Liverpool, and have been twenty years in the trade. I never go into the Duke's Dock; but the whole of our company, which is called the Manchester New Quay Company, are obliged to go into the New Quay Hole, at the south end of George's Pier. In the New Quay Hole, which is an open hole or basin without gates, we are allowed to have fires and lights on board the flats. We find them a great comfort. We sleep on board invariably. When we have bale goods to carry to the large trading vessels, we must go to the Corporation Docks where the vessels lie, chiefly to the Prince's Dock; we must put out our lights and fires under a penalty of ten shillings and costs. If we sleep on board to avoid expense, we suffer greatly from damp and cold. If we lie four or five nights in the docks, our beds are not only damp but wet. I sometimes wring the water out of them. The flats are not so thickly built as ships, and cannot resist the damp so well. I have been so afraid to go into my wet berth, that I have preferred to go and sleep on the boards in the dock office. I have often done so, as it is expensive to sleep in lodging-houses. In the long winter nights it is quite impossible to stay on board, either in bed or out of it. We have no place to go to but the public-house; we *can* get sight of a fire there. No place is pleasanter to a flatman than his own cabin, but when the fire is out his best friend is gone. It is all gloom and misery, and he has no longer any comfort in it. The flats have seldom more than two men to work them. One is obliged to remain on board during the tide watch, or the flat is fined; but the other man takes care to get off as fast as he can in the winter to warm himself wherever he can get near a fire, whether it be in a public-house, or a gin-shop, or anywhere else. We not only want fire, but we want light, and we must have it; I should go stark mad without light in the evenings. If we had fire and light we should read on board, and amuse or instruct ourselves in some harmless way, as we do when we lie in the New Quay Hole. We take groceries, madder, cotton, and sundries of all kinds in our return voyage to Manchester. We have fire and light on board all the way, and when we get to Manchester there is no restriction, as there is in Liverpool. There is no prohibition against fire and light in Manchester, or anywhere else that ever I heard of, except in Liverpool. It would be a great expense to poor men like us to have to pay for lodgings on shore when we are in Liverpool. We could not get a decent bed under a shilling a night. We save that sometimes, but not always. I save it by sleeping in the dock-office on the boards, with a rug round me. We are compelled, in spite of ourselves, to pay for our cooking on shore. It amounts to a very serious tax upon us. I can't afford it, in fact. I never heard of a flat taking fire in the Manchester Docks or in the Duke's Docks here. There is no danger of fire at all, in my opinion. The fear of fire in the Liverpool Docks is all a humbug—and worse than a humbug. It picks the pockets of poor men, and ruins their health besides. There surely can be no danger in flats, for fires never take place on board, although we carry large cargoes of naphtha and gunpowder. We scarcely make a voyage without inflammable materials on board. We have naphtha both in the hold and on the deck, as well as vitriol, turpentine, and spirits, and I never heard of an accident since I have been in the trade. I hope the public will take our parts, and that the law will be altered."

The next flatman was a very venerable and respectable-looking old man, and spoke with much earnestness. "I am," said he, "the oldest captain of a flat going in the Mersey at this time. I have been a captain of a flat for 55 years, and am now 73 years of age. I have left off coming to Liverpool during the winter, in consequence of the refusal of the dock committee to allow us fire and light. I have discontinued for two or three years. I was afraid of rheumatism, in being compelled to sleep on board of my flat. We bring salt from Northwich in Cheshire, and sometimes go to one dock, and sometimes to another. My daughter-in-law has been in a flat commanded by my son, lying in the Canning Dock for the last fortnight; she came on board my flat in the Mersey this afternoon with her baby, in order to have the comfort of a fire even for an hour or two. She remained until dark, when we went into dock, and had to put our fire out. I have been at Manchester with salt. At the Canal Docks there they allow us to have fire and light; and we can make ourselves comfortable. The flatmen sometimes bring their wives with them on their voyages—but not often, on account of the want of comfort in the docks, especially if they have young children with them. It is a great loss to me not to come to Liverpool in the winter months; but I am obliged to submit to the loss rather than catch my death of cold. The flat I command is my own; but if I were the master of another person's flat, and would not travel in the winter, I should have to go to the bastile—I mean the union workhouse. We are not even allowed to smoke a pipe on deck, but the flatmen will have their pipes, most of them. I don't smoke myself, and, therefore, I do not suffer in that way; but I know scores of flatmen who do, and who consider it a very hard case. When there is an alarm given that a policeman is near, they throw their pipes down anywhere; they have not time to reflect whether it is dangerous or not. When we come with a cargo of salt, not consigned to anybody in Liverpool, but awaiting the market or demand that may arise for it, we prefer going over to the Birkenhead Docks, because there we are allowed light and fire, and there we can await in something like comfort until we get a purchaser for our cargo. We pay 5s. for permission to enter the Birkenhead Docks, and we do not begrudge it, for we can get fire and light by it. The wages of a flatman—that is of a 'hand'—are not, on the average, much above 10s. or 11s. a week. The wages of a captain are not quite double, but sometimes they may be about twice as much as a 'hand.' It is a great expense, both to the captain and his 'hand,' to be denied fire. He has to pay a penny a morning for a kettle of hot water for his breakfast, a penny for cooking his dinner at a baker's, and a penny for his hot water for tea in the evening. All this expense falls upon the captain of the flat. The flats get as damp as any coal-cellar in Liverpool; and I have often seen them when you could wipe the wet off the sides of the sleeping berths. The bedding gets very damp; the pillows are often as wet as if they had been rained upon. No woman could live in such places. It is as much as a man can do; and more than I can suffer at my time of life. I should come to Liverpool all the year round if the regulations were the same as at Birkenhead. I have often been in the Duke's Docks—have known them for forty-five years. Flats have always been allowed to have light and fire in that dock; and I never knew of any accident taking place there from fire. Never heard of such a thing in the Duke's Dock, but I have heard of fires in the Prince's Dock and other docks, where they won't allow fire and light on board. We are often forced to go on shore, for the sake of warming ourselves, and sometimes have found our flats robbed on our return. This has happened to me. I wish the dock committee could prevent robberies in the docks as well as fires, and they would do a little more good to poor and honest men than they do now."

The next witness, a young man, stated—"I am a 'hand' on board a flat, and have been for eight years. The want of fire on board is a great hardship. I have often got wet through coming up river, and have changed the whole of my clothes. In steering into the docks, when it rains hard, I have not had a dry stitch upon me, and have been obliged to go on shore to a public-house to get my clothes dried, and they don't want flatmen there unless they spend their money. This has happened to me many a time, and has cost me a good deal of money in drink one way or another. If I didn't drink I could not get my clothes dried. I have often caught a severe cold from this alone, besides making my cold worse by going to bed in a wet berth. I am always more glad to leave Liverpool than to come into it; and if I could make my living anywhere else, I never would come into it. I have heard of and seen men whose health has been ruined in this manner, and who might at this day have been strong men if all the docks of Liverpool were conducted like the Duke's Dock. In the long winter evenings we go ashore to a public-house, and come on board again as well as we can at the latest possible moment. The regulations are hard upon us in every way—on our comfort, on our health, and on our pockets. They are quite the ruin of all seafaring men."

I visited the Duke's Dock so often alluded to in the statements made upon the subject, and entered into conversation with the flat-men. It is a narrow dock, with abundance of quay room. It contained, on the day of my visit, twenty-four flats, and two schooners, of about ninety tons. From every one of these flats, and from the galleys of the two schooners, the smoke was curling up in wreaths. Every ves-sel had a fire. The quays were covered with cotton bales, barrels of tar and oil, and kegs of naphtha and spirits. Several of the flats were laden with cotton, which they carry both on deck and in the hold. One in particular engaged my attention. It was so heavily laden with cotton that, unable to stow the cargo otherwise, the flatmen had piled the bales to a height above the chimney, and the smoke seemed to be issuing from the cotton. The dockmaster said there was no danger— no accident had ever occurred from fire in that dock as long as he remembered it, or that he had ever heard of. "What was more," he said, "the Duke's Dock was the principal powder dock in Liverpool, and independently of the gunpowder, of which large quantities were shipped and unshipped on the quays, no dock had such inflammable matter entering and leaving it as this had, and yet there never was an accident." It was mentioned in my last letter that a large stack of warehouses belonging to this dock had taken fire twice in the year 1843; the first time on the 4th and the second on the 27th of May. It was said by some persons that the fires in the flats were the causes of the two catastrophes, and an order against fire and light was in consequence issued by the Earl of Ellesmere. It was evident, however, from the height at which the fires originated—in the fourth story of the building, upwards of 80 feet above the chimneys of the flats—that no spark from them could have entered the windows and set fire to the warehouses; and it was afterwards satisfactorily proved that the fires must have been the work of an incendiary. The flatmen laughed at the idea of either of the two fires having been caused by the use of fire and light on board of the flats. They also complained of the new regulation of the Earl of Ellesmere. His lordship, it appears, had a galley built on the quay for their accommodation, in which they might cook, instead of cooking on board; but the galley was not found to answer. The flatmen broke the earl's law, and kindled their fires as usual. The offenders were so numerous (in fact every flatman that came into the dock was an offender) that it was found impossible to enforce the regulation, or wean the men from their old habit of making themselves comfortable on board. It was therefore deemed expedient to tolerate the practice; and in the Duke's Dock, with its gunpowder, its tar, its naphtha, and its spirits, the flatmen make homes of their vessels.

On reference to the chronological annals of the town, it appears that three fires have occurred in the docks since the passing of the act prohibiting the use of fire and light. The first occurred in 1824, on board the ship Dorset from Savannah, lying in the Prince's Dock. She was got out of the dock and scuttled in the basin. The second took place in 1836, on board the American ship Hibernia in the same dock. She was scuttled in the dock without doing any damage to the other shipping. The third took place in December, 1843, on board the

The Duke's Dock & Warehouses

Meg of Meldon, in the Waterloo Dock. She also was scuttled without doing damage to other ships.

Another feature of this question is, that which relates to emigrants. By the Passenger Act, the emigrants are entitled to come on board twenty-four hours before the advertised time of sailing, to use the ship as if they were at sea, and to be supplied with provisions for that time. Even in the spring and summer months—the most busy periods for emigration—the deprivation of fire and light during the twenty-four hours is some hardship upon the poorer class of emigrants, great numbers of whom do not avail themselves of their privilege of living on board where no cooking is allowed, but prefer to spend a few shillings extra in the boarding houses, where they have previously resided. It often happens, however, that a ship cannot sail on the advertised day of sailing, but is detained three or four days, or even a week, by a variety of causes. It is then that the case becomes one of greater hardship. No cooking of any kind can take place on board—they cannot even have hot water for a cup of tea—and bread and cheese and cold water is their principal fare. At night, when three or four hundred people are cooped up between decks, and utterly in the dark, their discomfort is extreme. The people, however, brave the regulations, and light lucifer-matches, if only to have half a minute's light to find their way to their berths or to their luggage. The danger of this practice is palpable, and might be obviated by a few masked lanterns, if the act of Parliament obtained by the dock committee did not stand in the way.

It will be seen that this question, on account of its effects upon the health and morality of the maritime population, is a very important one. There seems no other argument than that of terror to be brought forward in defence of the Liverpool practice of denying the sailor the comfort of fire and light. Whenever a man eats, there is a danger of his being choked. Wherever there is a candle, there is a danger of fire. It is doubtful, however, whether it would be more rational to prohibit eating lest men should be choked, than to prohibit fire and light in the docks lest the shipping should be destroyed.

LABOUR AND THE POOR.

LIVERPOOL.

[FROM OUR SPECIAL CORRESPONDENT.]

THE PORTERAGE SYSTEM.

LETTER IV.

As I stated in my previous Letter, the persons employed in discharging vessels in the magnificent docks of Liverpool are estimated, without including warehousemen, to amount to about 15,000 or 16,000 men. This estimate may be erroneous. There is no means of arriving at the real numbers, because no record is kept, nor is any licence or certificate required for carrying on the business of an operative porter or dock labourer, skilled or unskilled. As far as I can judge from inquiries made of different parties, 16,000 is about the number, divisible into three classes—namely, the lumpers, and the dock labourers, who discharge the ships, and do all the work in the hold; the master porters and the operative porters, who take charge of the cargo on the quay, weigh it, look after the marks, sample it, enter the weights, and place it in carts for transmission to the warehouses; and the carters, who cart it off.

First in order are the dock labourers. But I commence my inquiry with the most numerous body—that of the operative porters—not only because they *are* the most numerous, and their condition the most interesting, but because a change of system with respect to them has been legalized by Parliament, which, as alleged by a numerous section of their body, has had the effect of throwing thousands of them out of work. They bear a high character for industry, honesty, and sobriety—the magistrates, merchants, and master porters of Liverpool vying with each other in praising their general behaviour at all times, as well as their patience and good conduct under very trying circumstances. It is a melancholy sight, in walking through the open space of the Liverpool Exchange, or through any of the streets leading thence to the docks and river, at any time during the business hours of the day, to notice the multitudes of men hanging about in every corner awaiting the chance of employment in the docks and quays. The Exchange seems to belong as much to the operative porters as to the merchants; and each body seems to occupy its own particular half of the enclosure. On the one side is a great crowd of men, in good broad-cloth, talking upon business or politics, and possibly negotiating large transactions to be estimated by thousands of pounds sterling; on the other side is a still larger crowd of men, in fustian-jackets, and with horny hands, loitering about, or gathered into little knots at every corner, waiting, hour after hour and day after day, for the chance of obtaining a job that shall bring to each individual the price of a day's work. I counted upwards of 300 upon the Exchange-square one morning, and 300 men in groups make a very imposing appearance; whilst, in the adjoining streets towards the Mersey, there must have been at least ten times the number. It is impossible to avoid taking an interest in the condition of so large a body of industrious and well-behaved men, who have been seriously affected by the operations of the recent law—framed without any view to their interests, but upon considerations connected entirely with the important questions of the efficiency of the docks, the trade of the town, and the interests of merchants and shipowners.

I will endeavour to present the history of this change as briefly and succinctly as possible. For nearly ten years, from 1835 to 1845, the merchants and authorities of Liverpool had made application from time to time to the Government for an increase of landing waiters, the insufficiency of whose numbers greatly impeded the trade of the town. These applications were unsuccessful. In February, 1845, Mr. T. B. Horsfall, afterwards Mayor of Liverpool, brought the subject before the town council, and moved the appointment of a special committee, to consider and report upon it. Mr. Horsfall, in moving for this committee, stated that not a single additional Custom-house officer had been appointed for the port since April, 1835, although, in the interval, its trade had increased about 64 per cent. It was, he said, not an uncommon thing for fifty, sixty, or seventy sail of vessels to be detained for want of landing waiters; and one day, in the summer of 1844, no less than 131 vessels were delayed by this cause. On another day, in the beginning of July in that year, 104 vessels were enumerated as being in this predicament, sixty of which were in discharging berths in the docks. Although there were several other grievances, which it was in the power of the Treasury and the Custom-house Department to remedy, this appears to have been the most prejudicial to the interests of the town and port, and the one most strongly brought under the notice of the Government. The Town Council appointed the committee which Mr. Horsfall asked for, and, after repeated meetings and the collection of evidence upon the various subjects of complaint, it unanimously agreed upon its report. This document stated that, for the six months preceding, the daily average of vessels detained for want of landing-waiters was 28—and that the minimum loss to the merchants and owners was £10 per day per vessel, or upwards of £100,000 per annum; being more than the annual expense of the whole customs establishment of the port. A deputation was shortly afterwards appointed to proceed to London and lay the whole case before Sir Robert Peel, who was then in office. The result of this proceeding was, that 57 additional Custom-house officers were appointed for the port—and that, in a letter communicating this decision, Mr. Goulburn, the Chancellor of the Exchequer, brought under the notice of the authorities of the town the defective system of porterage, pointing it out as a principal source of the inconvenience, confusion, and delay complained of, and without remedying which no real benefit would accrue to the trade of the port, whatever might be the number of tide-waiters and other officers whom the Government might appoint. This subject, having been pressed upon the local authorities by the Customs Department for a long time previously—as long as thirty years—and being moreover acknowledged as a grievance by the principal merchants and shipowners, was taken into the consideration of the Town Council, with a view to a remedy. A report submitted to the Town Council on the 3d of December, 1845, by a special committee appointed on the 10th of November previously, exhibited the defects of the system.

It is here proper to explain more fully what this system was. When a vessel arrived in the docks, each consignee of goods on board, although there may have been twelve or twenty, or any other number, employed his own porters to weigh, weight off, mark, sample, and remove his consignments to the warehouse. The consequence was, that if there were twelve consignees, there were often twelve different and independent gangs of porters employed in discharging the vessel, none of them yielding obedience to any one but the consignee who employed them. The committee stated that this system "arose, in a great degree, from the force of circumstances, but that it was one which they conceived tended, in a great degree, to impede the trade of the port, to throw an increased expense on the merchant and shipowner, and to lessen most materially the efficiency of the Docks." They further said that they were enabled to state these facts by the perusal of official documents furnished by the Board of Customs, and that those results were the consequence of serious delays, "arising mainly from the non-attendance of porters at the proper hours, the confusion and waste of time occasioned by the unnecessary employment of several sets or gangs of porters at one vessel, and from the want of a proper and responsible superintendent." They also expressed their opinion that "nothing short of a legislative enactment would effectually provide a remedy, and recommended that they should be authorized to communicate with the Dock Committee, with the view of obtaining the insertion of a clause in their proposed new act, requiring the employment of one set of porters only in the discharge of the entire cargo of any vessel unloading in the Liverpool docks, the expense of such discharge to be borne respectively by each consignee of goods in fair proportion." The committee at the same time recommended a revision of the scale of charges. These recommendations were afterwards embodied in the Dock Bill, and became the law of the land, power being given to the largest consignees of the cargo to appoint the master porter to unload the ship. This is the Act of the 9th and 10th of Vict., cap. 109, which received the Royal assent on the 26th of June, 1846, and has given rise to the present dissatisfaction of the operative porters. Section 35 of that statute enacts that the cargo of each vessel from any foreign port, entering or using any of the docks or basins of the trustees, or the quays of which no warehouses shall at the time have been erected, shall be received, weighed, and loaded off by one set of porters only, who shall be in the employ and under the direction and orders of one of the master porters, acting in pursuance of, and under the powers and provisions of, this act. The 36th section defines the position and responsibilities of the master porter, and enacts that every master porter, before he shall be capable of undertaking or receiving, weighing, and loading off the cargo of any vessel entering the docks, shall execute a bond, with two sufficient sureties, to be approved of by the Dock Trustees, in the penal sum of £200, to make good any loss or damage that may accrue to the cargo under his care in the process of receiving, weighing, and loading off, whether that loss or damage be caused by himself, or by the operative porters in his employ. The 40th section enacts a penalty of £50 against any master porter who shall undertake to discharge a ship, without having entered into the proper bond, as above stated;

and the 41st section gives the trustees the power, in the exercise of their discretion, to prohibit any person, for any cause, and for any period which they may think proper, from acting in the capacity of master porter.

This is, in a short compass, the history of the change in the porterage system of Liverpool. I shall now proceed to detail the complaints of the operative porters, and give their version of the manner in which it affects their interests, and deprives them of a large amount of employment which they formerly received. I shall follow up their statement by an impartial inquiry upon every other side of this complicated question, and shall show the opinion of those who oppose, as well as of those who support, the present system—of the shipowners as well as of the merchants, and of the master porters as well as of the working men. I found the inquiry exceedingly difficult, and, without expressing any opinion of my own, I give the various statements of the parties interested. My first inquiries were among the operative porters themselves. I endeavoured to discover not only the most intelligent among them, and those most suffering from the pressure of distress, but those who were still in tolerably full employ, that I might get exactly at the truth of the present position of the whole body. I should premise that at the time they waited upon me to state their grievances, they were making application to the Legislature for the repeal of the act which they complain of as bearing injuriously upon their interests, and as having thrown thousands of them partially out of employment. I give their statements as made to me, sometimes in reply to my questions, and sometimes as volunteered by themselves, without any questions on my part. I should mention, also, that in addition to two deputations of porters who waited upon me, I saw some others of the men at their own homes. The first person who made me a statement, and whose initials only I prefix, said:—

P—— H——: "I am an operative porter, and a Liverpool man. I was in the employment of one firm for ten years before the new system. I averaged all that time five days' work in the week, at 3s. 6d. a day. It is very different now. The firm must employ a master porter to discharge the vessels, and the master porter employs such men as he pleases. For the last sixteen weeks I have only had 13½ days' work—not a day's work a week. I have not had a single job for the last fortnight. Many hundreds—perhaps there may be thousands—in the parish of Liverpool are as badly off as I am; perhaps worse. I have no wife; but I have four children. If it had not been for the parish, I and my children must have starved. If things don't mend, we must all go to the workhouse."

E—— I——: "I am an operative porter. I was employed, off and on, by two houses in Liverpool. For six years before the new act came into operation, I scarcely lost a day's work. I had 3s. 6d. a day. I have not gained 5s. a week since the new act was passed. This week I have not had a day's work. I began to pawn my furniture about two years ago. I had some good furniture left to me by my father when he died. I could not manage to keep it. All that a pawnbroker would take of it is gone. I have a wife and a daughter. Last week I had three days' work. It was the best week I have had for six months, and I was able to get my boots out of pawn. I have got them on now, but I expect I shall have to send them back to the pawn-shop next week, if I don't get a job or two. I never applied to the parish; and I won't apply, if I can help it. I am a Liverpool man. I was born of English parents in the town. I am not one of the 'Grecians'" (*i.e.* raw Irish).

J—— C——: "I am an operative porter. I have a wife and four children. Before 'master-portering' came into operation, I had generally from four to five days' work in a week, at 3s. 6d. a day. Now—and ever since the master-portering began, I can't make above three days in the week at the best. For the last seven weeks I have only had fourteen days' work. This week I have earned nothing. I consider myself lucky, compared to some porters that I know. I know hundreds very badly off. One of my children, a boy, has a place at a carpenter's, and gets 5s. a week. His money helps us a good deal. He goes errands, and does other work about the shop. Without his money, I don't know how I should manage. Though not a teetotaller, I am a temperate man, and never give any of my money to the publican. I spend what I earn upon my family."

J. C——: "I have been for eight years a porter. Before the master-portering system began I could make from three to four days a week; but for the last twelvemonth I have not made two days a week. My wages used to be 3s. 6d. a day. Since the middle of October I have only made eleven days, or about £1 18s. 6d., to keep me for eighteen weeks. I have a widowed daughter, who is a dressmaker, who keeps house for me. She earns enough to help me a little. I don't pay my way. I can't do it. I have got credit at a store, where I have bought grocery and other things for three or four years. The people know me, and will not let me want, if a little credit can help to keep me above water.

Between the credit I have got, and the pawn-shop, I contrive to live somehow or other—but I scarcely know how I do it."

H. ——: "I am an Irishman. I am 64 years of age, and have been an operative porter in Liverpool for 32 years. Until about 15 years ago times were pretty good in the portering business. I have worked in the timber docks, the cotton docks, and the corn docks—anywhere where I could get a job. My wages are 3s. a day for cotton, and 4s. 6d. a day for timber. I used to get in the old times about a pound a week, one way or the other. Times have been very bad lately, since the master porters came into operation. They are the worst enemies of the poor porter. Some of them employ unskilled porters, who will take almost any wages they can get. Some of them will give eighteen pence or two shillings a day, instead of three shillings. The unskilled porters have got strength only. They don't know their business. They have no education to it. They can't mark, or weigh, or sample. The skilled porters are men who can weigh and sample, and do all sorts of porter's work. They have the best chance of work. I consider myself a skilled porter, equal to any work in the business. I don't know how many skilled and unskilled porters there are in Liverpool. There may be 2,000 skilled hands. There may be 15,000 or 16,000 porters of all kinds. There may be 20,000. I don't know how many there are. There are too many. For the last two years I have not had three days' work in the week, on an average. There are so many 'green hands' from Ireland, who come to do the warehouse and other work for almost nothing, that we haven't the same chance we used to have. We call them 'green hands,' or 'Grecians,' or 'foreigners.' I have not had one job for the last fortnight. I have twelve in family: a wife, two sons, a married daughter, and her seven children. Her husband is a cooper, and has gone to New Orleans to try his fortune there. He had not one farthing to leave them, and he has not sent them anything yet. He could not help it, poor fellow; he could get no work here. We do the best we can. One of my sons has 14s. a week. He lodges with us, and his money helps us."

D. W——: "I have been a porter for 26 years. I am experienced in every department. I can weigh, take weight, mark, lower, sample, and do all other parts of the business. Under the old system I was well employed. I got from five to six days' work in the week all the year round. Under the master-porter system I am not half employed. I never have more than three days' work in the week. I have the full wages. I have a wife and four children. One daughter used to do needlework to help us, but she has no work now. There are too many hands at the needle-work in Liverpool. No porter in Liverpool had cause to complain un-til these master porters came up. They are paid by the job—at a fixed rate—and the sooner the job is done the more money they can make. They save the wages of the porters, and put it in their own pockets. I have been obliged to pawn almost everything. I had a Bible that I gave £3 for, twenty years ago. All the children's names and ages were in it. It was beautifully bound, with pictures in it. I was obliged to pawn it for 5s., and it is now lost, as I could not pay the interest on it when the year was up. I have paid poor-rates in Liverpool for twelve years, and I expect that now the parish will have to keep me. I have buried eight of my children. I was very poor when the last died. I was out of work, and had no money to bury it. I borrowed the money of a friend. I owe it yet, and can't see how I shall ever be able to pay it. If I could get regular work, such work as I used to have before the master porters were invented, I could soon pay it."

D. B——: "I have been a porter for twelve years. I undertake all kinds of porter's work except the timber work. I do not work in the timber line, but principally in the cotton and corn. The master-porters' system has taken the bread out of my mouth. I used to get five days' work in the week. Since September last I have not had above two days' work in the week. I keep no note of the days in any book, only in my memory. I have a wife and two young children. I pay 5s. a week rent. For six months I have only gained 7s. a week, leaving 2s. to live on. We could not live on that. My wife keeps an infant-school, and gains about 3s. a week; and my brother-in-law lodges with me and pays me 2s. 6d. a week. If it was not for these two things I couldn't manage at all. It is this that keeps me out of the workhouse; but both these things are very uncertain."

W. M——: "I have been a porter in Liverpool since the year 1825. I am not a 'Grecian,' I am a Scotchman, and came from the west of Ross-shire. I was pretty well employed under the old system. I can take weight, mark, weigh, sample, and perform all kinds of porter work. I used to average 12s. or 15s. a week. For thirteen weeks, at the beginning of last year, I had only eight days' work. I got jobs at that time as an extra hand at the Albert Docks. From April to October, when things were not so slack in the port, I averaged three days a week; but for the last twelve weeks of the year, I only earned 7s. 9d. for the whole time. A warehouseman, who is my friend, lent me two or three shillings every now and then to help me on, and I owe him a good deal of money. One of our principal merchants used often to employ me under the old system. He knew me, and would give me a turn, and do me a kindness when he could. All the work goes through the master porters' hands now, and many of the master porters employ the cheapest hands they can get—'Grecians,' or others that perhaps have just come over from Ireland, and have not been in Liverpool a week. In the month of February last I had only eight and a half days' work. I have passed all the rest of my time about the Exchange, looking for jobs. Under the old system a man could get a job by looking about the docks, but now he cannot. His only chance is at the Exchange, and thereabouts. I have waited there for eight hours at a time, and all for nothing. The waiting is the most miserable part of it. I am often obliged to wait in the cold and rain, and uncertainty. I would rather work for nothing than wait for nothing. It is very hard to stand idle all day with your hands in your pockets, without being able to earn a crust."

L. S——: "I am an operative porter, and know all about the business. I don't know how many operative porters there are in the town, but I know that there are a great deal too many. The 'Grecians' are always coming over, and I think they are brought over on purpose, by the master porters and others, that they may pay them half wages, or anything they please. The operative porters have established an association. Their object is to procure the repeal of the Act 9th and 10th of Victoria, cap. 109, as far as it relates to the portering business. The effect of this act has been to create a large class of middlemen called master porters. They live—I don't mean all of them, but the new hands among them—by underbidding one another to the merchants and consignees, and making up their profits out of the wages of the operative porters. They employ the green hands—the 'Grecians'— unskilled porters, that are always coming over on the chance of work. Some of them keep lodgings for single men, and give their jobs to their own lodgers. Others keep provision shops, and give their jobs to those who 'run up scores with them.' Some keep public-houses. I know that the dock committee have power to refuse a licence to any master porter who keeps such places, and carries on the 'truck' with the porters; but it is easy to do it. The master porter can keep the lodging-house, or the public-house, or the store, in a friend's name, or a relation's, and the dock committee can't get at him. The single men who lodge with the master porter have a better chance of work than the married men. It is a very hard case upon a man with a family, who has been in the town all his life, and paid rates, to be kept out of his bread in this way. The system encourages men to come over from Ireland, when the town is too full already. Some of the warehouse-men also keep these houses, and carry on the same system. The Irish think that there is no end of work in Liverpool, but they soon find out their mistake when they come. Once they are here, they remain here. That is all the better for the master porter, for he gets his work cheap; that is to say, the unskilled work. He can't get the skilled work any cheaper. I have been between seven and eight years in the business. It has grown much worse since the new system was pursued. I have very good employment compared with some men. I have at least three days a week. I should have more if it were not for the system of importing 'Grecians' to keep down the price of labour."

I took the statements of several other men: their evidence was of the same tenor, and was generally to the effect that employment was diminished one-half at least under the new system, and that a certain class of master porters—new men to the business—and not the respectable master porters, and also some of the warehousemen, kept lodging-houses, public-houses, and provision shops, and confined the work they got to their lodgers or customers. It would be needless to give the evidence of a greater number of men. It was all to the same purpose. My next object of inquiry, having seen how the matter affected the merchants and shipowners, and the large body of operative porters, was to communicate with the respectable master porters, and learn their view of the case. I found them generally an intelligent body of men, quite willing to give information, even on the minutest points; and to show their books in corroboration of their statements. One and all spoke with the highest respect of the behaviour of the operative porters as a body.

The first gentleman I saw connected with the trade of the master-porterage begged, if I saw proper, that I would have no scruple in publishing his name as a voucher for the truth of his statement in every particular. He said, in answer to my inquiries, having fully explained my objects:—

"I am the representative of one of the oldest firms of master porters in the town of Liverpool. Our house has been established for upwards of 45 years. I succeeded my father in the business. The term 'master porter' is by no means a new one. There have been master porters in Liverpool for 60 or 70 years at the least—perhaps longer. The only difference made by the new act regulating the quay porterage of the port, is that master porters are now licensed; formerly they could act without a license. In the year 1841—I select that year because I have that year's Liverpool Directory now before me—there were only ten recognised master porters. You will see my name among the number, if you look in the 'Directory' for that date. There were perhaps a few others in a small way, but very few. In the 'Directory' for 1849 the names of only 24 master porters are inserted, but there were at least as many as two hundred in the town at that time. There are probably a great many more now, but I can't say exactly. Many of the principal merchants in the town are master porters. They take out licences for convenience, in order that they may act for themselves when they have consignments, and employ their own porterage. There are various kinds of porters employed in the unloading of a ship in the docks. There is, first, the Lumper, or stevedore, with his men, who are totally unaffected by the recent act; next, there is the Master porter and his operatives, who are the only persons affected by it. If the ship contains a cargo of rum, wine, molasses, oil, sugar, or any other commodity in casks, there are the Master cooper and his men, whose business it is to put the casks into proper condition on the quay, to prevent their being stove in. Next after the operative porters are the Carters, who cart the cargo from the quay to the several warehouses engaged by the consignee. The operative porters are again employed to hoist the cargo from the cart to the store or warehouse; but the act which they complain of, only refers to their labour on the quays—so that each consignee, whether large or small, may employ what men he pleases in the streets or at the warehouses. Most undoubtedly there are fewer men employed under the new system than there were under the old. The porterage work is done with much more rapidity, and there is a saving both of time and expense. When ships were detained under the old system much longer than they should have been, it was an injury to the shipowner, to the merchant, and to the docks. It was expensive to the shipowner and merchant, and injurious to the docks, because such ships continued to occupy berths that other ships were ready to fill. For instance, under the old system, a vessel of 300 tons, with a general cargo, would take seven days for the porterage. Each consignee would have had his own men hanging about, under pay, though perhaps not actually employed; awaiting the discharge from the ship of their employer's consignments, and not putting a finger on any other consignee's goods. From 18 to 20 men would be employed. Under the present system, when the master porter acts for all the consignees, the work could be done by 10 or 12 men in 5 days. You can easily imagine what a great saving this is—but I cannot at this moment give you the exact figures; because it would be necessary to specify exactly the various articles in a miscellaneous cargo. The master porters, I mean the old-established and respectable men, have no reason to be in favour of the present system. It has diminished their employment as well as that of the men. The licensing has brought a larger class of master porters into the business, who underbid each other, and resort to the disreputable system of canvassing the merchants. I will explain the canvassing system. By the insertion of a single letter in the act of Parliament, giving the power of employing the master porter to the largest consignees instead of the largest consignee, a system of canvassing the small consignees has sprung up, to the great annoyance of the merchants. The object of a canvasser is to get the small consignees, who together may represent the larger portion of the cargo, to sign a paper or 'round-robin,' authorizing him to obtain the porterage of the ship, from the ship's consignee. The effect of this system upon the respectable master porter is, to deprive him of business, for no respectable master porter will canvass the merchants. The canvasser in general offers a discount to the consignees—that is, he offers to do the job for a sum below the usual rates, as an inducement to the merchant to employ him. These are the class of men that reduce the wages of the operative porters, for such a person can only do the job at a cheaper rate, and make a profit out of it, by taking it off the wages of the men. The old operative porters will not work for less than the usual wages, and many of the new ones who accept such wages are quite unskilled and unfit for the business, and have not even the proper tools. There are many warehouse-keepers who take out licences as master porters, and offer to do the porterage at a lower rate than usual, upon condition that the cargo, or part of it, be warehoused with them. This system also tends to beat down the wages of the operative porters. The hours of working of the operative porters are from half-past eight to half-past three in winter, with a short interval for dinner. The hours in the summer are from 8 to 4, with an interval for dinner. The men get paid for over-hours. The establishment of the Albert Dock has had the effect of taking away work from the master porters and from the operative porters. I have heard a good deal about a low class of master porters, who keep lodging-houses for young men, and of others who keep public-houses or provision-shops. I believe there is some truth in the charge, and that they evade the dock committee by not keeping such places in their own name. I have heard of such men getting the porterage work from the consignees by offering to do it from 30 to 40 per cent. under the rates fixed in the new rate-book. They can make it answer, not only by reducing the wages, but by charging their own prices for their lodgings or their provisions, or by allowing the men to get in their debt for drink. I believe there is a good deal of this in Liverpool. It is very injurious to the town, and to the character of the respectable master porters, who would scorn to become parties to it; and, of course, still more injurious to the poor men. The operative porters never spoke a word against the master porters until the new system was introduced, and until this competition for work arose betwixt the licensed master porters of an inferior class. Many of these new men, canvassers, and others, have not even a place of business in the town. Many of them are warehousemen whose services have not been needed under the new system, and who have in consequence taken out licenses as master porters. The working porters are, I think, a very honest body of men. During all the time I have been in business, I never had a man convicted of theft or misdemeanor. They are well behaved, and have many temptations; and it is a wonder to me, considering the hardships they suffer, that theft is not more common among them."

The second master porter who was obliging enough to enter into the details of his business said, in answer to my inquiries:—"I have been a master porter since the establishment of the new system. I was previously head warehouseman to one of the principal firms in Liverpool for twelve years, managing both a large import and export trade. In that capacity I knew the whole details of the old system. The new system is, in my opinion, highly beneficial to the interests of the dock trustees and owners, because ships are discharged in a shorter time, and the same berth will accommodate a larger succession of vessels in a given time. There can be no mistake upon that question; but all the credit of this expedition is not due to the new system, but part of it most certainly to the abolition of duties upon the import of cotton wool, and upon a great variety of foreign produce, making a difference of about three working hours from March to October, and about two working hours in the other part of the year. Under the new system, the Custom-house regulations are also much more favourable to the merchant than they used to be; for instance, under the old Custom-house regulation, the ship's consignees had to pay 5s. per hour per ship to the landing surveyor; from 6 to 8 o'clock in the morning in the summer season, and from 4 to 6 in the afternoon, being four over-hours; to the landing waiters, 2s. 6d. per hour in the same way for each ship; and to the weighers, 6d. per hour for each ship; and to the two officers placed on board the ship, 6d. per hour per ship; and to the depot-keeper, 6d. per hour in the same manner; and if the goods were going to a bonded warehouse, two officers stationed there were entitled to the same remuneration. There were some other charges of a similar kind, amounting in the whole to a very considerable sum for each ship. Under the present Custom-house system, if one ship only is working, these charges are still due; but if ten or any other number of ships are working, they count but as one ship, and divide this charge amongst them. This is one of the great causes of the present expedition. A great number of ships are attended to at once by the Custom-house authorities at a proportionately smaller charge to the merchants. Another reason is, that the weigher of a cargo of all free goods is the servant of the master porter, and not, as formerly, independent of him, and the servant of the Custom-house. The master porter can make him do his work. Under the old system he had no control over him, and could not make him work faster, if he were inclined to be lazy. I do not think that equal advantages result from the change to the importing merchants. They may save in expense; but I consider their own servants would be the most proper persons to look after their own produce, especially when of a peculiar or delicate nature. I think the large consignee of goods pays quite as much as ever he did. The change has had the effect of increasing very largely the number of master porters, many who were formerly head warehousemen having left that business to become master porters. I do not consider the business of master porter a very good one. The risk and responsibility are very great, and the profits very small. Upon one class of American produce, and that the principal import of Liverpool—I mean cotton—the profits of a master porter are so small as barely to pay him an amount as much as the wages of a warehouseman, while the risk he runs is considerable. I have sometimes done cotton ships, and have not realized within £3 of the men's wages; one reason being the bad stowage of some ships, which prevents the lumpers on board from working as fast as they might, and causes my men to be longer employed than they might otherwise be, and thus consuming all my profit. Even in the best cargoes of general produce, the profits of a master porter are not greater than the wages he would receive for his superintendence, were there no such system as master porterage. I have lost as much as £75 within five months in the busy time of 1847, in damage done to goods at the quay, or for goods lost. Under the new system less men are required than were employed under the old. The employment of one gang of men for the whole cargo leads to simplicity and expedition. Under the old system a vessel of 600 tons, with a cargo of cotton, consigned to various consignees, would take about eight days and about twenty men on a fair average to do the quay porterage. Under the present system a vessel of the same tonnage and cargo would take from three to four days—not more than four—and about ten men to do the quay porterage. This is a system that must evidently throw a great many men out of work. The effect of so many men being out of work is very injurious to the interests of all the retail shopkeepers of Liverpool, both for clothing and provisions. The poor-rates in Liverpool are very high, and the shopkeeper has hard work to pay them, even when things go right, and by losing his business from the men, is less able to pay them. In addition to this, the rates become heavier because so many operative porters are thrown upon the parish with their families. The charge against the master porters—or 'middlemen,' as they are sometimes called—of being worse employers of the operatives than the merchant master porters would be, I consider to be unjust and unfounded. The middleman master porter employs a greater number of men on the quay for any cargo than a merchant master porter would employ, and, as far as I ever knew, pays certainly as much and in some cases more wages. The reason why a middleman master porter employs a greater number of men is, that he is dependent upon other people for his business, and must give satisfaction to them, and by doing the work properly and with the utmost care, to establish a character for himself, and avoid coming into collision, and being found fault with by warehousemen, merchants' clerks, and merchants themselves, to all of whom he must submit if he hopes to prosper in his trade. The merchant master porter being quite independent has no such motives. In cases of slight damage or losses in the porterage of smaller consignees, the merchant master porter easily settles the matter with his friends; whereas the middleman master porter is called to strict account, and has the loss invariably deducted from his bill. It is his interest, therefore, to employ more men, in order that the work may be done satisfactorily to all parties and profitably to himself. Two of the heaviest losses in the above-named £75, which I had to pay, might, I think, have been successfully resisted in a court of law; but the middleman master porter is obliged to put up with such losses. He cannot afford to run the risk of losing his employment altogether, by offending the merchants, or resisting any claim for loss that they make against him. I never employed the inferior class of porters. It is against my interest to do so. I have always employed skilled men, the best I could get. I never offered or paid them less than 3s. 6d. a day. No respectable master porter, that I know of, pays less. I have sometimes paid more to men who thoroughly knew their business in all its details of weight-taking, counting off, weighing, marking, or taking general charge of the gang, or in fact acting as captain of the gang. The effect of the change has been to diminish the employment of the men generally, but not in the slightest degree in my business, or in that of any master porters I know, to diminish the rate of wages while they are employed; on the contrary, its effect has been to increase the rate of wages." [Here the master porter, who also said he had no objection to the publication of his name, showed me his books from the commencement of his business, from which it appeared that he had paid weekly a large amount of wages—sometimes as much as £150. The books fully bore out his statement]. "The canvassing system is carried on to a large extent. I consider it injurious to the master porter, and an annoyance to the merchant. It is not injurious to the operative-porters. It can make no difference to them; at least it never does in my business; for, as I have said before, I always pay the same wages. I think the canvassing system might be remedied, by giving the largest consignee, not the largest consignees, the power of employing the master porters, or else giving the power to the ship's consignee. Some of the merchants are themselves to blame for this system of canvassing. They will not give the work to a master-porter unless he offers under the usual charges, or at a discount of 20, 30, or 40 per cent. I consider that this system has been sanctioned by the dock-trustees, the secretary having decided in its favour in 1847, when the system of canvassing first commenced. It is a very bad system, and ought to be stopped. One charge made against the new system is, the irregularity in weighing, by which the ship might lose in freight, or the merchant might suffer in his goods. I consider this charge to be unfair, and not justly chargeable against the system; because every ship's consignee has the right of sending his own weigher; and in all cases has to pay for a weigher, whether he authorizes the master porter or sees to it himself. The charge against the middlemen master porters, of keeping lodging-houses, provision-shops, and public-shops is unfounded. This system is not carried on by them—at least I know of no master porter in town who keep such places, or who makes any profit out of the porters by such means. There was once a master porter who was proved upon investigation before the Dock Committee, after complaint being made, of keeping a public-house or beer-house. The Dock Committee gave him the choice of abandoning his public-house, or ceasing to act as a master porter. He chose to remain a publican, and he is no longer a master porter. I know of no other case, and never heard of any other. I know nothing as to the practices of warehousemen in this respect, but as regards the master porters I consider the charge to be unfounded. No respectable porter would enter into it. Nothing would be more agreeable or satisfactory to the master porters as a body, than that the Dock Committee should institute a full investigation into this subject, and give them an opportunity of meeting every charge of the kind, or any other that might be brought against them. I am quite sure on that point."

The above statement was made in the presence of five other master porters, who agreed entirely in the truth and correctness of all contained in it.

Another master porter, whom I subsequently saw, and who was represented to me as doing a larger business, both in lumping and master portering, than any other man in Liverpool, made the following statement in the presence of three other master porters:—

"I am both a lumper and a master porter. I have been a lumper for 21 years, and am the first who took out a licence as master porter under the new law. I do the lumping and porterage of two of the largest houses in Liverpool. I do not think that the new system has diminished the employment of the other master porters. It has nothing to do with the lumping department, but only with the quay-porterage. Formerly a warehouseman sent a certain quantity of men to do the porterage on the quay, and detained the goods on the quay until after Custom-house hours. During Custom-house hours the men were employed in receiving and weighing the produce; and after Custom-house hours they loaded the goods, and received them at the warehouses. The men received for this double work one day's wages. Under the present system the master porter pays his men a day's wages for the work actually done on the quay during Custom-house hours. For the warehousing work another gang is employed, and if they begin work after Custom-house hours, they get half a day's wages. There are no quarter day's wages in Liverpool; nothing less than half a day. It is in this manner that I think the chance of work is increased by the new system. Under the old system, the men were paid for their attendance whether they worked or not. Under the new system, it is the business and the interest of the master porter to see that the men do work, and consequently the work is done sooner and with less confusion than it used to be. Under the system which the ship-owners and others complained of, the porters about the Exchange would take their chance of work fairly as it came, because they were under pay whether they worked or not, and there was no one having such interest as at present to get the ship discharged, and to leave her berth free for another vessel. But under the new system, many of the men who complain of its operation are more particular. They must pick and choose their work, or they will not do any. They will not take the chance of work when it is offered them. For a general cargo we find no difficulty in getting men to do the porterage; but when a cotton ship, say from Mobile, very heavily laden is to be discharged, many of the men will not take the work. It is very hard work, as the heavy cotton bales have to be lifted on high carts. This kind of men prefer to hang about the Exchange and lose their day's work altogether, rather than work at the cotton ships." [Here another master porter corroborated this, by stating that on the arrival, some time ago, of a ship called the Adept, of 1,000 tons burden, from Mobile, with 2,500 bales of cotton, in the Brunswick Dock, working sufferance, he engaged 14 men to do the porterage, but on his arrival at the dock he found that only six of the 14 had come down. They never made their appearance at all, preferring to take the chance of easier work]. "Under the present system, men who will work, and who know their business, have better employment and better wages than ever. There are, no doubt, a great many unskilled hands, and old men, who are skilled, who do not get work."

Another deputation of operative-porters, men in full employ, and satisfied with the existing system, waited upon me, and one of them made the following statement:—

"I have been an operative porter for twenty-five years, ever since I was fourteen years of age. My father was a master porter. I have always had the same wages—at least, I began with 3s. 6d. a day, and have now 4s., as a weigher. I am employed every day; I am a skilled porter, and

I believe that all the skilled porters who are willing to work can get it. There are very great numbers in Liverpool of unskilled porters, a great number from Ireland, and different parts of Scotland and Wales, and, indeed, all parts, because they hear there is so much work at the docks. All kinds of mechanics, when their work is slack, try portering, and this increases the number of unskilled porters. I know of tailors, shoe-makers, joiners, watchmakers, plasterers, and all kinds of mechanics and operatives who do portering when they want a day's work. There are several warehousemen in Liverpool who let lodgings to porters, and give their lodgers whatever work they can. They only take single men, and give them lodgings where there are two or three beds in a room, and two or three in a bed. The usual charge is 2s. 6d. a week, and washing of a shirt, a pair of stockings, and a neckerchief. If they board as well as lodge, they pay 10s. or 12s. a week. It is this system which brings so many extra hands into the town, as it is the interest of the warehouseman to fill his house with such men, and he gives them employment in his department. When such porters can't get employment from the warehousemen, they try and get it from the master porters, but the master porter does not want such men. They are unskilled; and, as the master porter is responsible for all damage and loss, it is his interest only to employ the best men. For skilled porters the business is as good as ever it was. The new system has not, to my knowledge, deprived the really skilled porters of work—it has not taken any work from me. I work generally with fifteen others. We have all of us had as much work as we used to have. Perhaps some of the skilled porters, when they become old—above 50 or 55—don't get so much work as skilled porters who are young; but, generally the skilled porters get work. Some of the porters who complain of the new system would not do well under any system; for instance, if they are asked on the Exchange to go and work for a master at a cotton ship, they won't go, because the hours are longer than in the sugar, coffee, and rum ships; and harder labour is required at the bales of cotton than at any other porterage. Such men can't expect to be always em-ployed. They don't deserve it. I never heard of a master porter keeping a public-house, nor paying at a public-house. They have small offices of their own. I never heard of a master porter keeping a provision shop, nor a lodging-house. It is the warehousemen who do it. Neither did I ever hear of a master porter offering less than the usual wages, 3s. 6d., 3s. 8d., and 4s. The corn porters are a class by themselves, they work at nothing but corn, and their regular wages is 3s. a day, that is when they work for the merchants. When these men work for the master porters they get 3s. 6d. I do not see what good is to be done by the compromise proposed by Mr. Brown, or by any change. There will always be unskilled men out of work, as long as so many strangers or broken-down mechanics come crowding into the porterage business from all parts of the country. The new system is a good system for the good men, but all the merchants of Liverpool could not employ the crowds of men that call themselves porters. There is no work in the town for them, nor ever will be."

Another porter, who said he had been in the business for twenty-two years, corroborated the above statement, as far as his own experience went; and a third, who had been nine years in the town, and who had worked both for merchants and for master porters, made a similar statement. One of these men said he averaged five days a week work for the last twelve months. The other said he might have had six days' work in the week, but was occasionally negligent in looking for a job, and thus threw himself out of work from time to time, but this was not oftener than once in three months.

Desirous that no injustice might be done to any class or individual, and that not only the views of the working men and master porters should be stated, but that every party interested or concerned should have an opportunity of making known how this complicated business affected him, I called upon one of the partners in an extensive mercantile house largely engaged in the import trade of Liverpool. That gentleman obligingly furnished me with the following statement:—

"I can only give you my views as an importer of produce into Liverpool. That is the business of our firm. The interest of the shipowner and the dock committee in this question is different from that of the merchant. The shipowner naturally and very obviously wishes to get his vessel discharged with the utmost possible dispatch. The interest of the dock committee is the same. The object of the importing merchant, especially if he have delicate and valuable produce, is to have it landed and delivered with the utmost care, so as to prevent loss and injury. Under the old system the importer sent his most skilful men to attend to the particular produce which he had on board, giving them such instructions as were needful for its protection. These men took charge of it from the moment it left the vessel's hold until it was put into his warehouse. Under the new system he is prevented from employing those men whom he thinks best suited to receive his goods, and is prohibited from touching them until he finds them in the carts for conveyance to his warehouse. The consequence is that frequent loss and injury to the goods take place, besides minor inconveniences arising from the confusion of marks and the mixing of goods. The loss in an individual case may often be so small as not to be worth while litigating with a master porter; but, being of frequent occurrence, these losses become exceedingly vexatious as well as injurious. If the loss in any one instance were considerable the claim would be preferred against the master porter. For the protection of our firm we have taken out licenses as master porters, so that when we are the largest consignees we may have the porterage and control of our own goods as we had under the old system. But this proceeding is not unattended with loss and inconvenience to us. In one case we had a consignment of wool and oil, and were the largest consignees. In addition to our consignments the vessel brought a quantity of fruit and wine, and some perishable articles belonging to smaller consignees. All these articles we were obliged to receive on the quays and take charge of, and were responsible for their right handling. Not being engaged in the wine trade, or knowing anything about that business, our men were not skilled in handling wine, and caused some breakage—and a consequent claim, which we had to pay. Such cases are of frequent occurrence. We consider it a great hardship upon us who have men that we have employed for fifteen, and even twenty years, and skilled in the handling of all the produce that we usually import, that we cannot now make use of their services, and that we are often obliged to receive our produce after it has been handled by raw men that the interest of the master porter or his screwing disposition may cause him to employ. It may be to his gain, but it certainly is not to ours, that such raw hands should be employed, for he charges according to a legal scale, which scale does not regulate him in the rate of wages he has to pay. As regards the question of the comparative economy of the two systems, I think the present system is more economical to the importer where the consignments are small and unimportant. In imports of any magnitude the business was formerly managed quite as economically as at present. Merchants were not obliged to employ master porters at all, and had nothing to do with the book of rates. They employed their own men, and made the most of their time. If they chose to employ them after dock hours they could do so, without extra expense, up to six o'clock; but, by the present system, merchants, not being master porters for the occasion, must pay for extra hours to the master porters if the men work beyond half-past three in winter, or four in summer. The present law is constantly broken for mutual convenience of merchants having particular imports of delicate produce. Merchants who by right of being the largest consignees have the privilege of master-portering allow the other importers to receive their own produce, because they cannot get the skilled hands to attend to it. The present law seems to me to be unjust, as taking from the importer the power of looking after his own interests, and as transferring that power to unknown, and as it may be unskilful, parties, whose interests may be diametrically opposed to his own. The mere economy in landing produce is not the only question to be considered. The correct receiving and careful handling of his produce is of vital importance to the importer or consignee, in regard to its satisfactory sale and realization. The present system appears to me to have created much ill-will among the operative porters, and much inconvenience as well as loss to importers, without having afforded advantages at all equivalent to those whom it appears to have been intended to benefit—the dock trustees and the shipowners."

Another gentleman, a member of one of the most eminent firms in Liverpool, gave a different view of the question. He stated that under the new system a large importer would save in the porterage of a general cargo at least 25 per cent., taking one import with another. In a particular cargo, such as cotton, he would save quite as much, in addition to the advantage of despatch. He never found any loss resulting from the carelessness of master porters and their men; and did not believe that they habitually employed unskilled men, as it obviously would not answer their purpose to do so. He saw no hardship on any merchant, who for his own protection took out a license as master porter, in being required to act for the whole of the consignees, when he happened to be in the position of largest consignee. He was not compelled to act in that capacity unless he chose, for he could devolve the duty upon a middleman master porter, who would be grateful for the job, and accept it with all its responsibility. He considered the change of system highly advantageous to the dock trustees, to the shipowners, and to the trade of the town generally.

It will be seen from the above statements that the question is a very complicated one. Opinions vary very considerably upon it; but, as far as I could judge, the truth of the matter seems to be, that the change was forced upon the dock trustees and the town council by the Government; that it has worked exceedingly well for the docks, for the shipowners, and for the merchants generally—with a few exceptions, confined to the importers of delicate or peculiar produce; but, in producing these great advantages, it has been attended with a diminution of employment to a very large number of unskilled, and to a few skilled operative porters, principally old men. That it has caused great suffering and distress among the large and daily increasing body of men who thrust themselves into the business of quay-porterage, without any other qualification than their strong arms, is a fact that appears to me to be indisputable—and I believe that the evil has to some extent been fostered by the bad system of the persons, whether they be master porters or warehousemen, who keep lodging-houses for single men, making residence with them a *sine quâ non* for a chance of employment, or who keep public-houses and provision stores, to fleece the operative porters who happen to be married. A return to the old system is impossible, so that the parish of Liverpool, overburdened as it already is with pauperism, will, I fear, have to maintain from 4,000 to 5,000 men and their families, as the inevitable result of a change in other respects highly beneficial to the commercial interests of the port.

It only remains to add a few words upon the compromise suggested by Mr. William Brown, M.P., himself a master porter. That gentleman drew up the following resolutions, in concert with other parties:—

"Resolved—1. That the law as it now stands, empowering middlemen to step in between the employed and the employers, is not satisfactory to the parties most interested. The middlemen (master porters) must necessarily deduct from the operative porters' wages a remuneration for themselves, as they can only charge a fixed tariff to the consignees of the goods.

"Resolved—2. That those middlemen or master porters should not have the power of claiming the exclusive right of doing this description of business.

"Resolved—3. That as the captains of vessels, and also the owners and consignees of the ships on their behalf, are deeply interested for the safe delivery of the cargo in good condition, that they alone should have the right to employ one set of men to do this work, unless they wish to hand it over to the largest consignee of the cargo, which, in some cases, they may think desirable, if the description of goods comprising the cargo is of that kind that the management of them can be better attended to by those who are accustomed to deal in and handle those articles.

"Resolved—4. That as the owners and consignees of ships have a direct and positive interest in giving them despatch, it would not be just to make them depend for getting the quays cleared on any gang of men but those under their immediate control.

"Resolved—5. That the loading off the quays by one set of porters is the best security for economy and despatch, which has a direct tendency to increase the trade of the port, and necessarily a demand for more men to do the work.

"Resolved—6. That to resort to the former mode of each consignee of goods sending down a separate gang of porters to wait their goods coming out of the ships, caused more men to come from other places to Liverpool than was necessary to do the work, and in bad or slack times made greater competition for the little that was to be had, operating against the older established hands, and increasing our poor rates, without benefiting the merchants, as the wages paid by them fluctuate very little whether there is much or little work to be done, the usual wages being 3s. 6d. per day.

"Resolved—7. That we do not contemplate any interference with the dock committee in the Albert Dock, or sheds or warehouses attended to by their porters.

"Resolved—8. That we are desirous and hope that our recommendations will be satisfactory to the parties interested, and, if so, that the operative porters should not proceed further with their bill now before Parliament."

The operatives have in the meantime, and agreeably to the suggestion of Mr. Brown, abandoned their bill, and consented to abide by arbitration. The question is still under discussion. Should the above resolutions be adopted as a compromise, there will in reality be no change. It will be the present system under a new name. The master porter, apparently sacrificed to the wrath of the operative porters who have been thrown out of work, will still be employed, and must be employed, if the object set forth in the fifth of these resolutions is to be attained. A large portion of the unskilled porters will remain, as at present, without work; and considering that of the many thousands of operative porters in Liverpool not one-third are skilled men, it will be seen that the amount of distress and of consequent dissatisfaction cannot be diminished by any change which shall merely transfer the nominal or the real superintendence of the work at the quays to the ship's consignee, instead of to the master porter. In fact, there seems to be no remedy but to stop the importation of unskilled labourers into Liverpool, a course of proceeding which might be attended with many evils and disadvantages. As for the multitude of unskilled labourers at present in the town, it seems clear that although the merchants, the shipowners, and the dock trust have gained upon the one hand by the change of system, they will lose upon the other by being compelled to pay an additional poor rate for their negligence in having suffered an erroneous and mischievous system to encumber the town with unnecessary hands before they adopted a substitute.

LABOUR AND THE POOR.

—◆—

LIVERPOOL.

[FROM OUR SPECIAL CORRESPONDENT.]

THE DOCK LABOURERS AND THEIR FAMILIES:—THE "CHIP," "GRIT," AND "OAKUM" TRADES.

Letter V.

Next in numerical importance to the quay porters, or operative porters, whose condition I described in my last letter, are the dock-labourers of Liverpool. Their numbers are variously estimated at from 7,000 to 10,000 men; but as many of them act in the capacity of quay porters, when not employed in the discharge of vessels, and thus belong to both classes, it is obviously very difficult, especially in the absence of any record kept by the authorities of the docks, or of the town, to arrive at an accurate estimate of their numbers. Although as a body they are unaffected by the operation of the act of Parliament of which the quay porters have recently complained, they are not without grievances, which they share in common with all the other labourers about the docks. These grievances are reducible into two—the immense influx of unskilled labourers from Ireland and elsewhere, by whose competition the rate of wages is reduced; and the system carried on by lumpers and warehousemen in letting lodgings to single men, or in keeping public-houses and provision shops, and giving the preference of their employment to single men who lodge with them, in the one case, or to the single or married men who deal with them in the other. This system is highly prejudicial to the interests of the working men. Not only are their wages reduced in money value by it, but they are compelled to pay for their food and lodging, as well as for the drink they are induced to consume, those high credit prices which have no other limit than the conscientious scruples of the men who traffic upon them—a limit which is very elastic.

This class of men are employed both in loading and unloading ships; and are under the superintendence in both cases of "the Lumpers" or "Stevedores." The word "Lumper" is derived from the contract into which the master workman enters with the captain, agent, or owner of the ship, to unload it by the "lump" or bulk. The word "Stevedore" seems to be of American origin, and to be derived from the verb to "steeve"—equivalent to heave or hoist. The loading of a vessel is generally paid by the ton, and not by the lump; the unloading almost invariably by the lump, according to the contract which the lumper enters into with the captain or agent. The men who carry on this business, many of whom are highly respectable, and two of whom, as I was informed, do fully a third of all the business of the port, prefer to be called Stevedores, and have no particular liking for the more idiomatic and indigenous term of Lumper.

The following statement of the manner in which this business is conducted, and of the wages paid to the men, was made to me by a stevedore—who always used the word stevedore when he spoke of the better class of men in his trade, and the word "lumper" when he spoke of the inferior class amongst them. He said:—

"I am a stevedore, and have a fair business, but not one of the largest. When a stevedore undertakes to unload a ship, it is his business to engage and employ the men. He generally has men whom he knows and can depend upon. He makes his choice out of all the dock labourers, and takes the best he can find. There is no rotation of gangs. The leading man or foreman gets 4s. a day; the other men 3s. 6d. and 3s. If they begin at any time before twelve o'clock in the day, they are paid for a day's work. The steadier men in the best season, which is the timber season of July and August, get employment every day. The timber ships go to the south end of the town, to the Brunswick Dock, which is called the Timber Dock. The next most busy season is in April, May, and June, when the cotton ships arrive. The cotton work is not so good as the timber work, and does not last so long. I should say that about three hundred ships annually arrive in the port of Liverpool with cotton. The timber ships are not taken by the lump. There is a fixed customary rate of 6d. per ton for unloading timber ships. A ship of 1,200 tons burden would pay the stevedore £30 for unloading. The cotton vessels are taken by the lump, and one of the American liners, of the average tonnage, entirely laden with cotton, would have to pay from £25 to £30 for the lumping. Some of the agents beat down these prices; and if the stevedore is beaten down too much, he must either refuse the job, or employ raw hands at less than the usual wages to do it. If a stevedore gets £4 for his own super-intendence and responsibility out of a £30 job, he considers himself tolerably well paid. The other £26 goes for wages, and would employ thirty men for about a week. There are three rates of wages in the cotton ships and in ships with general cargoes: 3s. a day, 3s. 6d. a day, and 4s. a day. The common labourers get 3s.; those who 'bear off,' or act as foremen of the deck, get 3s. 6d., whilst the men who break bulk in the hold get 4s. The stevedores always, if possible, employ the same kind of men in each particular department. It would be of no use to fill the hold with common labourers, or with men who bear off; neither would it do to fill the hatchways with men accustomed to the hold. When the stevedore lands the cargo in safety on the quays his business is at an end; and the master porters and their operatives take charge of it. A great number of the dock labourers are Irishmen—I should say two-thirds of them; to say one-half only would be under the mark. Some of the lumpers cheat the men. By cheating, I mean that they give them less than the fair wages; and some that I have heard of keep public-houses and lodging-houses, and make a profit out of the men that way. The Dock Committee has no power over the stevedores, as it has over the master porters. Some are both stevedores and master porters. The labourers are not attached to any particular dock. They go from one to the other, as work requires. All the docks are worked in one way, except the Albert Dock, which has a system of its own. At the south end of the town, including the Brunswick, King's, Queen's, Salthouse, and other docks, there is no combination among the workmen. I have heard of a combination at the northern docks, of which the object is to keep out strangers and raw hands, but I don't know how it works."

I saw some other stevedores, but as the statements they made were not materially different from the above, and threw no new light upon the condition of the men, as influenced by excessive competition of raw hands upon the one side, or by the malpractices of publicans, lodging-house keepers, and provision-dealers on the other, it will be unnecessary to repeat their views of the matter. From the dock labourers themselves I procured a further insight into their present condition. I give the statements of two of them, principally but not entirely made in answer to my inquiries, for I found very few men of their class—indeed I may say not one of them—capable of telling a consecutive story.

O—— B——. "I am a dock labourer, and am fifty years of age. I have been a dock labourer for sixteen years. I came from the north of Ireland. I get 3s. a day wages, and managed to have employment about four days in the week until within the last two or three years. There are good and bad lumpers in Liverpool; some very good and some very bad, and some that couldn't be worse. I have worked for lumpers who never paid me my wages. I lost 14s. 6d. by one man, and 9s. by another. I never lost more than 14s. 6d. at a time. It was a very serious thing for a poor man like me to lose 14s. 6d.—a whole week's work. It drove me to the pawnshop with my clothes, my bed, and other things. I never got the things out from that day to this. I never had money enough to spare, even to pay the interest on them, and they were lost. Work is a great deal slacker with me than it used to be. I think the reason may be that there are so many new hands always coming into the town. Perhaps it is because I am getting old that the lumpers don't employ me as they used. Men are not so fit for dock labour at 50 as they are at 20 or 30, at least not for the heavy work. There are many hundreds as slack of work as I am. I only had two days' work from Christmas to the middle of March. Before Christmas I had three days' work in the week pretty regularly. I was obliged to go to the parish at Christmas, and was allowed five shillings a week. That allowance was stopped because I lived in a cellar that was not of the legal height. [By the Local Sanitary Act no cellar must be used as a sleeping-place that is not fully seven feet in height, and one-third of this height above the surface of the street. I shall have more to say upon this subject in another letter.] The relieving officer told me to leave the cellar: but I had nowhere else to go to, and I paid no rent for it. The landlord had pity on me, and allowed me to live rent free in it, because I was so poor. I was afraid that if I left the cellar I should be struck off the parish books all the same, and that I might have lost both my lodgings and my relief-money. I sometimes am allowed to pick up a few 'chips' about the Docks; and the children sell them. I have a wife and four children. I have sometimes made six pence and sometimes nine pence a day by 'chips.' The children can do nothing else to help me, but sell the chips. The eldest boy is eleven years old—he cries the chips about the streets. I have had no chips for some days. They are not always to be had about the docks. I sometimes buy sixpenny-worth of wood of a joiner to break into chips; but have not had a sixpence for two days— nor a penny. I made a shilling by chips within the last fortnight. My wife cannot leave the children to go out to work. She can sew, but she cannot make shirts, or do anything at the slop business. The children sometimes go to school—to the ragged school. I cannot pay for them to any other. The eldest boy that cries the chips knows his letters. The other children do not."

J—— D——. "I have been fifteen years a dock labourer, and am principally employed by a lumper in discharging timber and cotton ships. I get 4s. 6d. a day when employed in unloading timber. Formerly the wages were 4s. a day in money, and six penny-worth of drink; but about four years ago the men demanded to have the 6d. instead of the drink, and it was given to them. For cotton work the wages are 3s. and 3s. 6d. a day. The timber work is harder, and requires tools. No tools are required in cotton porterage. The tools for unloading and removing timber might cost about 16s., and include a 'cant-bar' to turn the timber over with; and a 'shod-bar' to assist in canting. It requires some skill for the timber porterage, but none for cotton. Any man who is strong enough can do the cotton work. It is now a very slack season for timber. The slack season lasts from January to the end of June or July. The timber ships come in after that, chiefly from Canada. The 'throng' or busy season for cotton is in the months of March, April, and May. I should think there are several hundreds of timber porters out of work at present, or catching a day's, or half-a-day's work in the week. The timber porters are, on the average, idle about six months out of the twelve; and they then try the cotton porterage or any other work that is to be got. I cannot tell how many dock labourers and quay porters there are in Liverpool. They are very thick; there is no end of them. About seven years ago the corporation gave out tickets, with numbers upon them—a kind of badge without which no porter was to be employed. I saw one ticket that was marked six thousand and odd. I heard that more than 14,000 tickets were given out. The system has been discontinued. The porters had to pay a shilling for their tickets; but they were never asked to show them. The system was found to be of no use to anybody. The lumpers ought to pay 3s. and 3s. 6d. a day; but so many fresh hands come over from all parts, and stand about the quays, that they fall into distress, and will work for anything. Most of them are in distress when they come, or we should not see them in Liverpool. They will take 2s. a day, or 1s. 6d.—anything they can get, when they are 'hard up.' The old hands will never work for less than the customary wages. Some of the lumpers carry on business as lodging-housekeepers. They keep lodgings for single men, and give their lodgers the preference. Their lodgers get into their debt, and they give them work in order to be paid. I know lumpers who keep public-houses, as well as lodgings. If a man will get two or three shillings in debt for drink on the Saturday night, the lumper will give him a job on the Monday morning, if he can. There are other lumpers who do not keep the lodging-houses and public-houses in their own names. They put their foreman or some other man into it, but it is all the same to the poor porters. Some of the lumpers are rich, and some are almost as poor as the porters. It requires no licence to be a lumper—only interest with the captain or owners. Some lumpers pay their men's wages in public-houses, but there is not so much of that as there used to be—indeed there is very little of it now."

J—— M——. "I have been eleven years a porter, principally in the cotton ships. I am forty-nine years of age. During the first ten weeks of the present year, I had only eighteen days' work at 3s. a day, or £2 14s. for all that time. I pay 4s. a week rent. I have a wife and a son. My son is learning to be a cooper, and can nearly earn his own living. Last year I may have had six months' work—but do not think I had so much. I have been reduced to the greatest want, and would be very happy to get four days' work in the week all the year round. Very few men in Liverpool can do so well as that. The business has got worse of late. There are too many porters by half. There was a time in Liverpool when all the porters found employment. But now, not more than half are at work on any one day even in the busiest times. The potato famine in Ireland brought over a great number of porters, and things have been worse in Liverpool ever since. The portering business is tried by every one who can do nothing else. Whenever a mechanic is out of work, he tries his hand at our trade. When a tradesman fails, he goes to the docks to pick up a job. There are people of all trades in the docks—from an anchor-smith to a jeweller. It all depends upon the lumpers to give them employment. Any man may be a lumper; but very few can do a large business. When a strange ship arrives in the Docks it is beset by lumpers; but the lumpers do not go among the regular traders. They know the connections of the captains and owners, and whether it is of any use to ask for the job. Dock labour is very slack at present. Freights are very low, and the owners scarcely get a farthing per lb. for cotton. I remember when it was a penny and three-halfpence. The Albert Docks keep a good many men out of work. It may be a good system for the docks which is carried on there, but it is a bad system for the working men."

As many of the dock labourers and porters complained of the system pursued in the Albert Docks, I made a point of ascertaining particularly in what manner the system of dock labour, as carried on in that dock, differed from the general practice in all the rest. The Albert Dock was opened with considerable ceremony by his Royal Highness Prince Albert in July, 1846. It is surrounded by its own sheds and warehouses, all within the dock premises. The warehouses are both bonded and free. Neither lumpers nor master porters are employed on their own responsibility—the trustees of the dock assuming the responsibility of properly discharging, landing, and warehousing the cargoes, and of employing the proper porters for the purpose. The chairman of the dock trustees and eight of the trustees are appointed by the Town Council of Liverpool. They have a permanent body of porters in their employ, amounting on the average to sixty men, whose wages are about 18s. a week. After these, when the business of the docks requires the employment of a larger number of men, the services of a 'preferable' class of porters and carmen are called in. The names of these men are entered in the books of the dock trust, and cards of preference are given to each individual. They have the same wages as the permanent body, as long as they are employed. If the dock is so full of vessels discharging as to require a still larger supply of porters to do the work, a choice is made among the general body of porters in the town. Sometimes as many as 1,200 men have been employed in one day, while at others the numbers do not exceed 200. The dock committee likewise appoints the warehouse-keepers, the warehouse clerks, and the landing clerks. This dock is an experimental one as regards management, and appears, as far as I could learn, to have given the highest satisfaction to the commercial interests of the town, but not to the warehouse-owners or the porters. The dock committee, with a laudable despotism—if I may be allowed the term—require that all the superior officers in their employment should ensure their lives in some insurance office; and that the porters in their permanent employ should belong to a benefit society. The permanent porters in the Albert Docks have established, it appears, a benefit society of their own, and by paying 6d. a week when in health, they receive 12s. a week when sick.

Another small class of dock labourers in Liverpool is composed of the coal trimmers and heavers. These men are employed in stowing the coal on board the American mail-steamers, the Dublin and Glasgow steam-packets, and other steam-boats that are connected with the port. One of these men gave me the following account of this business. He was a man of about five and thirty, neat and clean in his personal appearance, but had his head bound up with a handkerchief. He said:—

"I am a coal-trimmer, and finished a boat last night. It was an American mail steam-packet. I work for a coal-lumper. The coal-lumpers are employed to stow away coals on board steam-packets, and they engage and pay the 'trimmers,' 'heavers,' and 'wheelers.' About twenty-six men are required to put the coals on board, and properly 'trim' them in a first-class American liner. There are seventeen constant men in the 'gang' with which I work, and these are sufficient in most cases. If a steamer is beyond her time in arriving and must get away again at her appointed day, the coal must be put on board more rapidly; and it is then necessary to employ extra hands. It generally takes two days and a half to get in the coals, but sometimes not more than twenty-four hours can be allowed for the purpose. The coal-trimming is a very particular business, as the coals must be stowed very closely away. Not an inch of room must be lost. The 'heavers' and 'wheelers' bring the coal aboard from the quay, and the 'trimmers' trim it in the hold. The lumper who employs me is a very honest man, and pays our wages regularly. I made 16s. 3d. by the job I have just finished. It took me two days and a half. I do not expect another job this week. I consider it an average week. I am generally idle half the week, and gain enough during the other half to support me. Some weeks I have made as much as 30s., and I have often made 25s. and 20s. I have been five years at the work, and have contrived to live, and perhaps a little more. The foreman of the gangs earns 2s. 6d. a week over and above the trimmers. The largest steamers carry 750 tons of coals. Some carry 650 tons, and some 600 tons. I have worked two days and a night at trimming without sleeping, or any other rest, except for meals. Among the seventeen constant men in our gang there are five teetotallers. The men in this business drink a good deal of beer—they seem to require it; but they do not drink to excess. Some of them 'break out' now and then. I left the trimming for nearly nine months during the five years that I have been at it. I was engaged to go out as a labourer to Ichaboe to dig guano. I signed an agreement for 35s. a month before I went out. It was a bad business for me. The work among the guano affected my hands, and brought all the nails off. It also affected my skin and my bodily health generally. I have had a bad neck ever since. It is now bound up, as you see. I prefer the coal trimming to guano digging."

After having taken the statements of the dock labourers, I proceeded to visit some of the worst districts in the southern parts of the town, where the labourers reside. Notwithstanding all the daily and most laborious exertions made by the sanitary officers of Liverpool for the removal of nuisances, and the cleaning of the streets, there are districts both in the southern and northern parts which are unsurpassed, if not unsurpassable, for filth, squalor, and unwholesomeness, by any large town in the kingdom. The cellars and courts of Liverpool are in this respect notorious. I shall have much to say upon this subject in a future letter, but must confine myself for the present to the subject more immediately in hand—the condition of the porters and labourers and their families, and the means by which they endeavour to eke out a scanty subsistence when work in the docks or on the quays is not to be obtained. There are three sources of profit open to them, in all of which the women and children are employed—oakum picking, the pounding and sale of "grit," and the chopping and sale of fire-wood or "chips." In the numerous courts that abound in every part of the town these various branches of industry are carried on. In Liverpool, court branches from court; and it is a peculiar sight, in threading their labyrinths, to observe the multitudes of poor women of all ages, sitting outside of their miserable hovels, engaged at one or the other of these occupations. The oakum pickers buy old rope from the marine store dealers at 1½d. per lb., and pick it into oakum, which they sell back to the marine store dealers for 2d. per lb. The oakum is used principally for the caulking of vessels. At this work a woman, if she labours hard for 10 or 12 hours a day, may manage to pick about 12 or 14 lbs. of rope into oakum, making a profit of 6d. or 7d. The pounding of the "grit" is a business that will bring in about the same sum to an industrious person. These two trades are entirely carried on by women. I never saw a man engaged at either of them, but at both I observed in the courts, or in the interior of the hovels, females of all ages, from seventy years of age down to seven, or even lower, hard at work. "Grit" is the name given to pounded sandstone, which is sold about the streets in half-pennyworths and pennyworths by the girls who break it. It is used for scouring door-steps. They procure the soft stone from the quarries, generally without payment, and convey it to their courts and alleys, where they pound it into powder, on the pavement, by beating it with pieces of granite. They never seem to employ hammers or mallets for the purpose. In one court I noticed a half-clad, dirty child, of eleven years of age, with a heap of the "grit" before her, very busily at work. I asked her for a sight of the stone which she used as a hammer. On taking it up I observed an indentation on one side. It fitted to her thumb. Her elder sister, who sat beside her, with four or five others engaged in the same occupation, said the indentation was caused by the constant work and pressure of the thumb, and that after two or three years' work at grit-pounding, the granite or paving stone generally had a thumb mark upon it. She showed me her own, and the thumb mark was plainly perceptible, and about a quarter of an inch in depth. Who shall calculate the amount of labour represented by such a hollowing and scooping out as that? and what faculties, physical, intellectual, and moral may not have been deadened and deprived of all opportunity of growth and development, by such incessant and scantily-rewarded labour? Not one of this group of girls could either read or write, or had ever been to a school. The chip business seemed to employ almost as many people as the oakum and the grit—with this difference, that strong men and lads are employed in its manufacture, and both boys and girls in its sale. New Bird-street and Brick-street, with their crowded and filthy courts, were the seats of these three humble manufactures that I visited, in company with the reverend Mr. Bishop, a gentleman, well known in Liverpool for his unostentatious benevolence and kindly sympathy with the poor population. His presence procured me a cordial greeting wherever I went. The poor people knew him as their friend; and although they could not well understand what object I could have in visiting them, and in asking so many questions about their humble trade and mode of life, they took it for granted that my object must be a good one, if *he* took an interest in it. Guided by him through a perfect maze of dingy streets, rank with fetid smells, swarming with ragged and dirty children, some of whom were at play, but by far the greater number engaged in picking oakum or pounding "grit" at their door-steps; and stooping occasionally to avoid coming in contact with the yellow, reeking, patched and ragged garments that were hung across courts and alleys to dry, we entered the apartment of an Irishwoman engaged in the chip trade. The apartment was occupied by the old woman and her son—the latter a burly, healthy, good-humoured-looking young man of twenty, who was seated on the floor engaged in tying up the chips in bundles. The apartment was also occupied by two Irish lads, who had come to Liverpool a few weeks previously to look for employment as dock labourers, or operative porters, but who had failed in obtaining it. All four lodged together in this one dark and small room, not above twelve feet square—the three young men sleeping in one bed on the floor, and the old woman in another. The old lady seemed very much puzzled to know what interest I could possibly have in the 'chip' business; and though she spoke very little English, she contrived to let me know how surprised she was that I could think such small matters worthy of notice; as well as to express sometimes very considerable contempt for my ignorance upon one or two points on which I requested information. The son, like all the strong Irish of Liverpool, worked in the docks or on the quays, whenever he could get a chance from a friendly lumper or master porter; but being an unskilled labourer; not being able to read or write, and knowing in consequence nothing of weights or marks, his chance of employment was but small. He contrived to live, however, in the chip business, with his mother's help. Around him on the floor was a large heap of chips of wood of all sizes and shapes, which he was engaged in making into bundles. He continued his work while he answered my questions—the old woman occasionally interposing a word, and occasionally turning her attention to a pot upon the fire containing a mess of Indian meal stirabout, that she was preparing for dinner for the family and the lodgers.

"I do," said he, "a pretty good business in the chip line. I buy wood and shavings at the timber-yards. I also buy old bacon boxes and pork barrels from the provision dealers—boxes that come from America principally, and some that come from Cork and Dublin. I split them up into chips and sell the bundles to the retail dealers, or chandler's shops. The wholesale price is 4d. a dozen bundles. They are retailed by the shops at a half-penny a piece, or 6d. a dozen. With my mother's assistance in doing up the bundles, I can gain about 6s. a week. It would be a pretty fair week when I could make 6s. I do not cry the chips about the streets, as some do—all our business is with the retail shops. The best week's work I ever had in chips was when I sold fifty dozen of bundles. A dozen bundles would cost me 2d. for wood, and I should have 2d. a doz. for labour. The fifty dozen would bring me in a profit of 8s. 4d. That was the best week I remember. I would not tell you these things if I thought you were in the trade, but you don't look like a chip-dealer, and I dare say you mean something for our good, or Mr. Bishop would not have brought you. I generally buy about 12s. or 15s. worth of wood at a time, which very few can afford to do. I make the best kind of chips, and sell the large bundles. My bundles are 4d. a dozen; but some make smaller bundles, which they can afford to sell at twelve a penny, or twenty a penny. The bundles are not tied with rope or string, but with wisps that come off the cotton bales. Boys and girls go about the ships to pick up the wisps, and sell them at one-halfpenny per pound to the marine store and rag shops. There is very little to be got in that way, as the captains, or lumpers, sell what they call the sweepings of the hold, and the wisps among the rest. A penny worth of wisps would tie a great number of bundles—perhaps a hundred." [I afterwards learned, in reference to this family, the whole of whose furniture was not worth five shillings, that the woman had amassed the sum of £10, which she had placed in the savings bank. There was not a chair in her wretched apartment. Her son either sat upon the floor, or on an old box; the mistress of the establishment retaining a three-legged stool for herself. For ten shillings out of her £10 she could have provided herself with four very tidy chairs, and given her apartment an air of comfort. It was supposed that she and her son were saving the money to enable them to emigrate to the United States.]

My next informant was the inhabitant of a very dirty cellar eleven feet square. He was an old and sickly-looking man, in ragged attire, with the exception of a striped waistcoat—a good deal too large for him, but new, clean, and strong. He said "I am fifty-two years of age. I have a wife and three children. I cannot get any work at portering, though I have tried hard for a job in the docks. I have had nothing to do for many months. I came to Liverpool from the county of Mayo. There are thousands of porters out of work. I am obliged to do something else when I can't get a job at portering. I can't do heavy work. The wife and myself and the three children all do what we can. We try both the 'chip' and the 'grit' business, but not the oakum picking. The children break the grit with bits of paving stone, just as all the others do that work in the 'grit' line. I sometimes get stone for nothing at the quarries, and have to carry it here on my back. I often have to pay a halfpenny or a penny a bag for the stone to the quarrymen. The children cry the grit about the streets after we have made it. Grit is sold by halfpennyworths and pennyworths. The servants buy it to clean their hearths or their door-steps with. It is very good for that purpose. It takes a long time to make sixpennyworth of grit, and often still longer to sell it. There are so many in it now to what there used to be, that people can't live. I also do a little in 'chips.' I think it a better business. There are some old bacon-boxes in the corner, which I bought for fifteen pence. I shall have to break and cut them into chips, which will take me two or three days. I shall send the children out with them for sale in the streets; and if I get half-a-crown for them I shall get as much as I can expect. I make bundles of various sizes—some to be sold at six or seven a penny, and some of the smaller ones at twenty-four a penny. The most that the wife, myself, and the three children can gain in a day by chips and grit is eightpence. I never made more. My eldest boy is seventeen years of age. He generally cuts up the wood; I look about at the bacon-shops and buy it, or go to the carpenter's yards, and sometimes get a little for nothing, but not often. The wife ties up the bundles with wisps, and the two younger children cry 'chips, chips,' about the streets all day—from morning to night. Two or three years ago I made more by the chips than I make now. I could earn 10d. a day at the trade, when there were fewer people engaged about it. There are many days now when we can only sell eight pennyworth. The profit on that would only be 4d. The whole five of us live for a day on two pounds of Indian meal made into stirabout, and a halfpennyworth of milk. That would be 2½d. a day. As for clothes, we are all naked almost. Three years ago I had some clothes, but everything belonging to me is pawned except what I have got on. This is a good waistcoat that I wear, almost as warm as a coat. It was given to me by a farmer's wife, when I went harvesting last autumn. I always try the harvest work. I get 1s. 6d. a day at it, and save some of it to keep the house at home. I have no chance of porter's work. I tried to get among the sweepers employed by the town to do the sweeping work of the streets. It is good wages that they get, nine shillings a week all the year round. But I have no friends, and cannot get on the sweeping. I wish I could. It would be the making of me to get on the sweeping. A kind lady gave me two shillings about a fortnight ago, which helped me on a little. Things are very bad for the poor in Liverpool, and are getting much worse. There are too many people at all kinds of work—too many porters, and too many chip-sellers—more than the town wants. I pay 1s. 6d. a week rent for this cellar, but we have not got it all to ourselves— only a part of it. There is another lodger who sleeps here, he pays 1s. a week—not to us, but to the landlord."

Here the lodger, a cripple, who had descended into the cellar while the old man was telling his story, and who had been listening for some time to the questions and replies which I have embodied in the foregoing statement, gave a history of his condition and of the circumstances which brought him into it. He looked exceedingly ill, and was shockingly dirty. I took down his statement, and give it in his own words:—

"My name is Michael D——. My father was a labouring man. I am 40 years of age. In the year 1835, I was employed as a school-teacher in Dublin, in connection with the Church Educational Society. I had a salary of £40 a year, which I received for about three years in one situation in Dublin. I had a similar situation in Drogheda, where I remained for five years. From Drogheda I went to a place in the county of Waterford, where I remained for four years. That brings me, I think, to 1847. At that time I had been reading the Irish Bible to the Irish scholars; and had left the Church Educational Society in consequence of some difference I had about reading it. I was opposed for reading the Bible in Irish. I made myself enemies and the place grew unpleasant to me. I at last made up my mind to leave Ireland and come to England. I had no friends in England, and did not even know the name of any one in Liverpool when I landed in it. I buried my wife in Dublin, and also my child, and was alone in the world when I came here. I had not saved any money, but I paid my passage over, and arrived in Liverpool with a shilling, a silver watch, and a good stock of clothes. I pawned my watch and clothes the first week, and, seeing nothing that I could do in Liverpool, I went on to Bolton. I don't know what induced me to go there. I knew nobody in Bolton, but I had good testimonials, and showed them to the teacher at Trinity School in that town. He gave me some employment. In fact I gave him private lessons in mathematics. I was a pretty good mathematician; and he paid me a shilling an hour, for two hours in the evening. I also got another scholar, who paid me 15s. in all, for giving him lessons in ornamental writing, I gained in one way or another about 12s. a week during the two months I remained in Bolton, and saved a little money. I wanted to visit Liverpool to get my watch out of pawn, and had occasion, also, to stop at St. Helen's. When the train arrived at St. Helen's, I did not hear the guard cry out the name of the place. I was paying no attention; but when the train was in motion, I noticed the name of the place written up at the station. Without thinking what I was doing, I jumped out of the train. The concussion was so great that it broke three of my ribs, and I received other injuries. I have never had a day's health since, and have been a poor object in the great town of Liverpool from that time to the present. I was picked up and taken to a doctor's shop. I paid his expenses; and when sufficiently recovered to move about again, I went to Prescott, thinking to get employed in teaching. From Prescott I came to Liverpool, but never got any employment. I knew nobody—not a creature—and had neither friends nor money, and was too weak for porters' work of any kind. I remembered that when I was a teacher in Waterford, I had seen the children at Lord Waterford's school make little work-baskets of wire and cotton—very flimsy things—and that I had made one or two for my amusement. I resolved, being in the greatest distress in Liverpool, to try my hand at them. I made a good many of them, and for awhile contrived to earn about five shillings a week. They were a novelty at first, and went off very well. People are tired of them now; and there is no sale for them. They are very light and frail. There is no substance in them. Last winter I sold a few at 6d. and 4d. each. I do nothing now. I have an allowance of 2s. a week from the parish; and pay 1s. for my lodging, and 1s. for my food. I don't know how I shall get clothes when these rags are done. I prefer the out-door relief, and have no wish to go into the workhouse. My only earnings besides the work-boxes, was 4d. that I got some weeks ago, for writing a letter for an Irishman. I have not strength to undertake a school, or to make chips. I have no other prospect than that of being turned over to my parish in Ireland, and of ending my days in the union workhouse. I could give lessons in Trigonometry and Navigation; but I have no means of getting pupils."

I should add to this story that I afterwards saw some letters written by this Irish teacher, and that neither the calligraphy, the orthography, nor the syntax was of a nature to prove his alleged proficiency in *these* branches of education. As regards mathematics, it is a singular fact that the Irish, of the class above the lowest, have a great partiality for this study. Cheap mathematical works find a readier sale in Ireland than any other books.

The next family I visited inhabited a room in a court leading out of Jordan-street—a street of the worst kind. A privy was close to the door, which, as I was informed, was common to four houses, and used by upwards of fifty people. The people of these four houses kept their windows close shut to keep out the smell. The man made the following statement:—

"I am out of work, and have not dirtied my hands with a job for nine weeks. I have a wife and four children—three daughters and a son. Two girls and a boy have got employment in a rope-walk, and earn four shillings a week each. The youngest girl, 'Biddy,' goes about the streets crying 'chips.' I try the chip-making. Everybody does when work fails. All the poor people in the town take to chips, or grit, or else to oakum-picking, when they can get nothing else to do. I do not know how many poor people there may be in the chip trade. I never heard and never thought about it; but there must be a great number. I remember the time when something like a living might be made out of 'chips.' I sometimes sell seven shillingsworth in a week, which is half profit, or sevenpence a day. I chop up the wood, my wife ties it in bundles, and little Biddy cries them about the streets. I buy the wood from carpenters and joiners, as well as from shipbuilders. I never tried the grit business. The chip business is bad enough but 'grit' is worse. There are three rooms in this house, and I pay 4s. a week rent for them. I let one room for 1s. 6d. a week to a family of six persons. I was visited by the police some months ago, who found fifteen people in the house; for I had given a night's lodging to some poor lads from Ireland. The police reported me for keeping too many lodgers, and I was had up before Mr. Rushton, and fined £1 4s. 6d. I have not paid the fine. I can't pay it. I do not know what number of lodgers I am entitled to keep. No demand has been made for the money; but if it is asked of me I must go to prison for it, I suppose." [Here "Biddy" made her appearance—a fresh, pretty-looking girl of ten years of age, with a boy's greatcoat on, and her empty chip-basket upside down on her head, in guise of a bonnet. Her mother at sight of her exclaimed—"Ah Biddy—you hussy—what sort of a head-dress is that you have got? Ain't you ashamed before the gentlemen?" Biddy took it off, doffed her great coat, handed over sixpence to her mother as the produce of her day's work, and took her seat beside the fire]. The father continued, "Biddy is a good girl. She has been out since seven in the morning; it is now two; she will go out again with chips after dinner. She complains of her head sometimes. The load is rather heavy for her, and makes her head ache. She goes to the ragged school in the evening." [I afterwards ascertained that this poor man was fined, not for keeping too many lodgers, but for letting lodgings by the night without having a licence as a nightly lodging-house keeper, as required by the Liverpool Sanitary Act. I shall have occasion to refer to this subject in reference to the sanitary state of the town, and the operation of the Sanitary Act.]

I shall describe but one more scene. In the most miserable room I had yet beheld, I found a poor creature—an Irish woman—sitting upon the floor tying up chips. The room was on the first floor of a house in a narrow court. In ascending the stair I could see into the apartment, although the door was shut. The plaster, both outside and in, had fallen from the lath work, and through the interstices I could plainly distinguish the woman at her work. I afterwards took an inventory of her furniture. The room was 6 feet by 12. The windows were broken, and partly patched with paper, rags, and boards, but not in such a manner as to exclude the cold air. One pane was stuffed with a broken basket. The door also was broken, and permitted any passer-by to look into the apartment. In fact, the place was more like a cage than a room. On the floor was what I supposed to be the bed, a bundle of something rolled up in a piece of old, ragged, dirty, red carpeting. There was neither table nor chair, nor any other article that could be called furniture, except one small three-legged stool. Besides this, there was a dish, two broken tea-cups, a broken basin, an iron pot, and a bit of soap. Other articles there were none of any kind, except the chips upon the floor, in the midst of which the poor woman was seated. She did not rise from her work. She knew my companion, and his kindness to the poor. She said, in answer to my inquiries, still tying up her chips as she spoke—

"My husband is out of work. He is a dock labourer. He has had nothing to do—not half a day, for six months. We have four children. They never go to school. One of them is going. We have been starving with cold all the winter on account of the state of the wall. The landlord will not repair it, although we pay 1s. 6d. a week rent. We have nothing to live on but what we get by 'chips,' and begging. The children sell them in the streets at 22 bundles a penny. My husband cuts them, and I tie them up. I can tie up eighteen pennyworth in a day—[396 bundles]. It would take me a whole day; and if we could sell them all I should earn ninepence. The children beg in the streets. Begging is a better trade than selling chips; but we try both—God help us. There are 29 people in this house. They are all poor like ourselves. Some of them are beggars and some of them are in the chip business. I don't like to let the children go to the school because they are so ragged. I know the schools are meant for ragged children, but mine are too ragged. I shall let one boy go. He has been out begging to-day, but has not brought home anything. He is not a cotton-picker. The police are very severe upon the children who pick up cotton in the street. It is not a good business; begging is far better than that. I hope to sell all these chips to-day. When any of the children come home I will send them out with chips. A few tickets for soup would be a great blessing to us (my companion gave her a handful). May the Lord reward you! My husband would like to get on the sweepings. He cannot get work in the docks." [I learned afterwards that the child alluded to by this woman was sent for one day to the Industrial Ragged School, where the children are fed as well as taught; but that the mother took it away on the second day, and sent it out begging again. She said she could not afford to let the boy go to school—he was more profitable to her as a beggar!]

I shall conclude this letter with a few words relative to the "sweeping," to get connected with which I found to be a great object of ambition among the poorer class of people in Liverpool. The sweeping of the town is conducted under the superintendence of the Borough Engineer's Office—a branch of the sanitary establishment. In the week before my inquiries commenced, the number of sweepers employed in cleansing the streets from rubbish, in Liverpool, and in the surrounding townships of Toxteth Park, Everton, Kirkdale, and West Derby, was 250. This is about the average number employed. The work is steady, and the wages are 1s. 6d. a day, or 9s. a week. Pauper labour is not employed for the purpose, being found unprofitable.

LABOUR AND THE POOR.

—◆—

LIVERPOOL.

[FROM OUR SPECIAL CORRESPONDENT.]

SHIRTMAKERS AND NEEDLEWOMEN.—THE SLOP TRADE AND SWEATING SYSTEM.

LETTER VI.

The position of Liverpool, as a port crowded with sailors and emigrants, and as the great outlet to the western world, renders it a place of much importance to the slop-sellers. In addition to the great bulk of the public, to whom the slop-sellers appeal by the cheapness of their goods, the clothing of sailors and emigrants furnishes a constant trade. The slop trade generally is divisible into two great branches—in one of which women are actively employed as the workpeople, and in the other both men and women, but men principally. The first includes such work as canvas and duck trowsers, flannel drawers and jackets, cotton shirts (both plain and striped), and waistcoats of all materials, except of woollen cloth. The second branch of the trade employs men who avail themselves very often of the labour of the female members of their families to augment their scanty earnings; make the garments of sailors and emigrants, and clothes for exportation, besides and who supplying the home demand for ready-made apparel. I shall take these branches separately, and commence my inquiries with the female slop-workers. It is very difficult to ascertain the number of women employed in needlework and slop-work in Liverpool. Indeed I may say that the science of statistics is one which does not flourish in this town. There is no account to be depended upon, even of the amount of the population—one account stating it to be under 300,000, and another to be above 400,000. I could not ascertain with any exactitude the number of porters and labourers employed at the docks; nor, in a matter which vitally affects the interests of the inhabitants of Liverpool—the burden upon the pockets of the rate-payers, caused by the constant immigration of pauper Irish people—was I able to obtain anything like a complete estimate of the money pressure of the evil. As regards the needle-women and slop-workers, I endeavoured, by diligent inquiry among various parties from whom I judged it likely that I might gather the information, to arrive at something like an approximative estimate of the number of female slop-workers; but neither from the employers or from the employed could I elicit any statement founded upon reliable data. Some employers seem to be of opinion that from three to four thousand needlewomen are employed in the town, while others think that five or even ten thousand would be nearer the truth. The needlewomen themselves have no precise ideas upon the subject. They have a notion of some overwhelming and inexpressible number of competitors in the trade; a number that can only be vaguely designated by such phrases as an "immense quantity," "many thousands," "almost every poor woman," "a great deal too many," and others equally indefinite. The impression ultimately left upon my mind was, that the number of needlewomen in Liverpool is unintentionally exaggerated by both parties; and that, considering the great home, colonial, and foreign trade in articles of slop-manufacture carried on by the town, comparatively few needle-women find direct employment, although a great number may be employed to assist their husbands or fathers, who take slop tailors' work. The "Liverpool Directory" does not give the names and addresses of those outfitters and others who may strictly be called slopsellers in the wholesale and retail trade; but in a list of upwards of 250 tailors and woollen-drapers, 75 are entered as "outfitters." Among the linen-drapers and mercers, as well as among the tailors, a slop business is extensively carried on; but, on inquiry, I learned that the greater portion of the female slopwork required by Liverpool is done in the north of Ireland. There appears to be very great and permanent distress among the needle-women in Liverpool, whatever their numbers may be; a fact which may arise from two causes—first, from the superior manner in which the slopwork is executed in Ireland, owing to the perfect organization of the business; and, secondly, from the want of such organization in Liverpool, and the daily increase of the numbers employed in the work, by all the unskilled women who fall into distress, and who betake themselves to needlework as their only resource. The slop-sellers in Liverpool may be divided into three classes. The first are the wholesale houses who carry on the foreign and colonial trade in shirts, and cloth and flannel goods; the second are the retail houses; and the third are the slop-tailors. Some of the retail outfitters and slop-sellers employ a kind of "men-catchers," whose business it is to look out for emigrants and sailors, and to induce them to purchase outfits. The retail houses are the principal employers of the women of Liverpool.

The following statements, taken down from the needlewomen—some of them in constant, and some of them in precarious employ, some of them old hands at the business, and some of them new beginners, some of them employed in slop-work, and some in the fine description of goods—will show the condition of the class:—

Mrs. K——: "I work at shirt-making for one of the principal shops in Liverpool. I can earn about 4s. 6d. a week—or, to be more correct, I should say 4s. 4d. The most I can do is to make four shirts in the week, at 1s. 1d. each. It is very particular work—strong and plain. I have been at this work for a twelvemonth, but could not make more than three shirts a week at first, until I got into the way of it. I make four now, by working very closely. The shop for which I work finds the workpeople in thread. We have not to buy it. Some of the shops in Liverpool make the workpeople provide the thread. I am sometimes obliged to work till one and two in the morning, and very seldom have done till twelve. I begin work at eight in the morning in winter, and at six in summer. I have made shirts as low as 8d. each—they are inferior in quality, and are sold cheaper. They have only two buttonholes in front instead of three, and only one row of stitching round the wristband, instead of two, and only three plaits in front instead of five. I could only make four of these shirts in a week. Perhaps I might make five by sitting very late, but I could not continue at such work. My strength would not bear it. I should have no time for rest. There are very many at this kind of work in Liverpool. I have a child to keep out of my earnings; but I could not have lived if I had not had friends to keep me. My husband is dead. I have no rent to pay, which is a great assistance to me. I cannot afford to buy any clothes. I have had nothing new for a twelvemonth or more. I am a native of the county Tipperary, and live with my brother, who has a situation in Liverpool."

E. —— and J. ——, two young women, sisters, of the ages of about 20 and 22, made the following statement: "We work for a slop-shop, and make jean trowsers and other articles. Each of us can make three pair of boy's, or two pair of men's trowsers in a day. The price for boy's trowsers is 4d. a pair, and for men's 6d. We could make three pair between eight in the morning and seven or eight at night. We have to find thread and twist. The thread for one pair of trowsers would cost near upon a penny, and the twist for one pair the same. The flannel-drawer work is better paid. We could each make 9d. a day at them, clear of all expense for thread. Neither of us ever made more than 4s. in a week since we have been at needlework. We served our time to the dress-making, but we can get no work in any of the shops in Liverpool. They are all full of hands. There is no end of fresh people who come into the dress-making business. Our employer is a slopseller, and exports his goods. We do not know where he sends them to, but they are not sold in the town. The trowsers that we make for 6d. a pair sell at 2s. 9d. a pair. For making flannel jackets he pays 1s. a piece, but it takes two days to make one, and the thread costs 2d. It is very hard work, and does not bring in above half-a-crown a week. We do not always get these to make, but if there are any we must take our chance of them. We could not live upon needlework without assistance from our friends. We could not earn 6s. a week each if we were to work for eighteen or twenty hours a day."

Mrs. C——, a middle-aged woman, of very clean and respectable appearance, said: "I work at fine shirtmaking. I make calico and linen shirts at 1s. 4d., 1s. 8d., 2s., and 2s. 3d. each, according to the quality and work. I could make a shirt at 1s. 4d. in a day, if I sat very close and worked very late; say from seven in the morning until ten at night. If I had constant work at this I could make 8s. a week, but not easily. I could make four of the 2s. 3d. shirts in a week, if I could get them to do. It would be very hard work, and would take from six in the morning till past twelve at night. I have often worked all night. I have done so for two nights in a week without going to bed. I was obliged to do it, as my father, a labourer, was for twenty-one weeks without work, and depended on me to keep him from starving. I did not make 2s. 6d. extra by sitting up for these two nights, as a good deal of the profit went for coals and candle. I never worked for the slop-shops. I had no work for six weeks before Christmas until last week, when I got a private job to put new sleeves and bodies to four shirts. I received 2s. 8d. for it. This week I have only had one shirt to make, for which I shall get 8d. I have other means of living, as my husband is a sailor. He has gone to Savannah, and has left me his monthly money. If I depended upon needlework I must starve, or go into the workhouse."

Mrs. H——: "I am sixty-seven years of age, and have been for thirty years employed in Liverpool at all sorts of needlework. I have made jackets, vests, sailors' trowsers, shirts, everything. I mostly make flannel drawers now, as my eyes are so bad that I cannot undertake fine work. I could make two pairs in a day, but I cannot get constant employment. The shops are all very slack. I have only earned 3s. for the last three weeks. About two years ago I used to make calico striped shirts, and got three shillings a dozen for them. I had to find the thread out of that. I could not make a dozen in a week—not above eight. It was miserable work. I could work faster at that time than I can now, as my eyes were better. The shop I work for gives me the flannel drawers to make as a favour, because I am old, and because of my failing sight. I have worked for one shop for 25 years. I never was able to save a farthing. My husband was a seafaring man, who was often ailing, and I had to support him. He has been dead since the first cholera; I forget when that was, but I think it is 20 years ago. He died coming home from Jamaica. The work was much better in 1832, and for some years afterwards, than it is now. In *them* times I could make half-a-crown a day by making petticoats for the black women, and bedgowns lined with baize, also for the black women in the West Indies. I received 4s. a dozen for the bedgowns, and 2s. 6d. a dozen for the petticoats. I could make a dozen petticoats in the day by sitting late, but not a dozen bedgowns. I used to make check chemises for the black women. I do not remember what I got for them, but I remember that it was a much better business than needlework is now. I could almost make as much in a day as I can now make in a week. None of the shops pay as well as they did. Since slavery was abolished there has been a great falling-off in this kind of work; and no other work so good has come up to supply its place. The slaves were good customers to Liverpool. The abolition of slavery is the worst thing that has ever happened to the needle-workers. It has reduced wages at least one-fifth. I have no son—nobody to help me, and nobody to support but myself. I never made any application to the parish. I let lodgings, but I do not manage to live rent free by them; but still every lodger is a help. I very seldom have meat for dinner, but I try to afford it once a week—on Sunday. My dinner on other days is bread and butter. I like potatoes, but I find bread more nourishing. A cup of tea is the nicest thing I get. I could not do without my tea. I should drink more of it, and take it stronger, if it was not so dear. The cheapness of sugar is a great blessing to such poor people as me that likes a cup of tea. Indian meal is cheap, but I don't like it, and never heard of any one that did, unless they could get nothing else. I use oatmeal sometimes, but my chief diet is bread and butter, and tea. I cannot do without my tea."

I put a variety of questions to this old lady, with the view of ascertaining in what manner the abolition of slavery in the British West Indian colonies had either diminished her chances of employment or lowered her wages; but I found her quite incapable of explaining the matter, or throwing any light upon it. She repeated very earnestly that it had done so; but she did not appear to have even the shadow of a notion what the reason could have been. Upon making inquiries some days afterwards of a gentleman largely engaged in the wholesale slop-trade, it was explained that, prior to the passing of the act for the emancipation of the negroes, their masters supplied them with coarse calico shirts of a certain pattern and colour, which they were compelled to wear. A large trade in the article was carried on from Liverpool, and it gave employment and good wages to a considerable number of women. When the negroes became their own masters this trade immediately declined. They did not look with any favour upon an article which appeared to them the livery of their ancient slavery, and they would not be tempted to purchase such shirts at any price, however small. In fact, they would not look at them. They made their own choice, and patronized shirts of a more expensive fabric, of a better quality, and of more flaring colours, especially those gaudy intermixtures of white, red, and yellow, which are known to be so agreeable to negro eyes, and generally to uncultivated people. There is at present considerable trade in these showy articles, but it does not give employment exclusively to the women of Liverpool, as many houses, for reasons which will be explained in the course of this letter, prefer to employ the needlewomen of the north of Ireland.

Mrs. V——: "I have worked for five years at trowser-making and other needlework. My husband is a stevedore, or lumper in a small way, but does not get regular employment. He does not earn 10s. a week, one week with another; but between his work and mine we manage to live—that is all. We are five in family. The eldest boy is in an attorney's office. He runs errands and does other things, and gets 4s. 6d. a week. The other two children are too young to earn anything. I make duck and canvas trowsers, and duck and moleskin jackets. The moleskin is the best paid work. I get a shilling a pair for the best made duck or canvas trowsers. It requires to be strong work. I should have no thread to buy out of the shilling—only the wax, which is not much. To make one pair of this kind, the best, I should have to work from five or six in the morning to twelve at night, with a rest for dinner. Taking one week with another I make 3s. 6d., or it may be 4s., but certainly not more. Some shops pay less prices than I get. I, myself, have made trowsers for three pence a pair, but it was not fine work. I have always worked for one shop. For making duck jackets I have generally got 10d., though sometimes I have been paid as much as 1s., or 1s. 3d. I could make one duck jacket in a day, but do not often get the chance. I should starve if I had no husband to rely upon. Needlework is a bad trade, but it helps us to live, and while my husband can earn anything I do not complain."

Mrs. G——: "I work for several shops in Liverpool, and employ other women under me. I have six in my employ at present. The principal work we do is in making sailors' trowsers of light canvas or duck. They are sometimes called Tecklenburger trowsers in the trade. I am responsible to the shops for the work, and receive 4d. a pair for the trowsers. I cut them out, superintend the work, and press them. I pay the women 3d. a piece for making. One of my best hands would make six pair of such trowsers in a day—that would be 9s. a week. A common hand would make four pair a day. The best hands could not make a pair of trowsers in less than three hours. Eighteen hours a day is hard work, but some women can do it. It is not many that can; it is too great a strain on their health. I calculate that I can make 9s., or, perhaps 10s. a week for my own labour, superintendence, and responsibility. I do not include house room or coals and candle, which I have to supply; but, after these expenses are paid, my profits are 9s. or 10s., on the average. I also have to find thread. All these expenses are heavy, and I cannot afford to pay the workwomen more than 3d. per pair for merely making the trowsers. A penny a pair is small profit to me, and to make up the 9s. I am obliged to work as hard as any of the women. I often work harder, I am sure, than some of them. I don't know of any fall in wages. I never had more than I have now."

The next two needlewomen I saw I visited at their own homes. The first was a young woman under thirty, with three children, of whom the eldest was a girl aged eleven, the second a boy of nine, and the third a boy of three years of age. She lived in one small room on the first floor, in a pestilential street. The room was dirty, and scantily furnished, and had an air of misery and squalor in every part of it. The tent bedstead was without curtains, and very scantily provided with mattress and covering. The domestic articles were scattered about in confusion—the two chairs and the table, which, with the bed, formed the whole furniture of the place, were filthy—the window panes were stuffed with paper and rags. On the table was a quantity of coarse blue woollen stuff, which she was engaged in making into shirts for sailors. She gave me the following history of her earnings:—"I have myself and these three children to support by slopwork. My husband was a sailor. He died at Quebec three years ago. He used to give me his monthly money regularly; and when he died I was obliged to earn my own living by needlework, as I could do nothing else. I am an Irishwoman, but I was brought up in Liverpool. I never applied to the parish for relief. I principally make canvas and duck trowsers. They are hard work, but I could manage to earn 10s. a week, if I could get the work to do. I should be obliged to work from six in the morning to eleven at night to gain as much as that. I am considered a very rapid worker, and have a good character in the trade. The duck trowsers and canvas trowsers are equally troublesome to make, and the price paid for the work is the same. I prefer the work to shirt-making, as it is better paid. At shirt-making I could not earn above six or seven shillings a week if I worked eighteen hours a day. Shirts take a great deal of making, there is so much stitching. I have been fourteen years at needlework. The pay was much better six years ago than it is now. The duck trowsers were then paid 6s. a dozen—they are only paid 4s. a dozen now. I can't tell the reason. They are sold much cheaper than they used to be. The shirt-making does not appear to be any lower than formerly. It is so low that it can't be reduced. People starve at shirt-making, and you can't well bring them lower than starvation, if you expect them to be able to move their fingers at all. I try all sorts of needlework. I take it as it offers. I make red flannel shirts for sailors, and also for the Californian trade. I do not consider it well-paid work—not so good as the canvas trowsers. The price of making is 4s. a dozen. There is no thread to find out of this. They give out at the shop what thread they think will do, and ought to do, but it sometimes runs short, and then the needle-women must buy what is deficient. I have a job on hand that must be finished by to-morrow morning, and I shall have to work all night to get it done. I shall make about a shilling by the night's work. The whole job will bring me in 3s. 6d., and will have occupied me two days and a night. One week with another I earn about 5s. I do not know how much that would amount to in a year. Last week I only earned eighteen-pence, for half a dozen white duck frocks for sailors. I pay two shillings a week rent. The worst year I remember was 1849. Before that I managed pretty well, and could get a little clothes, but last year I could not buy even a rag for myself or my children—indeed I could scarcely get food, let alone clothes. I do not send my little girl to the evening school, although I know she might go free. She has no clothes to go in. I know that is no objection at the Ragged School, but I don't like to let her go without proper clothes. She is eleven years old, and I make her useful to me. She can sew, and do the common work. She fetches the work home from the shop for me, and takes it back, and saves my time in this way when I am very busy. It is but seldom that I am too busy to take the things home myself. The elder of the boys does not go to school. He has never been at one. He has no teaching at all. I should like to send him to the school if I could afford to pay for him, and could get him a little better clothes."

The next woman I visited was one of a different class, and her neat house, her clean and highly respectable appearance, and the air of humble comfort and great propriety in everything about her impressed me at once in her favour. Her house was in one of the numerous small courts of Liverpool, but the court itself was much cleaner than these places usually are, as it appeared to have been recently washed out. Her little room was carpeted, and contained several very good articles of plain furniture, as well as a few humble but not unsuccessful attempts at luxuries, in the shape of prints and china figures of somewhat coarse execution. She was neatly attired in black, and wore a little collar and a cap, both as white as "the driven snow." She was engaged, spectacles on nose, in making linen shirts, and at the table beside her sat two other elderly women, both respectably dressed, but neither of them offering the steady, comfortable, matronly appearance that she did. One of them was her sister, who lived with her, and assisted her in her business. The other was a lodger, whose husband was at sea, and who was eking out her subsistence by needlework. The mistress of the house no sooner opened her mouth than the accent betrayed her country. She was from Dumfries, and spoke the Scotch *patois* in all its native broadness. She said, in answer to a few questions that I put to her, "I do not work for the shops, and have not done so for some years. I know very little about the slop-work, except what I hear from others. All our work is bespoke work. We are employed by families and by ladies who know us, to make shirts for gentlemen, and various articles for the ladies. We also do the mending for families. I have never occasion to go out and ask for work. One lady recommends another, and I have always enough to do, for which I am very grateful, when I know that so many poor creatures are starving. We are paid 2s. a shirt, which is almost as much as some of the slop-workers get for a dozen. I am seldom employed on cotton shirts; mostly always on linen. They are well made, and have a deal of work in them. My sister and I make a shirt a day, at the least—that is about 12s. a week between us. We sometimes make more than that—scarcely ever less. We are well paid for the mending also; but we always put strong and careful work in it. Our eyes are not so good as they were; and we can't work more than eight or ten hours a day. I should say we generally work ten hours. We are very thankful that we can pay our way. We get a little bit of meat almost every day, and our tea, and we can afford to dress ourselves respectably. We are very careful and saving, and are obliged to be. It is trying work for our eyes, but a little cold tea rubbed on them, when I am tired, always brighten mine up, and refreshes me. I don't think the constant looking at needlework, or at the brick walls, is very good for the sight. We see nothing but brick walls in this court, but I have no great desire to go out walking now to look at the fields. I used to like the sight of trees and flowers; and often think, as I sit over my work, of the pleasant place I lived at before I came to Liverpool. It was on the river Nith, about five miles from Dumfries; and I could sit at my window and look over the 'bonnie' river, and the fields. But somehow 'I'm no caring' to go out much now. I don't seem to want to go out. We have the whole of this house to ourselves. It contains three rooms, and we pay a rent of 3s. 2d. a week. The 2d. over is for the water, which the landlord pays, and I am never 'fashed' with the tax-collector, either for water or anything else. The landlord pays all the taxes out of the 3s. 2d. We have a good supply of water. It comes in once every day, and I never hear any of the people in our court complain that they have not water enough. I am a widow, without children. I had a son, but he is dead. I have gone through a great deal of trouble. My father was killed at Dumfries, by falling from a cart and being run over, and my 'mither' died broken-hearted three months afterwards, leaving me a 'young lassie' with the charge of seven brothers and my sister. My brothers managed to get work at one thing or another. They are now all dead, but two. These two are doing pretty well, and my sister and I are left to get our living in this way. We are very thankful that we can do so."

It will be seen from the above statements, that the slopworkers and needlewomen of Liverpool, if they have no husbands whose wages may help them to live, or no friends to whom they can look for assistance—work in a state of much poverty and suffering; but that such as are fortunate enough to work for private families, and for the better class of shops, manage to procure a humble subsistence, correspondent with their moderate wants. I shall only append to their little histories the results of my inquiries among the slopdealers and outfitters. The reader will then be enabled to perceive some of the causes that operate to restrict the employment of the Liverpool needlewomen, and to transfer their work to the north of Ireland.

A large slopseller in the wholesale trade, to whom I applied for information on the subject, willingly showed me his books and accounts, and entered into the following particulars:—"I do not," he said, "employ many of the Liverpool needlewomen, unless I am compelled by the sudden arrival of a large order to take them on. It would not answer the purposes of my trade to employ uncertain and unskilled hands. The needlewomen of Liverpool are very often the wives of sailors. If they get their husbands' monthly money pretty regularly they do not care for needlework, but if there is any falling off in that they apply for slop-work. They are not regularly trained to the business, and I could not depend upon them for the execution of the orders that I have to supply. Great numbers of them take to needlework whenever they fall into distress from any cause. Some of them are the wives of porters and dock-labourers, who take to slop-work when their husbands are out of employ, and leave it off as soon as the husbands get a few jobs to keep them going. I do a large trade in shirts, both white and coloured. The coloured shirts find a ready market in the West Indies and in America. I get the greater portion of my work done in the north of Ireland—chiefly in Derry and Donegal. Whole parishes there are engaged in the business. The people are regularly trained to it, and do their work with the greatest neatness and promptitude. I send to a middleman, who is responsible to me for the proper state of the work. The lowest price I pay to the middleman is 2s. 6d. per dozen for striped cotton shirts; the next price is 2s. 9d. per dozen for regatta shirts; and for the better description of shirts the price varies from 6s. to 14s. per dozen. The middleman finds all the trimmings, except buttons, cuts out the shirts, pays the carriage of the goods to and fro, and allows a discount of five per cent. for ready money. In this way I have no trouble, and I get the work done in a satisfactory manner. I have often been in the villages in Derry and Donegal where this work is done. The needlewomen seem comfortable. They employ all their children in the business as soon as their little hands are able to thread a needle. The men do not work at the business, but boys of twelve or thirteen often do. The children do the hems and the simpler kind of work, and the women finish it off. Many boys, who afterwards become tailors, learn the first rudiments of the business at shirt-making. When they grow up they come over to England in search of employment as tailors, and generally have to resign themselves to work for the sweaters. They are not fit for better work. There are great numbers of Irish tailors of this class in Liverpool. As far as I know, an Irish needlewoman, in the employ of the middlemen who work for me, will average six shillings a week for her labour, and if she have children who are old enough to assist, she may make from a shilling to half-a-crown more. I speak of the superior work. In the inferior work, a woman will not perhaps earn more than 7d. a day, or 3s. 6d. a week. I find the Irish work in every respect the best. It is guaranteed by the middleman to be properly made; and he takes all the trouble off my hands, and pays the needle-women as much as they would be paid if they were employed directly. The system is such, that even if the price for an article be somewhat less to the workwoman, she is surer of constant work than under the system of working for the shops. The organization of the business is the great thing, and none but the skilled workpeople in Ireland get employment from the middlemen. It would not answer their purpose to employ such people as sailors' wives and porters' wives, who take to shirt-making as a temporary resource in distress. I am often obliged to employ gaol labour in consequence of having orders which I have not time to get executed in Ireland. I do not consider the prison labour to be at all satisfactory. I think that prisoners should be compelled to work out their own subsistence in some way or other; but, as far as shirt-making and needle-work generally are concerned, I do not think it by any means so satisfactory as the free labour of the Irish villages. It appears cheaper at first glance, but it is not so in reality. For instance, the shirts for which I pay 2s. 6d. a dozen making to the Irish middleman, cost me 2s. a dozen here. I pay 2s. to the corporation of Liverpool for such shirts made in the gaol. But the work is not guaranteed, as the Irish work is. I must take it with all its imperfections. I have to supply all the trimmings, and to do the cutting, and I have no discount of 5 per cent. It thus comes quite as expensive as the other, if not more so; and the work is decidedly inferior in every respect. You may be sure that for these reasons I employ as little gaol-labour as I possibly can. During the month of March I was obliged to employ gaol-labour on seven different occasions. You will see from these accounts sent by the corporation the quantity of work, and the rate at which it is charged. It amounts to 505 shirts, or 42 dozen—a very small matter—slightly exceeding £4. If there were a good organization of the business here by means of middlemen, or others, who would be responsible both for the goodness of the work and the regularity of the supply, I should not send to Ireland. The only attempt to systematize the work here is when a woman has half-a-dozen or a dozen other women to work under her. It is better to give out a quantity of work to one such woman, than to have the whole dozen of women coming to your establishment to ask for it; but even this is by no means so satisfactory as the Irish mode of conducting the trade. The middleman system, with its supervision, care, and punctuality, is what is wanted; and such a system would be far better for the really good and skilled workwoman who knows her business than the system, or no-system, of the Liverpool slopworkers."

I found, upon further investigation, that this statement was correct, both as regarded the superior quality of the Irish work and the uncertain nature of the work done by the needlewomen of Liverpool. I should mention, in addition to the facts above stated—and to prove that the constant accession of new, unskilled, and precarious hands into a business already scant enough for those who expect to live by it, inevitably diminishes wages—that it is not always the slopsellers who attempt to beat down the prices of their workpeople, but the workpeople themselves, who offer to work for less than the generally established or understood charges, in the hope of carrying away a greater portion than their competitors. Many instances of this were reported to me. In one case, a sailor having been drowned in America, his wife, left utterly destitute, with two children to support, applied to a slopseller, and offered to make shirts at any price he chose to give her, whether it was the regular price or not. Another was the wife of a dock labourer. Her husband had been confined to his bed for nine weeks. She had pawned everything that she possessed which she could part with, and she applied to a slop-seller for work with tears in her eyes, saying she would make cotton shirts at twopence a piece rather than starve any longer. Another woman, who did not make any plea of distress, offered to guarantee to make, or get made, all the shirts of one large establishment—cotton or linen, coarse or fine, sailors' or gentlemen's—at one uniform rate per dozen, considerably below the average prices formerly paid. I do not know whether this woman were in distress, or whether she were a speculator, or sweater, who calculated upon making a good income out of the work of the needier class of workpeople—but, in either case, it is the tendency of such offers, if constantly repeated, to bring down the rate of wages, and to cause destitution and misery among the working-classes.

An investigation into the condition of the Slop Tailors of Liverpool will conclude this branch of my subject. The same difficulty as regards ascertaining their numbers, which I found among the needle-women, exists also among the tailors.

There is no Trades Union or Society of Tailors in Liverpool, and there has not been any for four years. No statistics have been drawn up of the number of journeymen tailors in the town, but it is generally estimated to exceed 3,000, of whom about 800 are employed in shops by the respectable master tailors, leaving considerably upwards of 2,000 who work for the slop-tailors and show-shops. A movement has recently been made among the journeymen in Liverpool, in consequence of the disclosures made in *The Morning Chronicle* of the state of the trade in London. Their object is to abolish, if possible, the sweating and slop system, and to return to the old custom of the trade, which was, that the master should employ all his workmen upon his own premises.

There are but five or six great slop or show shops in Liverpool, and, as in London, a Hebrew is at the head of the trade, and pays large sums for placarding the walls, and advertising his goods in the local papers. The same firm has an establishment in London, and in several provincial towns. The greater portion of the slop journeymen tailors in Liverpool seem to be Irishmen, who come over at a cheap rate in the steamboats. They are mostly in great distress when they arrive, and are therefore willing to work for the sweater, at the sweater's prices. Within the last few years the number of men employed on the premises of the master tailors has gradually diminished. The respectable master tailors, as a body, complain that their trade is yearly falling off, and going into the hands of the show-shops and slop-sellers; and that the only means they have of competing with them is to lower the wages of their men. There are no regular houses of call for tailors in Liverpool, such as there are in London; but the men loiter about at the corners of the streets where the principal tailors reside—such as at Lord-street, Whitechapel, John-street, &c. This is a nuisance of which the masters make loud complaints—and which is anything but agreeable to the men. Some of them, when tired of waiting in the street, resort to public-houses, and sit drinking there.

Certain houses are known to the trade as houses which the men are in the habit of frequenting; and those who are in want of journeymen, when men are not to be found in the streets, hunt them out as they best can.

From the inquiries I made among the respectable portion of the trade, I learned that the introduction of the slop, and consequently of the sweating system, into Liverpool, has had a highly injurious effect both upon masters and men. In Liverpool, as elsewhere, not only the working and middle classes, but people in wealthy circumstances, are allured by the cheap prices of the show-shops, their ostentatious placards, and their constant advertisements in the newspapers, to bestow their patronage upon slop goods. One extensive tailoring establishment, where, before the slop system was introduced, 140 men were employed on the premises in making bespoke goods—doing what is called in London the honourable trade—has reduced the number of its hands to seventy. Another establishment, not so large, but doing, nevertheless, a considerable business, has been compelled, under the pressure of the same system, to reduce its hands to the extent of no less than two-thirds. Many similar instances were reported to me. Generally the respectable master tailors are in favour of the movement, commenced by the operative tailors, to place the true state of the trade before the public. There does not appear to be in Liverpool any fixed rate of wages. Each master tailor pays what he thinks proper; but, in what is called the respectable trade, it is considered that 4d. or 4½d. an hour is fair wages; and that from 24s. to 27s. a week is the average that should be paid for full work if the men were properly remunerated.

The statements made by the journeymen tailors of the operation of the slop system, seem, as far as I can gather, to resolve themselves into the following:—

First. That the rate of wages is so miserably small that a single man can barely manage to live, and that, if a married man wishes to avoid starvation, he must employ his wife and children to assist him in his work, to the neglect of his household, to the loss of all chance of education for his children, and to the still further reduction of the wages of the trade.

Second. That when the work is given out at the slop-shops, the operative must leave a deposit of £5, or obtain security for that amount; that large numbers of poor tailors in Liverpool, and of still poorer tailors who daily arrive from other parts of the country and from Ireland, are unable to do either the one or the other, and that consequently the services of a sweater, or middleman, are called into operation, who employs these men, and still further reduces the miserable wages paid by the slop shops.

Third. That the sweating system is not only in itself a hardship upon the poor men, as causing a reduction of their wages, but that it is a robbery and a cruelty besides, as the sweaters are generally hucksters and lodging-house keepers, and compel the operatives to board and lodge with them in wretched hovels and close unwholesome work-shops, that they may make a further profit out of them.

Fourth. That the slop clothes, from the badness of the material, require much stronger work and more skill and care than good material would do, in order to give them a "finish" and "appearance," to pass off the bad material—thus increasing the labour of the operative without increasing his wages.

Fifth. That the slop-sellers, in their competition with the whole trade and with one another, have no regard for the health or the morals of the men, or for their rest from labour on the Sunday; that they will give out work on Saturday night, and expect it to be re-turned on Monday morning; and that religious men and preachers of the Gospel, who purchase their cheap clothing of the slop-sellers, unwittingly encourage this system of desecration of the Sunday, and cause the physical and moral degradation of the operative.

Sixth. That slop-clothes, manufactured in the "sweating" estab-lishments and in the fetid courts and filthy apartments of the under-paid journeymen are not always wholesome; that slop-shirts and linen and cotton articles manufactured in similar places can be washed and purified before they are worn, but that this process cannot be resorted to with paletots, shooting-jackets, coats, and trowsers; and that con-sequently, to say nothing of the vermin that is sometimes found on such articles, there is, in times of fever—if not always—a danger of contagious disease to the wearers of them.

I made it my business to investigate the allegations of the men upon all these points. I visited the slop-workers in their wretched homes, and took down their statements from their own lips. I also called upon the sweaters, some of whom reluctantly gave, and some positively, if not rudely, withheld—information. I shall state the result of my inquiries in my next letter.

LABOUR AND THE POOR.

LIVERPOOL.

[FROM OUR SPECIAL CORRESPONDENT.]

THE TAILORS, THE SLOP TRADE, AND THE SWEATING SYSTEM.

LETTER VII.

I mentioned in my last letter the general state of the slop trade in Liverpool, and the agitation which has been recently commenced among the operative tailors in consequence of the misery they suffer. The tailors of Liverpool allege that the trade is even in a worse condition in their town than it is in the metropolis. However this may be, I am convinced, from the inquiries I have made among both employers and employed, and from the visits I have paid to the slop-workers at their own homes, that nothing can well be more deplorable than the condition to which these hard-working men and their families have been reduced in Liverpool. Before giving the detailed results of my inquiries amongst them, it will facilitate the reader's comprehension of the subject if I present a short history of the trade as it existed when the men were generally in the receipt of earnings sufficient for the support of their families, and when the work was carried on exclusively in the workshops of their employers. The object of the operatives who have stirred in the matter at the present time is to restore the trade to this condition.

The following information relative to this subject extends as far back as the year 1792, and was derived from an aged tailor, who was for nearly fifty years in the trade, but who has been for six or seven years engaged in the business of a furniture broker. Prior to the year 1792 the trade was solely carried on by respectable master tailors, who had regularly served their apprenticeship. The business of the woollen-drapers was entirely distinct. All the journeymen worked on the premises of their employers, and no journeyman was allowed to work in any shop who had not served his full time. This was a rule of the trade, observed both by masters and by men. The wages at that period were

16s. a week, and the hours of work were from six in the morning till seven in the evening, allowing an hour for dinner. All kinds of work were then done on the premises, including sailors' work, and such work as now goes under the name of slop-work. No women were employed in any portion of the business. The number of journeymen in the town was computed at between 200 and 280. In the year 1792 a man commenced business both as a tailor and as a draper; others followed the example who had not served their apprenticeship. The old master tailors felt aggrieved at this innovation, and insisted that the trades of the tailor and the draper should be kept separate. After the display of some angry feeling, they combined with some of the journeymen to prevent the operatives from working for any man who had not regularly served his time to the business. The drapers suffered so much inconvenience in consequence, that a few of them, on behalf of the rest, commenced proceedings against certain master tailors for a conspiracy to injure them. This case came on for trial at the Lancaster assizes, and excited much interest in the trade. The drapers gained the victory, and the business of tailoring was thus thrown open. Shortly afterwards, from 1797 to 1798, the journeymen tailors struck for an advance of wages, and claimed 3s. a day as a fair reward for their labour, alleging as their principal justification that the rise in the price of provisions was so great that they could not live upon their former wages. The contest did not last long. The drapers, of whom there were by this time a considerable number in the town, consented to the advance demanded by the men. The regular master tailors speedily followed their example. As provisions advanced in price, the men continued to demand more wages. In 1801 the price of flour was 6d. per lb., and gradually wages rose from 18s. to 21s. a week. About this time, slop-shops for the supply of seamen's clothes began to be established, but the slop-shops had all their work done upon the premises, and the system was introduced of working by the piece, instead of by the day. There existed at this time a society of tailors, for the protection of the trade, and for the purposes of a sick and burial club. This society gave its sanction to the new arrangement as regarded piece work, because a number of old and infirm journeymen were likely to become burthensome to its funds, unless this permission were accorded. The Society of Tailors, therefore, made the first great step towards breaking up the old system, for they not only sanctioned piece-work in the slop-shops, but they allowed the old members of the trade to take the work home and to employ the female members of their families.

Slop-work at this time was wholly confined to the clothing of sailors. The ultimate result of this change was to bring a number of women into competition with men, especially in waistcoat making.

In 1805 there was another strike for an advance of wages, from 21s. to 24s. a week; and as the drapers, notwithstanding the result of the trial in their favour, still dreaded the effects of another combination against them, they were generally well disposed to buy off such opposition, by agreeing to the terms of the journeymen. In all the strikes at this time the drapers invariably gave in first, and the old master tailors were compelled to follow. This contest was no exception, and the men obtained the 24s. In the year 1806 a society, called the "Blue Last," after the name of the tavern at which its members assembled, was formed for the purpose of more generally establishing the "piece-work" system. The men appear to have been dissatisfied with their weekly wages, and to have imagined that the more industrious and more rapid workers could earn more money if paid by the piece. Some of them also took work home from the shops, and thus made another innovation upon the ancient system, that all work should be done on the premises of the employer, except the work allowed to be taken home as a special privilege by aged members of the trade. The number of men in this society was between 60 and 80. They were looked upon with much ill-will by the rest of the trade, avoided as much as possible both in public and private, and called "Dungs." From this time up to the year 1808, the slop system in sailors' clothes was extensively carried on, and the women who had been engaged in making sailors' waistcoats applied to the drapers, and obtained waistcoats to make in the general trade. This gave much offence to the regular journeymen, and in that year a general strike took place against all drapers and master tailors who employed in the business any women except the wives and daughters of regular journeymen, who had served their apprenticeship. The contest was not a long or severe one, as the principal masters alleged that there was too much reason in the demand to justify them in resisting it. The next strike took place in April, 1810, when the number of journeymen in connection with the Tailors' Society, or Union, was upwards of 400. Their demand was for 27s. a week wages, and the prohibition of all out-door work whatsoever. The strike did not last above three or four days, when the masters gave in. In November of the same year, in consequence of the death of one of the Royal Family, the operative tailors claimed a privilege peculiar to their trade, which was, that they should have double wages during the whole time of public mourning. The masters resisted, and the men struck. After they had been out a fortnight, a proposition for a compromise was made by the masters, that the operatives should have their double wages, but only when engaged upon black clothes, and not when making coloured garments. The journeymen agreed without demur to these terms, and returned to their work. The price of flour at this time was 3d. per lb., and of butcher's meat from 8d. to 9d. per lb. In 1812 another contest took place between the old master tailors and the drapers, in consequence of a second combination by the former. The operatives only supported the master tailors to a limited extent, as the drapers were generally, if not always, the first to agree to any advance of wages, and had consequently made themselves popular. Another trial for conspiracy or combination was the result, and, as in the former case, the old master tailors were defeated. At this time the London system of "three books" was introduced. The object of this system was to classify the workmen, according to their standing and abilities. The qualification for a "first book" operative was a two-years' residence in the town, without fault having been found with his work by his employer; for the "second book" one year's residence, without fault found with his work. Town apprentices were admitted to this book. The "third book" included all strangers, and every other description of tailor, good, bad, and indifferent. The men in the first book had the first chance of work, those in the second were only employed when those on the first book were provided for, and the third came in last. The wages of all these operatives were the same—namely, 27s. a week. Things went on smoothly enough in the trade until April, 1813, during the American war, when the men once more struck for 5s. a day wages, or 30s. a week, in consequence, as they stated, of the high price of provisions—flour of an inferior quality selling at 1s. for 2 lbs., or 2 lbs. 8 oz., and butcher's meat ranging from 9d. to 10d. per lb. The men remained out for nine weeks—but the masters were enabled to resist them, by the aid of the "Dungs" and others who took work home, and by sending their work to other towns to be made. The men at last gave in—the masters not having yielded in the slightest degree. In May 1814, the men once more demanded an increase of wages to 30s. a week, and obtained the request without a strike. In consequence of the great stagnation of trade, and the general distress that prevailed in 1818, large numbers of tailors were glad to accept of work in constructing the "Prince's Dock." The distress continuing, the unemployed tailors formed themselves into a society to offer their services to the trade at the reduced wages of 24s. a week. The masters, however, did not approve of this movement. They seem to have imagined that if so large a reduction of wages was made, their customers would expect a corresponding reduction in the price of their goods. Ultimately, an arrangement was entered into, fixing the rate of wages at 27s. a week, and leaving the price to the consumer unaltered by the change. The members in connection with the Tailors' Society amounted at this time to nearly 600. The price of provisions was high, inferior flour being sold at 6d. per lb., and butcher's meat at 10d.

In the year 1823 there was much ill-feeling and agitation among the tailors in the town—arising out of the following circumstance. A large establishment in the trade took a number of out-door workers, not belonging to the Trade Society, to work upon their premises. They placed them in a separate workshop, apart from their regular journey-men. The Society men were indignant at what they considered an infringement of their rules, and sought every occasion to annoy and insult the "Dungs." Breaches of the peace occurred, and ultimately several of the ringleaders were arrested, tried at the Liverpool Quarter Sessions, and sentenced to three and six months' imprisonment in Kirkdale Gaol. The cost of defending these men was £335, which fell upon the Tailors' Society.

In 1824 wages rose to 30s., without a strike; but in 1826 the masters reduced them to 27s. The men struck in January, and held out till the 20th of April, when they gave in, and accepted the 27s. per week. The number of men on this strike was 750. It cost the Society £235, independently of the loss of wages. The number of out-door workmen was upwards of 200, amounting, with their wives and families, to probably 800. This was the last general strike of the Liverpool tailors; and the out-door system has continued gradually to increase from that time to the present. The regular operative tailors trace the growth of the out-door work, as well as the slop and sweating system, to this strike. It greatly exasperated the employers, who, even after it was concluded, continued to give the preference of their work to men who had not been engaged in it. The regular operatives have been un-organized and quite powerless since this time. The "Society" gradually fell off in numbers, and finally expired about four years ago. There are still two "benefit" societies for tailors for sickness and burials, but their numbers are very small.

The following statement was made to me by a master tailor and draper, now in business in the town:—

"In the year 1818, I first entered a tailor's establishment in Liverpool. I served seven years' apprenticeship, worked a few years as a journeyman, seven years as a master tailor, and about fifteen as a master tailor and draper. From 1818 to about 1827, the trade of the tailor was divided into master tailors and journeymen. Of the master tailors there were three classes. 1. Those who had served an apprenticeship of seven years, who sold cloth and everything appertaining to their business, took the part of foremen-cutters themselves, and inspected their journeymen's work. 2. Those who had served an apprenticeship, acted as their own foremen, and occasionally sat down to assist the journeymen in the making up of the garments. The cloth was generally purchased from the drapers, either by themselves or their clients. 3. Those who had not served an apprenticeship, but had capital sufficient to purchase cloth, and to employ a tailor as foreman-cutter, and others to inspect the work done for them. There has been a great number of this class of masters from time to time, who have had not the least knowledge of the trade, being decayed merchants, pawnbrokers, drapers' assistants, &c. &c.

"Previously to the year 1826 the journeymen tailors were also divided into three classes:

"1. Those who could do a full day's work of the best description, and in the best manner, in twelve hours.

"2. Those who could do a day's work in twelve hours, but inferior in its execution.

"3. Those who could not do twelve hours' work in that time.

"The journeymen had a trade society among themselves, and laws and regulations by which they were governed. The most important of these was the 'house of call,' where all who were out of employment assembled three times a–day, to answer to their names, and to receive information as to what masters were in want of workmen. If there were any of the first-class men out of employment, they had their option, according to their priority on the roll, of taking the work offered, or of refusing it. Should none of the first-class men be out of employment, the work was given to those of the second class, and so on until it came to the third class. Thus the work was distributed to all out of employment, according to their abilities as workmen. And, for the better distribution of the work amongst the unemployed, no man in employment was allowed to work more than twelve hours a day, as long as there was a man upon the roll unemployed. No man, under any pretence, was allowed to take a stitch of work home. Should he do so, he was branded as a 'Dung,' and fined one guinea. If this sum was not paid, he was expelled from the society. No man was allowed to work under the prices agreed upon between the master and the journeymen, under a similar penalty; nor for any shop which did not employ men from the house of call. Every man worked on the master's premises. The men had a sick club, and made subscriptions among themselves for charitable purposes. The men and masters of every shop had one day of their own, when they dined together in harmony, thus keeping up a kindly feeling between each other, called 'The Tailors' Bean Feast.'

"In the year 1826, a panic took place, which caused a great depression in trade; and, in order to retrench, the master tailors reduced the journeymen's wages from 30s. to 27s. per week. This caused a strike, which lasted from January, 1827, to April of the same year. The combination of the workmen was so strong, that it was impossible for the masters to get their work done without sending for men from other places. A number of runaway apprentices and unskilful workmen, who could get employment under no other circumstances, were introduced into the town from Ireland and elsewhere. They were placed under the superintendence of some skilful workmen, who were employed, at good wages, to examine their work. As it was not considered safe to employ these men in the workshop of the master, on account of the insults and assaults to which they might be subjected, they were taken to some private dwelling-house, where they could not be found out and enticed away by the workmen belonging to the strike. As many of them received good wages during this time, they were willing to be huddled together like pigs, and to work night and day to complete their work. When the strike ended, unskilful tailors could find no employment, and those who had superintended them during the strike lost their occupation. In order to get employment the best way they could, many offered the masters a still further reduction of wages if the work should be given them out of doors. Many masters were tempted by this, and these men employed unskilful tailors at still lower rates than were paid to themselves, and worked them longer hours per day. It was thus they acquired the name of '*Sweaters.*'

"The *Sweaters* may be arranged in three or four classes:—

"1. Sweaters for the public. These are men who cut and make up clothes and find the sewing materials, charging only journeymen's wages. To enable them to do this, they employ women and boys to assist them at less than one-half the general wages.

"2. Sweaters for drapers, who are men the drapers keep as customer-hunters, giving them 10s., 20s., or 30s. upon all custom they may bring, together with a chance of being recommended to those who may inquire of the draper for a tailor to make up their clothes. These men employ under them persons similar to the first class.

"3. Sweaters for master tailors and drapers, who have the work ready cut and the trimmings found. They make up the clothes at a less rate than the journeymen's wages, but employ less unskilful hands than the two first classes, though they work them longer.

"4. Sweaters for the ready made and slop shops. These are men who have a small sum of money sufficient to deposit as a guarantee for the work given out to them, and who take the work at about two-thirds less than the standard rate of wages. They employ the surplus labour, working them on an average 16 hours, Sundays included, and that at a rate at which the poor workmen can barely keep body and soul together.

"It is a fact that the ready-made clothes sellers and slop sellers have enough and more money than will pay the wages of all the work given out to these sweaters placed in their hands without interest, as a guarantee for the safe return, &c. of all the goods. Thus the men who are employed by them have to provide money for their own wages. This, as well as the fact of the public paying cash on delivery, enables the ready-made tailors to go into the best market with cash in their hands, and buy at the lowest prices. Thus, and by making an inferior article appear well by an unnecessary quantity of work in the making-up, they are able to display articles by which *apparently* they get little or no profit, whereas in reality they gain sometimes four times the amount of profit a respectable master tailor gets, whose prices appear higher. If the public would pay cash to all the respectable master tailors who have their work done on the premises, instead of taking twelve months' or two years' credit, tailors would be enabled to make a very great reduction in prices, and to give a much superior article for less profit than is taken at any of the ready-made shops. This would tend in a great measure to put an end to the demoralizing system of sweating."

Before personally commencing my inquiries into the state of the operatives, I notified my intention to the principal slop establishments, and expressed my willingness to give publicity to any statements upon the subject which they might feel inclined to make. I was not, however, favoured with any communication in reply. In company with an intelligent journeyman, deputed to wait upon me on behalf of the operatives, I proceeded on the two following days to visit the workmen at their own homes.

The first tailor upon whom we called resided in a narrow court leading from a street inhabited by the very poorest classes of the population, swarming with poultry and dirty children, and sending forth odours by no means pleasant or wholesome. Close to the door of his hovel—so close that standing on the threshold I could reach it with my hand—was the common privy of the whole court, with its door wide open. A girl of about eleven years of age, scantily clad and very dirty, who sat in the tailor's room nursing a baby, and whom at first I could scarcely distinguish amid the smoke, said that her father had gone to lie down, but that she would call him. She did so without moving from her place, and the next minute I saw a pair of feet, one of them closely bandaged, and with its bandages being about three times the size of an ordinary foot, projecting from the stair which led from the lower to the upper room. It was the tailor, who was unable to walk, and who was easing himself slowly down by sitting on each stair, and guiding himself with his hands without using his feet. He was a very pale, sickly-looking man, scarcely past the middle age. Without moving further into the room—and indeed he was incapable of such an exertion—he very freely explained his position. He said:—"I was formerly a master tailor in a small business; but having failed after a seven years' struggle, I was obliged to become a journeyman, and work for others. I contrived to make a living, partly by working for the regular trade, and partly by doing private work for some of my old customers both in and out of the town. Unfortunately for me, and many like me, a great slop tailor and others established themselves here, and all my work as a small master soon left me. The show shops quite ruined me. This was five or six years ago. I tried slopwork, but found that I could not live by it. The prices were starvation prices, nothing more. I then thought I would try the portering work on the quays, which I did, and succeeded pretty well in getting jobs. For the last four years I have not followed the tailoring trade, except to make a chance pair of trowsers now and then. The porters were jealous of me, and are still. They complain frequently that all sorts of tradesmen and workmen take to the portering instead of minding their own business. I am sure I have no reason to be thankful for having become a porter. Twenty weeks ago I broke my ankle at porter's work in the Albert Docks, and have been laid up ever since. I was only a chance hand at the Albert Docks—not one of their permanent men; but as I was disabled in the service of the company they have allowed me 10s. a week ever since. I am afraid that I am ruined both for tailoring and portering work. If the Albert Dock Company stop my allowance, I and my family must go to the parish."

The next tailor upon whom I called was represented to me as a sweater. He lived in a court off Cross-hall-street. I had to stop my nose in going up the little narrow entry that led from the street into the court. We found the "sweater" at home; and after a little parley, and an explanation that we had no other object in view than the good of the trade, he somewhat reluctantly allowed us to ascend to his work-shop. The stairs were so dark that we were obliged to grope our way; and on arriving at the attic, we found six men, sitting cross-legged on the bare floor, employed in making coats. The solitary window of the attic was wide open, and allowed the smoke of the adjoining chimneys to be occasionally wafted in; the "blacks" fell thickly upon my note-book, as I stood. The only furniture in the room was an old and wretchedly dirty bed in the corner. The walls were greasy and discoloured with dirt and steam, and did not appear to have been whitewashed for years. The men were in rags; their shirts were dingy brown, and allowed their elbows and shoulders to peer through; not one of them had either shoes or stockings, and their feet did not appear to have been washed for a twelvemonth. The sweater's wife came up to the attic with her husband that she might be informed of all that was going on. She was tall and strong, and had evidently once been a handsome woman, but her face was begrimed with smoke and dirt. She frequently interrupted the questions and replies by curses upon the heads of the slop-sellers and the keepers of show shops. The master of the place, an Irishman, explained that three of the workmen were his sons, and that the other three were men whom he employed. They all lodged together. They worked for a slop-shop. He himself had been a year in Liverpool engaged in the business, but during the whole time he had not been able to purchase a single article of cloth-ing for himself. I had no reason to doubt the truth of this statement. Although he had shoes to his feet and a coat to his back, his whole attire, from the crown of his head to the sole of his foot, was in a state of such miserable dilapidation that it would not have sold for a shilling to the most liberal of dealers in second-hand goods. He said he was a coat maker and made nothing but coats, and that trowser making and vest making were separate branches of the business.

I first asked the prices paid for making the coats, and how much a man could earn weekly by his labour. All the men began to speak at once, crying out that it was "starvation work," "cruel work," "slave work," "damnable work," &c.; but by dint of patience with them, and by getting one man to speak at a time, and asking the rest to correct his statement if he were wrong, I elicited generally the following facts, which I present in their own words, merely premising that the sweater and his wife stood by, and corroborated (the woman with loud and obscene oaths) the statements of their three sons and their fellow-workmen:—

"Eight shillings a week, and occasionally ten shillings, is about the sum we can each earn. We can sometimes get twelve shillings; but it takes hard, hard work, late and early, Sunday and Saturday, to gain as much as that. We must work long past hours and the whole of Sunday to make twelve shillings. We are often compelled to work on Sunday. To-day is Saturday, and if you call to-morrow you will find us at it. Out of the twelve shillings we should have to pay at least a shilling for trimmings, and perhaps be fined into the bargain. We are fined for various reasons. We work for two shops—a Jew shop and a Christian shop in the same business. They are much alike in their prices. There is a fine of one penny if there's a bug on the clothes, when we take them home. If there be a louse the fine is 6d. at one of the shops, but only a penny at the other. They put it in paper, and exhibit it in the shop, with the name of the tailor who brought it. They hold it up, and jeer at us. They also give us a printed ticket to sew on the clothes when we bring them back, and if that ticket be soiled—or if the foreman says it is soiled—which is all the same thing, we have to pay a penny. It is of no use to complain. If we attempt to show that a ticket is not dirty, we are turned out of the shop, and told not to kick up a row. There is no redress. We are obliged to submit. The coats we are now making are shooting jackets. They pay 4s. each for them. Some of the shops pay only 3s. 6d. each for the same kind of work. For a dress coat the price is 6s. Twist and sewing silk are to be found out of those prices, and would cost about sixpence for a shooting coat. The coats, in consequence of the inferiority of the cloth, require a deal of extra pressing, in order to give them a fine finish and appearance. They are very particular at the slop-shops, and if the articles are not pressed sufficiently to please the foreman they are returned upon our hands. A married man at this trade is no where at all. He can't live if he has young children. If he have children grown up and able to help, he may manage to starve. A dress-coat for which the slop-shops pay 6s. for making would take the best tailor in England three days to make, and very hard work too. The trimmings would cost about 8d. The dress-coats sold in the slop-shops are of the very best work. It is not possible to have better work, but the quality of the cloth is not so good. They require an immensity of pressing to make them show off at all, or give them anything like a good finish. They are also pieced more than coats made by the regular trade. At the slop-shop they keep the supply of cloth very short, and we are obliged to piece in order to screw out enough material. This adds greatly to our labour. It sometimes increases the length of the job by three or four hours, and not a farthing extra is paid. They sent us a dress-coat from the shop at nine o'clock last night, and wanted it made by twelve to-day. We could not have done it unless we had sat up all night. We refused the job. We were too much tired out. We could not have undertaken it. Late on a Saturday night we have received coats to make, to be returned on Monday. Of course, we must work on Sunday if we undertake them. We have now several coats on hand, that cannot be done to-night. If we do not finish them by twelve o'clock on Monday, we shall not get paid for them until twelve o'clock on Tuesday—neither shall we get any more work until Tuesday. By working to-morrow, and finishing them by Monday at noon, we shall get paid on Monday, and get another job to begin on Monday afternoon. The fact is, if we do not work on Sunday we shall lose two days' work. We shall have to starve on Monday—that's the plain truth of it. Monday is always a day on which we want money. It is the rent day over all Liverpool, for houses such as ours. The rent must be paid punctually every Monday, or we shall be sold up."

As the compulsory prevalence of Sunday labour is one of the greatest grievances of which the poor tailors complain, and one of the most disgraceful results of the slop system, I determined on the following day, which was Sunday, to judge for myself of the extent of the evil. I and my companion of the day before called upon this sweater at eleven o'clock on the Sunday morning. He did not at first seem very willing that we should go up stairs to the attic, among the men; but he ultimately consented that we should, if I would not publish his name, or say anything to get him into trouble with his employers.

This was promised, and on groping our way up stairs we found two out of the six men hard at work. One of them was the eldest son of the sweater, a young man of four or five and twenty, with a very intelligent countenance. He was, however, extremely pale and thin; and it was evident at a glance that he was consumptive. He was in his old position, bare-footed and cross-legged, and was pressing a shooting jacket, and exerting all the strength he possessed to press hard. I took down the following statement exactly as he spoke it:—

"For the last six months, there have not been three Sundays on which I have not been obliged to work; and to work hard. I work both for a Jew and a Christian slop-shop. It is not for a Christian shop that we are finishing these coats, but I have worked for 'Christians' on the Sunday—and often too. There is no secret about that. The foreman of one shop offered to give me 3s. to make a shooting coat, instead of 4s., the usual price. I objected, and he told me to go and drown myself. He could find plenty to do it, if I wouldn't. It would have taken me two days' very hard work to make it, and I should have had to pay trimmings out of it. All these coats take a dreadful deal of pressing with the iron. If the shopman does not think one of them pressed enough, he will throw it at the workman's head. I have been served so, and been forced to take it home and press it again. A short time ago, we had a black paletot to make, lined through with silk, and closely stitched, in diamond pattern. We used ten skeins of silk to it. It took three of us to make it, from three o'clock in the afternoon of one day until three o'clock in the afternoon of the next, working all night. We got 8s. for the job. The silk cost us 1s. 0½d., and candles 6d., leaving us 6s. 5½d. to divide between three of us, for 24 hours' work each, or nearly 1¼d. an hour, day and night. No niggers were ever such slaves as we are. I expect to be just as hard at work next Sunday as I am now. I dare say if you call you will find us just as we are now. The rent must be paid on Monday. Six days' work is not enough to keep us. It is nothing but work, work, work—day and night—without ceasing. We have no Sundays—no holidays—no anything but 'slavery.'"

The next tailor we called upon was a trowsers maker for the slop-shops, and lived in the same court as the preceding. I visited him on the Saturday, and saw him also on the Sunday. On my first visit I found him in a small attic, without a fire-place or furniture of any kind; sitting barefooted and cross-legged on the floor, along with two other men, also barefooted, and a woman. The woman sat cross-legged on the floor with the men. They were all engaged in making slop-trowsers. The master of this place was quite a young man, and very boyish in appearance. He was married to a daughter of the sweater upon whom we had previously called. He said:—"We work for a slop-shop and make nothing but trowsers. For a pair of the best slop dress-trowsers we get 2s.; for a pair of the best bespoke, or customer's trowsers, 2s. 6d.; and for a pair of lighter spring or summer trowsers, 1s. 9d. It would take 12 hours' hard work to make a pair of the best slop trowsers; and the trimmings would cost 2d. out of the two shillings. It would take 18 hours to make a pair of customer's trowsers. The slop-shops like to encourage more hands to come into the town than are wanted. That's my belief, but of course I don't know it for certain. It keeps down prices. One of them makes it a regular practice every now and then to post up large bills about the town, stating in big letters that '1,000 hands are wanted,' and will find constant employment at his shop. It encourages people to come and buy, and sends raw Irishmen to the shop to ask for work, which, if they are starving, they will take at almost any price. They give the waistcoats out to women to make, except the best black cloth ones, which they give to men. They pay 1s. 9d. for a black cloth waistcoat which takes 10 or 12 hours to make. Great numbers of waistcoats are now brought down from London. They are made still cheaper there than in Liverpool. One slop establishment gets down about 500 weekly. Coats also come in large quantities from London, and keep down prices in Liverpool. Many women are employed in tailoring here. The trade is ruined by the slop-shops—men cannot live."

One of the men, who was sitting at work, added to this statement that he had lived with a sweater, and paid him 2s. 10d. a week for his lodgings and coffee and milk in the morning. He had to pay extra for the sugar for the coffee, and for the bread and butter, if he wanted any. He had to work from daylight till twelve o'clock at night—and out of his earnings was not able to afford meat above once a week, and could not buy any clothes. He never went to church. He had no clothes to go in. He had not himself worked on Sundays, but he knew many who did, regularly. In the sweater's where he formerly worked, they only got 2s. 6d. for shooting jackets, and 1s. 3d. a pair for tweed trowsers.

It was represented to me that one of the principal sweating establishments in Liverpool was kept by a man in ——— street. I resolved to proceed thither and state my errand. I shall premise that this was on the Saturday. I was told that I should not be admitted, but at all events I determined to try. The character given of this place was to the effect that the sweater, who kept a lodging-house and a huckster's or chandler's shop, employed from 17 to 20 men at slop-work for some of the largest slop-shops in Liverpool, and that he was amassing a considerable sum of money by the three-fold profits he made out of his men—first, upon their wages; second, upon their board; and third, upon their lodgings—for he compelled all his tailors to board, and many of them to lodge with him. It was further stated that his workshop was dense and unwholesome in the extreme, and the worst place of the kind in Liverpool. We found the shop without difficulty. The wretched street swarmed with ragged children and dirty women—yellow clothes were stretched out of the windows to dry, and foul smells of sewerage, gas, and nameless filth arose in rank abundance. The pavement of the road was all turned up, and a deep trench for the improvement of the sewerage was in course of construction. Scores of ragged boys were frolicking upon the embankments on either side—jumping into the trench, or pelting each other with little pellets made of the soft clay, into which their feet sunk at every step. Many of these pellets struck against my hat and breast as I passed, and I saw from the grinning of the boys that they were intentionally thrown. On entering the sweater's shop I noticed on one side the usual articles kept by hucksters and chandlers—loaves of bread, cheese, bacon, candles, biscuits, flour, oatmeal, eggs, tea-canisters, &c. On the other side was a huge pile of corduroy and moleskin trowsers. The master of the establishment speedily made his appearance. He was dressed tolerably well, and had a clean shirt, a satin waistcoat, and a gold chain to his watch. I explained to him that I was engaged in an investigation into the state of the poor and the labouring population, and that I should be much obliged to him for any information he would give me relative to the tailoring trade. He curtly refused to give me any information whatever. After many attempts, I told him that I had been long engaged in similar inquiries, and that he was the first man who had ever refused to give me information. He said "he did not care: I should not go into his workshop, nor talk to any of his men, if he knew it." "The gentleman is not in the trade, and will do you no harm," said my companion. "You know quite as much of the trade as I do—I shan't tell you anything, and you shan't see my workshop," was the sole reply, in a tone and manner which made me think it was quite as well that I had not ventured alone into his premises. On turning to go away, I saw through the glass door at the back of the shop that a long table was laid out with hunks of bread, each with a tin can beside it. The hour was after twelve, and I conjecture, whether rightly or not, that the "sweater" was preparing for the dinner of the "sweated."

From this place I proceeded to ——— alley, where I found another trowser-maker at work, in a small room up a dark pair of stairs. The room was more comfortably furnished than any I had previously seen, although the clothes-line, stretched from end to end, and full of wet clothes, did not improve it. The tailor sat on a board; and not on the floor, and there were three or four chairs, a table, a chest of drawers, and other articles of furniture in the room. There was also a good fire. The tailor's wife stood by. A little boy of seven years of age sat on the board with his father amusing himself with a pair of scissors and some shreds of cloth; and a tidy girl, of eleven or twelve, stood gazing with wonder at the unusual appearance of two strangers in the room, one of them with a note-book in his hand. The tailor and his wife received us very civilly, and indeed cordially. He was a very sallow and lean, but intelligent-looking man, considerably beyond the middle age. He said:—

"I am a trowsers-maker, and work for a slop-shop. I have a wife and five children. I was formerly in business for myself at Birmingham, but lost it. I was afterwards a journeyman in Birmingham; but not getting constant work, I came to Liverpool. After some weeks' loitering about at the corner of Lord-street, I obtained employment from a slop-shop. I am now making a pair of the best black trowsers. They are the best as regards work, but not the best, nor anything like it, as regards the cloth. I shall get 2s. for making them, out of which I shall have to pay above 1½d. for sewing silk and twist. My wife helps me a little, and it will take her and me twelve hours to make such a pair of trowsers. When I was a journeyman in Birmingham, ten years ago, I got 4s. 9d. in the regular trade for such a job. The regular trade in Liverpool does not pay so much as that now. The slop-shops ruin the regular master tailors as well as the journeymen. My wife is a waistcoat maker. We both work very hard to make a bare living. She and I may earn, on an average, from 10s. to 12s. a week, but we have all our trimmings to buy out of that. This week we have both worked very hard indeed, and have earned 12s. It is slavish work. I see no way to extricate myself. It is of no use to complain at the shop. They say, 'If we don't like the work, we can leave it; there are plenty of others who will be glad of it.' We contrive with difficulty, though I scarcely know how, to get meat once a week. My wife is an excellent manager, and makes the money go as far as it possibly can. The children live on bread and Indian meal, and sometimes oatmeal. My wife now and then buys 2d. worth of bones, and makes soup for them. Tea is our greatest blessing. We could not do without that. We have been much better off since bread and flour became as cheap as they are now. They will take 3d. or 4d. off a job on various excuses, about bugs and dirty tickets, and such like. If I were employed by a respectable tailor on his premises, in the old fashion, I could earn, without wearing myself to death, as much as 18s. or 20s. a week, and my wife could attend to the family. But this slop system forces the regular tailor to lower his prices too."

The next tailor we visited was an old man—dirty, unshaven, and dispirited. He lived in a court, at the extreme corner, nearest to the privy and the ash pit. His workshop was on the ground-floor. The door was open, and puffs of coal smoke emerged from it. I was not able to endure the smoke, and stood at the door while he spoke, although by so doing I was brought into uncomfortable proximity to the abominations of the cess-pool. I made the visit as short as possible for this reason, but had time to take the following statement:—

"I am a trowsers maker, but I make anything that comes in my way—trowsers, coats, or waistcoats. I work for a slop-shop, and my daughter helps me. (The daughter, a girl of 18 or 19, sat at work at the window, engaged on a boy's jacket—a chance job from a neighbour). Between us we can earn 12s. a week by working very hard. We might earn 14s. or 15s. if we worked 18 hours a day each of us—but such work would soon bring me to the grave, and make an end of my troubles. I could not earn 12s. a week by my own hands, if I worked ever so hard. I have a wife and four children, but my wife is of no use in the business; she can't do the work. I have been six years working for one slop-shop in ―― street. The shop reduced its prices about two years ago. For shooting jackets that were formerly paid 5s., they now offer 3s. 6d. If we grumble, the foreman says, 'he pays as much as other folk, and we may either take it or leave it; there are plenty of people in the world to do it if we won't.' The slop-shops give bad materials, but good work. They are all very particular about the quality of the work; and are 'savage' at the slightest fault. I and my family manage to live—but that is all. I can't save a penny. I once belonged to a benefit club, but have been obliged to drop it. If I should be taken ill and unable to work, I don't know what I shall do. I suppose I must lie where I fall.

There is always the parish or the grave. I sometimes think it scarcely matters which."

The next man resided in Peter-street, and had the advantage of a thoroughfare—a great advantage in such a place as Liverpool—even although the thoroughfare was of the lowest and filthiest class of streets. Anything is better than the dreadful courts, with their narrow entries, not above a yard in width, and forming areas scarcely more than 20 feet square. He had a neat, clean room, and seemed, from the appearance of himself and family, as well as of his apartment, to be of a superior class of workmen. He said: "I work for a slop-shop, and call myself an 'out-door jur,' or slave. I am obliged to work for the ready-made shops, although they pay bad prices—not enough to enable a man to live. I have three sons in the trade. We all live together. One of them is employed in the regular trade, and gets decent wages, and so helps the whole of us. It is not only the slop-shops that injure the trade; the woollen-drapers do quite as much harm. They take orders from customers and call themselves tailors, although they never do a stitch of work. They employ small masters to do the work, and pay the same prices as the slop-shops. They only pay 1s. 10d. for making a monkey-jacket for sailors. That is the outside price. It would take a day to make one; and there would be trimmings to pay out of the 1s. 10d. I never work on Sundays; we can manage, the whole of us, by the help of my son's wages, to live without that, but many people can't." Here the wife interposed, "Work on Sundays!" she said, "oh no! we'll never do that, please the Lord. It's bad enough as it is. Those who work on Sunday never have any luck." "Aye! aye!" rejoined the husband—"it's all very well to talk that way, but a hungry belly neither cares for Sunday nor Saturday. There are plenty of 'jurs' in Liverpool who must work on Sunday, if they don't want to starve on Monday."

Having been informed that in —— road there resided a sweater, to whose workshops we might have access, we proceeded to the place indicated. It turned out that we were wrongly informed, but we found a tailor's wife who gave the following information. The woman said her husband was out. "He was a slop tailor, and worked for a Jew. He got 'shameful' wages, not enough to live upon. He had been a soldier in his young days, and had a pension of 1s. 1½d. a day, or she did not know how they could live. He only received 9d. for a pair of lads' moleskin trowsers, strongly sewed and lined, out of which he had to buy the trimmings." [Here she produced a pair of trowsers which had been thrown back on their hands because they were not properly made. My companion, a practical tailor, examined them, and declared that they were as well made a pair of trowsers as he had ever cast his eyes on.] Another tailor, the son-in-law of this woman, who lodged in the room above, hearing strange voices, came down stairs with his wife, and entered into explanations connected with his wages. He said: "I make shooting-coats as well as trowsers for a Jew slop-shop. They pay 3s. for a shooting-coat. I and my wife can make four a week. The trimmings of each would cost 3½d. That would be 1s. 2d. for the four, leaving us 10s. 10d. for ourselves. Perhaps we might contrive to make five, by getting up very early, and sitting up very late, or working part of Sunday; but it would be shameful hard work. Out of five pair of trowsers which I took home to a slop-shop on Friday, three were sent back, for nothing that I know of except the impudence of the foreman. I have often been obliged to work on the Sunday, or to starve on the Monday. It is killing work. If there is even so little as a basting stitch left in a coat, which might be taken out in the shop, they will send the workman home with it. They will not allow the stitch to be taken out in the shop. The operative must take it home, and come again on Monday. I can't pay anything to a friendly society. I can't live even. If I am taken ill, I must apply to the parish. There is no other chance for me."

Such were the results of two days' inquiries among the slop tailors of Liverpool.

I attended, three days subsequently, a meeting of about thirty operatives, called for the purpose of giving me any further explanation or evidence which I might require. The evidence generally was in corroboration of that which I had obtained by my personal visits to their homes; but I select out of the mass the following statements, as throwing additional light upon the condition of the slop-workers generally. Among the company was a respectable master tailor, who from time to time passed his judgment as a tradesman, thoroughly knowing the business, upon the quality of the work which the men exhibited. The first man whose statement I select was, like nineteen out of twenty of the tailors, exceedingly pale and thin. He looked careworn and dispirited, and was far from cleanly in his person or attire. He said:—

"I work for a sweater in —— street, along with thirteen other men whom he employs. He keeps a huckster's shop, and sometimes has more men at work than he has now. I do not lodge in the house, but he pays for my lodging out. I have a wife and one child, and my wife gets all the food we require from his shop. There is no regular bargain that we shall get our food from his shop; but I expect we should have a good chance of being turned off if we didn't. He pays from 2s. 6d. to 3s. 3d. for making a shooting coat. I can earn from 10s. to 11s. a week; but have once or twice earned as much as 14s. in a week by making Tweed trowsers. It costs 2s. a week for my lodgings, and about 9s. for food for myself and family. The sweater pays the lodgings. My wife gets during the week the things she wants—such as bread and oatmeal, butter, a little tea, and sometimes a bit of bacon. We sometimes send down to the shop for a few half-pence out of his till. He will let us have them if he is in the humour. He likes his own way. Bread and butter and tea are my chief diet. He sells good tea, but he makes us pay a good price for it. We buy it by the ounce, and he charges us 4d. I pay no money; indeed I scarcely ever see money. My wife gets what she wants; and on Saturday night the sweater reckons up the wages due to me, and deducts the lodgings and the food; and gives me the difference. Some weeks I do not earn enough to square the account; but I sometimes get a shilling over, and sometimes two shillings. One week I got 3s. 6d.; but that was the most that ever I got. No man can earn more than 14s. a week at this work, if he were to rise at six every morning and work till twelve or one every night."

The next statement was made by a very smart and clever-looking lad, about twenty years of age, with eyes very much inflamed. He said, "I live with my father, who is a shoemaker. We are five in family—father, mother, myself, and two young sisters, one about eleven, and the other three years of age. My father was once a master shoemaker in the town of Galway; but he failed there, and thought he would try Liverpool, as he has a brother here, who, he thought, might be of service to him. He can't do much work. He is too old, and I have to support the family with my mother's assistance. I work for a slop-shop, and am a coat maker. For a black shooting-coat, which I could make myself in two days and a quarter, I get 4s., and have to pay the trimmings out of it. My mother and I could make one in one day and three-quarters. My mother pads and stitches the collars, and sews the linings. I served five years to the business. The greatest sum that my mother and myself ever earned in one week was 14s. We worked from six in the morning till ten at night every day, and a great part of Sunday. Out of the 14s. I had to pay above a shilling for thread, silk, and twist. My eyes are very much inflamed with the work by candlelight, but they are better than they were. We can't afford more than one room. We all work, cook, wash, and sleep in it. I know pretty nearly the size of it. It is about fifteen feet one way by eight the other. My eldest sister goes to school. We pay three-halfpence a week for her. We have two meals a day, and contrive to get a little bit of meat about twice a week. We pay 4½d. a lb. for it, and one pound serves us all. We take tea morning and evening; and the evening tea, with or without meat, we call our dinner. We have been in Liverpool about ten months—and neither my father nor myself have bought a single article of clothing or shoes in that time. What we have we brought from Ireland with us. My mother has had one cotton gown new, but that is all we have been able to buy. My sisters have had nothing. They are very hard upon us at the shop, and very particular over the work. They are also very particular about bugs on the clothes. I was fined a penny because a bug was found on a coat I took back. The man in the shop gave me the bug, and I put it on the floor, and crushed it with my foot. I was fined another penny for that, as he said I ought to have taken it outside."

A third man made the following statement:—"I work for a shop that is called a 'sailors' outfitter's'—it is not one of the fine show-shops. My employer keeps three 'runners' about the docks to look after sailors. The 'runners' are sometimes called 'pikers,' and 'man-catchers.' They have weekly wages of a pound, and some of them twenty-four shillings, and are besides paid a shilling a man for every sailor they 'catch' and bring to the shop. Nothing but sailors' clothes is made in the establishment. I have served a regular apprenticeship to the tailoring business. For a blue naval jacket, finished with silk facings, and slashed sleeves, I get 4s. It takes me 21 hours to make. I have no trimmings to pay for. I could not make above three in a week, without working on Sunday or on extra hours of the night, when I might manage four. Trowsers are better paid in proportion. The price for shop trowsers, quite plain, with pockets, is 1s. 9d.; and I could make eight in a week. I have earned as much as 18s. in one week, but it was desperate hard work, and I could not continue at it long, even if I had the chance. It would destroy any man's health entirely."

Here a pair of black dress trowsers, for the making of which the slopsellers pay 2s., was exhibited in the room. The master tailor already alluded to examined them thoroughly, and gave the following technical description of the work which had been put upon them. He said "these trowsers are capitally well made, with fly fronts, pricked or prodded in, as thick as the needle can stitch; bound tops, thickly back-stitched; two pockets, bound and thickly stitched under; stitched tips, well tacked; back-stitched bottoms, strap buttons and cloth straps; button stays, back-stitched; fork lined back and front, silk waist-band linings, and brace-buttoned stays separately felled." The man who made them said he was employed fourteen hours upon the job, including an hour for meals. He received 2s., and the silk, twist, and thread cost him seven farthings, leaving 1s. 10¼d. for his labour. The master tailor stated that the best workmen in the trade could not make a better pair of trowsers. There was a great deal more work put upon the article than would be necessary if the cloth was good, but which was quite necessary on such trowsers, to make the bad stuff hold together. In the regular trade a man would be paid 4½d. an hour for making them, and the trimmings would be found him, making 5s. 4d. for the job, instead of 1s. 10¼d.

The man who made the following statement was a very sharp and decided kind of person; and expressed himself with great clearness and energy:—

"I formerly worked for a slop-shop, but have not worked for it for the last three months. I left it because I could not earn enough to keep soul and body together, and buy candles. I made shooting coats, for which they paid me 3s. I have heard that some tailors have got 4s. for the same articles. I could never screw out more than 3s. for one. I could scarcely make three such coats in a week, with the work they want in them. I should have to work very hard to do it—sixteen hours a day, including the going to the shop and coming back, and the waiting. I have been sometimes obliged to wait six hours for a job. I have to leave a deposit of a pound before I can get work. I have now £6 out on deposit at various shops I work for. I have sometimes other men to work for me, and am a kind of a small 'sweater,' or something in that way. I get a penny for every shilling the men earn, and think I am entitled to it for being responsible for the work, for superintending it, and for finding the money to leave as a deposit. At the time of the cholera seven of us worked together in one room, and three of the men took the disease. They remained all the time till they recovered, and the rest of us worked in the room with them. We had no other place to go to. I now work for a tailor and draper, not a slop-shop. I get 10s. for a dress coat of the same kind that two slop-shops only pay 6s. for. The work is exactly the same. I could earn from 16s. to 18s. a week at this kind of work, if fully occupied, but I don't always get the chance. I have nothing to pay for trimmings. The tailors and drapers always find trimmings, at least as far as I know. A man, not a regular tailor, but who came out of a pawnshop to try the tailoring business, sent for me at one o'clock on Friday afternoon last, to make two navy jackets with silk facings and slashed sleeves, four trowsers, and four waistcoats, which were all to be done on Monday morning at nine o'clock, or to be returned on my hands. Being in want of a job I undertook it, went with him to a draper's to buy the cloth, and engaged ten men upon it. We sat up all night, and finished the work in time. I made no bargain about price, expecting the regular prices of the trade. He has refused to pay me, unless I bring tickets of the slop-shop prices, when he says he will pay the same, and not a farthing more. The slop prices would be about 17s., without the cutting, which I did; the regular trade prices about 47s., with the cutting. I shall sue him to-morrow for 47s."

With this statement I conclude the subject, leaving the readers of these letters to form their own opinion of the slop and sweating system in Liverpool, and its effects upon the health, the morals, and the religion of the people.

LABOUR AND THE POOR.

LIVERPOOL.

[FROM OUR SPECIAL CORRESPONDENT.]

THE SANITARY OPERATIONS OF THE BOROUGH—THE WATER SUPPLY—BATHS AND WASH-HOUSES—THE CELLARS, AND DWELLINGS OF THE POOR.

LETTER VIII.

Like all the other great towns of England, Liverpool has grown into wealth and importance, without paying proper attention to the requirements of its population in the essential matters of health and pure air. It is imperfectly drained—its sewerage is incomplete—it has no sufficient supply of wholesome water—and the poorer classes congregate together in close, fetid, and pestilential courts and alleys, without regard either to health, to cleanliness, to comfort, or to decency. Yet it must not be forgotten that Liverpool has been long aware of its manifold deficiencies in all these respects, and that its authorities were among the first in England to set an example of sanitary improvement. The following summary of what it has already done in this respect, will enable the reader to understand how great is the task it has undertaken, and how much yet remains to be done, before it can be said that the 100,000 Irish, who live in its filthiest streets and courts, and the same number of the poorer classes of English birth, who live much in the same way, in the same and in other parts of the town, can be placed in a position of decency as regards their dwellings, or before the richer classes can be considered safe from the ravages of fever, the results of the filth and malaria amid which such large numbers of human beings habitually have their existence:—

"The borough of Liverpool," says the report of the local health committee, drawn up by the borough engineer, "occupies the slopes of a series of small hills, on the east margin of the Mersey. At the southern extremity is Park-hill, the summit of which is about 1,200 yards east from the line of the docks, and about 188 feet high above the old dock sill, to which datum all the heights mentioned here have reference. Nearly north from Park-hill, and about 3,000 yards east of the line of docks, is the summit of another hill, at the junction of Smithdown-lane and Parliament-street. The height is 192 feet, and the lowest point of the valley between the two summits, occurs at the crossing of Princes Park-road, at the height of about 152 feet. Proceeding northwards from Smithdown-lane, on a line nearly parallel with the river, we arrive at Edge-hill, the summit of which is near to St. Mary's Church, and is 228 feet high. From Edge-hill the ground slopes gently northward to Kensington, where there is an extensive flat, at the height of about 208 feet. It rises slightly at Low-hill, and proceeds in an irregular rise, interrupted by gentle knolls to the summit of Everton, in the neighbourhood of the church. This summit is the highest point in Liverpool—it is nearly north from Edge-hill, and is 248 feet high above the datum.

"From Everton the ground falls rapidly to the east, in the direction of Tue Brook, and to the north into the valley between Everton and Walton-hill. To the west it also falls, until, at the height of 104 feet, it meets the head of a valley formed between Everton and a lower ridge, which, commencing at Kirkdale at about 112 feet high, and 1,000 yards east from the river, returns in a southerly direction, with an irregular fall, interrupted by two knolls, the first at Bevington-hill, and the other at the crossing of Plumber-street and Prussia-street, to the site of the Old Castle of Liverpool, in Castle-street, where it terminates at the height of about fifty feet above the datum. The valley inclosed between the ridges, formed by the succession of hills first named, stretching northwards from Smithdown-lane to Everton, and the return ridge which extends from Kirkdale to Castle-street, terminates in a long level track in Paradise-street, the site of the Old Pool of Liverpool, and receives the drainage of the western slopes of the first ridge, and the eastern slopes of the other. The rise from the valley to Everton is very rapid; but as the valley expands, the slopes become less steep, and at about half-way between the bottom of the valley and the summit at Edge-hill, a slight intermediate hill, Brownlow-hill, occurs, between which and the slope of Edge-hill a long flat track, which is the site of the Old Moss-lake, is included.

"On the west and south sides of Park-hill the water flows directly into the river; on the east side, the natural outlets are the Dingles. The east slopes of Edge-hill drain into a brook which runs from the south of Kensington-road, by the Botanic Gardens, to Otterspool. The east slopes of Everton drain into Tue Brook, and its northern slopes into the valley between Everton and Walton.

"So long as Liverpool was circumscribed by the narrow limits of its early boundary, and while the Pool was washed by every tide, the drainage of the refuse matter of the town into the Pool, and thence into the river, although not quite in accordance with sanitary principles, as now received, was an evil of no great magnitude. But when the Pool and its tributary brook, with a short-sighted economy, were filled up together, and ultimately covered with buildings, without the precautions having been taken of raising sufficiently the new surface, and providing a proper sewer, this natural outlet was destroyed at the time when the increasing size of the town demanded increased facilities in draining it, and was converted into a source of disease. Gradually, too, the margin of the town, along the river side, became lined with docks and basins, into the latter of which the sewers were made to deliver their contents, to their manifest injury, and the deterioration of the health of the town, from the accumulation of putrid matter. When Mr. Rennie was called upon to report on the sewerage of Liverpool, in 1816, he remarked on this great evil as follows:—

" 'All the sewers in Liverpool (except the tunnel to the north shore, and that to the south shore) disembogued the water and soil into the basins of the docks. The sewers in Chapel-street and Water-street are discharged into St. George's Basin; the Whitechapel sewer, and the Hanover-street sewer, with all their branches, terminate in the old basins. These basins are, in consequence, so much loaded with soil, that their use as entrances to the docks is greatly abridged, and the expense of removing it is enormous. It would, therefore, be not only highly beneficial to the inhabitants, but also to ships frequenting the port, if new discharges could be provided, totally independent of the basins. This, I hope, may be effected to a certain extent, although it cannot be done to the extent which could be wished if the docks are to be enlarged, as proposed, and the trade of Liverpool imperiously demands; but, notwithstanding discharges for the sewers cannot in every case be made independent of the basins, I trust what I have so proposed will be much less objectionable than the present mode, and will in a great measure remove the objections I have stated.'

"It is to be regretted that, convinced as he was of the disadvantages of the outlets into the basins, Mr. Rennie did not suggest some comprehensive plan by which these might have been altogether dispensed with, or at least anticipate the extension of the docks, and the increase of the town, by providing outlets running fairly into the river along the then unbuilt dock sites.

"The evils arising from the sewers discharging into the dock basins are these:—

"First. The flow of the water in the sewers is exposed to a periodical stoppage during high water. This is an evil of great magnitude, and one from which the lower parts of the town suffer severely, particularly Paradise-street, Whitechapel, and the streets along the line of the docks. The cellar-floors in these places are in many instances below the level of the tide for six hours in the twenty-four, and not only are the drains of the houses to which these cellars belong stopped for that time, but the waters from the upper parts are pent up, and flowing back through the house drains, inundate the lower floors. When heavy rains occur during high water the evil is fearfully increased. A great evil arises in Liverpool, as in London, from the outlets being left open at low water, so that every blast of wind traverses the whole length of the sewers, and forces the foul gases up gully holes and into houses. The subsequent rise of the tide does the same by pressure.

"Second. Around the outlets into the basins an accumulation of deposit takes place, which materially affects the usefulness of the basins, and is also a fertile cause of disease.

"Third. The sewage water being discharged into the basins is wasted, and cannot be applied to its legitimate use of enriching the soil."

Such are the deficiencies of Liverpool on this important point, as stated by the officer of the local board—deficiencies the more surprising, because the town is well situated for a thorough system of sewerage, and has a noble tidal river or arm of the sea running alongside of it, into which its sewerage, if not preserved for manure, might be conveyed without injury to the river. The Mersey at Liverpool, unlike the Thames at London, could never, however pure from the pollution of sewage, be used for the supply of the town with water; and the strength of the tides is such as speedily to remove all offensive matter that may be poured into the stream. One of the chief causes of the inattention of Liverpool to this subject was the divided local jurisdictions that had power within its boundaries—jurisdictions always at war with one another, as happens in every part of the country where there is no authoritative central power to coerce them into unanimity for the good of the public.

The inquiry instituted, in 1839, by the Government, into the condition of the labouring population in the towns and rural districts, first drew the attention of the authorities of Liverpool to the deplorable condition of the town in a sanitary point of view. Nothing, however, was done until 1842. In that year, the admirable report of Mr. Chadwick upon the "Health of Towns" was the means of still more forcibly directing the minds of philanthropists to the subject, and the corporation of Liverpool began to move. In that year, it applied for and obtained two local acts, respectively entitled "The Liverpool Health of the Town and Buildings Act," and "An Act for the Improvement, good Government, and Police Regulation of the Borough of Liverpool." The provisions of both these acts had reference to the improvement of the health of the town, but the first especially so, as it made provision for appointing a Health Committee, and surveyors to assist them; for regulating the width of streets and preventing houses being built in confined courts; for making the ground-floor of every house to be built at least six inches above the road or street adjoining thereto; for regulating the size of rooms and windows; for preventing altogether the separate occupation of cellars in courts; for regulating the occupation of cellars in streets under certain provisions; for compelling the owner of every house to provide and keep in repair a privy and ash-pit for the same; for providing for the flagging and channeling of all courts and passages; for compelling the cleansing of private drains and cess-pools; for providing for the cleansing of unwholesome dwellings, and for regulating interment in cemeteries, &c. But with reference to enforcing the cleansing of private drains, this act was rendered almost useless by divided local authority. The corporation were expressly prevented, by the 18th section of their act, from cleansing any private sewer or drain which led into the sewers of the local commissioners. Consequently the benefits intended by the act in this respect were rendered entirely nugatory. At the same time, by a peculiar anomaly in the act of the then existing Liverpool highway board, parties were precluded, under heavy penalties, from either permitting any offensive matter to run into the sewers, or from connecting any water closets therewith. Thus the existing sewers within the parish of Liverpool were rendered useless for two of the chief purposes for which sewerage in towns is mainly valuable.

Having obtained these Acts of Parliament the corporation of Liverpool made vigorous exertions to do the best they could with them. They had all the cellars examined and surveyed, and they cleared of their inmates all those which were separately let in courts. Between the 1st of July, 1844, the time fixed by the act for the commencement of the clearance of cellars in streets, and the 1st of January, 1846, they cleared upwards of three thousand of these places in the worst streets in the town. They likewise caused, through the agency of their building surveyor, several hundreds of cesspools to be repaired where offensive matter soaked from them into adjoining property, and improved the construction of a great number of others. Through the medium of Mr. Fresh, the active and intelligent inspector of nuisances whom they appointed, they caused, between September, 1844, and the end of 1846, 1,732 unhealthy nuisances, complained of by inhabitants, to be inspected and suppressed. Through the operations of their Police Act they likewise caused, between the year 1842 and the end of 1846, 6,113 informations to be laid against parties creating nuisances of various kinds in the town—in 5,611 of which there were convictions. The result was that all such nuisances were considerably abated. It would be too much to say that they were finally removed.

On the issue of the Government Commission for inquiry into the Health of Towns, the corporation of Liverpool seem to have afforded Dr. Lyon Playfair every facility in their power for the furtherance of his objects. They entered at once into his views as to the evils resulting from divided local authority in their borough, and as to the inadequacy of the existing legal powers to grapple with the magnitude of the evils then in operation, for want of a proper sanitary act. It is well known that the result of the Government Commission was the introduction of Lord Lincoln's Health of Towns Bill in 1845. The Government, however, as is equally well known, did not proceed with the measure. In the following year, the corporation of Liverpool applied for a sanitary act of their own, based on the provisions of Lord Lincoln's bill, and with such alterations only as made their act better adapted to the peculiar requirements of Liverpool, especially with regard to the equitable arrangement of local taxation in the several amalgamated townships. Another great distinction made by this bill had reference to the cellars of the town. The bill provided that no cellars should be allowed to be separately occupied if the floor was more than four feet below the level of the adjoining street, if the roofs were less than three feet above the same, and if they were not also provided with sufficient windows, flues, &c. This bill, after considerable opposition from the commissioners of Toxteth Park, one of the local boards which it sought to extinguish, at length passed into a law, and the local powers of the various commissioners merged into the corporation.

The act came into operation on the 1st of January, 1847. The town council immediately appointed as their medical officer of health, Dr. Duncan, a gentleman of considerable eminence as a sanitary authority, and as their engineer, Mr. Newlands, also a gentleman of acknowledged ability and experience. They also organised, with as little delay as possible, an extensive and comprehensive staff in these and other departments. In order to provide properly for the cleansing of the borough, the Health Committee divided it into twelve districts or sections, to each of which they appointed an inspector, with sufficient gangs of scavengers, and with a superintendent over them acting under the engineer. Each inspector was made answerable for the efficient and continual cleansing of all the streets, courts, and passages in his district, and the superintendent was made responsible to the engineer for the whole work being properly and sufficiently done. Under this head alone, the corporation of Liverpool expended during the year the sum of £15,667, besides upwards of £1,600 for watering the streets. In addition to this they let by contract the removal of all the "middens" and ash-pits in the borough. Under this contract, they at the present time, pay upwards of £10,000 yearly to the contractor, besides giving him the benefit of selling and receiving all the proceeds of the manure. Lists of all applications to empty cesspools are daily given to him, and the inspectors report every morning (from lists furnished to them daily of middens to be got out) upon all which are removed or neglected on the previous night. By this means a continual check is kept upon the operations of the contractor. Lists are likewise made out every morning, in the inspector of nuisances office, of all the cesspools emptied on the previous night. These are furnished to the building surveyor, in order that they may be examined by his staff, and that any required repairs may be at once made. By this means, any leakage or nuisance proceeding therefrom is abated. Likewise, in order to correctly test the state of cellar occupation in the borough, the Health Committee had all the street cellars beneath small houses measured, and a registry of their dimensions made. It was found that there were 14,085 of these places, which were then, or had been previously, let as separate dwellings. 7,640 only were found occupied at that time. The number of lodgers or inmates was 27,128. It was likewise found that 5,841 of these places contained beneath their floors, wells of stagnant water sunk for the purposes of drainage, and from which foul exhalations highly prejudicial to health were continually arising. Between the 8th of October, 1847, and the 1st of April, 1848, the council compelled the reconstruction of 1,156 privies, and the effectual repairing of 1,539 others, making in all 2,695 of these places which were brought, during that short period, from a state of disgusting filth and utter dilapidation, into one of repair and comparative decency.

In the summer of 1847, however, the first year in which their Sanitary Act came into operation, the borough and parish of Liverpool experienced an awful visitation, which for several months defied all their sanitary remedial efforts, and which, for severity, was almost, if not quite, unexampled in the history of English provincial towns. The potato crop having failed in Ireland, and the chief means of support being thus swept away from the poor, the miserable, starving, sickly creatures, flocked to Liverpool, their most available English seaport, where upwards of 296,000 of them landed in a short time in a state of almost incredible destitution and filth. As filth and famine are the prolific generators of disease, they brought with them a pestilence which carried dismay and death wherever it came. In defiance of all preventive efforts, the cellars and smaller houses of the Irish residents in the most unhealthy streets became crowded to excess. In ministering to the relief of these wretched creatures many valuable lives were lost, and in providing for their necessities a tax was imposed upon the rate-payers of the town of Liverpool, which for weight was utterly unprecedented in parochial taxation.

Throughout the whole of this trying period the corporation and the parochial authorities of Liverpool acted in concert, and while the parish made every provision it possibly could for the relief of the sick and destitute, and for the extensive provision of medical attendance and fever hospitals, both in lazarettos on the river and in hospitals ashore, the corporation provided for the daily cleansing of filth from all the streets, courts, and passages, for the purification of unhealthy dwellings, and for the dispensation of chloride of lime gratis in all infected places. They likewise endeavoured, out of very limited means, to increase the supply of water. In defiance of all human efforts, however, many thousands of persons died, including a large number of the industrious tradesmen of Liverpool and their families.

It was the end of the autumn of 1847 before this great calamity passed away. As soon as the corporation found themselves at all in an ordinary condition to proceed with their work of sanitary reform they did so. Between that period and the end of the year 1848 they cleared of their inmates about 5,000 of the most unhealthy cellars, situate in 380 of the worst streets in the town, and likewise caused the cleansing and purification of 2,275 unhealthy dwellings, as well as of a great number of cellars. They effectually cleared all the cellars found separately occupied in courts, and caused the adoption of house drainage in very numerous instances, and the inspection and abatement of 2,075 nuisances complained of by the inhabitants. In addition to this, they laid 1,093 other informations for nuisances, in 1,021 of which cases they obtained convictions. They also delivered 960 notices for the consumption of smoke, and laid a number of informations against parties who neglected the warning. They caused an efficient medical inspection and survey to be made of 752 lodging-houses of an inferior description, and they adopted an excellent code of by-laws for preventing overcrowding.

The paramount necessity of an abundant supply of pure water did not escape the attention of the corporation. Typhus and cholera, and the filthy state of the streets inhabited by the poorer classes, were either of them quite sufficient to force this subject on the notice of any authority claiming to do its duty to the people. All these causes combined in Liverpool to render the subject one of the very highest importance to the health and safety of all classes. But unfortunately this question was too much debated among the rate-payers as a purely financial, and not as a sanitary one. The controversy on the water question, which was continued so long and produced so much acrimony, commenced some three years back, about which time the corporation were strongly advised to take the water supply into their own hands. The companies which previously supplied the town were the Bottle and the Harrington Companies. These companies applied to Parliament for powers to raise additional capital, on terms which were believed to be inimical to the interest of the town, and the corporation appeared as the opponents of the bill for which the companies were applying. The bills were withdrawn from Parliament on the understanding that the corporation would become the purchasers of the rights held by the companies. Negotiations were immediately commenced, and some differences of opinion arising as to the value of the property, Mr. Robert Stephenson, the most eminent of living engineers, was called in as arbitrator, and he placed a high figure on its value. Mr. Stephenson's award was £666,000—a sum which all but the owners of the property believed to be greatly in advance of its value.

Pending the award of Mr. Stephenson, a project for an increased supply of water from the lake of Bala, in North Wales, was brought before the public by Mr. Robert Rowlandson. The project was warmly taken up in a local newspaper of considerable influence, and as the four millions of gallons was notoriously inadequate to the wants of the town, the Bala Lake project was received with considerable favour.

The scheme was pronounced to be magnificent, and although the cost was looked upon by some as a serious impediment, others, regarding the supply as inexhaustible, felt inclined to view the pecuniary part of the question as of the least importance. A visit to the Bala district was made by the projector, accompanied by some members of the Town Council, and Mr. Hawksley, the engineer. This occurred about the middle of October, 1847. About this period, or a little previous, a public meeting of the inhabitants was held in the Sessions-house, at which it was determined to merge the powers of the Highway Board, a body which levied rates for paving, lighting, sewerage, and other purposes, in the Town Council; and measures were accordingly taken to comply with the standing orders of the House of Commons, one of the preliminaries of which is, the giving the requisite notices in the local papers of the intended application to Parliament. It was then found that the Bala Lake scheme had been superseded by the Rivington project, and that Mr. Rowlandson had been displaced by Mr. Hawksley. This was the first bone of contention, and the personal feeling with which the contest became subsequently tinged, may be said to have arisen at this stage of the proceedings. The district between Bala Lake and the Mersey had never been surveyed, and the estimate of Mr. Rowlandson was necessarily a rough one; he estimated the expense at some half-million sterling, while the friends of the other scheme contended that the cost would be at least double that amount. The storm gathered strength as it proceeded, and the Rivington Act was procured in the spring of the following year, at an enormous expense, as the bill was opposed by the bleachers and other persons in the district, who claimed compensation. When the bill passed, the opposition became still more furious. Endless discussion took place in the press and in the Town Council, and while the popular feeling was strongly against the "Pike," as it was called for brevity, that scheme received the steady support of Mr. William Rathbone, Mr. William Earle, Mr. Hugh Hornby, and other gentlemen of fortune and station, who have ever been foremost in promoting measures of sanitary and social reform. But the 1st of November was approaching—the day when a third of the councillors are elected—and the elections went decidedly against the "Pike" party. Of the sixteen wards into which the town is divided, the "Pike" advocates only succeeded in two or three; but the retiring mayor, Mr. T. B. Horsfall, took a step at this time, which had the effect—whether intended or not—of gaining the ultimate victory to the "Pike." He signed all the contracts for the piping, &c., involving an outlay of more than £150,000. The anti-"Pikeists" were so annoyed at this step, that they, in return, began to damage the credit of the corporation, for the purpose of frightening capitalists, and thereby, if possible, preventing the money from being furnished for carrying out the scheme. No corporation stands higher as regards financial character than that of Liverpool, and had the security of the corporation *per se* been offered to the lenders, any amount of money would have been forthcoming. But by the terms of the Rivington Act the security of the water-rates was the only security which the corporation could give to the lenders; and the water-rates, it was clearly shewn, were insufficient to meet the engagements which the Rivington scheme would entail on the town. This fact, which was bruited in the council, alarmed the capitalists out of doors, and no money was forthcoming on the water account. In the meantime the making of the pipes was proceeding, the contractors being bound to have them ready by a given time. The work being done, the parties wanted their money, of course, but there was no money from the only source from which it could be paid, namely, the water-rates. Actions were threatened, and as the contractors lived in Scotland, no means were left untried to satisfy their immediate demands, but in vain. It was evident that without going again to Parliament, the whole machinery of the water scheme would come to a stand. The water committee of the Town Council which favoured the "Pike" scheme retired, and were succeeded by a body of gentlemen who were opposed to that project, of which the late Mr. Harbord was elected chairman. The excitement connected with the duties of the office and the subject it is believed literally killed him, and his death added a melancholy intensity to the struggle. Again the November elections were approaching, and again the pro-"Pikeists" suffered another severe defeat, all their candidates being rejected by the municipal constituency.

The new Town Council, however, found itself in a difficulty. The contest, as far as it had hitherto gone, was a bitter and expensive one; and the friends of the Rivington Pike project, though turned out of office, manifested no disposition to allow their opponents to procure the repeal of the act of Parliament, which they had obtained at great cost, and in the carrying out of which they had already incurred liabilities to a large amount, which the town would have to pay if the scheme were abandoned. In this dilemma, and wishing to do nothing rashly, they resolved to fortify themselves by taking the opinion of Mr. Robert Stephenson, upon the questions whether the existing water supply was or was not deficient—whether if sufficient, an adequate supply of pure water could not be obtained by boring for additional wells in the stratum of new red sandstone on which the town is built; and if not, whether the Rivington Pike project was the one he would recommend. It was generally supposed that Mr. Stephenson would report in favour of the "home" supply, as the wells are called in the town; and against the "foreign" supply, as the Rivington Pike water is designated. But after a long and patient inquiry Mr. Stephenson delivered in his report at the beginning of April, in favour of the "Pike." In addressing himself to the main question, "under all the circumstances of the case, what course is recommended to be pursued?" Mr. Stephenson summed up his observations as follows:—

> "In the progress of this report I hope I have succeeded in explaining the conclusions to which I have arrived at each step of the investigation, and made intelligible the facts and reasons on which they are based. The following are the results, in my judgment, established as regards the supply from wells:—
>
> "That the new red sandstone in and about Liverpool does contain a very large reservoir of water.
>
> "That it is fissured most extensively.
>
> "That a sympathy, varying in degree, does in consequence exhibit itself between wells, and generally the mass of sandstone may, for all practical purposes, be regarded as exceedingly permeable.
>
> "That, notwithstanding this extensive permeability, individual wells sunk into it are not proved to be capable of yielding a supply, much, if at all, exceeding one million of gallons a day.
>
> "That a slight tendency has evinced itself of the salt water from the river making its way into the mass of sandstone rock upon which Liverpool stands.
>
> "That if any attempt be made to obtain an increased supply by deepening the present wells much below the range of the tide, this tendency will be accelerated in velocity and very materially increased in amount.
>
> "That there is no probability of an adequate increase of the supply of water being obtained from the existing wells by boring or sinking them deeper.
>
> "That the various proposals for obtaining water by sinking at one point in the immediate vicinity of Liverpool will not produce the stipulated quantity.
>
> "That no position offers itself as eligible for the construction of adequate reservoirs in the Childwall or Alt Valley.

"And, finally, that the most, if not the only feasible plan for making the water contained in the sandstone available for the purposes named in the instructions, is to sink a series of wells scattered over a large area of country lying to the east or north-east of the town."

Mr. Stephenson stated his opinion that to sink the wells alluded to in the last paragraph over a large area would be a very expensive process. "In addition to this," he continued,

"It is impossible to throw out of the balance of circumstances the position of the Rivington project. The powers have been obtained at a large expense of time and money, and numerous prospective interests have been dealt with and adjusted; large contracts have been entered into, and certain responsibilities must be met. These, from the authentic statements which have been laid before me, cannot fall far short of 70,000*l.* or 80,000*l.*, the interest of which, in the event of the abandonment of the Rivington plan, must of course become an annual charge on the well system.

"Such are the circumstances which, in any dispassionate mode of treating the subject, must be allowed their due weight; and with this conviction I have anxiously endeavoured to give to each its proper influence, both present and prospective. The contested parts of the project have had my uninterrupted study since I was on the ground, and I believe it has been made evident—

"That the Rivington scheme is adequate to the supply of an abundance of water to meet both the immediate wants of the town, and also the prospective demands which may arise from any probable increase of population for the next twenty years to come.

"That the reservoirs are fitted for such a storage as will secure an uniform and copious supply at all seasons.

"That little apprehension need be entertained respecting the mains being carried over the Wigan coalfield.

"And that with proper care the total cost should not come up to the amount which has been stated.

"Believing, as I do most sincerely, that these qualifications are possessed by the Rivington plan, I come to the deliberate opinion that, after having expended such large sums of money, and incurred such heavy responsibilities to obtain an abundant supply of water of unquestionable quality, from an unfailing source, by means of gravitation, and consequently at a comparatively inconsiderable annual outlay, the inhabitants of Liverpool would be deserting their true interests, both present and prospective, if they failed to hold fast the powers which they now possess, and may never be able again to obtain, for accomplishing, in the most perfect manner, a great social advantage now so much and so universally sought after, and were to abandon them for an alternative which I am convinced is surrounded with difficulty and uncertainty."

This report created very general disappointment amongst the rate-payers of Liverpool, but the first feeling of annoyance having worn off, they began to reflect that it would be utterly futile to proceed to Parliament for the repeal of the Rivington Pike Act, in face of such a report as this. In the first hot zeal of their opposition, many of them appear to have forgotten that a large town does not merely require an adequate supply of pure water for culinary purposes, but an abundant supply for sanitary purposes and the extinction of fires; and that although the better class of houses were well supplied, the houses of the poor were very inadequately provided with water upon the old system. When the Rivington Pike Works are completed, the corporation of Liverpool will be in a condition to afford a constant supply of soft and pure water at all times to the whole of the inhabitants, and as this water will be always placed on the mains at full pressure from large reservoirs, situate on high ground behind the town, it is intended to be made at any time instantly available for the extinction of fires. It is also contemplated to erect stand pipes in every court and passage and at every lamp post, in order that by means of hose the streets and courts may be daily washed and effectually cleansed from impurities, and that the sewers may be well flushed. Through such daily cleansing it is anticipated that an immense improvement will be effected in the general health of the people of Liverpool. If these anticipations should be realised, the apparent costliness of the Rivington Pike project will, perhaps, be no longer an objection among the rate-payers. They will doubtless confess that it is better to pay a large water-rate than to die of fever, or even to endure a minor evil—an enormous poor-rate.

To the corporation of Liverpool belongs the honour of being the first corporate founders of public baths and washhouses for the poor. The idea was suggested to them by the humble efforts of a poor woman, who resided in a small house in one of the unhealthy, dirty, pestilential streets of the town, and who observing, during a time of fever, that much discomfort was caused by the washing and drying of clothes in the miserable rooms in which sick people lay, offered the use of her back kitchen to her neighbours. They gladly availed themselves of the facilities afforded. In the course of a few months it was regularly used by about 85 families. These operations excited the attention of some benevolent ladies who passed their time in visiting and relieving the poor; and through the aid afforded by them this exemplary woman was enabled to keep up her little establishment, and the women who made use of her back kitchen gladly paid a penny each for the privilege of doing their washing out of their own homes. The corporation of Liverpool took the hint, and in the year 1842 erected, in Frederick-street, at the southern part of the town, at a cost of £3,341 11s. 1d., the first baths and washhouses for the poor. The good woman with whom the idea originated was appointed its keeper and superintendent; and she may still be seen doing her duty in the establishment. This experiment having answered the expectations of its founders, a second establishment was projected for the benefit of the poor in the populous districts of the north of Liverpool. This edifice was erected in Paul-street, Liverpool, at a cost of £8,534 8s. 3d. A third building, on a still larger scale, is now in course of erection, and the following statistics will show the extent to which the poor have availed themselves of the advantages of the two establishments already in operation, and the gain or loss per annum on each of them:—

RETURN OF THE PUBLIC BATHS AND WASHHOUSES IN THE BOROUGH OF LIVERPOOL, ON 31st AUGUST IN EACH YEAR RESPECTIVELY.

UPPER FREDERICK-STREET.—OPENED IN MAY, 1842.

Year.	Number of Baths paid for.	Receipts for Baths.	Number of Tubs used.	Number of Dozens of Clothes Washed.	Receipts for Washing.	Total Receipts for Baths and Washing.	Number of Baths gratis.	Total Number of Baths paid for and gratis.	Number of Dozens of Infected Clothes Washed.	Expense of Washing Infected Clothes.	Expenditure of Establish-ment.
1842	3,871	£36 3 0	1,557	2,809½	£6 9 9	£42 12 9	none.	—	none.	£0 0 0	£35 2 3
1843	14,548	152 15 9	10,584	22,834½	47 17 0	200 12 9	none.	—	45	1 11 4	259 13 11
1844	14,625	259 10 6	12,318	24,910	50 16 6	310 7 0	none.	—	97½	3 9 6	373 1 10
1845	15,231	306 3 11	12,640	23,590	52 14 2	358 18 1	none.	—	40	1 9 9	336 19 5
1846	22,423	389 8 4	12,765	23,401	53 4 8	442 13 0	none.	—	16	0 10 0	415 19 4
1847	27,802	350 13 7	12,149	24,006	50 15 4	401 8 11	none.	—	356	10 0 0	427 6 7
1848	22,663	321 15 6	14,770	29,448	61 6 9	387 0 11	220	22,883	125	3 18 0	495 15 11
1849	25,282	337 16 7	19,045	38,090	79 7 1	417 3 8	396	25,678	158	3 7 0	505 10 4

PAUL-STREET.—OPENED IN NOVEMBER, 1847.

Year.	Number of Baths paid for.	Receipts for Baths.	Number of Tubs used.	Number of Dozens of Clothes Washed.	Receipts for Washing.	Total Receipts for Baths and Washing.	Number of Baths gratis.	Total Number of Baths paid for and gratis.	Number of Dozens of Infected Clothes Washed.	Expense of Washing Infected Clothes.	Expenditure of Establish-ment.
For nine months in 1847	34,504	£426 16 9	22,732	46,297	£94 17 4	£521 14 1	8,152	42,656	495	£1 0 0	£542 9 11½
1848	43,761	531 8 8	38,090	76,180	158 14 2	690 2 10	21,300	64,061	911	1 18 0	973 1 7
1849	48,633	604 2 2	52,354	82,785	218 19 1	823 1 3	30,380	79,013	918	3 16 6	887 6 8

In Cornwallis-street, and Leveson-street, an open and airy situation, and very central as regards the class of the population to be benefited, are other Washhouses.

The building is in the Italian style. It is built of Liverpool red brick, with stone groins and dressings. The stone is a very light red colour, and is obtained from a quarry within the borough, and in the neighbourhood of the building. The bath accommodation comprises

> 10 First-class bath-rooms.
> 17 Second-class bath-rooms.
> 16 Third-class bath-rooms.
> ———
> 43 Bath-rooms.

Each bath-room has a slipper-bath, with hot and cold water, and a shower-bath, and each class has two vapour-baths and two douche-baths, making six vapour and six douche baths in all.

There are, besides, the two tepid swimming baths, one with a water area of 1,034 feet, and the other with an area of 1,113 feet.

The passages leading to the bath-rooms are so arranged that any number of the male baths can be shut off and included in the range of female baths, or *vice versa*, according to the preponderance of male or female bathers at the time.

The wash-house accommodation comprises:—

> 14 first class wash-stalls
> 24 second class do.
> 49 third class   do.
> 8 stalls for infected clothes
> ———
> 95 stalls in all.

In each stall there are two tubs, one with a close cover for steaming, the other for washing, and 25 of the stalls are made larger than the others, and have in addition a third tub—a dolly tub.

The drying place is made very large, in order to expedite this part of the process. The drying is effected by a blast of highly-heated and desiccated air. Previously to being submitted to the heated air, the superabundant moisture of the clothes is got rid of by hydro-extractors, of which there are three. A steam-engine drives the fan for the hot air, and gives motion to the hydro-extractors.

The water and steam boilers, the steam-engine, and the furnace for heated air, are situated in the middle of the area between the baths and washhouses. The boilers are six feet diameter, and twenty-four feet long, on the Cornish principle, with internal flues.

The pipes which supply the baths with hot water are very large, and there is some novelty in the apparatus for filling and emptying the baths, having for its object rapidity. The filling of a bath will occupy about fifteen seconds.

Altogether, there is accommodation for 1,000 bathers in a day of ten hours, allowing an hour for each bath.

The estimated cost of the baths and wash-houses, with all their fixtures, furniture, and apparatus, is £8,800. The value of the site is £1,070, making a total of £9,870.

It is believed that this establishment will not only be self-supporting, but will yield a surplus revenue, which may be applied in reducing the charges, or accumulated as a sinking fund to pay off the debt.

The corporation have just purchased the saltwater baths at St. George's Pier, so that when the Cornwallis-street baths are completed, the town of Liverpool will possess four public baths for the accommodation of all classes.

New Baths, George's Parade

The provision of public parks and places of recreation for the inhabitants has also been considered as a matter of duty by the authorities of Liverpool. In this respect they have received important aid from Mr. Richard Vaughan Yates, a philanthropic Liverpool merchant, who, at great individual expense, has purchased a beautiful park of about eighty acres for the free use of the public, and which he has drained and laid out with taste and skill. The Liverpool Corporation followed Mr. Yates in this important movement by purchasing and throwing open to the public the Liverpool Botanic Gardens. They have likewise purchased, for upwards of £80,000, the extensive estate of Newsham-house, on the confines of the borough, which they are about to convert into public pleasure grounds.

Another sanitary operation deserves mention. A great amendment has been lately effected in Liverpool in the regulation of slaughter-houses, by placing the garbage and refuse, while it is fresh, in tight boxes, and removing it at once out of the borough, instead of leaving it to be decomposed and to fester in cesspools. The council have also framed by-laws, which will compel the observance of this system.

The following figures contain abstracts of the operations of the nuisance staff for the year 1849, together with particulars of the whole cellar proceedings taken in this department under the Liverpool Sanitary Act since it came into operation:—

Nuisances complained of by inhabitants during the year 1849	2,755
Nuisances inspected and reported upon in the nuisance-book, and remedied as required by the act	3,373
Other nuisances reported upon	373
Nuisance notices issued	2,395
Notices given to remove stagnant water on land	731
Ditto from cellars	405
Notices given to complainants relative to the abatement of nuisances	1,146
Ditto to repair defective spouts	91
Ditto to fence dangerous excavations	203
Nuisances referred to the borough engineer for remedy by drainage or repairs	1,701
Nuisances referred for remedy to the building surveyor	702
Cases referred to the medical officer of health for his special examination	52
Cases reported of defective scavenging	30
Escapes of water by defective pipes in cellars and other places referred to the water engineer for remedy	263
Notices given to whitewash and purify the interiors of filthy and unhealthy dwellings	3,603

Renewed notices given to parties, who on re-inspection were found not to have complied with the previous notices to cleanse filthy houses 473

Notices given to whitewash the outsides of houses in courts during the prevalence of cholera, by order of Dr. Duncan 1,112

Lodging-house applications to register during the year 538

Notices given to lodging-house keepers to apply for license tickets 351

Lodging-house tickets issued 1,015

Lodging-house informations laid for overcrowding and neglecting to register 379

Amount of fines inflicted upon lodging-housekeepers, 395*l*. 12s. 6d.

Applications received to license slaughter houses under the "by-laws" 48

Orders issued to the contractors to empty middens .. 43,955

Middens returned as emptied during the year 53,109

Cesspools and ashpits taken from the returns and referred to the building surveyor for examination and repairs 14,045

Smoke notices issued 37

Ditto informations laid 136

Ditto proceeded with 9

The total number of cellars which have been measured in streets in the borough of Liverpool, and a registry thereof made, which is always available at the Nuisance-office for the information of the inhabitants, is 14,166

The number of cellars found occupied in streets at the time of measurement was 7,689

The number of inmates found in them was 27,254

When inspected there was found requiring draining and cleansing 5,871

The cellars which have been claimed as built or altered under the Health Act of 1842, and which are exempted from the operation of the Sanitary Act, are 1,221

The notices issued to owners of street-cellars, as required by the act, and duplicates of which have been kept for proof, are 9,426

Notices issued to obstinate tenants of street-cellars .. 1,069

Notices issued to owners of court-cellars found occupied 510

Notices to tenants of court-cellars who have refused to vacate them 79

Informations laid against owners of street-cellars for illegally letting them after notice 1,308

Informations laid against tenants of street-cellars who
  refused to quit at the request of the owners   284
Informations laid against owners of court-cellars   69
Informations laid against tenants of ditto   18
In the clearance of cellars, the worst and most
  unhealthy streets have been hitherto taken, and the
  number of such streets gone through is   495
In the above streets, the cellars found occupied were . 6,253
Of the above, there have been claimed as built or altered
  under the Health Act, and which can be now legally
  occupied 1,180
The number of cellars, therefore, thus cleared of
  inmates the first time over was 5,073
The number of cellars which, after being cleared, have
  been re-occupied, with beds in them, and have been
  again cleared, is 1,505
The number of cellars which on re-examination were
  found separately occupied, but without beds in them,
  and in evasion of the law, the parties pretending to
  occupy them during the day only, amounts to 1,427
Adding together the number of cellars originally
  cleared of inmates in streets, and those cleared again
  after their re-occupation, with the number of cellars
  cleared in courts, shows the total number of cellars
  cleared of inmates in the borough of Liverpool, from
  the time the Sanitary Act came into operation in
  1847 till the 1st day of January, 1849, to be 7,167
The actual number of inmates in the 5,073 cellars first
  cleared in the 495 streets gone through was, as taken
  by the officers 22,680

When the cellars were measured, the average rate of population
in them was found to be rather above 3½ for each cellar, and therefore, calculating the inmates of the cellars which have been cleared
in courts, and cleared a second time in streets at this rate, and which
together amount to 2,094, the inmates removed from them would
be 7,329, and would thus make the total number of cellar inmates removed from cellars in the borough of Liverpool within the last three
years to be about 30,009. From the above, however, should be deducted the inmates of the 1,427 cellars formerly cleared, but which, on
re-examination, have been found separately occupied without beds in
them, and taking these at the same average rate, the result would give
their population at 4,994, and taking this amount from 30,009 shows
the number of cellar inmates removed in the borough of Liverpool
since January, 1847, to be 25,015, and which is the closest approximation to the number actually ejected that can be obtained.

The questions remain, where have these 25,015 people gone? Have they left the town? or have they merely been shifted from the wretched cellars under ground into almost equally wretched rooms above ground? The corporation of Liverpool has endeavoured to do good. It has greatly improved the drainage and sewerage of the town; it has striven hard to procure an abundant supply of water; it has suppressed nuisances as far as it was able; it has provided baths and washhouses for the poor; it has opened parks and gardens to the people; but it has done nothing towards providing dwellings for the labouring classes. It is true that no new courts can be built in Liverpool upon the model of those abominable places; and that in the more modern courts that have been erected in the northern parts of the town the entrances are as wide as two courts, and admit a full current of air to circulate through them from end to end. But as long as the old courts exist, the people will inhabit them, unless better homes, equally central in situation and equally cheap, be provided for them. As regards cheapness, there will be no difficulty, for they pay from 3s. to 4s. a week (a large price) for the most wretched and unwholesome accommodations. Until better homes be provided for the poor, little good is done by hunting them from their cellars into rooms which may be a little larger, but which are slightly better ventilated or more comfortable than the places they have left. The wretched courts of Liverpool, notwithstanding all the exertions of the local authorities, still remain the close and fetid hotbeds of filth and disease. Court branches from court, and the entrance to them is sometimes so narrow as not to allow two people to pass each other. Streams of dirty water run down the sides of these entrances, which are encumbered with nameless filth, as well as garbage and refuse of all kinds. The interior of the courts allows no breath of air to circulate, and each has a privy at the end, common to all the inhabitants of the enclosure. In one small court of four houses, containing three rooms each, I inquired the number of inhabitants, and found it was upwards of eighty. In short, in all my experience of the filthiest streets in London, the most wretched "closes" of Edinburgh, and the purulent "wynds" of Glasgow, I never saw anything approaching to the dirt, discomfort, and squalor that I have seen in such streets of Liverpool, as Ben Jonson-street, Harrison-street, Lace-street, the Vauxhall-road, New Bird-street, Brick-street, Jordan-street, Crosshall-street, and some others, with the innumerable courts that branch from them on either side. All the sanitary operations in the power of the corporation to effect are but mitigations of this enormous evil. They can by no stretch of their authority make such places wholesome. They may punish day after day the offenders against the law of public health, but day after day the offences will be renewed, because the offenders are desperately ignorant, desperately poor, and desperately obstinate. Although the police is vigilant, and does its best to prevent the overcrowding of miserable creatures in small rooms, and in the licensed lodging-houses that keep lodgers by the night, the law is constantly broken. In one day (the day before that on which this letter was written) a man was brought before Mr. Rushton, the excellent stipendiary magistrate, for having 92 lodgers in his house, when he was only licensed, from the size and accommodation it afforded, to harbour 19. Another man not licensed at all was fined for having 11 lodgers in one room; and a second was fined for the offence of having 21 lodgers in one room being equally without a license. In several small houses in one court the police found 138 inmates, in addition to a pig, a description of lodger which the Irish are fond of, but which is expressly forbidden to be accommodated among human creatures by the by-laws of the corporation of Liverpool. These people are, in general, so ignorant of the necessity which forces the authorities to forbid pig-keeping and over-crowding, that they consider the law a cruelty and a tyranny; and make it a point of duty to evade it as often as they can; not often in the matter of pigs, but very often in the matter of poor travellers, emigrants, sailors, tramps, vagrants, and mendicants.

It will be seen from the foregoing statement that although the authorities of Liverpool have done much towards improving the sanitary condition of the town, much remains to be done. Everything testifies to their zeal in the cause of sanitary reform, and to the good feeling which has animated their efforts. But their task is Herculean. It is highly to their credit that, at such large expense, they have somewhat mitigated the evils. They will have the satisfaction of reflecting, that should pestilence again visit the banks of the Mersey, it may perhaps only slay hundreds, where, but for their efforts, it might again have destroyed its tens of thousands.

LABOUR AND THE POOR.

—◆—

LIVERPOOL.

[FROM OUR SPECIAL CORRESPONDENT.]

EMIGRATION.—EMIGRANTS AND MAN-CATCHERS.

LETTER IX.

The emigration from the United Kingdom has annually increased in a large ratio for the last ten years. The *Colonization Circular*, issued by her Majesty's Colonial Land and Emigration Commissioners in the spring of every year, furnishes the only authentic and complete account of the number of persons who leave the shores of the "old country" to seek their fortunes in the United States, the British North American colonies, Australia, the Cape, New Zealand, and our other possessions in all parts of the globe. The great bulk of the emigration is not, however, directed to the British possessions; and the advice and instruction afforded to the people by her Majesty's Commissioners in their annual twopenny pamphlet have no interest for at least three out of five of all those who quit the land of their birth to make trial of another. The United States absorb the largest share. The following table shows the progressive increase of the emigration to all parts of the world from 1839 to 1849 inclusive:—

Years.	North American Colonies.	United States.	Australian Colonies and New Zealand.	All other Places.	Total.
1839	12,658	33,536	15,786	227	62,207
1840	32,293	40,642	15,850	1,958	90,743
1841	38,164	45,017	32,625	2,786	118,592
1842	54,123	63,852	8,534	1,835	128,344
1843	23,518	28,335	3,478	1,881	57,212
1844	22,924	43,660	2,229	1,873	70,686
1845	31,803	58,538	830	2,330	93,501
1846	43,439	82,239	2,347	1,826	129,851
1847	109,680	142,154	4,949	1,487	258,270
1848	31,065	188,233	23,904	4,887	248,089
1849	41,367	219,450	32,091	6,590	299,498
Total...	441,034	945,656	142,623	27,680	1,556,993

A considerable proportion of this large emigration proceeds from Liverpool, which may be considered in this respect the principal port of the United Kingdom. It will be seen from the above table that for the last three years there has been an emigration much more extensive than usual to the United States of America; and that in the past year its amount far surpassed that of any year previous. During the present season it is probable that the emigration will be still greater. These swarming multitudes that embark at Liverpool for New York, Boston, and other transatlantic ports, to seek a home and happiness in the western world, where there is elbow room and to spare for the whole population of Europe, and where not only bread by the day, but independence for life, and an inheritance for the largest family, may usually be had for the seeking, are principally Irish of the most destitute classes. Nine out of ten of all the emigrants that leave Liverpool by the American liners are Irish people, and fully ninety-nine out of every hundred Irish are steerage passengers, crossing over at the cheapest rate. In the year 1847, the number of emigrant-ships (not including steam-boats) that left Liverpool for the United States, was 514, which conveyed 1,189 cabin passengers, and 128,447 steerage passengers, or a total of 129,636 persons. No record appears to have been kept which might have shown the exact numbers of English, Irish, and Scotch among them, but there can be no doubt in the mind of any one who has examined an emigrant ship with all her passengers on board, that the proportion of Irish to other emigrants approximates very closely to what I have already stated—nine out of ten. The above figures only apply to the emigrant ships under the inspection of the officer appointed by the Government, and take no account of an additional number of 4,888 persons who emigrated during the year in steam-vessels and other ships not under inspection; and who were mostly, if not entirely, of a higher class, principally English, Welsh, and Scotch people, emigrating to Canada or the other British possessions in North America. Including these, the total emigration of 1847 from the port of Liverpool would amount to 134,524 souls. In 1848 the number of emigrant ships that left Liverpool was 519; conveying 982 cabin and 124,522 steerage passengers, or a total of 125,504 souls. The number of emigrants of the higher grade for the same year, who took their passage in steam-boats and ships not under inspection, was 5,717; which, added to the previous numbers, give 131,221 as the total emigration of 1848. In 1849 the number of emigrants was still larger; the emigrant ships that left the port amounted to 565, conveying 1,614 cabin and 146,162 steerage passengers; in all 147,776. To these must be added 6,126 steam-boat emigrants, and others not under inspection; giving a total of 153,902 for the year. During the present year the tide of emigration runs even more strongly. In January, 32 emigrant ships left Liverpool, conveying 6,943 people, or an average of 217 passengers for each ship. In February, the number of ships that left was 37, conveying 8,779 emigrants, or an average of 235 passengers per ship. In March, the number of emigrant ships that left the port was 57, conveying 16,783 persons, or an average of 294 emigrants per ship. In April, the number of ships was 51, and of emigrants 17,458, making on an average 342 passengers per ship. In May, the number of ships was 62, and of emigrants 17,498, making on an average 282 per ship. In June the number of ships was 42, and of emigrants 13,453, or an average of 320 per ship. The total emigration for the half-year by ships under inspection, and exclusive of steam-boats, was 80,914.

The following table shows how large a proportion of the total emigration from the port of Liverpool, during the year 1847, was bound for the United States:—

	Cabin Passengers.	Steerage Passengers.	Total.
United States	3,499	100,166	103,665
Canada	79	28,078	28,175
New Brunswick	48	1,442	1,490
Nova Scotia	39	148	187
Newfoundland	31	88	119
West India Islands	137	18	155
Cape of Good Hope	16	none	16
Sydney	7	none	7
Western Australia	10	none	10

The returns for the year 1848 are of a similar character, and are as follows, with the addition of a Californian item:—

	Cabin Passengers.	Steerage Passengers.	Total.
United States	3,910	123,591	127,501
Central America and California	207	625	832
Canada	98	1,714	1,812
New Brunswick	52	31	83
Nova Scotia	66	40	106
Newfoundland	40	7	47
Prince Edward's Island	16	2	18
West Indies	173	26	199
The Cape	110	13	123
Australia and New Zealand	73	225	298

The emigration of the past year shows a considerable increase. The following is the return for 1849, including passengers by ships not under Government inspection:—

	Cabin Passengers.	Steerage Passengers.	Total.
United States	4,639	143,106	147,745
Texas and Central America	268	305	573
Canada	111	4,140	4,251
New Brunswick	53	153	206
Nova Scotia	32	69	101
Newfoundland	34	4	38
Prince Edward's Island	23	11	34
West India Islands	127	14	141
South Australia	37	405	442
Sydney	10	13	23
Port Phillip	43	165	208
New Zealand	none	none	none.

Great as is the present amount of emigration from Liverpool, it is likely to receive a still larger share of the general emigration of Europe, as operations are in progress to bring through this town the whole tide of German emigration to the United States, which is almost as large and strong as that from Ireland itself. Until the present year, the Germans that have left Liverpool for the United States have been but stragglers from the main army—the greater divisions of which have embarked from Hamburg, or other Hanse towns, or from Havre. It has been found, however, that all these routes are more expensive and inconvenient than the route by Liverpool, and that emigrants may be conveyed from the interior of Germany to New York *viâ* Liverpool, at a less rate and in better ships than from Hamburg or Havre. In consequence of this, efforts are being made by an enterprising firm of German merchants to bring the whole of this traffic into Liverpool, and it is very probable that their endeavours will be to a large extent successful, unless the bad character acquired by Liverpool for the plunder of emigrants, and for the absence of proper accommodation for them, should interfere to prejudice it in the minds of the German Governments. Upon this point, however, a reform has commenced, as I shall show hereafter.

There is great competition amongst the various owners and agents of the vessels that trade between Liverpool and the United States, as much of their profit depends upon the conveyance of emigrants. The price of steerage accommodation rises and falls considerably from week to week, and even from day to day. A year or two ago the average fare in the steerage was £5 for each adult, and half that sum for young children. During the present season the rate has sometimes been as low as £3 10s., and sometimes as high as £5. The fares in the second-class cabins vary from £4 10s. to £7, and in the first-class cabins the fare is pretty stationary at 16 guineas. In the steerage and second cabins the Government regulations make it imperative that a certain quantity of food and water shall be provided for each emigrant, whatever may be the passage-money received. If the owners and agents of emigrant vessels chose, in their rivalry, to take steerage passengers for a guinea or even half-a-guinea each, it would make no difference in the amount of accommodation and provisions which they would be compelled to supply. The regulation does not extend to the first-class cabin passengers, who are in general most liberally, and, indeed, luxuriously provided for. No emigrant ship is allowed to clear out or proceed on her voyage with a greater number of persons on board, including the master and crew and cabin passengers, than in the proportion of one person to every two tons of her registered burden. Besides this, whatever may be the registered tonnage of a ship, she is not allowed to have a greater number of passengers, exclusive of *bonâ fide* cabin passengers, than in the proportion of one passenger for every twelve clear superficial feet on the main deck, and in the deck immediately below the same. The penalty for an infraction of this law is fixed at not less than two, or more than five pounds, for each passenger in excess of the proper number. Before a ship is allowed to clear out, she must be surveyed under the direction of the Government Emigration Agent, at the expense of the owner or charterer, and certified to be in all respects seaworthy, and fit for her intended voyage. It is furthermore provided by the Passenger Act of 1849, the 12th and 13th Victoria, cap. 33, "that there shall not be more than two tiers of berths on any one deck in any such passage ship, and that the interval between the floor of the berths and the deck or platform immediately beneath them shall not be less than six inches; that the berths shall be securely constructed, and of dimensions not less than after the rate of six feet in length and eighteen inches in width for each passenger, and that persons of different sexes above the age of fourteen, unless husband and wife, shall not be placed in the same berth." In addition to and irrespective of any provisions of their own, which passengers may take on board, the captain "shall make to each passenger, during the voyage, including the time of detention, if any, at any place or port, before the termination of the voyage, the following issues of pure water and sweet and wholesome provisions; namely, at least three quarts of water daily, and of provisions at the rate per week of 2½ lbs. of bread or biscuit, not inferior in quality to navy biscuits; 1 lb. of wheaten flour, 5 lbs. of oatmeal, 2 lbs. of rice, 2 ounces of tea, ½ lb. of sugar, and ½ lb. of molasses: such issues to be made in advance and not less often than twice a week." It is at the option of the captains and owners to substitute good and sound potatoes, for either the oatmeal or rice, in the proportion of five pounds of potatoes to one pound of oatmeal or rice; but as a store of potatoes is bulky, and does not keep so well as rice and oatmeal, this arrangement is very seldom made. It is also optional at Liverpool, and in any Irish or Scotch port, to substitute oatmeal for the whole or any part of the rice. This allowance is considered very fair and liberal; but, as I learned from several of the captains, the poor people are often too ignorant to know what to do with the particular kind of food provided for them. One captain informed me—and his statement was confirmed by so many others as to appear to be a notorious fact—that not above one-half, or even one-third, of the poor emigrants know the use of tea; and that it is no uncommon thing to see an Irishman survey his allowance of tea for awhile, and then fill his pipe with a portion, and smoke it with evident satisfaction. Nor do Irish emigrants, as a body, appear to be any better acquainted with the uses of rice. They continually ask how they are to use it. I was informed of one man, who, after receiving his oatmeal, his rice, his molasses, his sugar, and his tea, very quietly set about and boiled up the whole mixture—tea and all—into a thick soup or pudding, beautifully speckled with expanded tea-leaves.

The arrangements for the health of the passengers are necessarily of the most stringent kind. The poorer class of Irish emigrants, at the best of times, are filthy in their persons, and appear to have but a very small sense of cleanliness and propriety. When sea-sickness overtakes them, their utter prostration of body and mind aggravates every dirty habit which they may have formed. To enforce cleanliness is, therefore, a most necessary part of the captain's duty, and he is obliged for the sake of all on board to enact the stern, unyielding despot. A surgeon or other duly qualified medical man must be taken on board every ship that carries above 100 passengers. But even in ships that clear out with a fewer number, a medical man is usually, if not always, engaged for the voyage, as a matter of precaution and expediency, if not of strict and compulsory duty. To enforce order and

The Emigrants

cleanliness on board, the captain either selects a dozen or two of the most respectable and intelligent of the passengers, whom he invests with magisterial authority for the voyage, or invites the passengers to elect their own monitors. This plan is generally found to answer its purpose; and whether nominated by the autocratic will and pleasure of the captain, or elected by the universal suffrage of the emigrants, these office-bearers have in most cases little or no difficulty in enforcing their authority, as a sanitary and general police.

As gratifying and striking proofs of the prosperity that attends the vast body of Irish settlers in the United States, and of their regard for and care of the relatives whom they may have left behind them in the "old country," I am enabled to state the following particulars. It is pretty generally understood that the Irish in America send home small sums by almost every packet that reaches Liverpool, to be transmitted through the various emigration agents and others, to their relatives in Ireland. These sums are principally intended to pay their passage to America, the land of promise—but, to the senders of this money, a land of realities. In the course of the year these small remittances run up to a very considerable sum. Few, however, know the aggregate amount. I had occasion some time ago in Ireland, when visiting a large union workhouse, containing between 2,000 and 3,000 inmates, to inquire if many such sums found their way to the paupers in that establishment, and I was informed that from six to eight persons weekly on an average were enabled to leave the workhouse by this means, and to pay their passage over to America. The captain of one American liner informed me of another highly gratifying fact of the same nature, of which he was personally cognizant. Several years ago, among the emigrants on board of his ship were two well-behaved Irish girls, who were going to New York to try their fortunes as domestic servants. Being pleased with their appearance and their testimonials of good conduct, he took them into his own family, where they have ever since remained. From time to time they have entrusted him with small sums, sufficient to convey from Liverpool to the United States no less than thirteen persons, including their father, mother, brothers and sisters, and cousins to the third and fourth remove. That such instances are by no means uncommon, the following figures will prove. I have before me the returns furnished by five well-known agency houses in Liverpool of the amount of money transmitted to them from New York, in small sums varying from £2 or £3 to £10 and £20, and seldom exceeding the last-named sum—the whole of it intended for the benefit of persons in Great Britain and Ireland, but principally in Ireland, to enable them to emigrate to the United States. The first house, having the smallest business in this way, received between the 1st of January, 1849, and the 6th of March, 1850—or a little more than fourteen months—the sum of £6,425 13s. 6d., for transmission to Ireland, exclusive of drafts on England, the amount of which I was unable to ascertain. The number of drafts was 1,934, or an average of £3 6s. 5½d. each. The second house received, in the same period of fourteen months, the sum of £24,658 12s. 1d., in 6,198 drafts, or an average of £3 19s. 4¾d. each, all for Ireland, and exclusive of drafts payable in Liverpool, and in other parts of England. The third house received in the same way, from the 1st of January, 1849, to the 1st of January, 1850, the sum of £53,279 1s. 3d., in 13,425 drafts, or an average of £3 19s. 4½d. The fourth house received in the year 1848 the sum of £51,628; and in the year 1849, ending the 1st of January, 1850, the sum of £72,628, or an increase over the former year of £21,000. I am not enabled to state the number of drafts, but taking the average of the other houses, or something less than £4 each, and calculating in the same way, the number would be found with tolerable accuracy, and would amount to 18,175. The fifth house received, from the 1st of January, 1849, to the 1st of January, 1850, the sum of £162,167 10s. 3d.

in the same way, principally for transmission to Ireland. This, in the same average of the amounts, would give the total number of drafts at 40,542. From the house of Baring Brothers and Co., which is supposed on competent authority to do a business still larger than the whole of the five here mentioned, no return has been received, but it is generally stated that their average receipts of this kind amount annually to nearly half a million. These six are far from being the only houses that are engaged in similar transactions, so that in all probability a million sterling at least is annually received from the United States of America on behalf of intending emigrants from Ireland. I should add that the passage money of a great number of emigrants is paid for them on the other side of the Atlantic. I could obtain no reliable statement of the aggregate amount, but an additional sum should fairly be allowed under this head, in stating the total amount paid by American settlers for the emigration of their Irish kinsfolk. The figures tell an affecting story, and are in the highest degree creditable to the character of the Irish in the United States. I could not help reflecting, when I remembered these facts, and looked upon the swarms of ragged, destitute, dirty, squalid Irishmen awaiting in the streets of Liverpool the sailing of the ships that were to convey them to America, that, however deplorable their present condition, they too, in the course of time, would, in all probability, go and do likewise, and not only elevate themselves far above the miseries of their former state, but help thousands of their friends and relatives to follow them into comfort and prosperity.

It would be interesting to know what portion of the total emigration that proceeds from the ports of Great Britain remains in the new world; and what portion, disheartened, disgusted, and disappointed, returns to England. I made some inquiries upon this subject, but was not able to ascertain any authentic particulars. Many captains of American packet ships informed me that they sometimes crossed from New York with forty or fifty disappointed emigrants; and one gentleman, a merchant in the town, corroborated the statement as far as his own experience went, by stating that on his return from a trip to the United States, there were between sixty and seventy English and Irish steerage passengers returning to this country, disappointed with their prospects, and quite sick of America. One captain informed me that during the present season, he took out as steerage passengers a sturdy English yeoman, with his wife and eight children, and a large quantity of boxes and packages, and that he met him a week after he had landed him in New York in a state of utter dejection, determined to return to England by the first packet. He had looked at a few farms within a circuit of fifty miles of New York, but neither approved of the farming, the land, the country, the people, the weather, the food, the drink, nor anything he had seen, felt, or heard since he had stepped out of the packet. He had not even unpacked his luggage, and returned to England, with his wife and eight children, after less than ten days' sojourn in America, a sadder, but scarcely a wiser, man.

As soon as a party of emigrants arrive in Liverpool they are beset by a tribe of people, both male and female, who are known by the name of "man-catchers," and "runners." The business of these people is, in common parlance, to "fleece" the emigrant, and to draw from his pocket, by fair means or by foul, as much of his cash as he can be persuaded, inveigled, or bullied into parting with. The first division of the man-catching fraternity are those who trade in commissions on the passage money, and call themselves the "runners" or agents of passenger-brokers. The business of the passenger-broker is a legitimate and necessary one—and many of the firms above alluded to as receiving such numerous remittances of small sums from America, are among the number. Under the Passenger Act of the 12th and 13th Victoria, cap. 33, the licences of all the passenger-brokers expired on the 1st of February, 1850, subject to renewal on their being approved of by the Government emigration agent, and to their entering into bonds, with two sureties, to the amount of £200, for the due fulfilment of all the requirements of the act of Parliament relating to the comfort and security of emigrants. The passenger-brokers of Liverpool, in common with the unwary and unsuspecting emigrants, have suffered greatly from the malpractices of the "runners" who pretend to be their agents. These man-catchers procure whatever sums they can from emigrants as passage-money—perhaps £5 or £6, or even more—and pay as little as they can to the passenger-broker, whose business they thus assume—often as little as £3 or £3 5s. In addition to these large and knavish profits, they demand a commission of 7½ per cent. from the passenger-broker, and they have been often known to claim and enforce this commission, although their whole concern in the matter may have been to watch the number of emigrants going into or coming out of the broker's office, and to put in a claim for having brought or "caught" them. It is obviously the interest of the brokers as well as of the emigrants that this system of plunder should be stopped; and the active and intelligent Government agent for emigration at Liverpool, without whose approval no license can be obtained, has done his best to extirpate this particular class of man-catchers. Before the renewal of their licences in February, he made it imperative that the passenger-brokers should sign a declaration to the effect that they would not give any fee, commission, or reward whatever, directly or indirectly, to any person or persons for procuring passengers in Liverpool for ships sailing to America. Such, nevertheless, is the competition among the passenger-brokers, even of the highest respectability, that it is in vain to expect that the system of paying commission for procuring passengers can be entirely stopped. If commission be not paid as per centage to the old race of man-catchers, it will be paid in salaries, or by some other means, to the accredited "runners" of each establishment, so that the system, somewhat modified and improved, will still continue. To form an idea of the sums paid in any one year, 1849 for instance, as commission to the man-catchers in the sole item of passage money, we have but to take the total steerage emigration of that year, and multiply it by £3 10s.—the average amount of passage money—and calculate what a per centage of 7½ per cent. would amount to. The total steerage emigration of 1849 was 146,162 souls, which at £3 10s. a head would amount to £511,567. A per centage of 7½ per cent. on this sum would amount to no less than £38,367 10s.; or, taking the commission at the low average of 6 per cent., to £30,694, which is generally stated to be about the sum actually paid to this particular class of people on the average of the last three years by the passenger-brokers of Liverpool.

But these are not the only class of the man-catching fraternity, nor do they confine their operations to an exorbitant profit upon passage money. The man-catchers keep lodging-houses for emigrants—wretched cellars and rooms, destitute of comfort and convenience, in which they cram them as thickly as the places can hold. The extra profits they draw from this source cannot be inferior in amount to their previously-mentioned gains, and the cherished hoards of the poor pay a large per centage to their unscrupulous rapacity. In addition to this trade, some of them deal in the various articles composing the outfit of emigrants, such as bedding, clothes, food, cooking utensils, and the knick-knacks of all kinds which they can persuade them to purchase. Some of the storekeepers in this line of business pay their "runners" or "man-catchers" as much as ten per cent. commission on the purchases effected by the emigrants; from which the reader may form some estimate of the enormous plunder that must be drained from the poor ignorant people. As every emigrant must provide his own bedding, the sale of mattresses, blankets, and counterpanes enters largely into this trade. After the bedding is provided, the "man-catchers," who are principally Irishmen themselves, and know both the strength and weakness of the Irish character, fasten upon their countrymen—many of whom, poor and miserable as they look, have sovereigns securely stitched amid the patches of their tattered garments—and persuade them into the purchase of various articles, both useful and useless. Among these may be mentioned clothes of all kinds—shirts, trowsers, waistcoats, shawls, petticoats, southwesters, caps, boots and shoes, slippers, cooking utensils, cans for the daily allowance of water, and tins to hold their meal, rice, and sugar. Provisions—such as bacon, herrings, salt-beef, and other articles not found them on board—and luxuries, in which whisky and tobacco are generally included, come next on the list, after reiterated assurances from the man-catchers that no emigrant will be taken on board without them. These being provided—and an Irishman being easily squeezable when a friend and a countryman is the "man-catcher" who has him in hand, and when he fears, too, that his passage-money will be lost for non-compliance with the regulations—his attention is next directed to such articles as pocket-mirrors, razors, bowie-knives, rifles, pistols, telescopes, &c. The stranger in Liverpool who takes a walk in the immediate vicinity of the Waterloo Dock, whence the greater number of emigrant vessels take their departure, will see a profuse display of the various articles upon which the "man-catcher" makes his gains—articles generally of the most inferior qualities, and sold at the most extravagant and ridiculous prices. The "man-catching" business in all its departments has been reduced to a regular system, and no London sharper can be more sharp than the Liverpool runners. Perhaps the most complicated and ingenious trick is the following. When a steam-vessel laden with emigrants leaves an Irish port for Liverpool, one of the Liverpool fraternity, dressed up as a raw Irishman, with the usual long-tailed, ragged, and patched grey frieze coat, the battered and napless hat, the dirty unbuttoned knee-breeches, the black stockings, the shillelah, and the short pipe, takes his passage among them, and pretends to be an emigrant. Before the vessel arrives at Liverpool he manages to make acquaintance with the greater portion of them, learns the parish they come from and the names of the relatives whom they have left behind, not forgetting those of the parish priest and the principal people of their neighbourhood. He also ascertains the names of the friends in America whom they are going to join. He tells them of the roguery of Liverpool, and warns them against thieves and man-catchers, bidding them take especial care of their money. On arriving at the quay in Liverpool he jumps ashore among the first, where a gang of his co-partners are waiting to receive him. He speedily communicates to them all the information he has gained, and the poor people on stepping ashore are beset by affectionate inquiries about their friends in Ireland, and that good man the parish priest. They imagine that they have fortunately dropped among old acquaintances, and their friend of the steam-boat takes care to inform them that he is not going to be "done" by the man-catchers, but will lodge while at Liverpool at such and such a place, which he recommends. They cannot imagine that men who know all about the priest and their friends and relatives can mean them any harm, and numbers of them are usually led off in triumph to the most wretched, but most expensive, lodging-houses. Once in the power of the man-catchers, a regular siege of their pockets is made, and the poor emigrant is victimized in a thousand ways—for his passage-money, for his clothes and utensils, and for his food. Even after they have drained him as dry as they can, they are loth to part with him entirely, and they write out, per next steamer, a full, true, and particular account of him—his parish, his relations, his priest, and his estimated stock of money—to a similar gang in New York. Paddy—simple fellow—arrives in New York in due time, and is greeted on landing by the same affectionate inquiries. If his eyes have not been opened by woful experience, he thinks once more that he has fallen among old friends, and is led off by the "smart" man-catchers of the New York gang, to be robbed of the last farthing that he can be persuaded to part with; and he is possibly induced to spend the savings of years in the purchase of land, supposed to be in the far west, but having no other existence but such as paper and lies can give it.

It is in the neighbourhood of the Waterloo and northwards to the Clarence Dock that the principal lodging-houses for poor emigrants are to be found, more especially about Denison-street, Regent-street, Carlton-street, Porter-street, Stewart-street, and Great Howard-street—most of them of the filthiest kind, externally and internally. The wretched accommodation provided for the multitudes of emigrants that daily pass into Liverpool, to await the departure of the vessels by which they have secured their passage, and the robberies of all kinds to which they are subjected during their stay, are evils that the philanthropic citizens of Liverpool, who feel for the misery of their fellow-creatures, might well hasten to remedy. An example of the mode in which this end might be accomplished has been set them by the enterprizing German alluded to in a previous part of this letter. This gentleman, who has entered upon the large speculation of drawing through Liverpool the tide of German emigration that now flows through Hamburg, Havre, and other continental ports, has taken a spacious and commodious building, almost immediately adjoining the new terminus of the Liverpool and Bury, or East Lancashire Railway, in Moorfields. This building was formerly a hotel, and was afterwards occupied as a temporary stock exchange, and for other commercial purposes. Mr. Sabel, the gentleman alluded to, having entered into arrangements for bringing over to Liverpool the first division of about 400 German emigrants, conceived it to be both his interest and his duty to provide proper accommodation for them on their arrival. For this purpose he engaged the building I have mentioned—a building ample enough to contain them all very comfortably, and indeed a much larger number. The establishment was not completely furnished, nor made ready in other respects, when I visited it, but workmen were busily employed in putting it into substantial and decorative order. The dormitories are large, light, and airy; the dining and sitting rooms are not only comfortable but luxurious, and the whole building is abundantly supplied with gas, water, and fresh air. The kitchens are also large and commodious, and it is part of the proprietor's plan to combine the advantages of a reading room and library with the other conveniences of the establishment. The emigrants will here be boarded and lodged at moderate rates, according to a fixed tariff, legibly printed, and exhibited conspicuously in every room of the house. Private rooms may be engaged by families; and the proprietor will provide, at a moderate and fair rate, for such as choose to use the establishment for the purpose, all the articles that emigrants really require on the voyage—such as bedding, clothes, cooking utensils, provisions, &c. Such an establishment is greatly needed in Liverpool for the Irish as well as for the Germans, and it would conduce very much to the prosperity of the port, and do credit to the character of the town, if half a dozen or a dozen of similar buildings were constructed in the neighbourhood of the Docks, and placed under proper superintendence. Not only would the health of the town be improved by the diminution in the number of low, dark, overcrowded, and pestilential lodging-houses, but thousands of poor people would be rescued during their stay in Liverpool from demoralizing and debasing influences, and would reach America purer in mind and richer in pocket than they can do under the present miserable system, under which they are in every sense "taken in and done for" by the man-catching lodging-house keepers. It is to be hoped that the speculation of Mr. Sabel may be successful, not only because success is due to him who originates a praiseworthy undertaking, but because his success will have the effect of inducing other enterprising men to imitate his example. The attention of the principal merchants and inhabitants has been already directed to the subject, and a public meeting has been held, at which a resolution was passed to the effect that those present, feeling the great importance of emigration to this country as well as to the colonies, deemed it necessary that measures should be immediately taken for the protection of emigrants, and for the improvement of their physical and moral condition during their stay in port. During the spring and summer months there cannot be less than 4,000 emigrants in Liverpool on any one day, and in the winter months about half that number; so that ten or twelve establishments, similar in size and appointments to that of Mr. Sabel, would not be too many for their accommodation. Some time ago the members of the Dock Committee, being fully impressed with the importance of the subject, both to the plundered emigrants and to the character and trade of the town of Liverpool, offered to co-operate with Government in providing the needful accommodation in the new Northern Docks; but the Government declined to contribute any portion of the funds, and the project fell to the ground. There is, however, no necessity for the aid of Government in such a matter as this. The appointment of a Government officer, to see that the ships are sea-worthy—that proper conveniences for health and comfort are established, and that a due stock of provisions and water be laid in—is all that can reasonably be expected from the State. Private enterprise, or the municipal aid of the town of Liverpool, which is peculiarly interested in the amount of traffic passing through it and in the preservation of its own good character, ought to be amply sufficient to provide accommodation and protection for emigrants, while they remain in the town.

It must not be supposed, from the statements in reference to the rogueries practised by "runners and man-catchers" upon the simple emigrants, that the emigrants themselves do not occasionally endeavour to commit frauds, both upon each other, and upon the owners and captains of ships. The Irish emigrant, with the passion for hoarding which is so common among his countrymen, often hides money in his rags, and tells a piteous tale of utter destitution in order to get a passage at a cheaper rate. The shameless beggary, which is perhaps the greatest vice of the lower classes of Irish, does not always forsake them, even when they have determined to bid farewell to the old country; and I have several times been accosted by men and women on board emigrant ships in dock, and asked for contributions to help them when they got to New York. "Sure, yer honor, and may the Lord spare you to long life;—I've paid my last farden for my passage," said a sturdy Irishwoman with a child in her arms, whom I saw on the quarter-deck of the fine ship the Isaac Webb, in the Waterloo Dock; "and when I get to New York I shall have to beg in the strates, unless yer honor will take pity on me." I asked her to show me her ticket. She said her husband had it; and her husband, a wretched-looking old man, making his appearance and repeating the same story, I pressed him to show me the document. He did so at last, and I saw that he had paid upwards of £17 for the passage of himself and wife, and his family of five children. "And do you mean to say that you have no money left?" I inquired of him. "Not one blessed penny," said the man: "No, nor a fardin," said the woman, "and God knows what'll become of us." "Do you know nobody in New York?" I next inquired. "Not a living sowle, yer honor." "Have you no luggage?" "Not a stick, or a stitch, but the clothes we wear." As I did not believe the story, I declined to give them anything. The Isaac Webb was detained two days beyond her advertised time of sailing, and all the emigrants, as usual, had liberty to pass to and from the ship to the streets, as caprice or convenience dictated. On the following day, I saw this sturdy woman and her husband entering the Waterloo Dock gates with a donkey-cart, tolerably well piled with boxes, bedding, and cooking utensils. I watched them on board the Isaac Webb, and when they were down in the steerage—where it was not very light, and I judged they would not recognise me—I asked the woman, who was busily assorting her bedding, whether that was her luggage? She replied that it was. "You told me yesterday, when you were begging, that you had no luggage." "Sure it's a hard world, yer honor, and we're poor people—God help us."

An incident of a kind not very dissimilar occurred on board of another American liner, the West Point. When the passenger roll was called over, it was found that one man, from the county Tipperary, had only paid an instalment upon his passage-money, and that the sum of 25s. each for three persons, or £3 15s., was still due from him. On being called upon to pay the difference, he asserted vehemently that he had been told in the broker's-office that there was no more to pay, and that to ask him for more was to attempt a robbery. The clerk coolly insisted upon the money, and showed him the tickets of other passengers to prove the correctness of the charge. The man then changed his tone, and declared that he had not a single farthing left in the world, and that it was quite impossible he could pay any more. "Then you and your family will be put on shore," said the clerk, "and lose the money you have already paid." The intending emigrant swore lustily at the injustice, and declared that, if put ashore, he would "get an act of Parliament" to put an end to such a system of robbery. The clerk, however, was obdurate; and the man disappeared, muttering as he went that he would have his "act of Parliament" to punish the broker, the clerk, and the captain. He returned in a few minutes from below; and, without saying a word of what had happened, and looking as unconcerned as a stranger, coolly presented a £5 note, and asked for his change.

Such is a specimen of the rogueries attempted by those who have money. Those who really have none at all, or who possibly have not sufficient to pay their passage, resort to other schemes for crossing the Atlantic at a reduced rate, or free of charge altogether, and "stow away." This is a practice which is carried on to a great and increasing extent. I reserve the particulars for a future letter.

LABOUR AND THE POOR.

LIVERPOOL.

[FROM OUR SPECIAL CORRESPONDENT.]

DEPARTURE OF EMIGRANT VESSELS—THE STOW-AWAYS—THE ROLL-CALL.

LETTER X.

The Passenger Act of the 12th and 13th Victoria, besides specifying the berth-room, general accommodation, and stock of provisions for each passenger, regulates in a variety of ways the observances to be adopted for the health and comfort of emigrants prior and subsequent to sailing. No passenger ship is allowed to proceed to sea until a medical practitioner, approved by the emigration officer of the port, shall have inspected the medicine chest and passengers, and certified that the medicines, &c., are sufficient, and that the emigrants are free from all contagious disease. For this service the medical practitioner receives a fee of a guinea per 100 passengers. The first business, therefore, that the intending emigrant has to perform after paying his passage-money, is to present himself at the medical inspector's office. Having done this, and been passed as free from disease, his ticket is stamped to show that he has undergone inspection. Three lists of all the passengers are made out:—One for the Government Emigration Agent, one for the Custom-house, and one for the ship. But the inspection alluded to is not the only medical examination the emigrant has to undergo. The city and state of New York, as well as Boston, Philadelphia, and other parts, have become very particular as to the kind of emigrants they will permit to land. They were so much alarmed by the appearance of the myriads of wretched creatures whom the potato rot and the cholera drove from Ireland across the Atlantic, that they issued stringent regulations, not only against the admission of persons suffering from contagious diseases, but against cripples and deformed people. Although the state of New York does not positively prohibit the immigration of the helpless, disabled, and deformed, it renders the captain of every emigrant vessel which brings them over, liable to a penalty of $75 for every such immigrant, and holds him responsible for the sustenance of every such person, for three years clear, without burdening the charities, public or private, of the city of New York. The only exception made is in the case of deformed or helpless immigrants who belong to families already settled in America, and who will undertake the charge of them. A pole-tax, or commutation money, of a dollar and a half per passenger is also levied upon all immigrants, the proceeds of which are devoted to the support of the hospitals of New York. The captain of every emigrant ship had formerly to sign a bond for the support, without charge on the public charity, for three full years of every steerage passenger whom he brought over, but the obligation was never enforced, and became, in fact, a dead letter. The regulation has since been abolished, and the commutation money has been raised from one dollar, its former amount, to one dollar and a half, at which it is now fixed. In consequence of these regulations a supplementary inspection of the emigrants by the medical officer of the ship takes place as soon after the ship has left the docks as the list of the passengers can be called over.

It sometimes happens that a ship cannot sail on the advertised day, either because she has not taken in her cargo, or because she has room for additional emigrants, or because the weather may be adverse. In this case, should the passengers themselves be ready to embark, they are entitled to recover from the owner, charterer, or master of the ship, "subsistence money," at the rate of 1s. a day each. Should the detention be solely caused by wind and weather, and the passengers be maintained on board with the same provisions and water as if they were at sea, the subsistence money is not payable. In consequence of the regulation of the Liverpool Dock Trust which prohibits the use of fire and light on board of ships in the docks, these detentions, as stated in a previous letter of this series, are often the cause of considerable hardship to the poor people.

The Waterloo Dock is the principal station of the American liners in the port of Liverpool. A description of the departure of one or two of these vessels, and of the scenes on board, both in the dock and in the Mersey, as well as an account of conversations held at various times with all classes of emigrants, may serve to convey an idea of that busy and interesting scene, the departure of a large emigrant ship with a full complement of passengers. It was a beautiful morning when I proceeded to witness the departure of the Star of the West, Captain

Lowber commander, a fine new ship, then on her first voyage, and registering 1,200 tons. The scene in the dock at half-past eight in the morning was busy and animated in the extreme. All the cargo was on board, consisting principally of iron rails, the exportation of which to America is very largely on the increase. The greater part of the passengers was also on board; but every minute until half-past nine there was a fresh arrival of emigrants and their luggage. In consequence of the regulations, both of the British and American Governments, it was to be presumed that the living freight of the Star of the West was in good condition, and duly certified to be unlikely to become chargeable to our Transatlantic brethren of New York. It must be confessed, however, that they did not present a very favourable specimen of the genus man. Destitution and suffering, long-continued, possibly for generations, had done their work upon the greater number of them. It was not alone their personal uncleanliness and their wretched attire, but the haggard, sallow, and prematurely aged expression of their faces, that conveyed the idea of degradation and deterioration. The retreating forehead—the small sunken nose—the projecting jaws—the protruding teeth—and the listless, vacant look, were common amongst both old and young, and forcibly recalled the description of the Irish of the southern and western districts, made by Mr. Gavan Duffy, himself an Irishman, and not disposed, it may be presumed, to exaggerate a description to the disadvantage of his countrymen. "I saw," said he, "in the streets of Galway, crowds of creatures more debased than the Yahoos of Swift; creatures having only a distant and hideous resemblance to human beings; grey-headed old men, whose faces had hardened into a settled leer of mendicancy, simeous and semi-human; and women filthier and more frightful than the harpies." There were many such Irish people as these on board the Star of the West on the morning of her departure; and the general appearance of the majority to whom such a description would not apply, was weakly and care-worn, bespeaking extreme poverty, neglect and apathy. There was one family of Germans on board—a father and mother, and four grown up and two younger children—whose appearance was in striking contrast with that of the Irish. The man was from Bavaria—a tall, well-formed, strapping "kerl" full fed and ruddy, and looking as if he could do no ordinary duty in felling the primeval forests of the Far West, and converting the wilderness into a garden. There were also two or three English families on board—the men easily recognizable by the smock-frock of the English peasantry, and the women by their superior neatness of attire. With these few exceptions the passengers were all Irish. The whole number of passengers was 385, of whom about 360 were Irish.

As the hour of departure drew nigh, the scene in the dock, on the quay, and on board, became more and more animated. The morning sun shone brightly—the sky was without a cloud—a forest of masts from all the surrounding docks pointed their delicate traceries against the deep blue of the heavens, and the star-spangled banner flapped to the fresh breeze. Another emigrant ship in the same dock, whose turn to be towed out was before ours, began to move slowly from her berth. This vessel was the Queen of the West. Like our own, she was filled as full as she could hold with Irish emigrants. It was an interesting scene as she moved slowly past us, to observe her decks crammed with passengers, her flags streaming to the wind, and to hear the sailors raising their peculiar and joyous chant as they trod in a circle at the windlass. As soon as she passed through the dock-gates it was our turn to move, but all our passengers were not on board. Until the very last moment, they kept arriving by twos and threes, with their luggage on their backs. Here might be seen a strong fellow carrying a chest or a barrel, and a whole assemblage of tin cans and cooking utensils; and there a woman with a child in one arm and her goods and chattels in the other. When the planks and gangways were removed, at least fifty of our emigrants had not arrived, and many of them had to toss their luggage on board from the quay, and to clamber on to the ship by the rigging, as she passed through the dock-gates. The men contrived to jump on board with comparative ease; but by the belated women, of whom there were nearly a score, the feat was not accomplished without much screaming and hesitation. One valiant fellow, who had been drinking overmuch with his friends on shore, made an attempt to leap aboard as the vessel was clearing the dock-gates, but miscalculating the distance he fell into the water. There was a general rush of people to the side of the ship, and a screaming among the women, but fortunately there was a boat alongside which rescued the man in less than a minute, and placed him on deck dripping wet, and considerably more sober than when he fell into the water.

We had not quite cleared the dock when another incident oc-curred. The cook had failed to keep his promise to be on board before the ship's departure, and the captain was informed that he had ex-pressed his determination to remain in Liverpool. This was an annoy-ing circumstance to occur at the last moment. The steward, it also appeared, had made a similar determination; he was a coloured man, and had come on board to tender to the captain the wages he had received in advance, and to state that he was too unwell to undertake a voyage across the Atlantic. Hearing some altercation on the quarter-deck, the passengers turned their eyes in that direction, where the steward was seen tendering the money, and declaring loudly, that he would not go back to America. "You cannot hang me for it," he said to the captain, "and I will not go." The captain, who displayed much equanimity, insisted, that as the steward was on board he would keep him there, and take him out to America, whether he liked it or not. The steward, who certainly looked ill, was of another mind; and, springing to the side of the vessel, jumped overboard into the dock before a hand could be raised to prevent him. He swam like a fish, and reached in safety another vessel at the distance of about fifty yards. This was provoking, but there was no redress, unless the captain chose to delay his voyage until he could arrest the man in Liverpool and bring the case before the stipendiary magistrate. In the meantime the steward was out of reach, and the captain had no other resource than to leave his ship in the Mersey and return to Liverpool for another cook and steward, to be picked up at an hour's notice.

We were towed towards New Brighton by a steam-tug for the distance of three or four miles, during which the scene in the steerage below was as animated, though scarcely so cheerful, as the scene on deck. The steerage was somewhat dark, but in the uncertain light a picture presented itself full of strange "effects." The floor was strewed with luggage, rendering it a matter of difficulty to walk—bundles, trunks, cases, chests, barrels, loaves of bread, sides of bacon, and tin cooking utensils, seemed to be piled together in hopeless and inextricable confusion, while amidst them all scrambled or crawled a perfect multitude of young children. All the berths were occupied. Some of the passengers seemed as if they had resolved to go to sleep even at that early period of the voyage. Some were eating their breakfasts in their berths, and some were making use of barrel-heads and trunks for tables and chairs, and regaling themselves with bread and coffee. Here and there a man might be seen shaving himself in the dim and uncertain light; while at other parts of the ample steerage, families were busily looking after their worldly goods, and establishing a demarcation between their own property and that of their neighbours. In some of the berths women were sitting up conversing; and in others children were singing, hallooing, and shouting, as if the excitement of the scene were to them a joy indeed. There was a constant rushing to and fro, a frequent stumbling over chests and barrels, and a perfect Babel of tongues. All was life, bustle, and confusion; but what seemed most singular, there was nothing like sorrow or regret at leaving England. There was not a wet eye on board—there had been no fond leave-takings, no farewells to England, no pangs of parting. Possibly there was no necessity for any. To ninety-nine out of every hundred of these emigrants the old country had been in all probability an unkind mother, a country of sorrow and distress, associated only with remembrances of poverty and suffering. I must confess that I expected to see something like the expression of a regret that the shores of old England would soon fade from their view for ever—something like melancholy at the thought that never more were they to revisit the shores of Europe; but nothing of the kind occurred. All was noise, hurry, and animation. They had made up their minds for a long journey; hope was before them, and nothing was behind them but the remembrance of misery. It was possible also that the leave-takings had taken place in Ireland, and that whatever sorrow they felt had been shown before their arrival in England. As soon as the steam-tug had drawn us about five miles up the Mersey, we dropped anchor, and disembarrassed ourselves of what the mate called the whole "fraternity" of orange girls, and other merchants of small wares, who had until that time accompanied us, to ply their trade among the emigrants. What with orange girls, cap merchants, and dealers in Everton-toffy, ribbons, laces, pocket mirrors, gingerbread nuts, sweetmeats, &c., there must have been nearly forty interlopers to be sent back to Liverpool. The steam-tug took charge of them all, as well as of the captain, who had to return in search of a cook and steward—and the Star of the West was left to the crew and passengers, and about half a dozen visitors.

The steam-tug had no sooner taken her departure than all the passengers were summoned on deck, that their names might be read over, their tickets produced, and a search made in the steerage, and in every hole and corner of the ship, for "stow-aways." The practice of stowing away has, it appears, very much increased of late years; and although the strictest search is invariably made before the emigrant ships leave the Mersey, a voyage is seldom completed without the discovery, when out in the Atlantic, of two or three of these unfortunates. In one voyage the captain of the Star of the West, then commanding the Montezuma, was favoured with the company of no less than ten stow-aways of both sexes, who had secreted themselves about the ship, until it was far out at sea, and had then presented themselves before him, without money or luggage. The manner in which the stow-aways contrive to elude the vigilance of the crew is surprising. They sometimes have accomplices among the steerage passengers, and sometimes have no other reliance than their own patience and impudence. In the first case, they are brought on board in barrels, or in large chests, with air holes bored in them, and placed among the luggage until the dreaded ceremony of the roll-call and production of the tickets is over, when they emerge from their hiding-places, and are fed during the voyage by the charity of those who are in their secret. In the instances where they have no friend on board they hide themselves in the hold, or about the steerage, in every unlikely corner they can find, and when starved into the necessity of avowing what they have done, boldly show themselves and claim their food. It is a puzzling matter how to deal with them. A captain can neither return with them nor throw them overboard, nor can he starve them to death by refusing them as much meal and water as will keep them alive till they reach New York; and if he punishes them by imprisonment they reconcile themselves to it, well knowing that after all they must be landed in America, and that the object they had in view will be accomplished. So great is their misery at home, and so exalted are their hopes of doing better in America, that they are contented to run all possible risks of the punishment or hardship that may be inflicted upon them on board. The practice, however, has other dangers than these, and cases have occurred in which the unhappy "stow-aways" have been suffocated in the chests or barrels in which they have been concealed. But such extreme cases are comparatively rare, and the worst fate that usually befalls the stow-away is the degradation of being compelled to perform all the dirty work of the ship. Sometimes a miserable wight is compelled to walk the deck in the bitter cold for a certain number of hours, without any protection from the weather; but it is seldom that a captain resorts to such useless and vindictive cruelty.

One captain, however, was so annoyed by the constant appearance of stow-aways in his vessel, in spite of all the precautions he adopted, that he resolved to tar and feather, in American backwood or "Lynch" fashion, the first he found. He was as good as his word, and sent a wretched stow-away back in the steam-tug to Liverpool in this painful plight. The man complained to Mr. Rushton, the magistrate, and the captain, aware that he had broken the law, and was liable to punishment for it, has not since returned to Liverpool. But, notwithstanding all the severity that is sometimes shown, and the fatal accidents that occur to the unhappy people who stow themselves away, the practice continues. A stow-away was lately discovered, almost dead, in a barrel of salt. A woman was taken out of a chest, after the vessel had been twenty-four hours at sea, with her limbs so cramped and benumbed, and so weak and exhausted as to be unable to stand up for a fortnight. On one occasion when a large cask was being hoisted over the side of an emigrant-vessel, the top of the cask gave way, and a man fell out, head-foremost into the dock, whence he was rescued with some difficulty. When a captain or any of the crew suspects a box or barrel to contain a stow-away, and he does not like to break it open, he resorts to the expedient of placing it on end, so that the stow-away, if one be concealed, must be made to stand on his head. This discipline, after a few minutes, seldom fails to make the wretched prisoner disclose himself, and call for mercy. It is generally extreme poverty that causes men, women, and children, to subject themselves to this danger; but cases have occurred in which the "stow-away" had money. A few weeks before the departure of the Star of the West, a stow-away was detected, before the ship left the Mersey, and sent ashore. He stated before the magistrate that he had paid a sovereign to a man-catcher for concealing him and taking him on board in a trunk. The statement was ascertained to be correct, and a warrant issued for the apprehension of the man-catcher. A remarkably stout man, six feet high, who had stowed himself away in a chest, was pointed out to me in the streets. The vessel in which he was concealed, the John R. Skiddy, was wrecked on the coast of Ireland, and he made his way back to Liverpool with the other passengers. How so bulky an individual could have crammed himself into a chest was difficult to imagine.

It was some time before the whole of our 385 passengers could be got together on the quarter-deck; but as soon as the matter was accomplished, and a rope drawn across, and men stationed at the gangways to prevent any access to the lower parts of the vessel, the search for stow-aways was commenced. The officer appointed by the agents and owners for the purpose, accompanied by the mate and a certain number of the crew, and by a few visitors, proceeded to the steerage, carrying lights, and armed with long sticks to poke under the berths, and to sound the depths of obscure and difficult corners, and with hammers to thump the bedding in the berths. Not a cranny in the Star of the West was left unsearched on this occasion; beds were unrolled, and mattresses hammered and shaken, lest men and women should be hidden amongst them. The long sticks [which some captains use with prongs at the end] were thrust under every berth, and into every nook of the vessel; suspicious-looking barrels were shaken, rolled about, or turned upside down; all trunks large enough to contain man, woman, or child, were subjected to the most jealous and persevering scrutiny, and turned upon end, back again, upside down, and in every way, to make a human being, if inside, manifest his presence by his shouts for release. No corner or hole was considered too small or unlikely to be searched; but this time the search was made in vain. No stow-aways were discovered, and we discontinued the scrutiny, not without a remark from one of the sailors—That, notwithstanding all the vigilance that had been exercised, some of the "creatures" would show themselves as soon as the ship was out at sea.

Searching for Stowaways

This ceremony over, the next ceremony, equally important— which was that of the "roll-call"—was commenced. Taking his stand upon the rail of the quarter-deck, that he might overlook the crowd, the clerk of the agents produced a list of the passengers, and began to call over their names. The first upon the list were Patrick Hoolaghan, his wife, Bridget Hoolaghan, and a family of seven children. The Hoolaghans, after some little difficulty, were all found; and, room being made for them, they passed to the gangway, produced their tickets, and were then ushered to the steerage, free to their berths and to all the privileges of the passage. The next was Bernard McDermott and a family of six. Not making his appearance with proper speed, the man on the rail raised a loud shout for "Barney," and made a touching appeal to his justice not to keep the ship waiting. Barney turned up in due time, and proved to be an utter Irishman—in face, voice, vesture, and attire—and skipped triumphantly down the gangway with his ticket in his hand, followed by the whole of the younger generation of the McDermotts. The next were Philip Smith, his wife, and eight children—a congregation of Smiths whose name and numbers excited a shout of laughter among the passengers. A request was made by some one in the crowd that if there were any more Smiths on the list their names might be called out at once, so that the whole tribe might be done with. The man on the rail was condescending enough to comply, and five other families of Smiths were duly called and as duly made their appearance amid the laughter and jeers of the assemblage. Patrick Boyle was next in order. Patrick, it appeared, was rather deaf, and did not answer to his name—

> "Paddy Bile,
> Come here awhile,"

shouted the man on the rail. The rhyme had no effect, and it was begun to be surmised that Paddy was not on board, when he was led forward by the collar by a fellow-passenger, as if he had been a culprit who had been caught in the act of picking a pocket. He looked nothing abashed or angry at the treatment, and after fumbling in his breast, in his coat, and in his waistcoat pocket, produced the proper receipt for his passage money; and was ushered down the gangway amid expressions from every side that were far from complimentary to his beauty or his sagacity. "Joseph Brown" was told to "come down." "William Jones" was asked to "show his bones," and various other rhymes were perpetrated upon the names of the laggards, to the great amusement of all the people on deck. The whole ceremony lasted for upwards of an hour and a half, and offered nothing remarkable but the discovery of an attempted fraud on the part of a very old couple of Irish people. In procuring their ticket they had represented their son, who was to accompany them, as under twelve years of age, and had only paid half price for him. The boy of twelve years of age, on being compelled to show himself, turned out to be a strapping young man of eighteen or nineteen. "You must pay full price," said the man on the rail, "or I shall be under the necessity of taking 'this little boy' ashore with me, and of allowing you to go to New York without him." The old woman burst into tears, and expressed her determination not to be parted from her child. The old man thrust his hands into his pockets and said nothing. "Come, pay the money," said the agent, "I have not a penny in the world nor so much as a farthing," replied the old man, "so you must just put us all ashore." "Get up their luggage and send them ashore," was the order given—but the old man said they need not trouble themselves, they had no luggage, nothing but the clothes they stood up in, and tin cans for their day's allowance of water. The old woman all this time was weeping bitterly, and cling-ing fast hold to her son, whose breast heaved violently, although he neither shed a tear nor spoke a word. It afterwards appeared, from the old man's statement, that he had a son in a situation in New York, and some of the passengers came forward and offered to be security that the son in New York would pay the amount of his defalcation. After considerable discussion, it was agreed that if they would pay 10s. down, the lad should be permitted to cross the Atlantic, and the sum was speedily raised by subscription among the passengers. This ended the roll-call.

This ceremony had scarcely concluded when a small boat from the town came alongside. It contained the coloured steward, who had jumped overboard in the Waterloo Dock. He still wore his wet boots and trowsers, but had obtained a dry shirt and jacket; he shook as if he had the ague, and his teeth chattered audibly. The two boatmen had him prisoner, and entreated very earnestly that the mate, who leaned over the side of the vessel to see what was the matter, would relieve them of their charge. They said the captain had met him in the town, and put him in their boat, with orders to take him out to the ship. They had been obliged to hold him forcibly down all the way for fear of his jumping overboard and being drowned. The mate remonstrated with the steward on his folly, and asked him to come on board peaceably, without making "such an ass of himself." The steward peremptorily declined. "If you force me on board, you will murder me," he said,

Quarter-deck of an Emigrant Ship—The Roll-Call

"for I swear, by heaven, I will jump overboard at the first opportunity." "Nonsense," said the mate, "I must do my duty. Lift him up." "Take care, I beg of you," said the steward, crying like a child, "I am a ruined man. I am ruptured already, and I ought to go to the hospital. Do not commit murder by forcing me on board. I know you are only doing your duty; but don't, don't, don't murder me." He made a desperate attempt to break from the two boatmen, who held him by the arms, and to leap overboard, and it was with the utmost difficulty that he could be retained in his seat. The mate descended into the boat, amid the earnest entreaties of all the passengers that he would let the poor man return to Liverpool. It soon became evident to the mate that the steward was in earnest, and that there was no possibility of getting him into the ship, unless by tying his arms and legs and lifting him up like a bale of goods, and that the determination and desperation of the man was such, that even if on board, it would be necessary to place him under restraint, to prevent his laying violent hands upon himself. It was clear that such a steward would be of no use on board. After a long parley, during which the moans and prayers of the steward that they would not be guilty of taking his life by forcing him on board were painful to hear, the mate gave up the contest as hopeless, and the boat returned towards Liverpool. There was now no necessity for holding him down, and the sick man stood up in the boat, and waved his cap to bid farewell to the ship, and to his late companions.

The visitors shortly afterwards quitted the Star of the West, with the clerk of the agents, and returned to Liverpool in a small boat. The vessel remained at anchor awaiting the return of her captain, with a new cook and steward. On the following morning, when I walked along the noble esplanade of the Prince's Dock, and looked towards the place where I left her, she was not to be seen. She had proceeded out to sea with a favourable wind.

The ceremonies of the search for "stow-aways" and the roll-call occupied too much of my attention in my visit to the Star of the West to permit me to make inquiries among the emigrants themselves as to their ideas of the New World, their prospects in it, and their reasons for preferring the United States to the British colonies. But in subsequent visits to other vessels that sailed within the succeeding five or six weeks, more especially the West Point, Captain Allen, the New World, Captain Knight, the Isaac Webb, Captain Cropper, and the Yorkshire, Captain Shearman, I took occasion to enter more fully into this part of the subject. The West Point sailed with nearly 400 emigrants, of whom about 60 were Welsh and English, and the remainder Irish, of the same class as those which sailed in the Star of the West. The Isaac Webb, a splendid new vessel, with a double steerage, took out no less than 780 souls, of whom, as usual, the large majority were Irish. The second-class cabins on board of this ship were exclusively occupied by English emigrants, the price of a berth varying from £6 to £7, while the price paid by the Irish in the steerage ranged at about £4. The New World took out about 450 emigrants, as nearly as I could ascertain, more than three-fourths of whom were Irish. The Yorkshire left the Waterloo Dock with nearly 400, but as she had room for many more, she lay in the Mersey for four-and-twenty hours, and ultimately sailed with a full complement. The second-class passengers, as indeed was the case in all the vessels that I visited, were English farm-labourers, small farmers, and respectable mechanics, while the steerage was invariably occupied by the Irish. Occasionally a few English, Welsh, and Scotch were to be found among the steerage passengers; but, generally speaking, the Irish had the steerage to themselves.

On going down into the steerage of the Isaac Webb, on the day originally fixed for her departure, a characteristic scene presented itself. Just under the hatchway, though not within view of the people on deck, two young men were seated, each upon a barrel, vehemently engaged in fiddling, for the amusement of a crowd of about seventy emigrants, composed of men and women of all ages, and of attentive and delighted children who had gathered around them. These young men were emigrants, and not straggling fiddlers, picking up a livelihood in this manner. They were dressed in the ordinary garb of the Irish peasantry, patched and ragged enough, and were fiddling to the people for love, not money. After a time a space was cleared between decks—the emigrants, young and old, sat down upon their boxes or barrels, or upon the edges of their berths, while the children formed a ring at a little distance. An Irish reel was then got up. A ruddy-cheeked young woman, with all the beauty peculiar to the people of the south of Ireland in their youth, but which privation and suffering do not suffer to adorn them until the prime of their womanhood, accepted the hand of an Irish gallant of about forty years of age, in a very ragged long-tailed coat; while another damsel, not so good looking, but brisk and cheerful, granted a similar favour to an Irish lad about her own age; and the reel began. What the exhibition wanted in elegance, it made up for in vigorous joyousness. The four danced as if dancing were a business to be gone into with all the mind, with all the soul, and with all the strength, and kept at it till mortal limbs could endure it no longer without a reviving period of repose. As soon as they were thoroughly exhausted, another party of four, including an old dame who looked nearly sixty, stepped into their vacant places, the whole assemblage at this time amounting to upwards of a hundred spectators, looking on with delighted gravity. The children were in ecstacies, and many of them kept time with their feet and hands to the music of the fiddlers. When this party, like the previous one, was tired out with the exertion, a very decently-dressed middle-aged man, with a good black coat and trowsers, and a clean neck-cloth, stepped forward and claimed the privilege of dancing a jig with a comely-looking woman who was nursing her child. No sooner said than done. His fair partner handed the child to a woman who sat next to her, and was up and ready in an instant. The man danced with a vigour that I never saw surpassed; and as I admired his evident satisfaction with the exercise, a young lad standing beside me volunteered the information that the dancer had originally been the manager of a large mill in the North of Ireland, and a person very well to do in the world. He danced until his partner could dance no longer, and kept up the jig by himself for fully ten minutes after she had slid back to her seat to resume possession of her child. A loud burst of applause greeted him when he sat down, and the fiddlers took a rest and refreshed themselves with cakes and oranges. After an interval of ten minutes, or a quarter of an hour, the dance was recommenced, and I left the group in the full enjoyment of their pastime. I was afterwards assured by the captain that such scenes were of common occurrence; and that very often the bagpipes, instead of the violin, was the instrument that set the feet of his passengers in motion. The ex-manager of the mill, who seemed a person of considerable education and experience, although so much reduced as to be compelled by hard fortune to emigrate in the steerage with the poorest classes of his countrymen, said he had brought a flute with him to make music for his fellow-travellers on their voyage, and thought that between him and the two violinists they might manage to amuse the people pretty well, and make the time pass agreeably on the Atlantic.

The scene when the Isaac Webb—crowded with passengers both above and below—passed through the dock gates was lively and peculiar. As usual, although the vessel was two days beyond the time of sailing, a great number of her passengers had delayed coming on board until the last moment. A considerable portion of those who had already placed their luggage on board, and who preferred to stroll about the town, or sit drinking in the beer-shops, to lingering in the dark steerage, were also among the absentees—and their sole chance of getting on board was at the dock gates, where the passage was not many inches wider than the deck of the vessel. At the critical moment, donkey-carts laden with luggage drove up—and the rush of those belated to get on board with their goods and chattels, was tremendous. Thick as flies upon a honey pot, they might be seen clambering over the side of the vessel, threading their difficult way among ropes and cordage. Here and there a woman becoming entangled, with her drapery sadly discomposed, and her legs still more sadly exposed to the loiterers on shore, might be heard imploring aid from the sailors or passengers above. Men might be seen, impeded with luggage, and hurling small casks and boxes on to the deck, and climbing after them with hot haste. Many a package, containing property of value to these poor people, missed its mark and fell into the dock, whence it was rescued, and handed up by a man in a small boat, who followed in the wake of the mighty ship. Ultimately the whole of the passengers got safely on board—although it is difficult to say how they managed it, amid the uproar, turmoil, confusion, and pressing of one over another, that occurred within the few minutes that the ship lay between the walls of the dock-gate. It was as difficult to get out of her as to get in, but several visitors took this opportunity of leaving her, and I among the number. When, at last, the ship cleared the gate, and floated right out into the Mersey, her full proportions became disentangled from the maze of shipping in which she had been formerly involved, and she seemed indeed to be a Leviathan. The spectators on shore took off their hats and cheered lustily, and the cheer was repeated by the whole body of emigrants on deck, who raised a shout that I supposed, must have been heard at the distance of a mile even in the noisy and busy thoroughfares of Liverpool.

The Departure

The departures of the West Point, the New World, and the York-shire were equally characteristic. The wind and weather being highly favourable on the day appointed for the sailing of the West Point, I proceeded twenty miles to sea in that vessel. We were nominally towed out by a "tug," but as soon as the broad sails of the West Point were spread to the propitious wind, the sailing vessel outstripped the steam-boat and we tugged the "tug." In conversation with the pas-sengers during the short but agreeable sail of twenty miles, I found that very many of them were going out to join friends and relatives in the United States who had preceded them years before, and who had forwarded them money to pay their passage. Some few were going to remain in the state of New York; but by far the greater proportion were bound for Ohio, Illinois, Wisconsin, and Missouri. Very few of them seemed to know whether Canada was, or was not, a British possession; and not one of the Irish to whom I put the question had ever heard of Nova Scotia, Newfoundland, or New Brunswick. One respectable-looking lad, of about twenty, said he had five pounds in his pocket. He knew no person in America, but as he had heard of the state of Ohio, and that land was cheap, and labour well paid, he was going thither to try his fortune. He was not, he said, afraid of hard work, and had no fear but that he should get on. The English emigrants in the second-class cabins knew all about Canada and the British North American possessions, but thought the United States preferable to either of them. "Besides," said one sturdy man from Lincolnshire, "we don't know what's to happen in Canada. It won't always belong to England, and there may be a 'rumpus.' It's all right in the States, and that's the place for my money." This man and his family were bound for Wisconsin. In conversation with him upon the generally respectable appearance of the English, the squalid appearance of the Irish emigrants, and the probability that a few years' residence in the New World would much improve the latter, both physically and morally, he showed me a passage in a cheap tract, just published, entitled "Nine Years in America. By Thomas Mooney; in a Series of Letters to his Cousin, Patrick Mooney, a farmer in Ireland," which bore upon the subject of our discourse. I re-produce the passage. "I have seen a thousand times," says Mr. Mooney, "the two growths of children from the same Irish parentage present a remarkable difference. Those born in America were brave, beautiful, and intellectual-looking—high foreheads, bright eyes, quick and intelligent. Those of the *same* parents, born before they left Ireland, wearing still the stamp of sorrow on their brow, and the stoop of suffering in their gait." Mr. Mooney, whose little tract contains much valuable information upon the subject of emigration, precedes this remark by the following statement of his experience:—

"In my travels in America, I was ever anxious to learn what effect political and religious freedom has put upon the moral tendencies of my own countrymen—the Irish. I now give a few of the results as indicated by the public prisons which I have personally visited. In Auburn state prison, the principal prison of New York state, there were in 1848, 680 criminals condemned for serious crimes, from periods of two years to the end of life. Of these but 45 were Irishmen. Though the Irish in

New York state bear a proportion of 1 to 6 of the whole, the criminals of Irish birth are but 1 to 15. There are two other prisons of this state, from which I have not yet got reports, but as this is the chief prison, I may be permitted to average the two at twice the relative numbers of Auburn, which will give us 1,360 criminals, of which say a hundred are Irish. In the chief prison of Pennsylvania, in 1848, the total number of prisoners was 120; of these only 12 were Irish. From the foundation of the prison in 1829, the total number of prisoners was 2,421; of these 199 were Irish, or 10 a year for twenty years. It must be noted the state of Pennsylvania is the most Irish in the Union; perhaps one-fourth of all are of that nation. In the chief prison of Massachusetts, at Charlestown, near Boston, in 1849, the whole number of criminals was 281; of these but 30 were Irish, though one in seven of the whole population is Irish. In the city of Boston and its suburbs, in a population of 120,000, full 40,000 are Irish. In the state of New Hampshire, at Concord, the state prison contains 77; of these the Irish are but twelve. The state prison of Connecticut, near to Hartford, in 1849, contained 150, of which 13 only were Irishmen. The state is crowded with Irishmen in the factories, and making railroads. The chief prison of the state of Illinois is at Alton, and the total number of prisoners in 1849 was 196; of these eight only were Irish. Though the Irish bear a proportion of one to eight of the whole population, the Irish criminals are one to fourteen and a half. These figures prove a wondrous and most gratifying result. The above returns are from six of the greatest states in the Union as to population, business, factories, and dense cities. In these six states, containing eight millions of people—more than one third of the whole—there are but 220 Irish criminals, though the Irish population in these six states is fully one million and a half! Taking the remaining states (from which I have not been able to procure returns), according to this showing, we have but some 500 or 600 Irishmen in prison, in the year 1848-49, in the republic. We may proudly compare this improvement in the moral condition of our countrymen, Patrick, with their condition in Ireland."

The large sums annually forwarded from the United States to Ireland for the purpose of paying the passage of friends and relations to the New World, prove to some extent that the statement of Mr. Mooney is founded in truth. It seems clear, however miserable and degraded the Irishman may be in his own country and in England, that his miseries and degradation are the consequences of social or political evils, which in the Old World he has not power to remedy, or even to struggle against, and that they are not the results of any innate imperfection in the Irish character. No man works harder than the Irishman, and his prosperity in the United States is a gratifying proof that he only requires a "fair field and no favour" to become a useful and happy member of society.

The emigrational movement, it will be seen, is much on the increase, both in England and in Ireland. Intending emigrants should beware, however, how they listen to the statements put forth by pretended "land associations." With regard to the colonies, the British Government, in its annual pamphlet, gives nearly all the information that is either useful or desirable; but as regards the United States, the emigrant has nothing to guide him truly, but the reports of friends who may have gone before him. Swindling associations take advantage of the popular ignorance, and placard the walls of our great towns with prospectuses, setting forth the advantages of particular districts, with the sole view of procuring a deposit of passage money. A placard, setting forth as follows the objects of "The United States Land and Emigration Society, and Working Men's Mutual Mining and Manufacturing Association," has been lately issued. It bears a number of names as directors, treasurers, engineers, managers of works, head miners, &c.; but none of them resident in England. It also bears the highly respectable names of the eminent Liverpool house of Brown, Shipley, and Co., as the bankers of the association. The attention of that firm was first directed to the concern by the following letter of inquiry:—

"Bolton, April 23, 1850.

"Gentlemen—Will you please to say, per return, if Mr. S. T., Manchester, is an agent for the Working Men's Mutual Mining and Manufacturing Association, or if you think it would repay me going so far, for I am a practical mechanic, and am well acquainted with spinning and manufacturing, and he pledges himself that I shall have work and remunerating wages for the same?

"I have a bill before me with your name as bankers for this association.

"Your answer will oblige your obedient servant,

(Signed)   "J. A.

"Messrs. Brown, Shipley, and Co."

Messrs. Brown, Shipley, and Co., immediately, on receipt of this letter, wrote to say that they had no knowledge whatever of the party who had thus made use of their name. They also placed the document in the hands of the police, both of Liverpool and Manchester, but hitherto all efforts to discover the parties who concocted the fraud have proved unavailing. Its publication in this place may perhaps be a warning to the working classes. The document ran as follows:—

> "Emigration to the Western States of America!—Under the Sanction and Charter of the United States Government for Mining and Manufacturing Purposes—The United States Land and Emigration Society, and Working Men's Mutual Mining and Manufacturing Association. Established 1846.
>
> "This society and association has been formed for operations in the 'Great Valley of the Ohio west of Alleghany Mountains,' for mining and manufacturing purposes, thereby assisting the oppressed working men in over-populated districts of the United Kingdom, and establishing them in a locality teeming with abundance in the richest mineral treasures of the earth, requiring only the aid of man to produce almost every article suited to the wants of mankind in general, with the greatest facility, on associative principles; having in abundance coal, iron, copper, lead, zinc, &c., with a soil equally prolific, reproducing luxuriantly all seeds committed to it, and bordered by the most extensive cotton districts, with a delightful and salubrious climate, pure air, and excellent water, as may be proved by the writings of every traveller through the Western region. As an encouragement to workmen, and for the bettering the condition of their families, twenty acres of land will be conveyed to each operative as a free gift, as in this state (Virginia) it is only required that each settler should have a property qualification of 25 dollars value, and a residence of two years to entitle them to citizenship. To secure which conditionally the society make the free gift, thereby entitling such parties to every privilege (except that of voting for two years), which they have to wait until after the declaration of intention, each head of a family being required to enter into arrangements for the purchase of 100 or more acres adjoining, with choice and privilege of selection, whereby their children may be instructed early in agriculture when not otherwise employed.
>
> "This grand work of philanthropy has been brought forward by American gentlemen, merchants, &c., and its works are in full operation, whereby they guarantee to every settler constant employment and remunerative wages, numbers of which are fast locating not only from Great Britain, but from Canada and the more eastern states.
>
> "All settlers are privileged to join with any or all of the several branches, as well as the manufacturing department. It is intended to manufacture all articles from the raw material of the mine as well as the cotton, for which works and mills are in course of erection.
>
> "The situation is most central, and bordered by 'the Great River Ohio,' which connects with the Mississippi, and is also intersected by

several fine navigable rivers, streams, &c., with turnpike roads to and from the leading cities and towns; so that there is every facility in the communication and transit of goods to the seaboard.

"There has several new towns lately sprung up as if by magic, showing at once that a rapid improvement has commenced in this portion of the United States; beside which, one line of railroad is now under construction, crossing the centre of these lands, with two others in preparations offering abundant employment to settlers.

"The proprietors of the foregoing sincerely hope that their care in the selection of settlers of good moral character may not be wrongly understood; as their object is purely the future welfare of all settlers and families, as well as present benefits, by selecting temperate, industrious persons as citizens, whereby a virtuous settlement may be formed in conjunction with the original, which are of the earliest origin, and they, therefore, use every discretion in laying the foundation of what must hereafter be the great manufacturing district of America. Therefore, we say, 'Judge ye of the future by the past.'

"For further information, see 'Emigrants' Directory,' price 2d.

"Every particular and necessary information to be had on application to the agent, at his office, Manchester, who is despatching ships every two days, at the lowest rates, for the comfort and convenience of passengers."

LABOUR AND THE POOR.

—◆—

LIVERPOOL.

[FROM OUR SPECIAL CORRESPONDENT.]

THE MORMONS, AND MORMON EMIGRATION.

LETTER XI.

During the course of my inquiry into the extent of emigration from the port of Liverpool, I learned that the followers of Joseph Smith, the Mormon Prophet, who are known by the names of "Mormons," "Mormonites," and "Latter-Day Saints," had many years ago established an emigrational agency in the town, having ramifications in all parts of England, Wales, and Scotland. I learned that the number of Mormon emigrants sailing from the port of Liverpool to New Orleans, on their way to Deseret and Upper California, during the year 1849, was no less than 2,500—chiefly farmers and mechanics of a superior class, from Wales, Lancashire and Yorkshire, and the southern counties of Scotland—and that since 1840 the total emigration of the sect from Great Britain has been between 13,000 and 14,000. Before entering into any further details of their emigrational proceedings, which, as will appear from the sequel, are highly interesting, and may be fraught with momentous consequences to the future peace of America, a slight sketch of the origin, progress, and present position of this remarkable sect, both in the United States and in Great Britain, will put the reader in possession of the facts necessary to the due comprehension of the subject. They unfold one of the most curious episodes in the modern history of the world, and certainly the most singular story in the recent annals of fanaticism.

The founder of the sect—Joseph Smith, jun., as he was called till within a year or two of his death—was born in 1805. The first congregation of Latter-day Saints was organized in 1831, and now, in less than twenty years, the sect numbers nearly 30,000 people in Great Britain, and about four times, or according to some statements six times, that number in America. Joseph Smith was a digger for gold before he took up the trade of preaching and prophesying; and to his people after his death belongs the merit, or the credit, of discovering the gold of California. The Mormons are now the principal inhabitants of a State to which they have given the name of "Deseret," a word that occurs in their new Bible, or Book of Mormon, and which is said to signify a "honey-bee." They expect, within a short time, by means of immigration from Great Britain, and by the gathering together of their people from all parts of the Union, to muster a sufficient number in Deseret to claim formal admission into the American Union. The number of inhabitants requisite for this purpose is 60,000, and there can be little, if any, doubt, that, in a few years, the object of the Mormons will be accomplished. The irritating and embarrassing, yet interesting and important, question of slavery in the Union will be again raised by their claim of admission, so that, if the statesmanship of the Union devise some plan for the admission of California which shall not displease the Southern slaveholders, this question will be merely adjourned. It may be tided over by a Californian compromise, but will revive in full vigour on the question of Deseret. Such is the present position of the Latter-day Saints. The growth of Mahomedanism, rapid as it was, is not to be compared to the rise and growth of Mormonism.

I now proceed to detail more particularly the history of Joseph Smith and the sect he founded—appending an abstract of their religious belief. To avoid the appearance of unfriendliness towards men who—whatever the character, or views of their leader may have been, or whatever may be thought of their own fanaticism—are carrying on a remarkable work, but little understood, or even heard of, in this country beyond the limits of their own body, I shall, whenever it is possible to do so, present their history in the words of their own writers, appending such statements as may be necessary for the exposition of the truth. The following particulars are extracted from the "Remarkable Visions" of Mr. Orson Pratt, their emigrational agent at Liverpool, a gentleman who styles himself, in the title-page, "One of the twelve Apostles of the Church of Jesus Christ of Latter-day Saints;" but who is styled in Liverpool, "Head Apostle of the Latter-day Saints in England, and chief Agent for the Church of Jesus Christ for all Europe:"—

"Mr. Joseph Smith, jun.," says Mr. Orson Pratt, "was born in the town of Sharon, Windsor County, Vermont, on the 23d December, 1805. When ten years old his parents, with their family, moved to

Palmyra, New York, in the vicinity of which he resided for about eleven years, the latter part in the town of Manchester. He was a farmer by occupation. His advantages for acquiring scientific knowledge were exceedingly small, being limited to a slight acquaintance with two or three of the common branches of learning. He could read without much difficulty, and write a very imperfect hand, and had a very limited understanding of the elementary rules of arithmetic. These were his highest and only attainments, while the rest of those branches so universally taught in the common schools throughout the United States were entirely unknown to him. When somewhere about fourteen or fifteen years old, he began seriously to reflect upon the necessity of being prepared for a future state of existence; but how, or in what way to prepare himself, was a question as yet undetermined in his own mind. He perceived that it was a question of infinite importance, and that the salvation of his soul depended upon a correct understanding of the same. He retired to a secret place in a grove, but a short distance from his father's house, and knelt down and began to call upon the Lord. At first he was severely tempted by the powers of darkness, which endeavoured to overcome him, but he continued to seek for deliverance until darkness gave way from his mind, and he was enabled to pray in fervency of the spirit, and in faith; and while thus pouring out his soul, anxiously desiring an answer from God, he at length saw a very bright and glorious light in the heavens above, which at first seemed to be at a considerable distance. He continued praying, while the light appeared to be gradually descending towards him; and as it drew nearer it increased in brightness and magnitude, so that by the time it reached the tops of the trees the whole wilderness around was illuminated in a most glorious and brilliant manner. He expected to see the leaves and boughs of the trees consumed as soon as the light came in contact with them; but perceiving that it did not produce that effect he was encouraged with the hopes of being able to endure its presence. It continued descending slowly, until it rested upon the earth, and he was enveloped in the midst of it. When it first came upon him, it produced a peculiar sensation throughout his whole system; and immediately his mind was caught away from the natural objects with which he was surrounded, and he was enwrapped in a heavenly vision, and saw two glorious personages, who exactly resembled each other in their features or likeness. He was informed that his sins were forgiven. He was also informed upon the subjects which had for some time previously agitated his mind—namely, that all the religious denominations were believing in incorrect doctrines, and consequently that none of them was acknowledged of God as his church and kingdom. And he was expressly commanded to go not after them; and he received a promise that the true doctrine, the fulness of the gospel, should at some future time be made known to him; after which the vision withdrew, leaving his mind in a state of calmness and peace indescribable. Some time after having received this glorious manifestation, being young, he was again entangled in the vanities of the world, of which he afterwards sincerely and truly repented.

"And it pleased God, on the evening of the 21st Sept., A.D. 1823, to again hear his prayer. It seemed as though the house was filled with consuming fire. This sudden appearance of a light so bright, as must naturally be expected, occasioned a shock of sensation visible to the extremities of the body. It was, however, followed with a calmness and serenity of mind, and an overwhelming rapture of joy, that surpassed understanding, and, in a moment, a personage stood before him.

"Notwithstanding the brightness of the light which previously illuminated the room, yet there seemed to be an additional glory surrounding or accompanying this personage, which shone with an increased degree of brilliancy, of which he was in the midst, and though his countenance was as lightning, yet it was of a pleasing, innocent, and glorious appearance, so much so, that every fear was banished from the heart, and nothing but calmness pervaded the soul.

"The stature of this personage was a little above the common size of men in his age; his garment was perfectly white, and had the appearance of being without seam.

"This glorious being declared himself to be an angel of God, sent forth by commandment to communicate to him that his sins were forgiven, and that his prayers were heard; and also to bring the joyful tidings that the covenant which God made with ancient Israel concerning their posterity was at hand to be fulfilled; that the great preparatory work for the second coming of the Messiah was speedily to commence; that the time was at hand for the gospel, in its fullness, to be preached in power unto all nations, that a people might be prepared with faith and righteousness for the Millennial reign of universal peace and joy.

"He was informed that he was called and chosen to be an instrument in the hands of God, to bring about some of his marvellous purposes in this glorious dispensation. It was also made manifest to him that the 'American Indians' were a remnant of Israel; that when they first emigrated to America they were an enlightened people, possessing a knowledge of the true God, enjoying his favour and peculiar blessings from his hand; that the prophets and inspired writers among them were required to keep a sacred history of the most important events transpiring among them, which history was handed down for many generations, till at length they fell into great wickedness. The greatest part of them were destroyed, and the records were safely deposited, to preserve them from the hands of the wicked, who sought to destroy them. He was informed that these records contained many sacred revelations pertaining to the Gospel of the kingdom, as well as prophesies relating to the great events of the last days; and that to fulfil his promises to the ancients, who wrote the records, and to accomplish his purposes in the restitution of their children, they were to come forth to the knowledge of the people. If faithful, he was to be the instrument who should be thus highly favoured in bringing these sacred writings, who should endeavour to aggrandize himself by converting sacred things to unrighteous and speculative purposes. After giving him many instructions concerning things past and to come, he disappeared, and the light and glory of God withdrew, leaving his mind in perfect peace, while a calmness and serenity indescribable pervaded the soul. But before morning the vision was twice renewed, instructing him further and still further concerning the great work of God about to be performed on the earth. In the morning he went out to his labour as usual, but soon the vision was renewed—the angel again appeared, and having been informed, by the previous visions of the night, concerning the place where those records were deposited, he was instructed to go immediately and view them.

"Accordingly he repaired to the place, a brief description of which shall be given in the words of a gentleman named Oliver Cowdery, who has visited the spot:

" 'As you pass on the mail-road from Palmyra, Mayne county, to Canandigua, Ontario county, New York, before arriving at the little village of Manchester, say from three to four, or about four miles from Palmyra, you pass a large hill on the east side of the road.

" 'It was at the second mentioned place where the record was found to be deposited, on the west side of the hill, not far from the top down its side; and when myself visited the spot in the year 1830 there were several trees standing—enough to cause a shade in summer, but not so much as to prevent the surface being covered with grass, which was also the case when the record was first found.

" 'How far below the surface these records were placed I am unable to say, but from the fact that they had been some fourteen hundred years buried, and that, too, on the side of a hill so steep, one is ready to conclude that they were some feet below, as the earth would naturally wear, more or less, in that length of time. But being placed towards the top of the hill, the ground would not remove as much as two-thirds perhaps. Another circumstance would prevent another wearing of the earth—in all probability, as soon as timber had time to grow, the hill was covered, and the roots of the same would hold the surface.

" 'However, on this point I shall leave every man to draw his own conclusion, and form his own speculation: but, suffice to say, a hole of sufficient depth was dug. At the bottom of this laid a stone of suitable size, the upper surface being smooth. At each edge was placed a large quantity of cement, and into this cement, at the four edges of this stone were placed erect four others, their bottom edges resting in the cement at the outer edges of the first stone. The four last named, when placed erect, formed a box; the corners, or where the edges of the four came in contact, were also cemented so firmly that the moisture from without was prevented from entering. It is to be observed also that the inner surfaces of the four erect or side stones were smooth. This box was sufficiently large to admit a breastplate such as was used by the ancients to defend the chest from the arrows and weapons of their enemy. From the bottom of the box, or from the breastplate, arose three small pillars, composed of the same description of cement used on the edges; and upon these three pillars were placed the records. This box containing the records was covered, with another stone, the bottom surface being flat, and the upper crowning.' When it was first visited by Mr. Smith, on the morning of the 22d of September, 1823, 'a part of the crowning stone was visible above the surface, while the edges were concealed by the soil and grass.' From which circumstance it may be seen 'that, however deep this box might have been placed at first, the time had been sufficient to wear the earth, so that it was easily discovered, when once directed, and yet not enough to make a perceivable difference to the passer-by.' 'After arriving at the repository, a little exertion in removing the soil from the edges of the top of the box, and a light lever, brought to his natural vision its contents.' While viewing and contemplating this sacred treasure, with wonder and astonishment—behold! the angel of the Lord, who had previously visited him, again stood in his presence, and his soul was again enlightened as it was the evening before, and he was filled with the Holy Spirit, and the heavens were opened, and the glory of the Lord shone round about and rested upon him. While he thus stood gazing and admiring, the angel said, 'Look!' And, as he thus spake, he beheld the Prince of Darkness, surrounded by his innumerable train of associates. All this passed before him, and the heavenly messenger said, 'All this is shown, the good and the evil, the holy and impure, the glory of God and the power of darkness, that you may know hereafter the two powers, and never be influenced or overcome by the wicked one. You cannot at this time obtain this record, for the commandment of God is strict, and if ever these sacred things are obtained, they must be by prayer and faithfulness in obeying the Lord. They are not deposited here for the sake of accumulating gain and wealth for the glory of this world; they were sealed by the prayer of faith, and because of the knowledge which they contained; they are of no worth among the children of men only for their knowledge. In them is contained the fulness of the Gospel of Jesus Christ, as it was given to his people on this land; and when it shall be brought forth by the power of God, it shall be carried to the Gentiles, of whom many will receive it, and after will the seed of Israel be brought into the fold of their Redeemer by obeying it also.'

"During the period of the four following years, he frequently received instruction from the mouth of the heavenly messenger. And on the morning of the 22d of September, A.D. 1827, the angel of the Lord delivered the records into his hands.

"These records were engraved on plates, which had the appearance of gold. Each plate was not far from seven by eight inches in width and length, being not quite as thick as common tin. They were filled on both sides with engravings in Egyptian characters, and bound together in a volume as the leaves of a book, and fastened at one edge with three rings running through the whole. This volume was something near six inches in thickness, a part of which was sealed. The characters or letters upon the unsealed part were small and beautifully engraved. The whole book exhibited many marks of antiquity in its construction, as well as much skill in the art of engraving. With the records was found 'a curious instrument, called by the ancients the Urim and Thummim, which consisted of two transparent stones, clear as crystal, set in the two rims of a bow. This was in use in ancient times, by persons called seers. It was an instrument by the use of which they received revelation of things distant, or of things past or future.'

"Having provided himself with a home, he commenced translating the record, by the gift and power of God, through the means of the Urim and Thummim; and being a poor writer, he was under the necessity of employing a scribe to write the translation as it came from his mouth.

"In the meantime, a few of the original characters were accurately described and translated by Mr. Smith, which, with the translation, were taken by a gentleman by the name of Martin Harris to the city of New York, where they were presented to a learned gentleman of the name of Anthon, who professed to be extensively acquainted with many languages, both ancient and modern. He examined them, but was unable to decipher them correctly; but he presumed that if the original records could be brought, he could assist in translating them.

"But to return—Mr. Smith continued the work of translation, as his pecuniary circumstances would permit, until he finished the unsealed part of the records. The part translated is entitled 'Book of Mormon,' which contains nearly as much reading as the Old Testament.

"After the book was translated, the Lord raised up witnesses to the nations of its truth, who, at the close of the volume, send forth their testimony, which reads as follows:—

" 'TESTIMONY OF THREE WITNESSES.

" 'Be it known unto all nations, kindreds, tongues, and people, unto whom this work shall come, that we through the Grace of God the Father, and our Lord Jesus Christ, have seen the plates which contain this record, which is a record of the people of Nephi and also of the Lamanites, their brethren, and also of the people of Jared, who came from the tower of which hath been spoken; and we also know that they have been translated by the gift and power of God, for his voice hath declared it unto us; wherefore we know of a surety that the work is true, and we also testify that we have seen the engravings which are upon the plates; and they have been shown unto us by the power of God, and not of man. And we declare, with words of soberness, that an angel of God came down from heaven, and he brought and laid before our eyes, that we beheld and saw the plates, and the engravings thereon; and we know that it is by the grace of God the Father and our Lord Jesus Christ that we beheld and bear record that these things are true, and it is marvellous in our eyes; nevertheless, the voice of the Lord commanded us that we should bear record of it; wherefore, to be obedient unto the commandments of God, we bear testimony of these things. And we know that if we are faithful in Christ we shall rid our garments of the blood of all men, and be found spotless before the judgment seat of Christ, and shall dwell with him eternally in the heavens. And the honour be to the Father, and to the Son, and to the Holy Ghost, which is one God. Amen.

" 'OLIVER COWDERY.
DAVID WHITMER.
MARTIN HARRIS.'

" 'TESTIMONY OF EIGHT WITNESSES.

" 'Be it known unto all nations, kindreds, tongues, and people, unto whom this work shall come, that Joseph Smith, jun., the translator of this work, has shown unto us the plates of which hath been spoken, which have the appearance of gold: as many of the leaves as the said Smith has translated we did handle with our hands; and we also saw the engravings thereon, all of which has the appearance of ancient work and of curious workmanship. And this we bear record with words of soberness, that the said Smith has shown unto us, for we have seen and lighted, and know of a surety that the said Smith has got the plates of which we have spoken; and we give our names unto the world that which we have seen; and we lie not, God bearing witness of it.

> "'John Whitmer.
> Christian Whitmer.
> Jacob Whitmer.
> Peter Whitmer, jun.
> Hiram Page.
> Joseph Smith, sen.
> Hyram Smith.
> Samuel H. Smith.'"

So far the story of Mr. Orson Pratt, derived from statements made at various times by the "Prophet" himself, and so far also the corroboration of the witnesses. It will be seen that the latter were principally of the two families of Whitmer and Smith. The Smiths were the father and brothers of Joseph. The next incident is the appointment of Joseph to the priesthood. It is related by Joseph himself in the following terms in the "Millennial Star," vol. 3, page 148:—

"While we (Joseph Smith and Oliver Cowdery) were thus employed, praying and calling upon the Lord, a messenger from Heaven descended in a cloud of light, and having laid his hands upon us, he ordained us, saying unto us, 'Upon you, my fellow-servants, in the name of the Messiah, I confer the priesthood of Aaron, which holds the keys of the ministering of angels, and of the gospel of repentance and of baptism by immersion for the remission of sins; and this shall never be taken away from the earth until the sons of Levi do offer again an offering unto the Lord in righteousness.' He said this Aaronic priesthood had not the power of laying on of hands for the gift of the Holy Ghost, but this should be conferred on us hereafter; and he commanded us to go and be baptized, and gave us directions that I should baptize Oliver Cowdery, and afterwards that he should baptize me. Accordingly we went and were baptized. I baptized him first, and afterwards he baptized me. After which I laid my hands upon his head, and ordained him to the Aaronic priesthood; afterwards he laid his hands on me, and ordained me to the same priesthood, for so we were commanded. The messenger who visited us on this occasion, and conferred this priesthood upon us, said that his name was John, the same that is called John the Baptist in the New Testament, and that he acted under the direction of Peter, James, and John, who held the keys of the priesthood of Melchizedek, which priesthood, he said, should in due time be conferred on us, and that I should be called the first elder, and he the second. It was on the 15th day of May, 1829, that we were baptized and ordained under the hand of the messenger."

Joseph Smith having made known his doctrine to these men, as illiterate as himself, and to various others, the wonderful plates began to be talked about. Among the persons who were originally most disposed to join the new sect was Mr. Martin Harris, whose name appears along with those of other witnesses in the above testimony.

Mr. Orson Pratt does not, however, state the whole of the facts connected with the interview of Martin Harris with Mr. Anthon, of New York, the learned professor to whom he alludes. A report having been spread abroad by the Mormons, that Professor Anthon had seen the plates, and pronounced the inscriptions to be in the Egyptian character, that gentleman was requested by a letter, directed to him by Mr. E. D. Howe, of Painesville, Ohio, to declare whether such was the fact. Professor Anthon returned the following answer:—

"New York, Feb. 17, 1834.

"Dear Sir—I received your letter of the 9th, and lose no time in making a reply. The whole story about my pronouncing the Mormonite inscription to be 'Reformed Egyptian Hieroglyphics,' is perfectly false. Some years ago a plain, apparently simple-hearted, farmer called on me with a note from Dr. Mitchell, of our city, now dead, requesting me to decipher, if possible, a paper which the farmer would hand me. Upon examining the paper in question, I soon came to the conclusion that it was all a trick, perhaps a hoax. When I asked the person who brought it how he obtained the writing he gave me the following account:—A 'gold book,' consisting of a number of gold plates fastened together by wires of the same material, had been dug up in the northern part of the State of New York, and along with it an enormous pair of 'spectacles!' These spectacles were so large, that if any person attempted to look through them, his two eyes would look through one glass only; the spectacles in question being altogether too large for the human face. 'Whoever (he said) examined the plates through the glasses was enabled not only to read them, but fully to understand their meaning. All this knowledge, however, was confined to a young man, who had the trunk containing the book and spectacles in his sole possession. This young man was placed behind a curtain, in a garret, in a farm-house, and being thus concealed from view, he put on the spectacles occasionally, or rather, looked through one of the glasses, deciphered the characters in the book, and having committed some of them to paper, handed copies from behind the curtain to those who stood outside.' Not a word was said about their having been deciphered by 'the gift of God.' Everything in this way was effected by the large pair of spectacles. The farmer added, that he had been requested to contribute a sum of money towards the publication of the 'golden book,' the contents of which would, as he was told, produce an entire change in the world, and save it from ruin. So urgent had been these solicitations, that he intended selling his farm, and giving the amount to those who wished to publish the plates. As a last precautionary step, he had resolved to come to New York, and obtain the opinion of the learned about the meaning of the paper which he had brought with him, and which had been given him as part of the contents of the book, although no translation had at that time been made by the young man with the spectacles. On hearing this odd story, I changed my opinion about the paper, and instead of viewing it any longer as a hoax, I began to regard it as part of a scheme to cheat the farmer of his money, and I communicated my suspicions to him, warning him to beware of rogues. He requested an opinion from me in writing, which of course I declined to give, and he then took his leave, taking his paper with him.

"This paper, in question, was in fact a singular scroll. It consisted of all kinds of crooked characters, disposed in columns, and had evidently been prepared by some person who had before him at the time a book containing various alphabets, Greek and Hebrew letters, crosses, and flourishes; Roman letters inverted or placed sideways, were arranged and placed in perpendicular columns; and the whole ended in a rude delineation of a circle, divided into various compartments, decked with various strange marks, and evidently copied after the Mexican calendar, given by Humboldt, but copied in such a way as not to betray the source whence it was derived. I am thus particular as to the contents of the paper, inasmuch as I have frequently conversed with my friends on the subject since the Mormon excitement began, and well remember that the paper contained anything else but 'Egyptian Hieroglyphics.'

"Some time after, the same farmer paid me a second visit. He brought with him the 'gold book' in print, and offered it to me for sale. I declined purchasing. He then asked permission to leave the book with me for examination. I declined receiving it, although his manner was strangely urgent. I adverted once more to the roguery which, in my opinion, had been practised upon him, and asked him what had become of the gold plates. He informed me that they were in a trunk with the spectacles. I advised him to go to a magistrate and have the trunk examined. He said, 'The curse of God' would come upon him if he did. On my pressing him, however, to go to a magistrate, he told me he would open the trunk if I would take the 'curse of God' upon myself. I replied I would do so with the greatest willingness, and would incur every risk of that nature, provided I could only extricate him from the grasp of rogues; he then left me. I have given you a full statement of all that I know respecting the origin of Mormonism, and must beg you, as a personal favour, to publish this letter immediately, should you find my name mentioned again by these wretched fanatics.

"Yours respectfully,

"CHARLES ANTHON."

This letter speaks for itself, and needs no comment. The following summary of the contents of the Book of Mormon, thus strangely issued into the world, is from a publication called the "Voice of Warning," by Parley P. Pratt, another apostle:—

"The Book of Mormon contains the history of the ancient inhabitants of America, who were a branch of the house of Israel, of the tribe of Joseph; of whom the Indians are still a remnant; but the principal nation of them having fallen in battle, in the fourth or fifth century, one of their prophets, whose name was Mormon, saw fit to make an abridgment of their history, their prophecies, and their doctrine, which he engraved on plates, and afterwards being slain, the record fell into the hands of his son Moroni, who, being hunted by his enemies, was directed to deposit the record safely in the earth, with a promise from God that it should be preserved, and should be brought to light in the latter days by means of a Gentile nation, who should possess the land. The deposit was made about the year 420 on a hill then called Cumora, now in Ontario county, where it was preserved in safety until it was brought to light by no less than the ministry of angels, and translated by inspiration. And the great Jehovah bore record of the same to chosen witnesses, who declare it to the world."

The question will be asked, could Joseph Smith, a notoriously illiterate man, really write even so clumsy a composition as the Book of Mormon? The following short history will throw some light upon the matter. It appears that in the year 1809 a man of the name of Solomon Spaulding, who had formerly been a clergyman, failed in business at a place called Cherry Vale, in the State of New York. Being a person of literary tastes, and his attention having been directed to a notion which at that time excited some interest, namely, that the North American Indians were the descendants of the lost ten tribes of Israel, it struck him that the idea afforded a good groundwork for a religious tale, history, or novel. For three years he laboured upon this work, which he entitled, "The Manuscript Found." "Mormon" and his son "Moroni" were two of the principal characters in it. In 1812 the MS. was presented to a printer or bookseller, residing at Pittsburg, Pennsylvania, with a view to its publication. Before any satisfactory arrangement could be made, the author died, and the manuscript remained in the possession of the printer, apparently unnoticed and uncared for. The printer also died in 1826, having previously lent the manuscript to one Sidney Rigdon, a compositor in his employ, who afterwards became, next to Joseph Smith himself, the principal leader of the Mormons. How Joseph Smith and Sidney Rigdon became connected is not very clearly known, and which of the two originated the idea of making a new Bible out of Solomon Spaulding's novel is equally uncertain. The wife, the partner, several friends, and the brother of Solomon Spaulding, affirmed, however, the identity of the principal portions of the "Book of Mormon" with the novel of "The Manuscript Found," which the author had from time to time, and in separate portions, read over to them. John Spaulding, brother to Solomon, declared upon oath that his brother's missing book was "An historical romance of the first settlers in America, endeavouring to show that the American Indians are the descendants of Jews, or the lost ten tribes. It gave a detailed account of their journey from Jerusalem by land and by sea, till they arrived in America under the command of Nephi and Lehi. He also mentioned the Lamanites. I have recently read the Book of Mormon, and to my great surprise, I find nearly the same historical matter, names, &c., as they were in my brother's writings. To the best of my recollection and belief, it is the same as my brother Solomon wrote, with the exception of the religious matter."

The religious matter derived from the Old and New Testaments has been engrafted upon Solomon Spaulding's romance in a manner that shows the clumsy, the ignorant, and the illiterate workman. Such phrases as the following are of frequent occurrence:—"Ye are like unto they." "Do as ye hath hitherto done." "I—the Lord delighteth in the chastity of women." "I saith unto them." "I who ye call your King." "These things had not ought to be." "Ye saith unto him." "For a more history part are written upon my other plates." Anachronisms are also frequent. The mariner's compass is spoken of before the date of the Christian era; and the Saviour of the world is represented as appearing immediately after his resurrection to the Jews in America—a people whom Joseph Smith affirms to have known no Greek, and to have spoken Hebrew, or reformed Egyptian, and saying to them, "Behold, I am Jesus Christ, the son of God. I created the heavens and the earth, and all things that in them are. I am the light and the life of the world. I am Alpha and Omega, the beginning and the end."

Joseph did not know that "Jesus" is the Greek for the Hebrew name of Joshua, and that "Christ" is the Greek of "anointed"—or that "Alpha" and "Omega" were the first and last letters of the Greek alphabet, and could, like the other two words, have had no meaning to a Hebrew people in America utterly ignorant of Greek. Many other similar instances could be cited.

Joseph Smith was often asked, both by friends and foes, the meaning of the word "Mormon," which occurred originally in Solomon Spaulding's novel, and appears to have been derived by him from the Greek. The following reply of Joseph, as published in a letter to the editor of the "Times and Seasons," is highly characteristic both of his cool audacity and his self-sufficient ignorance:—

"Sir—Through the medium of your paper, I wish to correct an error among men that profess to be learned, liberal, and wise; and I do it the more cheerfully, because I hope sober-thinking and sound-reasoning people will sooner listen to the voice of truth than be led astray by the vain pretensions of the self-wise. The error I speak of is the definition of the word 'Mormon.' It has been stated that this word was derived from the Greek word *mormo*. This is not the case. There was no Greek or Latin upon the plates from which I, through the grace of God, translated the Book of Mormon. Let the language of that book speak for itself. On the 523d page of the fourth edition, it reads:—'And now behold we have written the record according to our knowledge in the characters, which are called among us the Reformed Egyptian, being handed down and altered by us according to our manner of speech; and if our plates were sufficiently large, we should have written in Hebrew, Behold ye would have had no imperfection in our record, but the Lord knoweth the things which we have written, and also, that none other people knoweth our language; therefore he hath prepared means for the interpretation thereof.'

"Here, then, the subject is put to silence, for 'none other people knoweth our language;' therefore the Lord, and not man, hath to interpret, after the people were all dead. And, as Paul said, 'the world by wisdom know not God,' and the world by speculation are destitute of revelation; and as God, in his superior wisdom, has always given his saints, wherever he had any on the earth, the same spirit, and that spirit (as John says) is the true spirit of prophecy, which is the testimony of Jesus, I may safely say that the word Mormon stands independent of the learning and wisdom of this generation. Before I give a definition, however, to the word, let me say that the Bible, in its widest sense, means good; for the Saviour says, according to the gospel of St. John, 'I am the good shepherd;' and it will not be beyond the common use of terms to say, that good is amongst the most important in use, and though known by various names in different languages, still its meaning is the same, and is ever in opposition to bad. We say from the Saxon, good; the Dane, god; the Goth, goda; the German, gut; the Dutch, goed; the Latin, bonus; the Greek, kalos; the Hebrew, tob; and the Egyptian, mon. Hence, with the addition of more, or the contraction mor, we have the word Mormon, which means, literally, *more good.*—Yours,

"JOSEPH SMITH."

In addition to the Book of Mormon, the Latter-day Saints have a book of "Doctrines" and "Covenants," purporting to be direct revelations from heaven to Joseph Smith and others, upon the temporal government of their church, the support of the poor, the tithing or taxation of the members, the establishment of cities and temples, the allotment of lands, the emigration of the "saints," the education of the people, the gathering of moneys and other matters. This book abounds in grammatical inaccuracies, even to a greater extent than the Book of Mormon. "God, that knowest thy thoughts"—"A *literal* descendant of Aaron," meaning a lineal descendant—"An hair of his head shall not fall." "Your father who art in Heaven knoweth"—"And the spirit and the body is the soul of man"—"The stars also giveth their light as they roll upon their wings in glory"—"Her who sitteth upon many waters"—"Thou shalt not covet thine own property, but impart it freely to the printing of the Book of Mormon"—form but a sample of hundreds of similar sentences that might be culled, were it worth while. A few specimens of the kind of "Revelations"—and the style in which Joseph Smith represents the Almighty as speaking to him—will show the height of knavery, the depth of folly, and what absurdity men will believe under the influence of strong fanaticism. The following is part of a "revelation" purporting to have been given by Jesus Christ, in February 1831. In these revelations the Almighty is invariably represented as giving Joseph his proper designation of Smith *junior,* that he might not be mistaken for his father, Joseph Smith, *senior:*—

"Hearken, oh ye elders of my church, who have assembled yourselves together in my name, even Jesus Christ, the Son of the living God, the Saviour of the world. Behold, verily, I say unto you, I give unto you this first commandment that you shall go forth in my name, every one of you, except my servants, Joseph Smith, jun., and Sidney

Rigdon. ... If there shall be properties in the hands of the church, or any individuals of it, more than is necessary for their support, it shall be kept to administer to those who have not."

The following is part of a "Revelation" given to Joseph Smith in March, 1829, when Martin Harris desired to see the golden plates, and before he was put off with the paper transcript, which he showed to Professor Anthon:—

"Behold, I say unto you, that as my servant Martin Harris has desired a witness at my hand, that you, my servant Joseph Smith jun., have got the plates of which you have testified and borne record that you have received of me; and now, behold, this shall you say unto him—'He who spake unto you, said unto you I the Lord am God, and have given those things unto you my servant Joseph Smith jun. and have commanded you that you should stand as a witness of these things: and I have caused you that you should enter into a covenant with me that you should not show them except to those persons that I commanded you; and you have no power over them, except I grant it you ... And now, again, I speak unto you my servant Joseph, concerning the man that denies the witness. Behold, I say unto him, he exalts himself and does not sufficiently humble himself before me. But if he will bow down before me and humble himself in mighty prayer and faith, in the sincerity of his heart, then will I grant unto him a view of the things which he desires to see."

The "Prophet," and his principal assistant, Sidney Rigdon, appear to have soon quarrelled with the three witnesses. The first witness to the truth of his book of Mormon was declared by Smith himself in a revelation given in November, 1831, to be unfit to be trusted with "moneys:"—

"Hearken unto me, saith the Lord your God, for my servant Oliver Cowdery's sake. It is not wisdom in me that he should be entrusted with the commandments *and the moneys* which he shall carry into the land of Zion, *except one go with him who shall be true and faithful.*"

In a paper drawn up by Sidney Rigdon in June, 1838, when a great schism took place in the church, it is stated that Oliver Cowdery, David Whitmer, and another were united with a gang of counterfeiters, thieves, liars, and blacklegs of the deepest dye, to deceive, cheat, and defraud "the saints." Martin Harris, the last of the three, is spoken of at the time of the schism by Joseph himself in the following terms, in a paper called the *Elder's Journal:*—

"There are negroes who wear white skins as well as black ones. Grames Parish and others who acted as lackies, such as Martin Harris &c., but they are so far beneath contempt that a notice of them would be too great a sacrifice for a gentleman to make."

While, by means of "revelations," those who were not longer to be trusted, were pointed out to the true believers, Joseph Smith took care to have "revelations" upon matters relating to his own comfort. "It is meet," says a "revelation" of the Lord in February, 1831, "that my servant Joseph Smith, jun., should have a house built, in which to live and translate." A second "revelation" of the same month says, "If ye desire the mysteries of my kingdom, provide for him (Joseph Smith, jun.) food and raiment, and whatsoever thing he needeth."

Nor was Smith, according to the revelations, to labour for his living. "In temporal labours," says another revelation of July, 1830, "thou shalt not have strength, for that is not thy calling. Attend to thy calling, and thou shall have wherewith to magnify thine office, and to expound all scriptures."

An extract from one more "Revelation" will suffice for the present. It purports to have been given in July, 1830, to Emma Smith, the wife of Joseph, through Joseph himself:—

"The office of thy calling shall be for a comfort unto my servant Joseph Smith jun. thy husband. And thou shall go with him at the time of his going and be unto him for a scribe, while there is no one to be a scribe for him, that I may send my servant Oliver Cowdery, whithersoever I will. And it shall be given to thee also to make a selection of sacred hymns, as it shall be given thee, which is pleasing unto me to be had in my church."

The Hymn-book of Emma Smith does not appear to have been published; but a little Hymn-book, containing hymns selected by Brigham Young, the present head of the church and successor of Joseph Smith, has gone through eight editions. The eighth was published in Liverpool, in 1849, by "Apostle" Orson Pratt. A few extracts will not be out of place. The following hymn, which is said to be sometimes sung on shipboard in Liverpool, prior to the departure of Mormon emigrants, is, in point of literary merit, among the best in the volume:—

" Yes, my native land, I love thee;
    All thy scenes, I love them well;
Friends, connections, happy country,
    Can I bid you all farewell?
      Can I leave thee,
    Far in distant lands to dwell?

" Home! thy joys are passing lovely;
    Joys no stranger heart can tell;
Happy home! 'tis sure I love thee,
    Can I—can I—say 'Farewell?'
      Can I leave thee?
    Far in distant lands to dwell?

" Holy scenes of joy and gladness,
    Every fond emotion swell;
Can I banish heartfelt sadness
    While I bid my home farewell?
      Can I leave thee,
    Far in distant lands to dwell?

" Yes! I hasten from you gladly,
    From the scenes I love so well;
Far away, ye billows, bear me,
    Lovely native land, farewell!
      Pleased I leave thee
    Far in distant lands to dwell.

" In the deserts let me labour,
    On the mountains let me tell
How he died—the blessed Saviour,
    To redeem a world from hell!
      Let me hasten,
    Far in distant lands to dwell!

" Bear me on, thou restless ocean;
    Let the winds my canvass swell;
Heaves my heart with warm emotion,
    While I go far hence to dwell!
      Glad I bid thee,
    Native land, farewell! farewell!"

The next is a hymn for the Twelve Apostles, who are now engaged in different parts of Europe, in procuring emigrants and gathering the saints to the Salt-lake Valley in Deseret:—

> "Ye chosen twelve to ye are given
>   The keys of this last ministry—
> To every nation under Heaven,
>   From land to land, from sea to sea.
>
> "First to the Gentiles sound the news,
>   Throughout Columbia's happy land;
> And then before it reach the Jews,
>   Prepare on Europe's shores to stand.
>
> "Let Europe's towns and cities hear
>   The Gospel tidings angels bring;
> The Gentile nations, far and near,
>   Prepare their hearts his praise to sing.
>
> "India and Afric's sultry plains,
>   Must hear the tidings as they roll—
> Where darkness, death, and sorrow reign,
>   And tyranny has held control.
>
> "Listen! ye islands of the sea,
>   For every isle shall hear the sound;
> Nations and tongues before unknown,
>   Though long since lost, shall soon be found.
>
> "And then again shall Asia hear,
>   Where angels first the news proclaimed;
> Eternity shall record bear
>   And earth repeat the loud Amen.
>
> "The nations catch the pleasing sound,
>   And Jew and Gentile swell the strain,
> Hosannah o'er the earth resound,
>   Messiah then will come to reign."

Many of their hymns and songs are adapted to popular tunes, such as "The sea, the sea, the open sea," "Away, away to the mountain's brow," &c. One to the first mentioned tune is inserted in the "Times and Seasons," page 895, and commences—

> "The sky, the sky, the clear blue sky,
>   Oh, how I love to gaze upon it!
> The upper realms of deep on high,
>   I wonder when the Lord began it!"

But the following, to the tune of "The rose that all are praising," is perhaps the most characteristic, and with it I conclude the specimens of Mormon devotional poetry:—

> "The God that others worship is not the God for me;
> He has no parts nor body, and cannot hear nor see;
>   But I've a God that lives above—
>   A God of Power and of Love—
> A God of Revelation—O that's the God for me;
> O that's the God for me; O that's the God for me!

> "A church without apostles is not the church for me;
> It's like a ship dismasted, afloat upon the sea.
>   But I've a church that's always led
>   By the twelve stars round its head;
> A church with good foundations—O that's the church for me;
> O that's the church for me; oh that's the church for me!

> "A church without a prophet is not the church for me;
> It has no head to lead it, in it I would not be;
>   But I've a church not built by man,
>   Cut from the mountain without hands;
> A church with gifts and blessings—oh that's the church for me;
> Oh that's the church for me; oh that's the church for me!

> "The hope that Gentiles cherish is not the hope for me;
> It has no hope nor knowledge, far from it I would be;
>   But I've a hope that will not fail,
>   That reaches safe within the veil;
> Which hope is like an anchor—oh that's the hope for me;
> Oh that's the hope for me; oh that's the hope for me!

> "The heaven of sectarians is not the heaven for me;
> So doubtful its location, neither on land nor sea;
>   But I've a heaven on the earth,
>   The land and home that gave me birth;
> A heaven of light and knowledge—oh that's the heaven for me;
> Oh that's the heaven for me; oh that's the heaven for me!

" A church without a gathering is not the church for me;
The Saviour would not order it, whatever it might be;
  But I've a church that's called out,
  From false traditions, fear, and doubt,
A gathering dispensation—oh that's the church for me;
Oh that's the church for me; oh that's the church for me!"

It only remains to add that the Mormons recognize two orders of priesthood, the "Aaronic" and the "Melchizedek;" that they are governed by a prophet or president, twelve apostles, the "seventies," and a number of bishops, high priests, deacons, elders, and teachers; that they assert that the gifts of prophecy and the power of working miracles have not ceased; that Joseph Smith and many other Mormons wrought miracles and cast out devils; that the end of the world is close at hand; and that they are the "saints" spoken of in the Apocalypse, who will reign with Christ in a temporal kingdom in this world. They assert also that the seat of this kingdom is to be either Missouri—the place originally intended—or their present location of the Great Salt Lake Valley of Deseret. They allege that their book of Mormon and the Doctrine and Covenants form the fulness of the Gospel—that they take nothing from the Old or the New Testament—both of which they complete. They seem, however, not to have formed the same ideas of God which are stated in the Gospel—but to acknowledge a material Deity. This idea appears in the song or hymn to the tune of the "Rose that all are praising," above quoted, but is stated more broadly in the "Times and Seasons," and other works. The following extract from a kind of Confession of Faith, signed by Orson Spencer, one of the apostles of the church, gives the views of the sect upon this and other subjects:—"In some, and indeed in many respects, do we differ from some sectarian denominations. We believe that God is a being who hath both body and parts, and also passions. Also of the existence of the gifts, in the true church, spoken of in Paul's letter to the Corinthians. I do not believe that the career of sacred Scripture was closed with the Revelation of John, but that wherever God has a true church there he makes frequent revelations of his will; and as God takes cognizance of all things, both temporal and spiritual, his revelations will pertain to all things whereby his glory may be promoted."

Joseph Smith is more explicit. The following passage occurs in the "Millennial Star," vol. 6, under the "prophet's" authority, and signed with his name:—

"What is God? He is a material organized intelligence, possessing both body and parts. He is in the form of a man, and is, in fact, of the same species, and is a model or standard of perfection, to which man is destined to attain, he being the Great Father and Head of the whole family. This being cannot occupy two distinct places at once, therefore he cannot be everywhere present.

"What are Angels? They are intelligences, of the human species. Many of them are offsprings of Adam and Eve—of men, it is said, 'being Gods, or sons of God, endowed with the same powers, attributes, and capacities that their heavenly Father and Jesus Christ possess.'

"The weakest child of God, which now exists upon the earth, will possess more dominion, more property, more subjects, and more power and glory than is possessed by Jesus Christ or by his Father; while, at the same time, Jesus Christ and his Father will have their dominion, kingdom and subjects increased in proportion."

"Materialism" is in fact the strong point of the Mormons; and one of the pamphlets, which they circulate most largely, is entitled "The Absurdities of Immaterialism."

The Mormons lay claim to the power of working miracles; and many ludicrous stories are told by their enemies of the attempts made by Joe Smith and others, to get out of difficulties with their own people, after having promised too much in this respect. These stories are, of course, considered false and scandalous by the Mormons. I shall not reproduce them, but select, in preference, a specimen of their "miracles," as recorded by themselves, in their own publication, the "Millennial Star." It will answer the purpose far better than any statement made by their opponents. In a letter addressed to Mr. Orson Spencer, and published in the "Millennial Star" for August 1, 1847, the writer, a Mormon, who dates from Leamington Spa, Warwickshire, England, after detailing the attempts made to ordain one Currell to the Mormon priesthood—attempts which were defeated by the devil, says:—

"When we laid our hands upon him the devil entered him, and tried to prevent us from ordaining him, but the power of Jesus Christ in the holy priesthood was stronger than the devil, and after all the endeavours of the powers of darkness to prevent us, in the name of Jesus Christ, we ordained brother Richard Currell to the office of a priest in the church of Jesus Christ of Latter-day Saints. In consequence of what had taken place, many came to our meeting in the evening, and paid great attention. The scenes of the twentieth of June will long be remembered by us as a day of rejoicing in the glorious manifestation of the power of God, confirming the faith of the saints, and spreading the sound of the gospel further than we could have done it in a long time.

"I should inform you that when the devil found he was defeated in brother C——, he entered a sister, and kept coming in for several hours; as fast as one lot were expelled another lot entered; at one time we counted 27 come out of her. When we rebuked them they would come out, but as soon returned again. How was it they could acknowledge the power, and would damn our power, damn our gospel, and tear and bite? The sight was awful, but it has done us all good. I may as well say that some of the devils told us they were sent some by Cain, some by Kite, Judas, Kilo, Kelo, Kalmonia, and Lucifer; some of these, they informed us, were presidents over seventies in hell. The last that came, previous to our going to prison, told us he was Kilo, one of the presidents, and his six councillers. We cast them out thirty times, and had 319 devils, from three to thirty-seven coming out at a time. I shall feel obliged for any instruction you can give me on this subject.

"Yours,   Thomas Smith."

But enough as regards the doctrines and the miraculous pretensions of the Mormons. The reader has by this time acquired a sufficient knowledge of them. The full extent of their fanaticism is not portrayed in these extracts, but enough has been said in their own words to show what kind of men they are in a religious point of view. In my next letter I shall proceed to detail the remarkable growth of this extraordinary sect, first amid contempt and laughter, and ultimately amid the most relentless and vindictive animosity and persecution through good and evil fortune, until the present day, when they number themselves by hundreds of thousands—when they boast of having an emigration fund of three-and-a-half tons of Californian gold—when they have emissaries in every country in Europe—and when they are a prosperous and daily increasing people, and carry on emigration on a larger scale than was ever attempted in modern times by any political or religious society.

LABOUR AND THE POOR.

——◆——

LIVERPOOL.

[FROM OUR SPECIAL CORRESPONDENT.]

THE MORMONS—THEIR RISE AND PROGRESS—MORMON EMIGRATION FROM LIVERPOOL.

LETTER XII.

The truth that no absurdity of fanaticism is too outrageous to attract believers, finds continual corroboration. The learned and the unlearned, the rich and the poor, the gentle and the simple, alike break through the trammels of reason, and become the dupes of religious impostors, or of persons who are still more dangerous—the religious maniacs, who strengthen their cause by their own conscientious belief in it. To which ever of these two classes Joseph Smith is most properly consignable, it is certain that his doctrine was no sooner preached than he began to make converts of the people around him. The idea of the "Latter Days," or days immediately prior to the second coming of Christ to establish the millennium, is one that has a great hold upon the imagination of large classes of persons. Joseph Smith worked upon this idea, and every earthquake recorded in the newspapers—every new comet discovered—every falling meteor that was observed—every war and rumour of a war in Europe or America—every monstrous birth among inferior animals—every great public calamity, tempest, fire, or explosion—was skilfully and pertinaciously adduced as a proof and a warning of the "Latter Days." He had two great elements of success in his favour—sufficient novelty and unconquerable perseverance. His doctrine was both old and new. It had sufficient of the old to attract those who would have been repelled by a creed entirely new, and it had sufficient of the new to rivet the attention and inflame the imagination of those on whose minds an old creed, however ably preached, would have fallen and taken no root. Basing his doctrine upon isolated passages of the Bible—claiming direct inspiration from the Almighty, promising to true believers possession of the earth, temporal power and glory, and the blessing of Heaven—and being gifted with a courage and audacity that despised difficulty and danger, Joseph Smith soon found himself the recognised head of a small but increasing body of ardent disciples. On the 1st of June, 1830, the first conference of the sect, as an organised church, was held at Fayette, which place was for many years the "prophet's" residence, and the head-quarters of the sect. The numbers of the believers, including the whole family of the Smiths, was thirty. Even at this early period in the history of the sect, they met considerable opposition from the people. Joseph ordered the construction of a dam across a stream of water for the purpose of baptizing his disciples. A mob collected and broke it down, and used language towards Joseph that was anything but flattering to him or his followers, threatening him with violence and assassination. He was nothing daunted, however. With a rare skill he broke the keen edge of detraction by confessing boldly that he had once led an improper and immoral life; but, unworthy as he was, "the Lord had chosen him—had forgiven him all his sins, and intended, in his own inscrutable purposes, to make him—weak and erring as he might have been—the instrument of his glory."

But notwithstanding all this, Palmyra and Fayette, the first seats of the sect, and of the family of the Smiths, father and brothers, who all joined in the scheme of Joseph for founding a new religion, were somewhat too well known. They therefore removed, after a short time, to Kirtland, in Ohio. The attention of the whole fraternity was directed from the very commencement of their organization to the policy and expediency of fixing the head-quarters of the sect in the Far West, in the thinly-settled and but partially explored territories belonging to the United States, where they might squat upon good lands, clear the primeval wilderness, and purchase large estates with small means. Oliver Cowdery, having been sent on an exploratory expedition of this sort, reported so favourably of Jackson county in Missouri, that Joseph Smith, after remaining but a few weeks in Kirtland, determined to visit Missouri himself. Leaving his family and principal connections in Kirtland, he proceeded with his then faithful Sidney Rigdon and some others upon a long and arduous journey to the wilderness to fix upon a site for the "New Jerusalem" and future City of Christ, where the Lord was to reign over the saints as a temporal king, in "power and great glory." They started about the middle of June, travelling by waggons or by canal boat, and sometimes on foot, as far as Cincinnati. From this place they proceeded by steamer to Louisville and St. Louis. At the last-mentioned village all further means of transport failed them, and they walked a distance of three hundred miles to Independence, in Jackson county, Missouri, the seat of the promised inheritance of the saints. They arrived at their destination, foot-sore and weary, in the middle of July. Joseph was in raptures with the beauty and fertility of the country, and his delight broke out into the following description, which occurs in his autobiography, published in the "Times and Seasons:"—

"Unlike the timbered states in the east, except upon the rivers and water-courses, which were verdantly dotted with trees from one to three miles wide, as far as the eye can glance, the beautiful rolling prairies lay spread around like a sea of meadows. The timber is a mixture of oak, hickory, black walnut, elm, cherry, honey locus, mulberry, coffee bean, hackberry, box, elder, and bass wood, together with the addition of cotton wood, button wood, pecon—soft and hard maples upon the bottoms. The shrubbery was beautiful, and consisted in part of plums, grapes, crab-apples, and parsimmons. The prairies were decorated with a growth of flowers that seemed as gorgeous and grand as the brilliancy of stars in the heavens, and exceed description. The soil is rich and fertile, from three to ten feet deep, and generally composed of a rich black mould, intermingled with clay and sand. It produces in abundance wheat, corn, and many other commodities, together with sweet potatoes and cotton. Horses, cattle, and hogs, though of an inferior breed, are tolerably plenty, and seem nearly to raise themselves by grazing in the vast prairie range in summer, and feeding upon the bottoms in winter. The wild game is less plenty where man has commenced the cultivation of the soil, than it is a little distance further in the wild prairies. Buffalo, elk, deer, bears, wolves, beaver, and many lesser animals roam at pleasure. Turkies, geese, swans, duck, yea, a variety of the feathered race, are among the rich abundance that graces the delightful regions of this goodly land of the heritage of the children of God. Nothing is more fruitful, or a richer stockholder in the blooming prairies, than the honey-bee; honey is but about twenty-five cents per gallon.

"The season is mild and delightful nearly three-quarters of the year, and as the land of Zion is situated at about equal distances from the Atlantic and Pacific oceans, as well as from the Alleghany and Rocky mountains, in the thirty-ninth degree of north latitude, and between the tenth and twentieth degrees of west longitude, it bids fair to become one of the most blessed places on the globe."

The longer he stayed in Missouri the more delighted he was with the "location" fixed upon for the saints; and that there might be no difference of opinion upon the subject in the church, he had a direct "revelation" from the Almighty upon the subject;—establishing it as the future Zion, and setting forth his views relative to the organization of the church, the building of a temple, the allotment of lands, and the means of living of the people. This extraordinary document ran as follows:—

"Hearken, O ye elders of my church, saith the Lord your God, who have assembled yourselves together, according to my commandments, in this land which I have appointed and consecrated for the gathering of the saints; wherefore this is the land of promise, and the place for the city of Zion. And thus saith the Lord your God, if you will receive wisdom, here is wisdom. Behold, the place which is now called Independence, is the centre place, and a spot for the temple is lying westward, upon a lot which is not far from the court-house: wherefore it is wisdom that the land should be purchased by the Saints; and also every tract lying westward, even unto the line running directly between Jew and Gentile. And also every tract bordering by the prairies, in as much as my disciples are enabled to buy lands. Behold, this is wisdom, that they may obtain it for an everlasting inheritance.

"And let my servant, Sidney Gilbert, stand in the office which I have appointed him, to receive moneys, to be an agent unto the church, to buy land in all the regions round about, in as much as can be in righteousness, and as wisdom shall direct.

"And let my servant, Edward Partridge, stand in the office which I have appointed him, to divide the Saints their inheritance, even as I have commanded; and also those whom he has appointed to assist him.

"And, again, verily I say unto you, let my servant Sidney Gilbert plant himself in this place, and establish a store, that he may sell goods without fraud, that he may obtain money to buy lands for the good of the Saints; and that he may obtain whatsoever things the disciples may need to plant them in inheritance. And also let my servant, Sidney Gilbert, obtain a licence, that he may send goods also unto the people, even by whom he will, as clerks employed in his service, and thus provide for my Saints, that my gospel may be preached unto those who sit in darkness, and in the region and shadow of death.

"And again, verily I say unto you, let my servant William W. Phelps be planted in this place, and be established as a printer unto the church; and lo, if the world receiveth his writings, let him obtain whatsoever he can obtain in righteousness, for the good of the Saints. And let my servant Oliver Cowdery assist him, even as I have commanded, in whatsoever place I shall appoint unto him, to copy, and to correct, and select, that all things may be right before me, as it shall be proved by the Spirit through him. And thus let those of whom I have spoken be planted in the land of Zion, and speedily as can be, with their families, to do those things even as I have spoken.

"And now, concerning the gathering. Let the bishop and the agent make preparations for those families which have been commanded to come to this land, as soon as possible, and plant them in their inheritance. And unto the residue of both elders and members further directions shall be given hereafter. Even so. Amen."

On the first Sunday after their arrival, Joseph preached in the wilderness to a crowd of Indians, squatters, and, as he himself records, "to quite a respectable company of negroes." He made a few converts. On the 3d of August, after a sojourn of less than three weeks, the spot for the temple was solemnly laid out, and dedicated to the Lord; and Joseph in a day or two afterwards—having completed all his arrangements, established a bishop, and acquired, as he thought, a firm footing for his sect in this remote but lovely and fertile spot—prepared to return into Ohio, to look after his business in Kirtland. Some dispute, of which the nature is not clearly known, appears to have arisen between Joseph and his friend Sidney Rigdon before their departure. It is probable, from the course of subsequent events, that Sidney even at this time aspired to greater power in the church than suited the purposes of the "prophet;" but whatever the disagreement was, Joseph thought fit to rebuke his chief disciple by a revelation from Heaven, in which he accused him of "being exalted in his heart, and despising the counsel of the Lord." They afterwards became good friends again, and in partnership, or conjunction of some kind, and by the aid of other saints and elders of the church, they established a mill and a store in Kirtland, and set up a bank, with Joseph as its president, and Sidney Rigdon as cashier. To Kirtland they gave the name of a "stake," or support of Zion, intending to remain there for at least five years, and make money, until the wilderness was cleared and the temple built in Zion.

From this time until January, 1832, Joseph continued preaching in various parts of the United States, making converts with considerable rapidity, and combating some charges which were brought against his character by one Ezra Booth, formerly in his council, and whom he denounced as an apostate. His strange doctrines, and these charges against his character, united to the hatred with which other fanatics as violent as himself regarded his preaching, created much ill-feeling against him, and on the 25th of that month, being then resident at a village called "Hiram," he was dragged out of his bed at midnight, from the side of his wife, by a mob of Methodists, Baptists, and "Campbellites," who stripped him naked, and tarred and feathered him. Sidney Rigdon was similarly treated by the same lawless assemblage. Joseph now thought it high time to absent himself for a little, and on the 2d of April he started, in company with some of his adherents, for Missouri, "to fulfil the revelation." Although he left secretly, his persecutors received notice of his design, and tracked him for several hundred miles, until he arrived at Louisville, where he was sheltered and protected from his assailants by the captain of a steamboat. He arrived at "Zion" or Independence on the 26th, where he was enthusiastically received by a large congregation of thriving "Saints," and solemnly acknowledged as "prophet" and "seer," and president of the high priesthood of the church. He found that in his absence, but in obedience to a revelation which he had given, a printing-press had been procured, and a monthly newspaper or magazine established, under the title of the *Evening and Morning Star.* A weekly paper was also planned and established, called the *Upper Missouri Advertiser.* Both of these journals were exclusively devoted to the interests of Mormonism, which by this time numbered between 2,000 and 3,000 disciples, principally in Missouri. The number of the Saints in Kirtland, including women and children, was but 150. Joseph, however, had his mill, his store, and his farm to look after at Kirtland, and although while in that town he lived among enemies, it was necessary that he should return to it. He therefore left Zion, with the full confidence that all was going on prosperously. In January, 1833, while attending to his worldly business, a schism broke out in "Zion" itself, which threatened, and, in combination with other circumstances, ultimately produced, the greatest calamities, and led to the violent expulsion of the Mormons from the whole State of Missouri. The manner in which the Mormons behaved in their "Zion" was not calculated to make friends. The superiority they assumed gave offence, and the rumours that were spread by their opponents, as well as by some "renegades," who had been turned out of the church for misconduct, excited against them an intense feeling of alarm and hatred. They were accused of Communism, and not simply of a community of goods and chattels, but of wives. Both these charges were utterly unfounded; but they were renewed from day to day, and found constant believers, in spite of denials and refutations on the part of the Mormons. In addition to the odium unjustly cast upon them for these reasons, they talked so imprudently of their determination to possess the whole state of Missouri, and to suffer no one to live in it who would not conform to their faith, that a party was secretly formed against them, of which the object was nothing less than their total and immediate expulsion from their promised "Zion." In a letter to Mr. Phelps, the editor of the Mormon paper, the *Morning and Evening Star,* dated from Kirtland Mill, Joseph threatens the vengeance of God upon all the schismatics of "Zion." "I say to you (and what I say to you I say to all), hear the warning voice of God, lest Zion fall, and the Lord swear in his wrath the inhabitants of Zion shall not enter into my rest. The brethren in Kirtland pray for you unceasingly, for, knowing the terrors of the Lord, they greatly fear for you." Some of the Missouri saints, it appeared, had accused Joseph Smith of aiming at "monarchical power and authority;" and two of the high priests, in a letter written at the time, in support of the rebuke of the prophet to these "rebels," speak of "low, dark, and blind insinuations against Joseph's character and intentions." Whatever Joseph's views in this respect may have been, he found it necessary to take the sting out of this accusation, by associating with him in the supreme government of the church his old colleague, Sidney Rigdon, and another "saint." As usual, when any great movement was to be made, he had a "revelation." Under the date of the 8th of March, 1833, the Lord is represented as declaring that the sins of Sidney Rigdon and Frederick G. Williams were forgiven, and "that they were henceforth to be accounted as equal with Joseph Smith, junior, in holding the keys of his last kingdom." As it appears that Sidney Rigdon was too ambitious of power to be safely trusted among the saints of Missouri, he was commanded by this revelation to remain in Kirtland. The bishop was also ordered by the same authority to "search diligently for an agent," who was to be a "man who *had got riches in store—a man of God and of strong faith,* that thereby he might be enabled to discharge every debt, that the storehouse of the Lord might not be brought into disrepute before the people." Joseph also condescended to forgive the rebellious of Zion. "Behold, I say unto you," said the revelation, "your brethren in Zion begin to repent, and the angels rejoice over them. Nevertheless, I am not well pleased with many things, and I am not well pleased with my servant William E. Maclellin, neither with my servant Sidney Gilbert, and the bishop also; and others have many things to repent of. But verily I say unto you that I the Lord will contend with Zion, and plead with her strong ones, and chasten her, until she overcomes and is clean before me, for she shall not be removed out of her place. I the Lord have spoken it. Amen." On the same day Joseph "laid his hands on Brothers Sidney and Frederick, and ordained them to take part with him in holding the keys of the last kingdom, and to assist in the presidency of the high priesthood as his councillors. After which he exhorted the brethren to faithfulness and diligence in keeping the commandments of God; and gave much instruction for the benefit of the Saints, with a promise that the pure in heart should see a heavenly vision, and after remaining a short time in secret prayer the promise was verified. He then blessed the bread and wine, and distributed a portion to each, after which many of the brethren saw a heavenly vision of the Saviour and concourses of angels, and many other things."

But although the dissensions in the church were apparently healed by the judicious step thus taken, the old settlers of Missouri caused Joseph much alarm by the daily increasing hostility they expressed against the whole sect. The Mormon paper of June, 1833, published an article entitled "Free people of colour," which roused against them the hostility of the whole pro-slavery party—then as now peculiarly sensitive upon the question of abolition. The anti-Mormon press contained at the same time an article entitled "Beware of false prophets," written by a person whom Joseph called "a black rod in the hand of Satan." This article was distributed from house to house in Independence and its neighbourhood, and contained many true as well as false charges against Smith and his associates, reiterating the calumny about the community of goods and wives. The Mormons were insulted wherever they made their appearance, and quarrels and fights were of frequent occurrence. In the beginning of April a meeting of 300 people, enemies of the Mormons, had been held in Independence, or "Zion" itself, at which a resolution was unanimously agreed to, "that the Mormons should be removed out of their diggings;" but after the publication of these two articles, other meetings were held in various parts of Jackson county, at which still more violent resolutions were agreed to. A general meeting of the citizens of Jackson county, expressly convened, as the requisition stated, "for the purpose of adopting measures to rid themselves of the sect of fanatics called Mormons," was held on the 20th of July. Between four and five hundred people attended from every part of the county, and an address to the public was agreed upon. The address stated that little more than two years previously "some two or three of these people made their appearance in Missouri; that they now numbered upwards of 1,200; that each successive autumn and spring poured forth a new swarm of them into the country, as if the places from which they came were flooding Missouri with the very dregs of their composition; that they were but little above the condition of the blacks in regard to property and education; and that, in addition to other causes of scandal and offence, they exercised a corrupting influence over the slaves." The boast of the Mormons, that the whole country of Missouri was their destined inheritance, and that all the "Gentiles," or unbelievers in Joe Smith, were to be cut off in the Lord's good time, was not forgotten. The address concluded—

> "Of their pretended revelations from heaven—their personal intercourse with God and his angels—the maladies they pretend to heal by the laying on of hands—and the contemptible gibberish with which they habitually profane the Sabbath, and which they dignify with the appellation of unknown tongues, we have nothing to say; vengeance belongs to God alone. But as to the other matters set forth in this paper, we feel called on by every consideration of self-preservation, good society, public morals, and the fair prospects that, if it is not blasted in the germ, await this young and beautiful country, at once to declare, and we do hereby most solemnly declare—
>
> "That no Mormon shall in future move and settle in this country.
>
> "That those now here, who shall give a definite pledge of their intention within a reasonable time to remove out of the county, shall be allowed to remain unmolested until they have sufficient time to sell their property and close their business without any material sacrifice.
>
> "That the editor of the *Star* be required forthwith to close his office, and discontinue the business of printing in this country; and, as to all other stores and shops belonging to the sect, their owners must in every case comply with the terms of the second article of this declaration, and upon failure, prompt and efficient measures will be taken to close the same.
>
> "That the Mormon leaders here, are required to use their influence in preventing any further emigration of their distant brethren to this county, and to counsel and advise their brethren here to comply with the above requisitions.
>
> "That those who fail to comply with these requisitions be referred to those of their brethren who have the gifts of divination and of unknown tongues, to inform them of the lot that awaits them."

This address being read and duly proposed and seconded, was unanimously adopted. The meeting adjourned for two hours, and a deputation waited upon Mr. Phelps, the Mormon editor, upon Mr. Partridge, the bishop, and upon the keeper of the Mormon store, and urged upon them the expediency of complying with the terms above stated. The deputation reported to the meeting that they could not procure any direct answer to the terms proposed, and that the Mormons wished an unreasonable time for consultation upon the matter, not only among themselves in Independence, but with Joseph Smith, their prophet, in Kirtland. It was therefore resolved, *nem. con.*, that the *Star* printing-office should be immediately razed to the ground, and the type and presses secured. "This resolution," said the anti-Mormons, in an account of the occurrence published under their authority, "was with the utmost order and the least noise and disturbance possible, forthwith carried into execution, *as also some other steps of a similar tendency,* but no blood was spilled, nor any blows inflicted." The meeting then adjourned for three days, to give the Mormons an opportunity of considering their position and prospects, in case of refusal to leave the country.

The "other steps of a similar tendency," alluded to in this extract, appear to have been the tarring and feathering of two Mormons. Phelps, the editor, managed to escape from the mob, but Partridge, the Mormon bishop, and another Saint named Allen, were not so fortunate. These two were seized, stripped naked, tarred and feathered and set loose. The Lieutenant-Governor of the State of Missouri, Lilburn W. Boggs—a man who from thenceforward appears to have pursued the Mormons with unrelenting hostility, and whom they appear to consider as one of the chief agents of the untimely end of their Prophet, and worse than Pontius Pilate—was in the immediate neighbourhood of the riot, but declined to take any part in preserving the peace. Joseph Smith afterwards stated that he actually looked on, and aided the movement, saying to the Mormons, "You know what we Jackson boys can do. You must all leave the country." A Presbyterian preacher declared from the pulpit that "the Mormons were the common enemies of mankind, and ought to be destroyed." On the morning of the 23d of July the meeting again assembled. It was composed of several hundred persons, well armed, and bearing a red flag. They declared their intention of driving the whole of the sect forcibly out of Missouri if they would not go out peaceably. The Mormons saw it was useless to resist, and their leaders agreed, if time were given, that the whole sect would remove westward into the wilderness. It was arranged, and an agreement was duly signed to that effect, that one half of the Mormons, with their wives and families, should leave by the 1st of January and the other half by the 1st of April next ensuing, that the paper should be discontinued, and that no more Mormons should be allowed to come into the country in the interval. The opposite party pledged themselves that no violence should be done to any Mormon, provided these conditions were complied with.

Oliver Cowdery was immediately despatched to Kirtland with a message to the "Prophet." On his arrival it was resolved in solemn conclave, Joseph himself presiding, that the *Morning and Evening Star* should be published in Kirtland, and that a new paper, to be called, the *Latter Day Saints' Messenger and Advocate,* should be forthwith started. It was also resolved to appeal for protection to Mr. Dunklin, the governor of the state of Missouri, and demand justice for the outrages inflicted upon the sect. Joseph himself did not venture into "Zion," in the dangerous circumstances of his people, but undertook a journey to Canada with Sidney Rigdon and another, where they made some converts to the Book of Mormon. In the meantime Governor Dunklin wrote a sensible and conciliatory letter in reply to the Mormon petition, stating that the attack upon them was illegal and unjustifiable, and recommending them to apply for redress to the ordinary tribunals of the country. This letter was widely circulated, and the Mormons upon the strength of it resolved to remain in Independence, and "proceed with the building up of Zion." They commenced actions against the ringleaders of the mob, and engaged, for a fee of $1,000, the best counsel they could procure to support their cause. On the 30th of October the mob was once again in arms to expel them. Ten houses of the "saints" were unroofed and partially demolished at a place called Big Blue; and on the following days several houses were sacked at Independence. The Mormons in some instances defended their property, and a regular battle ultimately ensued between thirty of the saints, armed with rifles, and a large company of their opponents, also well armed. In this encounter two of the anti-Mormons were killed. Things assumed so alarming an aspect that the militia, under the command of Lieutenant-Governor Boggs, was called out. The militia, however, was anti-Mormon to a man, and the unhappy "saints" saw that they had no alternative but in flight. The blood that had been shed had caused such an exasperation against them, that it was unsafe for a solitary Mormon to show himself. The women took the alarm, and fled, with their children, across the Missouri river.

"On Thursday, November 7th," says the account in the "Times and Seasons," "the shore began to be lined on both sides of the ferry with men, women, and children, goods, waggons, boxes, chests, provisions; while the ferrymen were busily employed in crossing them over; and when night again closed upon the saints, the wilderness had much the appearance of a camp meeting. Hundreds of people were seen in every direction, some in tents, and some in the open air, around their fires, while the rain descended in torrents. Husbands were inquiring for their wives, and women for their husbands; parents for children, and children for parents. Some had the good fortune to escape with their family, household goods, and some provisions; while others knew not the fate of their friends, and had lost all their goods. The scene was indescribable, and would have melted the hearts of any people upon earth, except the blind oppressor, and prejudiced and ignorant bigot. Next day the company increased, and they were chiefly engaged in felling small cotton trees, and erecting them into temporary cabins, so that when night came on, they had the appearance of a village of wigwams, and the night being clear, the occupants began to enjoy some degree of comfort. The saints who fled, took refuge in the neighbouring counties, mostly in Clay county, which received them with some degree of kindness. Those who fled to the county of Van Buren were again driven and compelled to flee, and those who fled to Lafayette county were soon expelled, or the most of them, and had to move wherever they could find protection."

The public authorities of the State of Missouri, and indeed all the principal people, except those of Jackson county, were scandalized at these lawless proceedings, and sympathized with the efforts made by the Mormon leaders to obtain redress. The Attorney-General of the state wrote to say that if the Mormons desired to be re-established in their possessions, an adequate public force would be sent for their protection. He also advised that the Mormons should organize themselves into a regular company of militia, in which case they would be supplied with public arms. The "Prophet" having by this time returned to Kirtland, wrote to the "saints" in their distress, though he did not take the bold step of personally appearing among them. He reiterated that "Independence" or "Zion" was the place divinely appointed by God for the inheritance of the saints; that, therefore, they should not sell any land to which they had a legal title within its boundaries, but hold on "until the Lord in his wisdom should open a way for their return." He also advised that they should, if possible, purchase a tract of land in Clay county for present emergencies. He also had a "revelation," in which the Lord is represented as saying that these calamities were a punishment on the saints for their "jarrings, contentions, and envyings and strifes, and lustful and covetous desires." Zion, however, was the appointed place, and thither, in due time, the saints should return "with songs of everlasting joy." The "revelation," which was of unusual length, and contained a long parable, commanded the saints to "importune at the feet of the Judge; and if he did not heed, to importune at the feet of the Governor; and if the Governor did not heed, to importune at the feet of the President of the United States; and if the President did not heed, then the Lord God Himself would arise, and come forth out of his hiding-place, and in his fury vex the nation."

The saints, however, did not succeed in their object. They never returned to their "Zion," but remained for upwards of four years in Clay county. It was mostly uncleared land where they settled or squatted, but being a most industrious and persevering people, they laid out farms, erected mills and stores, and carried on their business successfully. They also laid the foundation of the towns of Far-West, and Adam-Ondiahman—but their blind fanaticism, here as well as in their former location, soon proved the cause of their expulsion from the whole State of Missouri. The slavery question, the calumny about their open adulteries and community of wives, their loud vaunts of their supreme holiness, their continually repeated declarations that the whole of Missouri was to be theirs by Divine command, and the quarrels that were the constant result, led to the same ill-feeling in Clay county. But before the final consummation, when, as one of their hymns says—

> " Missouri,
>   Like a whirlwind in its fury,
>   And without a judge or jury,
>   Drove the saints and spilled their blood"—

various interesting events in their history took place. On the 5th of May, 1834, Joseph resolved to proceed to Clay county and put the affairs of the scattered and dispirited church into order. Having organized a company of one hundred persons, mostly young men, and nearly all elders, priests, deacons, and teachers, he started at their head for Missouri. They travelled on foot; several waggons with their baggage and provisions, and relief to the destitute saints in Clay county, following behind. They were well provided with "fire arms and all sorts of munition of war of the most portable kind for self-defence." They were joined in two days by fifty more "saints" similarly armed. Their baggage waggons now amounted to twenty. Joseph divided his band into companies of twelve—consisting of two cooks, two firemen, two tent makers, two watermen, one runner or scout, one commissary, and two waggoners. Every night "at the sound of the trumpet they bowed down before the Lord in their several tents; and at the sound of the morning trumpet every man was again on his knees before the Lord." They passed through extensive wilds, and forded many streams and rivers; and though, as Joseph says, "their enemies were continually breathing threats of violence, they did not fear, neither did they hesitate to prosecute their journey, for God was with them, and his angels were before them, and the faith of the little band was unwavering." We knew, he adds, "that angels were our companions, for we saw them."

On their arrival in June at the Illinois river, the people were very anxious to know who and what they were. Many questions were asked, but the Mormons evaded them all, and gave no information as to their names, profession, business, or destination. Joseph himself travelled *incognito,* and though the settlers in Illinois vehemently suspected the band to be Mormons, they did not think it prudent to molest them. Having been safely ferried over the river, with all their baggage, they encamped two days afterwards amid some mounds, or ancient burial places of the Indians. Here Joseph played the "prophet," and gave his followers an additional proof of the authenticity of the Book of Mormon, and of the history of the Lamanites, the descendants of the Jews, therein recorded. This was intended as a master-stroke of policy, and doubtless was so under the circumstances. "The contemplation of the scenery," says Joseph, "produced peculiar sensations in our bosoms. The brethren procured a shovel and a hoe, and removing the earth of one of the mounds, to the depth of about a foot, discovered the skeleton of a man almost entire, and between his ribs was a Lamanitish arrow. The visions of the past being opened to my understanding by the spirit of the Almighty, I discovered that the person whose skeleton was before us was a white Lamanite, a large thick-set man, and a man of God. He was a warrior and chieftain under the great prophet Omandagus, who was known from the hill Cumorah, or Easter Sea, to the Rocky Mountains. His name was Zelph. He was killed in battle by the arrow, found among his ribs, during the last great struggle of the Lamanites and Nephites." On the next day, refreshed by this incident, and marvellously confirmed in the faith by the wisdom and knowledge of their prophet, they moved onwards, and crossed the Mississippi river, into the limits of the State of Missouri. Joseph was now on dangerous ground, and chose twenty men for his body-guards, appointing his brother Hyram Smith as their captain, and George Smith as his armour-bearer. He also appointed a "general," who daily inspected the little army, examined their fire-locks, and drilled them on the prairies. The people of Jackson county by this time were informed of Joseph Smith's arrival with his army. A deputation of them, who were in Clay county, to submit a proposal for the purchase of all the Mormon lands in Independence, no sooner heard that Mr. Smith was in the field in person, than they returned towards their own county to raise a force with which to meet and chastise the "prophet." One of their leaders, named Campbell, swore, as he adjusted his pistols in his holsters, "that the eagles and turkey buzzards should eat his flesh if he did not before two days fix Joe Smith and his army, so that their skins should not hold shucks." Joseph, who relates this story, adds, that Campbell and his men "went to the ferry, and undertook to cross the Missouri river after dusk; but the angel of God saw fit to sink the boat about the middle of the river, and seven out of the twelve that attempted to cross were drowned. Thus suddenly and justly," he adds, with great complacency, "they went to their own place by water; Campbell was among the missing. He floated down the river some four or five miles, and lodged upon a pile of drift wood, when the eagles, buzzards, ravens, crows, and wild animals ate his flesh from his bones, to fulfil his own words, and left him a horrible-looking skeleton of God's vengeance, which was discovered about three weeks afterwards by one Mr. Purtle."

Joseph, much delighted at the death of Campbell and his men, continued his march, and had a new "Revelation" from the Lord to comfort and excite his people. The cholera, however, broke out in his camp on the 24th of June, and Joseph attempted to cure it by "laying on of his hands and prayer." He failed, however, to do any good, and accounted for his failure by stating that "he quickly learned by painful experience that when the Great Jehovah decrees destruction, man must not attempt to stay his hand." Though he could not cure the cholera, he endeavoured to maintain his influence over the minds of his credulous followers, and impress them more forcibly with the miraculous nature of his mission, by stating that the enemies of the Mormons would suffer more severely from the visitation than the Mormons themselves. He laid particular stress upon the case of a woman who refused a "saint" some water to drink. "Before a week," said the "prophet," "the cholera entered that house, and that woman and three others of the family were dead." Joseph lost thirteen of his band by the ravages of the cholera. On the 1st of July he crossed into Jackson county, with a few friends, "to set his feet once more on that goodly land;" and, after remaining one day, proceeded with the remainder of his company to Clay county. He did not remain long with the saints, for we find that he arrived on the 2d and started back for Kirtland on the 9th. It was not prudent, it appears, that he should make himself too familiar with his believers. The great man was not to be seen too closely with impunity, for some of his travelling companions began to accuse him of "prophesying lies in the name of the Lord," and also of appropriating "moneys" to which he had no right. He did not leave, however, without organizing and encouraging the main body of the fugitives from Jackson county, and establishing the community in Clay county on a better footing than when he arrived. On his return to Kirtland, his first step was to bring to trial before his church the brother who accused him of "prophesying lies" and of appropriating moneys. The brother confessed his error, retracted his charge, and was forgiven.

The history of the sect for the next three years is one of strife and contention with their unrelenting and vindictive enemies in Missouri. The numbers of the Mormons increased with the numbers of their opponents, and the warfare raged so bitterly that the whole people of Missouri were ranged either on one side or the other. In the autumn of 1837 Joseph's bank at Kirtland stopped payment, the district was flooded with its worthless paper, and Joseph had a "revelation" commanding him to depart finally for Missouri, and live among the saints in the land of their inheritance. Joseph obeyed the "revelation" by departing secretly in the night, or "between two days," as it is called in America, leaving his creditors to their remedy. He found the affairs of his "church" in considerable confusion on his arrival. The "saints" formed a numerous and powerful body, but they did not agree among themselves; and occasional seceders and deserters from their camp—many of them consisting of men who were ashamed of their own delusions, besides others who were actuated by vindictive motives or disappointed ambition—spread abroad all sorts of rumours and stories to the disadvantage of the sect. The great schism alluded to in a previous part of this Letter broke out in 1838, when Joseph Smith found it necessary to denounce some of his oldest confederates, among others "Oliver Cowdery," one of the three witnesses to the authenticity of the Book of Mormon, and to the existence of the gold plates; Martin Harris, another witness; Sidney Rigdon, his co-equal in the government of the church, and various disciples and apostles. Sidney Rigdon was afterwards forgiven, being too important a personage to be turned into an enemy. In the midst of these squabbles, the people of Jackson county, joined by the people of Clay county, Caldwell county, and others, made a series of pertinacious efforts to expel them finally from Missouri. The Mormons were all well armed, and a body of them, instituted expressly for the defence of the sect, was organized under the name of the "Danite Band," or, as they were sometimes called, the "Destroying Angels." An affidavit made before a justice of the peace in Ray county, Missouri, on the 24th of October, 1838, and sworn by a man named Marsh, who had held office in the Mormon Church, and another affidavit, signed by Orson Hyde, an ex-apostle of the church, alleged the following facts with reference to these "Danites," and their proceedings:—

"They have among them a company consisting of all that are considered true Mormons, called the Danites, who have taken an oath to support the heads of the church in all things that they say or do, whether right or wrong. Many, however, of this band are much dissatisfied with this oath, as being against moral and religious principles. On Saturday last, I am informed by the Mormons that they had a meeting at Far West, at which they appointed a company of twelve, by the name of the Destruction Company, for the purpose of burning and destroying; and that if the people of Buncombe came to do mischief upon the people of Caldwell, and committed depredations upon the Mormons, they were to burn Buncombe; and if the people of Clay and Ray made any movements against them, this destroying company were to burn Liberty and Richmond. The plan of said Smith, the prophet, is to take this State; and he professes to his people to intend taking the United States, and ultimately the whole world. This is the belief of the church, and my own opinion of the prophet's plans and intentions. The prophet inculcates the notion, and it is believed by every true Mormon that Smith's prophecies are superior to the law of the land. I have heard the prophet say that he would yet tread down his enemies, and walk over their dead bodies; that if he was not let alone, he would be a second Mahomet to this generation, and that he would make it one gore of blood from the Rocky Mountains to the Atlantic Ocean; that like Mahomet, whose motto, in treating for peace, was 'the Alcoran or the sword,' so should it be eventually with us, 'Joseph Smith or the sword.' These last statements were made during the last summer. The number of armed men at Adam-on-diahmon was between three and four hundred.

"THOMAS B. MARCH.

"Sworn to and subscribed before me, the day herein written.
"HENRY JACOBS, J.P., Ray county, Missouri.

"Richmond, Missouri, Oct. 24, 1838."

AFFIDAVIT OF ORSON HYDE.

"The most of the statements in the foregoing disclosure of T.B. March I know to be true; the remainder I believe to be true.
"ORSON HYDE, Richmond, Oct. 24, 1838.

"Sworn to and subscribed before me on the day above written,
"HENRY JACOBS, J.P."

CERTIFICATE OF THOMAS C. BURCH AND OTHERS.

"The undersigned committee, on the part of the citizens of Ray county, have no doubt but Thomas B. March and Orson Hyde, whose names are signed to the foregoing certificates, have been members of the Mormon church in full fellowship until very recently, when they voluntarily abandoned the Mormon church and faith, and that said March was, at the time of his dissenting, the president of the twelve Apostles, and president of the Church at Far West; and that said Hyde was at that time one of the twelve Apostles, and that they left the Church, and abandoned the faith of the Mormons, from a conviction of their immorality and impiety.

"Thos. C. Burch; William Hudgins; Henry Jacobs; George Woodward; J. R. Hendley; C. R. Morehead; O. H. Searcy.—Richmond, October 24, 1838."

These and other statements of a similar kind, whether true or false, were daily inculcated, and produced the effect of exasperating the people against Joseph and his disciples. The Mormons, seeing the law broken by their opponents, refused obedience to the law themselves. They fortified their farms and towns, and treated with contempt the legal processes which it was attempted to serve upon them. The militia of the state was ultimately called out against them, under the command of General Doniphan. His measures were so vigorous, and the exasperation of the people against Joseph was so great, that the Mormons, dreading a general massacre of their sect, resolved to leave the state of Missouri and take refuge in Illinois, then very partially cleared and settled. Joseph Smith also, dreading assassination, and remembering the opinion formerly expressed by Governor Dunklin against the lawless proceedings of the mob of Jackson county, surrendered to answer the various charges of treason, murder, and felony, which were brought against him. The "treason" was for making war against the state of Missouri, the "murder" was the death of the two men in the affray in Jackson county, and the "felony" was the destruction and robbery of property committed by the Danite band. Joseph anticipated an acquittal upon the whole of these charges, and remained in prison for several months awaiting his trial. In the meantime the Mormons were hunted out of Missouri, no opportunity being allowed them to sell their farms, or enter into arrangements for the disposal of their property. In the midst of an inclement winter—in December and January, 1838 and 1839—men, women, and children—the sick and the aged, as well as the young and strong—were turned out into the prairies or forests, without food or sufficient protection from the weather. In this miserable plight they arrived in Illinois in small detachments, and were most kindly received by the settlers, as well as by the Indians. Subscriptions were entered into for their relief, and many of them procured situations in farms, mills, and stores. After a time they began to hold up their heads again. Their numbers had become formidable in Illinois. Persecution was doing its ordinary work in making proselytes, and the congregations of the saints were increased daily by new converts from among the people of Illinois. Early in the spring of 1839 the prophet escaped from prison, and made his appearance among his followers at a place called Quincey, in Illinois. His rude eloquence, his confident appeals to Heaven, his magnificent promises, his tact and skill, and the joy of the sect that he was once more among them, all combined to restore confidence. The great bulk of the Mormons were speedily gathered about a village called "Commerce," just above the Desmoines Rapids, on the Mississippi river. Here they soon made arrangements for settling down. The "Saints" joined them from various parts of the United States, many of them bringing considerable sums of money. As land was cheap, and purchasing almost as easy as squatting, they entered into possession of large tracts in the neighbourhood of "Commerce." Their numbers speedily amounted to fifteen thousand souls, including men, women, and children. They planned a city upon the site of Commerce, to which they gave the name of "Nauvoo," or "the beautiful," a word that occurs in the Book of Mormon. In the course of a year and a half they built about 2,000 houses, besides schools and other public buildings. They now called the place the Holy City. Joseph Smith was appointed its mayor, and for a brief period in his troubled life enjoyed the supremacy which was the great object of his existence, and the darling dream of his ambition. His word was law. He was both the temporal and spiritual head of his people, and enjoyed, beside the titles of "Prophet," "President," and "Mayor," the military title of "General" Smith, in right of his command over a body of militia, which he organized under the name of the Nauvoo Legion. Joseph became rather chary of giving forth "revelations" after he finally left Kirtland, but it was necessary to have a revelation with reference to Nauvoo, the Holy City. It was published accordingly in the month of January, 1841, and directed the building of a magnificent temple, to which all the saints were to contribute a tithe of their possessions, or of their time and labour. "Let all my saints come from afar," said this "revelation," the last that the prophet appears to have issued, "and send ye swift messengers, yea, chosen messengers, and say unto them, 'Come ye with all your gold, and your silver, and your precious stones, and with all your antiquities, and with all who have knowledge of antiquities, that will come, may come, and bring the box tree, and the fir tree, and the pine tree, together with all the precious trees of the earth, and with iron, and with copper, and with brass, and with zinc, and with all your precious things of the earth, and build a house to my name for the Most High to dwell therein.'" The saints were also commanded to build "a boarding-house" for the boarding of strangers, "Let it be built in my name, and let my name be named upon it, and let my servant Joseph Smith and his house have place therein from generation to generation, for ever and ever, saith the Lord; and let the name of the house be called the Nauvoo House, and let it be a delightful habitation for man, and a resting-place for the weary traveller, that he may contemplate the glory of Zion, and the glory of this, the corner-stone thereof." This "revelation" was not only the last, but the most elaborate of all the compositions issued under this name by the "prophet." It is divided into forty-six heads or paragraphs, and enters minutely into directions for raising the funds for these undertakings, and also for governing the church in all its various departments.

The building of the temple was immediately commenced. The site chosen was exceedingly fine, being on a hill commanding a magnificent view on every side. It was built of a polished white lime-stone, almost as hard as marble, and was 138 feet in length by 88 in breadth. It was surrounded by a pyramidal tower, ascending by steps 170 feet from the ground, and the internal decorations are described as having been very costly. The Mormons expended nearly a million of dollars upon this edifice. Shortly previous to this time the sect first began to be heard of in England. In a short sketch of the rise, progress, and faith of the Mormons, inserted in the fifth volume of the "Times and Seasons," it is stated that in 1837 the first mission to England was undertaken, under the direction of Elders O. Hyde, the same whose signature appears to the discharging affidavits relative to the "Saints," and H. C. Kimball. These two baptised two thousand people into the faith, chiefly in Manchester, Birmingham, Leeds, Liverpool, Glasgow, and South Wales. In 1843 the number of the sect in England had increased to upwards of 10,000. In 1844, Elder Lorenzo Snow being then in England, forwarded, by desire of the prophet, a copy of the Book of Mormon to Queen Victoria, and another to his Royal Highness Prince Albert, a circumstance at which the saints in Nauvoo seemed greatly to rejoice. A Mormon poet exclaimed, in reference to it—

> "Oh! would she now her influence lend—
>   The influence of royalty—
> Messiah's kingdom to extend,
>   And Zion's nursing mother be.
>
> "Then with the glory of her name
>   Inscribed on Zion's lofty spire,
> She'd win a wreath of endless fame,
>   To last when other wreaths expire."

Before entering, however, upon any statements relative to the past doings of the Mormons in this country, and their present emigrational proceedings, it will be desirable to conclude the personal history of the "prophet."

The length to which this Letter has already extended, compels me to postpone it until my next.

LABOUR AND THE POOR.

—◆—

LIVERPOOL.

[FROM OUR SPECIAL CORRESPONDENT.]

THE MORMONS—DEATH OF THE PROPHET—ENGLISH EMIGRATION OF THE SECT (CONCLUDED).

LETTER XIII.

My last Letter brought down the history of Joseph Smith to his establishment in Nauvoo, as mayor of that city, and his self-appointment to the rank of General of the Nauvoo Militia. For a time, the "prophet" and his followers were warned by sad experience, and were less haughty, less overbearing, and less presumptuous, in their intercourse with the "Gentiles," as they called all who were not Mormons. But the prosperity which attended them in Illinois, and the rapid growth of Nauvoo, soon filled them again with insolence and spiritual pride. The dissensions, which had subsided in adversity, were renewed in prosperity. The power and influence of Joseph were too great not to excite envy, and Sidney Rigdon did great mischief by introducing a novelty called the "spiritual wife" doctrine. This caused great scandal, both among the Mormons and among the Gentiles. Joseph himself appears, unless he has been grievously maligned, and unless the affidavits published by his opponents were forgeries, to have had as great a *penchant* for a plurality of wives as Mahomet himself. Sidney Rigdon, according to the same authority, outdid him in this respect, and had "revelations" of his own, which he made subservient to the gratification of his passions. There was possibly some exaggeration in these stories, but they do not appear to have been wholly unfounded.

A public lecturer of the name of Newhall published, in the *Salem* (Massachusetts) *Advertiser,* an account of a visit made to Nauvoo, in 1843. He described the Temple as a very "magnificent structure, different from anything in ancient or modern history," and "General" Smith's legion as a very fine body of men. He was present at a grand review of the corps by Joseph himself, accompanied by "six ladies on horseback—who were dressed in black velvet, and wore waving plumes of white feathers, and rode up and down in front of the regiment." He described Joseph himself as "very sociable, easy, cheerful, obliging and kind, and very hospitable—in a word—a jolly fellow— and one of the last persons whom he would have supposed God would have raised up as a prophet or a priest." Another account of Joseph was published about the same time by a Methodist preacher of the name of Prior. This gentleman says:—

"I will not attempt to describe the various feelings of my bosom as I took my seat in a conspicuous place in the congregation, who were waiting in breathless silence for his appearance. While he tarried I had plenty of time to revolve in my mind the character and common report of that truly singular personage. I fancied that I should behold a countenance sad and sorrowful, yet containing the fiery marks of rage and exasperation. I supposed that I should be enabled to discover in him some of those thoughtful and reserved features, those mystic and sarcastic glances, which I had fancied the ancient sages to possess. I expected to see that fearful faltering look of conscious shame which, from what I had heard of him, he might be expected to evince. He appeared at last; but how was I disappointed when, instead of the heads and horns of the beast and false prophet, I beheld only the appearance of a common man, of tolerably large proportions. I was sadly disappointed, and thought that, although his appearance could not be wrested to indicate anything against him, yet he would manifest all I had heard of him when he began to preach. I sat uneasy, and watched him closely. He commenced preaching, not from the book of Mormon, however, but from the Bible; the first chapter of the first of Peter was his text. He commenced calmly and continued dispassionately to pursue his subject, while I sat in breathless silence, waiting to hear that foul aspersion of the other sects, that diabolical disposition of revenge, and to hear that rancorous denunciation of every individual but a Mormon. I waited in vain; I listened with surprise; I sat uneasy in my seat, and could hardly persuade myself but that he had been apprised of my presence, and so ordered his discourse on my account, that I might not be able to find fault with it, for instead of a jumbled jargon of half connected sentences, and a volley of imprecations, and diabolical and malignant denunciations heaped upon the heads of all who differed from him, and the dreadful twisting and wresting of the Scriptures to suit his own peculiar views, and attempts to weave a web of dark and mystic sophistry around the Gospel truths, which I had anticipated, he glided along through a very interesting and elaborate discourse with all the care and happy facility of one who was well aware of his important station and his duty to God and man."

The same writer thus describes Nauvoo:—

"At length the city burst upon my sight. Instead of seeing a few miserable log cabins and mud hovels, which I had expected to find, I was surprised to see one of the most romantic places that I had visited in the west. The buildings, though many of them were small, and of wood, yet bore the marks of neatness which I have not seen equalled in this country. The far-spread plain at the bottom of the hill was dotted over with the habitations of men, with such majestic profusion, that I was almost willing to believe myself mistaken, and instead of being in Nauvoo of Illinois, among Mormons, that I was in Italy at the city of Leghorn (which the location of Nauvoo resembles very much), and among the eccentric Italians. I gazed for some time with fond admiration upon the plain below. Here and there arose a tall majestic brick house, speaking loudly of the genius and untiring labour of the inhabitants, who have snatched the place from the clutches of obscurity, and wrested it from the bonds of disease; and in two or three short years rescued it from a dreary waste to transform it into one of the first cities in the west. The hill upon which I stood was covered over with the dwellings of men, and amid them was seen to rise the hewn stone and already accomplished work of the Temple, which is now raised fifteen or twenty feet above the ground. The few trees that were permitted to stand are now in full foliage, and are scattered with a sort of fantastic irregularity over the slope of the hill.

"But there was one object which was far more noble to behold, and far more majestic than any other yet presented to my sight, and that was the wide-spread and unrivalled father of waters, the Mississippi river, whose mirror-bedded waters lay in majestic extension before the city, and in one general curve seemed to sweep gallantly by the beautiful place. On the farther side was seen the dark-green woodland, bending under its deep foliage, with here and there an interstice bearing the marks of cultivation. A few houses could be seen through the trees on the other side of the river, directly opposite to which is spread a fairy isle, covered with beautiful timber. The isle and the romantic swell of the river soon brought my mind back to days of yore, and to the bright emerald isles of the far-famed fairy land. The bold and prominent rise of the hill, fitting to the plain with exact regularity, and the plain pushing itself into the river, forcing it to bend around its obstacle with becoming grandeur, and fondly to cling around it to add to the heightened and refined lustre of this sequestered land.

"I passed on into the more active parts of the city, looking into every street and lane to observe all that was passing. I found all the people engaged in some useful and healthy employment. The place was alive with business—much more so than any place I have visited since the hard times commenced. I sought in vain for anything that bore the marks of immorality, but was both astonished and highly pleased at my ill success. I could see no loungers about the streets, nor any drunkards about the taverns. I did not meet with those distorted features of ruffians, or with the ill-bred and impudent. I heard not an oath in the place, I saw not a gloomy countenance; all were cheerful, polite, and industrious."

From this time until 1844, the wealth and power of the sect continued to increase, their numbers being augmented from time to time by the English immigration from Liverpool. The "Times and Seasons," of the 15th of May in that year, announced to the Saints "that Nauvoo was becoming a large city, and that a number of splendid houses were erected. Three ships' companies had arrived in the spring from England, and the Prophet was in good health and spirits." In 1844, they carried their heads so high that they put Joseph forward as a candidate for the Presidentship of the United States, and his still faithful Sidney Rigdon as a candidate for the Vice-Presidentship. Joseph was of course aware that his candidature was an act which had no other meaning than to please his disciples; and he wrote to Mr. Clay, who was supposed to have a good chance of being elected to that office, to know what course he would pursue towards the Mormons? As Joseph Smith could influence many votes, the answer of Mr. Clay was studiously courteous. "I have viewed," said he, "with a lively interest the progress of the Latter-day Saints. I have sympathized in their sufferings under injustice, and I think in common with all other religious communities they ought to enjoy the security and the protection of the constitution and the laws." Joseph was at the climax of his earthly glory; and might have been comparatively happy even amid the persecutions of his neighbours the "Gentiles," had it not been for secessions from his church, and the annoyances springing out of the "spiritual wife" doctrine of his indiscreet friend Rigdon. The population of Nauvoo was almost wholly composed of Mormons. The corporation over which the "Prophet" presided as "mayor" assumed a jurisdiction independent of, and sometimes hostile to, that of the state of Illinois. They denied validity to the legal documents of the state, unless countersigned by the mayor of Nauvoo, and they passed a law to punish any stranger in the city who should use disrespectful language about Smith. As time wore on, hostility against the sect increased. They waged a constant warfare with the nine counties that adjoin Handcock county, in which Nauvoo is situated, and their old feud with Missouri was kept up by legal proceedings, which, in a somewhat vexatious manner, were instituted against Smith. Lieut.-Governor Boggs, of Missouri, was fired at through a window by a Mormon, and narrowly escaped assassination. He swore that to the best of his belief Joseph Smith was a party to this attempt to murder him. The legal proceedings consequent upon this charge, tended to excite and maintain the bitterest animosity between the "Saints" and the "Gentiles." But the "spiritual-wife" doctrine of Sidney Rigdon was the cause of the greatest scandal, and ultimately produced an unlooked for catastrophe—the murder of Joseph Smith and his brother Hiram, by an exasperated mob in the gaol of Carthage.

It appears from many conflicting stories which have been published, that one Dr. Foster, a Mormon, and member of the Danite Band, or society of the "Destroying Angels," having been absent from home, suddenly returned without giving notice to his wife. He found the carriage of the prophet at the door. Being the leader of a secession from the Mormon church, and having, it is alleged, had previous suspicions of an improper intercourse, he questioned his wife as soon as Smith took his departure. The enemies of the "prophet" assert that she confessed that he had been endeavouring to prevail upon her to become his "spiritual wife." Dr. Foster brooded over this grievance for some time, and finding among the seceders that many were inclined to support him in attacking the characters of Joseph Smith and Sidney Rigdon, he, and another person named Law, commenced the publication, in the city of Nauvoo itself, of a newspaper, called the *Expositor.* In the first number they published the affidavits of sixteen women, to the effect that Smith, Rigdon, and others, had endeavoured to convert them to the spiritual wife doctrine, and to seduce them under the plea of having had especial permission from Heaven. This was somewhat too daring, and Joseph Smith in his capacity of Mayor of Nauvoo immediately summoned the corporation to consider the publication. They unanimously declared it to be a public nuisance, and ordered the city marshal to "abate it forthwith." A body of the "prophet's" adherents, to the number of two hundred and upwards, sallied forth in obedience to this order, and, proceeding to the office of the *Expositor,* speedily razed it to the ground. They then destroyed the presses, and made a bonfire of the papers and furniture. Foster and Law fled for their lives, and took refuge in Carthage. The Mormons, it must not be forgotten, indignantly deny the charges brought against Joseph Smith upon this subject of "spiritual wives," and especially the story of Mrs. Foster, which they treat as a base and utterly unfounded calumny. As regards Sidney Rigdon they are not so emphatic in their denial. Whatever the truth may have been, the consequences to the sect were momentous. Foster and Law applied for a warrant against Joseph and Hiram Smith, in the County Court at Carthage. The warrant was granted and served upon the Mayor of Nauvoo. He refused to acknowledge its validity, and the constable who served it was marched out of Nauvoo by the city marshal. The authorities of the county could not suffer this affront to the law; and the militia were ordered out to support the county officer in arresting the Smiths. The Mormons in Nauvoo fortified the city, and determined to fight to the last extremity in support of the "Prophet." The "brethren" from all parts of the country hastened to give assistance. Illinois, like Missouri, divided itself into two great camps, the Mormons and the Anti-Mormons, and the circumstances were so menacing that the governor took the field in person. In a proclamation to the people of Illinois, he stated that he had discovered that nothing but the utter destruction of the city of Nauvoo would satisfy the troops under his command, and that if he marched into the city pretexts would not be wanting on their part for the commencement of slaughter. Anxious to spare the effusion of blood, he called upon the two Smiths to surrender peaceably, pledging his word and the honour of the State that they should be protected. He also called upon the Mormons to surrender their public arms, and upon the Nauvoo legion to submit to the command of a state officer. The Mormons agreed to the terms, and Joseph and his brother surrendered to take their trial for the riot, and for the destruction of the office of the "Expositor." The prophet had a presentiment of evil, and said as he surrendered, "I am going like a lamb to the slaughter, but I have a conscience void of offence, and shall die innocent." While in prison at Carthage, another writ was served upon him and his brother for high treason against the state of Illinois. As the mob breathed vengeance against both prisoners, and as the militia of the country very indecently sided with them, and were not to be depended on in case of any violence being offered to the two Smiths by the people, the Governor was requested by the Mormons to set a guard over the gaol. On the morning of the 26th of

June, 1844, the Governor visited the prisoners in gaol, and pledged his word to protect them against the threatened violence. It now began to be rumoured among the mob that there would be no case against the Smiths on either of the charges brought against them, and that the Governor was anxious that they should escape. A band of ruffians accordingly resolved that as "law could not reach them, powder and shot should." About six o'clock in the evening of the 27th the small guard stationed at the gaol was overpowered by a band of nearly two hundred men, with blackened faces, who rushed into the prison where the unfortunate men were confined. They were at the time in consultation with two of their friends. The mob fired upon the whole four. Hiram was shot first, and fell immediately, exclaiming "I am a dead man." Joseph endeavoured to leap from the window, and was shot in the attempt, exclaiming "Oh Lord, my God." They were both shot after they were dead, receiving four balls. John Taylor, one of the two Mormons in the room, was seriously wounded, but afterwards recovered. Thus died this remarkable man. "In the short space of twenty years," says the account of his "Martyrdom," appended to the Book of Doctrines and Covenants, "he brought forth the Book of Mormon, which he translated by the gift and power of God, and was the means of publishing in two continents. He sent the fulness of the everlasting Gospel which it contained to the four quarters of the earth. He brought forth the revelations and commandments which compose the Book of Doctrines and Covenants, and many other wise documents and instructions for the benefit of the children of men. He gathered many thousands of the Latter-day Saints, founded a great city, and left a fame and a name that cannot be slain. He lived great, and died great in the eyes of God and his people; and like most of the Lord's anointed in ancient times, sealed his mission and his works with his own blood; and so did his own brother Hiram. In life they were not divided, and in death they were not separated."

The "Christian Reflector," a less friendly critic of his character and actions, thus spoke of his life and death:—

> "It is but a few weeks since the death of Joe Smith was announced. His body now sleeps, and his spirit has gone to its reward. Various are the opinions of men concerning this singular personage; but whatever may be the views of any in reference to his principles, objects, or moral character, all agree that he was one of the most remarkable men of the age. Not fifteen years have elapsed since a band, composed of six persons, was formed in Palmyra, New York, of which Joseph Smith, jun.,

was the presiding genius. Most of these were connected with the family of Smith the senior. They were notorious for breach of contracts, and the repudiation of their honest debts. All of them were addicted to vice. They obtained their living not by honourable labour, but by deceiving their neighbours with their marvellous tales of money-digging. Notwithstanding the low origin, poverty, and profligacy of the members of that band of mountebanks, they have augmented their numbers till more than 100,000 persons are now numbered among the followers of the Mormon prophet, and never were increasing so rapidly as at the time of his death. Born in the very lowest walks of life, reared in poverty, educated in vice, having no claims to even common intelligence, coarse and vulgar in deportment, the Prophet Smith succeeded in establishing a religious creed, the tenets of which have been taught throughout the length and breadth of America. The prophet's virtues have been rehearsed and admired in Europe; the ministers of Nauvoo have ever found a welcome in Asia; and Africa has listened to the grave sayings of the seer of Palmyra. The standard of the Latter-day Saints has been reared on the banks of the Nile, and even the Holy Land has been entered by the emissaries of this wicked impostor.

"He founded a city in one of the most beautiful situations in the world, in a beautiful curve of the 'father of waters,' of no mean pretension, and in it he has collected a population of twenty-five thousand, from every part of the world. He planned the architecture of a magnificent temple, and reared its walls nearly fifty feet, which, if completed, will be the most beautiful, most costly, and the most noble building in America. Its walls are of solid stone, four feet in thickness, supported by thirty stone pillars. That building is a monument pointing the traveller to the genius of its founder.

"The acts of his life exhibit a character as incongruous as it is remarkable. If we can credit his own words, and the testimony of eyewitnesses, he was at the same time the vicegerent of God—a tavernkeeper and prophet of Jehovah, and a base libertine—a minister of the religion of peace, and a lieutenant-general—a ruler of tens of thousands, and a slave to all his own base, unbridled passions—a preacher of righteousness, and a profane swearer—a worshipper of Bacchus, mayor of a city, and a miserable bar-room fiddler—a judge upon the judicial bench, and an invader of the civil, social, and moral relations of men; and, notwithstanding these inconsistencies of character, there are not wanting thousands who are willing to stake their souls' eternal salvation upon his veracity. For aught we know, time and distance will embellish his life with some new and rare virtues which his most intimate friends failed to discover while living with him.

"Reasoning from effect to cause, we must conclude that the Mormon Prophet was of no common genius; few are able to commence and carry out an imposition like his, so long, and to such an extent. And we see, in the history of his success, most striking proofs of the gullibility of a large portion of the human family. What may not men be induced to believe?"

The perpetrators of the shameful murder of the two brothers were never discovered. Several persons were arrested on suspicion, but there was not sufficient proof to convict them. The event was greatly deplored. The sincerest opponents of Mormonism were those who were most grieved at it. Joseph Smith murdered was a greater prophet than Joseph Smith alive; and it was predicted, both by friends and foes, that, however rapid the progress of the sect might have been in past times, it would be still more rapid when fanaticism might point to the martyrs of the faith—when the faults of Smith would be buried in the oblivion of the tomb, and when his virtues would be enhanced by the remembrance of his fate. The prediction was speedily verified, but not however until the Mormons had passed through another long period of persecution and suffering.

No sooner had the Smiths been removed from the way of his long-concealed but violent ambition, than Sidney Rigdon strove to vault into the vacant place of the deceased "prophet." Sidney, however, miscalculated his power and influence. Joseph had long been mistrustful of him. Sidney knew too much, and Joseph, without quarrelling with him, had kept him at arm's length. The mistrust of the prophet was shared by the principal Mormons, and his "spiritual wife" doctrine had alienated from him the confidence of many who had once looked upon him as a founder of the faith, and a pillar of the church. After the death of Joseph, Sidney Rigdon had a "revelation," commanding the saints to withdraw from their enemies, and leave Nauvoo, and establish themselves in Pittsburg. This "revelation" contradicted the "revelations" of Joseph; and the Saints under the guidance of Brigham Young, who had his own ambitious views to serve, treated Sidney's "revelations" as the unwarrantable innovations of a man who "lied before the Lord," and sought the destruction of his Saints. He was summoned to answer for his misdeeds before the high quorum of the priesthood. He refused to appear, and, evidence having been given in his absence, he was expelled from the church, and, to use the words of his sentence, "handed over to the buffetings of Satan."

The Missourians and anti-Mormons relaxed in their hostility after the death of the prophet and his brother, and for a twelvemonth affairs went on more quietly in the city of Nauvoo. Brigham Young succeeded to the chief presidency of the church, and the Saints carried on with vigour the building of the temple and the Nauvoo House, in order, as they said, to fulfil the "revelation," and prove to the Gentiles, not only the divinity of their mission, but their power, wealth, and perseverance. Quarrels occasionally took place. The Mormons, when insulted or oppressed, had not always the patience to forbear from retaliation; and among men who habitually bore arms to protect themselves it is not surprising that the conflicts should not in all cases have been confined to words. Skirmish succeeded skirmish, until it became once more necessary to call out the militia for the preservation of the peace. Regular battles ensued, blood was shed, lives were lost, and the exasperation of both parties was raised even beyond its former height. The Governor was called upon to interfere actively, and a meeting of delegates from the nine counties surrounding Nauvoo was convened, at which it was asserted by all the speakers that there would be no peace for Illinois as long as the Mormons remained within its boundaries. The delegates pledged themselves to support each other to the last extremity in expelling them forcibly, if they could not otherwise be induced to go. After a series of struggles and negotiations, and a regular siege of the city of Nauvoo by the Anti-Mormons, the Saints agreed to leave Illinois in the spring of 1846, or as "soon as grass grew and water ran," provided that in the interval they should not be molested, and that they should be allowed time and opportunity to sell their farms and properties, and remove beyond the limits of civilization. The first companies of the Mormons commenced crossing the Mississippi on the 3d February, 1846. They amounted to 1,600, men, women, and children, and passed the river on the ice. They continued to leave in detachments or companies of similar magnitude until July and August, travelling by ox-teams towards California, then almost unknown, and quite unpeopled by the Anglo-Saxon race. The Anti-Mormons asserted that the intention of the Saints was to excite the Indians against the commonwealth, and that they would return at the head of a multitude of the red skins to take vengeance upon the white people for the indignities they had suffered. Nothing appears to have been further from the intentions of the Mormons. Their sole object was to plant their church in some fertile and hitherto undiscovered spot, where they might worship God in their own fashion, unmolested by any other sect of Christians. The war against Mexico was then raging, and, to test the loyalty of the Mormons, it was suggested by their foes that a demand should be made upon them to raise 500 men for the service of the country. The Mormons obeyed, and 500 of their best men enrolled themselves under the command of General Kearney, and marched 2,400 miles with the armies of the United States. At the conclusion of the Mexican war they were disbanded in Upper California. The Mormons allege that it was one of this band who, in working at a mill, first discovered the golden treasures of California, and the Saints are said to have succeeded in amassing large quantities of the precious metal before the secret was made generally known to the "Gentiles."

The "Great Salt Lake Valley" was ultimately fixed upon as the halting-place and future home of the sect; and thither large detachments of Mormons have since directed their steps. In 1846, whilst one party went overland to Upper California another party chartered the ship Brooklyn at New York, and sailed round to the Pacific, by Cape Horn. This party was amongst the earliest of the arrivals in California, and its members are said to have been exceedingly fortunate at the "diggings," and to have amassed large quantities of gold. The courage of the sect revived, and they were never more elated at any period of their history than now. The Salt Lake Valley, in Deseret, is about eighty miles in length by twenty or thirty in breadth. Through the middle runs a beautiful stream, to which they have given the name of the "Western Jordan." They laid out a large city in 1847, and commenced the building of a new Temple. The climate is said to be excellent and the soil highly fertile. Fifteen thousand Mormons, exclusive of Indians, already inhabit the valley. About 5,000, in detachments of 400 and 500 each, are at present on their road overland from New Orleans, by St. Louis and Council Bluffs, the whole of whom are expected to reach their destination in August, September, and October of the present year. At their half-way station at Council Bluffs there is a Mormon population of about 20,000 people, who have squatted on a vast plain or prairie extending for about 100 miles, by 50 or 60 in breadth. Here they raise provisions and buy cattle, make and mend waggons, and save money to establish themselves ultimately in the Great Salt Lake City. Many of them remain a year or two before they move onward, so that these settlements are always filling with the new, and thinning of the old immigration. The principal town in this district is Kanesville, where there are said to be about 1,000 Mormons.

Several emissaries, or "Apostles," of the sect were despatched to Europe at the commencement of the present year, to "gather" the European Saints to the New Zion. Some have proceeded to Germany, to France, to Norway, and to Russia, but the strongholds of the sect are in England, Wales, and Scotland. Their elders state that nearly 30,000 people in Great Britain are members of their church, and that there is not a considerable town in which they have not a congregation. The number of Mormons in London is about 1,200; in Liverpool, 600; in Manchester, 700; in Birmingham, 1,100; in Glasgow, 500; in Edinburgh, 300; in Sheffield, 400; in Macclesfield, 200; in Paisley, 100; in Dundee, 100—while "branches" of from 20 to 50 members are to be found in all the minor towns. The Mormon emigration from Liverpool, by means of an agency established there in 1841, has amounted, according to a statement furnished by a principal Mormon "Apostle" now in Liverpool on an emigrational mission, to about 13,500. For the two years prior to the death of Joseph Smith, thirteen vessels wholly engaged by the Mormons for the emigration of their people quitted Liverpool for New Orleans; the largest number proceeding by one vessel being 314, and the smallest 60. During the last year the Mormon emigration amounted to nearly 2,500. Being desirous to know something of the class of persons who emigrate under Mormon auspices, to establish themselves in the Salt Lake City, and to ascertain from what parts of the country their ranks were principally recruited, I made inquiries at the office in Liverpool of Messrs. Pilkington and Wilson, the highly respectable shipping agents for the New Orleans packets. The gentleman who is the principal manager of this branch of their business, and who is thus thrown into frequent intercourse with the Mormons, was kind enough to furnish me with the following statement:—

"With regard to 'Mormon' emigration and the class of persons of which it is composed, they are principally farmers and mechanics, with some few clerks, surgeons, &c. They are generally intelligent and well-behaved, and many of them are highly respectable. Since the 1st of October, when, according to the new act, a note of the trades, professions, and avocations of emigrants was first required to be taken by the emigration officer, until March in the present year, the following seems to be the numbers of each who have gone out in our ships as far as I can ascertain. I find in our books the names of 16 miners, 20 engineers, 19 farmers, 108 labourers, 10 joiners, 25 power-loom weavers, 15 shoemakers, 12 smiths, 19 tailors, 8 watchmakers, 25 stone-masons, 5 butchers,

4 bakers, 4 potters, 10 painters, 7 shipwrights, 4 ironmoulders, 3 bas- ketmakers, 5 dyers, 5 ropers, 4 papermakers, 4 glasscutters, 5 nailors, 5 saddlers, 6 sawyers, 4 gunmakers, &c. These emigrants generally take with them the implements necessary to pursue their occupation in the Salt Lake Valley, and it is no unusual thing to perceive (previous to the ship leaving the dock) a watchmaker with his tools spread out upon his box, busy examining and repairing the watches of the 'brethren,' or a cutler displaying to his fellow-passengers samples of his handicraft which he is bringing out with him. Of course the stock thus taken out is small when placed in the scale with the speculations of commercial men; but judging from the enormous quantity of boxes generally taken by these people, in the aggregate it is large indeed. Many of these fam- ilies have four, five, or six boxes, bound and hooped with iron, marked 'Not wanted on the passage,' and which are stowed down in the ship's hold; these all contain implements of husbandry or trade. I have seen with Mormons on board ship a piano placed before one berth, and op- posite the very next a travelling-cutler's machine for grinding knives, &c.; indeed it is a general complaint with captains that the quantity of luggage put on board with Mormons quite takes them by surprise, and often sinks the ships upwards of an inch deeper in the water than they would otherwise have allowed her to go. Their provisions are always supplied by their agent here, of the very best description, and more than ample; for while the law requires that a certain quantity shall be put on board for each passenger, the Mormon superior puts in all cases twenty pounds per head above this quantity, and in addition a supply of butter and cheese. Everything is good. The bread always is good, frequently better than that used by the ship. The surplus provisions are given to the passengers on their arrival at New Orleans, and distributed by their superiors to each family in proportion to its numbers. As to the localities from which they come—the majority are from the manu- facturing districts, Birmingham, Sheffield, the Potteries, &c. Scotland and Wales have also despatched a large quantity. When the Scotch or Welsh determine on going, it is generally in large companies. It may perhaps be worthy of remark, that no Irish 'Saints' have yet made their appearance. The Mormons have the greatest objection against going in any ship carrying other passengers than themselves, and when such is the case, they invariably stipulate that a partition shall be erected across the ship's lower decks, so as to separate them from all other passengers.

"The means taken by these people for the preservation of order and cleanliness on board are admirable, and worthy of imitation. Their first act, on arrival here, is to hold a general meeting, at which they appoint a 'president of the company,' and 'six committee-men.' The president ex- ercises a complete superintendence over everything connected with the passengers; he allots the berths, settles disputes, attends to all wants, complaints, or inquiries, whether for or by the passengers; advises each how to proceed the most economically whether in purchasing provisions, bedding, or other articles, and he being in constant communication with the superiors here, the people are thus safely guarded from the hands of 'Man-catchers' and all others of the many who frequent our quays, and whose profession it is to entrap and prey upon the unwary stranger. The duty of the committee-men is to assist in getting the luggage on board, and to make a proper arrangement in the ship, &c. They also stand sentinel alternately at the hatchway day and night during the period the ship remains in dock, to prevent the intrusion of strangers. To show how effectually this is done, I may just mention that while in *every* ship taking the general class of emigrants, persons are found concealed on board, or 'stow aways,' *in no instance* has such been the case in a ship wholly laden with Mormons. To those acquainted with the slovenly and dirty arrangements of emigrants on shipboard, those of the Mormons, for the preservation of decency and morality, are deserving of the highest commendation. Each berth, or at least a great majority of the berths, have their little curtains spread before them so as to prevent the inmates from being seen, and also to dress and undress behind. In allotting the berths, each family or relatives are all placed in the berths next each other; and in case the passengers are from different parts—say from England and Scotland—the Scotch are berthed on one side of the ship, the English on the other. The duties of the president and committee do not cease after the ship leaves dock, but are continued during the entire voyage. The president still exercises his superintendence over the general conduct of the passengers, the delivery of provisions, water, &c. The committee act at sea as police. Three of them take each side of the between decks, and see that every person is in bed by eight o'clock in the evening, and in the morning that every passenger is up, the beds made, and the rubbish swept together, hauled up in buckets, and thrown overboard before seven o'clock. It is remarkable the implicit obedience paid by the passengers to those whom they thus elect over them; their slightest word is law, always respected, and cheerfully obeyed; in their social intercourse they address each other as 'brother' and 'sister;' and with regard to their care of the things entrusted to their charge, I have been told by an American captain who carried them, that having delivered to their committee a quantity of water which he told them was to serve for three days, he found at the end of the third day a fourth day's supply left; whereas had he given it into the charge of one of his sailors for distribution, it would not have lasted the three days. From my knowledge of the emigration at present going on from Liverpool, I can truly say that it would, indeed, be not only conducive to the comfort and health, but would absolutely save the lives of many who now die on shipboard, could the same rules for cleanliness, order, &c., be introduced amongst the general class of emigrants who leave this port for America."

The Mormons have, it is said, put aside 3½ tons, or 94,080 ounces, of gold, gathered in California, for the purpose of "gathering" the poor Saints from England and other parts of Europe, as well as from the remote districts of the American union, into the great Salt Lake Valley. At £4 an ounce, this would amount to £376,320. It is possible that they may have exaggerated their resources in this respect, but the fact is presented on Mormon authority. I was shown at Liverpool some of the gold coinage of their new state of Deseret. The five-dollar pieces are of pure Californian gold, without alloy, and somewhat smaller, but much heavier, than a sovereign. The reverse bears the inscription "Holiness to the Lord," surmounting the eye of Jehovah, and a cap somewhat like a mitre, both very rudely executed. The obverse bears two hands joined, and the words "Five dollars." The Mormons have established a perpetual emigration fund, the nature and objects of which are stated in the following epistle from the present head of the church, the successor of Joseph Smith, to their emigration agent in Liverpool:—

"Great Salt Lake City, Oct. 14, 1849.

"To Elder Orson Pratt—Dear Brother—You will learn from our General Epistle, the principal events occurring with us, but we have thought proper to write you, more particularly in relation to some matters of general interest, in an especial manner, the perpetual emigration fund for the poor saints. This fund, we wish all to understand, is perpetual, and in order to be kept good, will need constant accessions. To further this end, we expect all who are benefited by its operations will be willing to reimburse that amount as soon as they are able, facilities for which will very soon after their arrival here present themselves in the shape of public works; donations will also continue to be taken from all parts of the world, and expended for the gathering of the poor saints. This is no Joint-Stock Company arrangement, but free donations. Your office in Liverpool is the place of deposit for all funds received, either for this or the tithing funds, for all Europe, and you will not pay out only upon our order, and to such persons as we shall direct. We wish to have machinery of all kinds introduced in these valleys as soon as practicable. If you commence operations now, before you can get men to engage in the business, the material for cotton and woollen factories will be produced. Our settlements another season will extend over the rim of the basin, where we can raise the cotton, the sugar cane, rice, &c. Therefore, if you can find those who will engage in manufacturing cloth for this market in the valley, we want you should let these cotton factory proprietors, operatives, and all, with all the necessary fixtures, come to this place. We have a carrying company started, who will accommodate all emigrants to this place with passage and freight from Missouri river; they need not be obliged under this arrangement to buy oxen and waggons when they arrive there, and can be immediately transported through the entire route. We have considered it policy for us to collect tithing in money, instead of labour, as heretofore, therefore we employ constant hands upon our public works, and pay them the money, or such things as they need for themselves and families. We therefore have appointed Joseph L. Heywood and Edwin D. Wooley our agents to go east, and purchase such things as we need to supply our public works with, such as are necessary, such as glass, nails, paint, &c., and furnish workmen; these agents will probably call upon you from Boston for funds, if they should, you will send them accordingly. It is distinctly understood that these arrangements are entirely disconnected with the Perpetual Emigrating Fund; that is, sacred to its proper use in gathering the poor saints. Our true policy is, to do our own work, make our own goods as soon as possible; therefore do all you can to further the emigration of artisans and mechanics of all kinds; also continue to collect tithing.

"Our beloved brother Franklin D. Richards, who is appointed to go on a mission to England, will co-operate with you, and give you more particular items, policy, &c.

"With sentiments of the highest esteem, love, and kindness, we remain your brethren in the new and everlasting covenant,

"Brigham Young.

"P.S.—We want a company of woollen manufacturers to come with machinery, and take our wool from the sheep, and convert it into the best clothes—and the wool is ready. We want a company of cotton manufacturers, who will convert cotton into cloth and calico, &c., and we will raise the cotton before the machinery can be ready. We want a company of potters. We need them. The clay is ready, and dishes wanted. Send a company of each, if possible, next spring. Silk manufacturers and all others will follow in rapid succession. We want some men to start a furnace forthwith; the coal, iron, and moulders are waiting. B. Y."

It will be seen, from the foregoing statements, that the Mormons have made a great movement in advance since the death of Joseph Smith. California has been their golden land, and the source of their present prosperity and hope in the future.

"When the saints were about leaving Nauvoo," says an epistle in the *Millennial Star*, "Heber C. Kimball prophesied that in five years they would be better off than at this time. Little more than three years have elapsed when we behold the poor exiled Mormons in flourishing circumstances, counting amongst their riches a thousand hills and valleys, situate in the most remarkable, interesting, and auspicious portion of the globe; having the fountains of rivers that must speedily command the commerce of the world, in the midst of their territories. Thus the banishment of the church has become her freedom, the greatest boon her opponents could confer, and the glad signal for her to arise and shine. Forcibly ejected from the mother country on her arrival at the age of puberty, and thrown back upon her own unaided resources, the development of her wonderful constitution, capabilities, and organization, strikes the whole world with astonishment and admiration. They who have plundered, robbed, and driven her into the wilderness, and thought she was dead, now turn their eyes, and discover to their great surprise that she lives, and nobly aspires to power, honour, might, majesty, glory, and dominion. She has triumphed over every form of persecution and every species of cruelty. Under circumstances the most extraordinary and discouraging, she has proved herself not a whit behind the very first and foremost in all the characteristics necessary to constitute a great people. She has earned a title to a fair name and place amongst the nations. Yes, Zion is firmly established in the strongholds of the land. Riches unknown are at her disposal. And it is to be hoped that her oppressors will rejoice over her no more; and that no weapon formed against her shall prosper. Every one is aware of the impracticability of subduing a brave people, entrenched in the fastnesses of the mountains. A nation of mountaineers is not easily subjected. Even our enemies begin to acknowledge the manifest natural advantages and rising importance of the peculiar locality of the city 'sought out,' and are not backward in foretelling the proud and enviable station we must shortly occupy. They look to her for support, and think of calculating on her assistance, whom they have driven to the last extremity.

"All things work together for good. When an iron highway shall be cast up in the desert, not only will the flight of the righteous be greatly facilitated, but the kings, nobles, and rulers of the earth, with the great men, will flock to the city of refuge, painfully aware that in Zion alone will be found peace and safety. The signs of the times augur an unparalleled growth for the city in the midst of the everlasting hills."

The following particulars, with reference to the Great Salt Lake City, are of interest:—

"The Nauvoo Legion," says a general epistle to the saints signed by the new Premier, Bingham Joy, and dated on the 12th of October last, "has been re-organised in the valley, and it would have been a source of joy to the saints throughout the earth, could they have witnessed its movements on the day of its great parade; to see a whole army of mighty men in martial array, ground their arms, not by command, but simply by request, repair to the temple block, and with pick and spade open the foundation for a place of worship, and erect the pilasters, beams, and roof, so that we now have a commodious edifice, 100 by 60 feet, with brick walls, where we assemble with the saints from Sabbath to Sabbath, and almost every evening in the week, to teach, counsel, and devise ways and means for the prosperity of the kingdom of God; and we feel thankful that we have a better house or bowery for public worship the coming winter, than we have heretofore had any winter in this dispensation.

"The 24th of July last was a day long to be remembered by all present in this valley, and all saints who shall learn of our celebration, as the anniversary of the arrival of the Pioneers two years previous. To behold 1,200 or 1,500 feet of tables, filling the bowery and all adjoining grounds, loaded with all luxuries of the field and gardens, and nearly all the varieties that any vegetable market in the world could produce, and to see the seats around those tables filled and re-filled by a people who had been deprived of those luxuries for years by the cruel hand of oppression, and freely offering seats to every stranger within their borders, and this, too, in the valley of the mountains, a thousand miles from civilization, where two years before, nought was to be found save the wild root of the prairie, and the mountain cricket, was a theme of unbounded thanksgiving and praise to the Giver of all good, as the dawning of a day when the children of the Kingdom, can sit under their own vines and fig-trees, and inhabit their own houses, having none to make them afraid. May the time be hastened when the scattered Israel may partake of such like banquets from the gardens of Joseph.

"Thousands of emigrants from the States to the gold mines have passed through our city this season, leaving large quantities of domestic clothing, waggons, &c., in exchange for horses and mules, which exchange has been a mutual blessing to both parties.

"The direct emigration of the saints to this place will be some five or six hundred waggons this season, besides many who came in search of gold, have heard the Gospel for the first time and will go no further, having believed and been baptised.

"On the 28th September, fourteen or fifteen of the brethren arrived from the gold country, some of whom were very comfortably supplied with the precious metal, and others, who had been sick, came as destitute as they went on the ship Brooklyn in 1846. That there is plenty of gold in Western California is beyond doubt, but the valley of the Sacramento is an unhealthy place, and the saints can be better employed in raising grain, and building houses in this vicinity, than digging for gold in the Sacramento, unless they are counselled so to do. The true use of gold is for paving streets, covering houses, and making culinary dishes, and when the saints shall have preached the gospel, raised grain, and built up cities enough, the Lord will open up the way for a supply of gold to the perfect satisfaction of His people; until then, let them not be over-anxious, for the treasures of the earth are in the Lord's store-house, and he will open the doors thereof, when and where He pleases.

"The grain crops in the valley have been good this season; wheat, barley, oats, rye, and peas, more particularly. The late corn and buck-wheat, and some lesser grains and vegetables, have been materially injured by the recent frosts; and some early corn at Brownsville, forty miles north, a month since; and the buckwheat was severely damaged by hail at the Utah settlement, sixty miles south, about three weeks since; but we have great occasion for thanksgiving to Him who giveth the increase, that He has blest our labours, so that with prudence we shall have a comfortable supply for ourselves, and our brethren on the way, who may be in need, until another harvest; but we feel the need of more labourers, for more efficient help, and multiplied means of farming and building at this place. We want men. Brethren, come from the States, from the nations, come! and help us to build and grow, until we can say, enough—the valleys of Ephraim are full."

The following letter from a Mormon to his father in England, gives some additional particulars of the city and the journey overland from New York:—

"City of the Great Salt Lake,
"Rocky Mountains, October 6, 1849.
"My dear Father—I scarcely know how to commence the chequered history of my journey from New York, but will endeavour to give you a very abbreviated account, reserving my journal until we again meet, which happiness will, I trust, yet be permitted to us. We started 24 in number, on 10th of March, armed and equipped for a long and toilsome journey. During the first part, having the advantage of hotels, we were very merry, and enjoyed ourselves amazingly, but this was not to last long, as we had yet to experience the toils of a camp life. We travelled some 1,000 miles upon the Mississippi and Ohio rivers in American steamers, a mode of transit I am by no means partial to, as I was in a fever of apprehension the whole time, the accidents on these rivers being innumerable. They arise from 'snags' (pieces of timber sticking up in the muddy waters), from fire, collision, and bursting of the thin boilers, which are placed under the saloon. This part of our travel was, however, accomplished, with

only the loss of a few goods; and in the early part of May our mules were purchased, and we were ready for a start across the prairie. Our party had four waggons, each drawn by eight mules, and, in addition, we rode upon these combinations of all that is stupid, spiteful, and obstinate. For some little time I enjoyed the change—the novelty of this predatory mode of life. At day-break we left our tents, and were soon busy around the camp fire, preparing breakfast. Our stores did not admit of much variety; coffee, bacon, and hard biscuit, forming the staple of our provisions. The weather soon became oppressively hot, the thermometer rising to 100 and 110. This was rendered very trying by the entire absence of shade upon this ocean of land; indeed these vast plains closely resemble in atmospheric phenomena and in the appearance of the ground, the dry bed of some mighty sea. ... The heat, with the quality of our food, soon produced bilious fever, and before our journey thus far was accomplished, half our number had suffered from this complaint. We were much mistaken in believing the route a healthy one, the road being marked with the graves of victims to the California fever. About the middle of June I was taken ill, and with slight interruptions continued so till we reached this 'city.' You will perhaps imagine that being so styled, it resembles an English city, but it is only in prospect. The houses are either of logs, or built of mud bricks, called 'dobies,' and but in a few instances are not larger than one or two rooms; but time will accomplish much for this energetic and faithful people. Each house stands in 1¼ acre of garden ground, eight lots in a block, forming squares. The streets, which are wide, are to be lined with trees, with a canal, for the purpose of irrigation, running through the centre. As our waggon entered this beautiful valley, with the long absent comforts of a home in prospect, I experienced a considerable change for the better; and when, to my surprise and gratitude, I met a pious, kind, and intelligent artist, and a countryman also, who took me, emaciated, sick, and dirty, to his humble home, my happiness seemed completed. ... You must, from their own works, read the history of the Mormonites, and you will then learn how this despised people have been persecuted and driven from place to place, until they have at length found a haven in the all but inaccessible valley of the Rocky Mountains, where are gathered together, almost from every nation, some 10,000 of those who felt happy in sacrificing all that the world holds dear for the sake of their faith; and after struggling with innumerable difficulties and hardships, are building their temple in the wilderness, and are rapidly increasing both in spiritual and temporal wealth, having a church organised according to the New Testament pattern, and endeavouring to live by every word that proceedeth from the mouth of the Lord. The land here is most fruitful—I am told it produces 80 bushels of wheat to the acre; and vines, delicious melons, with other fruits and vegetables, grow in profusion. A city lot—that is, 1¼ acre—may be purchased at $1 50c., and would produce food sufficient for my wants the whole year. No man with ordinary intelligence can be poor in such a place; and then, glorious privilege, he can be free from the harassments and perplexities which continually destroy the peace of those who live in an artificial state of society. ... When recruited, in order to accomplish the remaining 600 miles, the distance that still intervened between the city and California, the waggons were sold, and ten of our number started for their original destination, through mountains covered with snow, with a prospect of being slain by Indians, or of feeding either upon their mules or each other. The other thirteen remained, earned their living in different ways, until later in the season; and have since started upon a southern route of 1,600 miles, for the gold mines, leaving me still too unwell to accompany them."...

The constitution of the New State of Deseret has already been drawn up and promulgated. It does not differ materially from the constitution of the other states of the Union. The preamble, which is as follows, shows its geographical position and limits:—

"THE CONSTITUTION OF THE NEW STATE OF DESERET.
"Whereas a large number of the citizens of the United States, before and since the treaty of peace with the Republic of Mexico, emigrated to and settled in that portion of the territory of the United States lying west of the Rocky Mountains, and in the great interior basin of Upper California; and

"Whereas, by reason of said treaty, all civil organization originating from the republic of Mexico became abrogated; and

"Whereas, the Congress of the United States has failed to provide a form of civil government for the territory so acquired, or any portion thereof; and

"Whereas, civil government and laws are necessary, for the security, peace, and prosperity of society; and

"Whereas, it is a fundamental principle in all the republican governments, that all political power is inherent in the people; and governments instituted for their protection, security, and benefit, should emanate from the same—

"Therefore, your committee beg leave to recommend the adoption of the following constitution, until the Congress of the United States shall otherwise provide for the government of the territory hereinafter named and described.

"We, the people, grateful to the Supreme Being for the blessings hitherto enjoyed, and feeling our dependence on Him for a continuation of those blessings, do ordain and establish a free and independent government, by the name of the State of Deseret; including all the territory of the United States within the following boundaries, to wit: commencing at the 33d degree of north latitude, where it crosses the 108th degree of longitude, west of Greenwich; thence running south and west to the northern boundary of Mexico; thence west to, and down the main channel of the Gila river, on the northern line of Mexico, and on the northern boundary of Lower California to the Pacific Ocean; thence along the coast north-westerly to 118 deg. 30 min. of west longitude; thence north to where said line intersects the dividing ridge of the Sierra Nevada mountains; thence north along the summit of the Sierra Nevada mountains to the dividing range of mountains that separates the waters flowing into the Columbia river—from the waters running into the Great Basin; thence easterly, along the dividing range of mountains that separates said waters flowing into the Columbia river on the north from the waters flowing into the Great Basin on the south, to the summit of the Wind river chain of mountains; thence south-east and south, by the dividing range of mountains that separate the waters flowing into the Gulf of Mexico from the waters flowing into the Gulf of California; to the place of beginning, as set forth in a map drawn by Charles Preuss, and published by order of the Senate of the United States in 1848," &c.

The following particulars respecting the route of the emigrants after their arrival at New Orleans will conclude this part of the subject. After remaining a few days in New Orleans, the emigrants start in companies, sometimes of two or three hundred or more, to St. Louis, by steamboat on the Mississippi. The distance is 1,300 miles. The next stage, also by steamboat, is a distance of 800 miles from St. Louis, to the settlements of Council Bluffs, already mentioned. Here they either remain to fatten their young cattle on the prairies, or squat upon the rich lands, until they are ready to go forward to the Great Salt Lake City. The distance from Council Bluffs to their final destination is 1,030 miles. The emigrants travel in ox teams, and their large caravans present a singular spectacle. Each waggon is drawn generally by six or eight oxen, and there are sometimes as many as 600 waggons in the procession. Each contains a bed-room and sitting-room. They cook on the road side while they give their cattle an hour's grazing in the prairies. They take three months to complete the journey from Council Bluffs to the Salt Lake City, and being supplied with provisions purchased at St. Louis, they want nothing but the occasional proceeds of the chase, in pursuing which the male emigrants amuse themselves on the way. They trade with the Indians as they go for buffalo robes and peltries, which the Indians exchange for fire-arms and ammunition.

I might extend the history of these remarkable fanatics to a much greater length. Enough, however, has been said, to prove the greatness of the work in which their leaders are engaged, and to which the discovery of the treasures of California has given a strong impetus. When their formal claim for admission into the American Union shall be made, some important debates will doubtless take place in Congress, and the old sore of slavery will once more be laid bare. Deseret is to be a free, and not a slave state; and the whole question will have again to be argued. It is probable that it will lose none of its bitterness when the once despised but now powerful Mormons shall be the means of bringing it forward.

It only remains to add, that the Mormons believe in the approaching destruction of all the kingdoms of the earth, and the immediate establishment of Christ's kingdom, under Mormon auspices, in Deseret first, and ultimately over all the continent of America. They expect the coming of Christ as a temporal sovereign, and the establishment of a Millennium, of which none shall share the blessings but the Mormons.

LABOUR AND THE POOR.

—◆—

LIVERPOOL.

[FROM OUR SPECIAL CORRESPONDENT.]

EDUCATION IN LIVERPOOL.

LETTER XIV.

The subject of education is one so extensive even in reference to the deficiencies of a single town, that I can do no more than present its leading features and outlines in connection with Liverpool. It was computed by an eminent statist, the late Dr. Watt, of Glasgow, that the number of children in that city between the ages of six and sixteen—the ages at which, to use a German phrase, they were "*schulpflichtig,*" or "due to the school"—was in proportion to the whole population as 18.30 to 100. Dr. Watt was of opinion that the same proportion, or one very near it, would apply to all other large manufacturing and commercial towns in the kingdom. If we apply this calculation to the town of Liverpool, and take its population at 400,000, the number of children that ought to be attending school would amount to 73,200. If we take the population at 350,000, the number of children due to the school would be 64,050. It does not appear, however, that in fixing the school years between the ages of six and sixteen, a correct estimate was made, either of the general practice or of the necessities of the great bulk of the people. Those parents who can afford to send their children to school very commonly send them before the age of six, often as early as the age of four; and with a large number of the youth of both sexes who are obliged to turn out into the busy world in search of their subsistence, the age of fourteen is the extreme limit of school attendance. The school years seem, therefore, to be more properly the years between four and fourteen. In the valuable statistics relating to the district of Vauxhall in Liverpool, drawn up with great care and labour by the Rev. Dr. Hume, and published in his pamphlet entitled "Missions at Home, or a Clergyman's Account of a portion of the Town of Liverpool," that gentleman considers the school age to be from 3½ to 12; and he computes that in a population of 13,028 residing in the Vauxhall district, the number of children between those ages was 3,228, or in the proportion of 24.77 to 100, or nearly one-fourth of the whole population. But as this district is densely peopled and poor, and as poor families are generally numerous, it would in all probability lead to error if the proportion of children within its boundaries should be taken as the general proportion for the whole town of Liverpool. If we take one-sixth of the population as the number that are fairly of an age to attend school, which is, as far as I am enabled to judge, a moderate and probable calculation, we should have for Liverpool, estimating its population at 350,000, an aggregate amount of 58,333 above the age of four, or "due to the school."

What is done for the education of this large number of children? Are the whole or the greater portion of them educated? Liverpool, it must be acknowledged, does as much in the cause of education as any other town in the kingdom—perhaps more. There is no deficiency of zeal or liberality among the ministers and members of the Established Church. There is no deficiency of either among the various Dissenting bodies. The Establishment and all the Dissenting congregations, as well as the Roman Catholics, have their day-schools and their Sunday-schools in every part of the town, and a large educational machinery is constantly at work, levying subscriptions, publishing reports, holding anniversaries, and teaching the children of the people. A return of the 34 schools in connection with the Church of England, within the Parliamentary boundary of Liverpool, states the total number of daily and Sunday scholars, for the year ending the 1st of January, 1850, to have been 14,090, including many infants under the age of four. The number of schools in connection with the various Dissenting bodies is not so easily ascertained, because there is no authorized annual or other publication issued by any of the Christian denominations in the name or behalf of the rest. It appears, however, from a list in "Gore's Directory," that the Dissenting bodies, exclusive of the Roman Catholic schools, have established day schools, where they educate 4,452 children. I learn from a return, drawn up with care, and furnished to me, that the Dissenters have, besides these, as many as 41 Sunday schools, in which the number of children on the books is 7,825, also including many infants under the age of four. The return was procured for the purposes of this inquiry, and is as follows:—

STATISTICS OF SUNDAY SCHOOLS IN LIVERPOOL.

Schools.	Denomination.	Teachers.	Children on books.	Attendance.
Great George-street	Independent	32	333	234
Crescent	,,	35	369	201
Wavertree	,,	10	110	80
Jordan-street	Wesleyan	42	367	234
Brunswick	,,	50	430	304
Great Homer-street	,,	50	440	350
Wavertree	,,	20	110	90
Windsor	,,	23	144	90
Mount Pleasant ...	,,	48	220	176
Pitt-street	,,	25	160	90
Rodney-street	Presbyterian	1	...	30
Canning-street ...	,,	24	130	105
Mount Pleasant ...	,,	30	190	155
Islington	,,	26	211	168
Pleasant-street	Wesleyan Association	24	147	112
Bispham-street ...	,,	20	150	117
Scotland-road	,,	19	233	170
Heath-street	,,	18	161	122
Lime-street	,,	16	71	53
Bird-street	,,	13	128	80
Grange-road	,,	10	54	24
Lime Kiln-lane ...	,,	17	116	91
Herculaneum	,,	22	146	130
Bovington-hill	New Connexion ...	24	149	120
Bethesda	,,	20	154	80
Park-place	,,	28	250	210
Burlington	Independent	18	222	180
Hanover	,,	16	139	91
Myrtle-street ... Wilde-street ... Ashton-street .. }	Baptist	75	710	475
Soho-street	,,	18	170	100
Pembroke	,,	24	189	130
Mulberry-street ...	Welsh Methodist ...	40	229	221
Salem	Welsh Independent .	26	68	166
Zion	Free Gospel	8	159	82
Bedford-street	Independent	26	216	170
Claremont	,,	18	160	90
Toxteth	,,	28	213	193
Newington	,,	22	206	140
Walnut-street	Baptist	21	180	158
			7825	

Besides the schools in connection with the Church of England
and with the various Dissenting bodies, there are five Roman Catholic
schools, which, according the statements of their patrons and man-

agers, educate among them 3,070 children. There are also the Corporation schools, educating upwards of 1,200 children; the workhouse schools of the parish of Liverpool, and the extra-parochial district of Toxteth Park; and the Liverpool Industrial Schools, established at Kirkdale, to aid the parish in the work of education, and affording food, lodging, clothing, and instruction in various trades, besides in the elements of a plain education, to an average of 1,150 children. There is also the Royal Hibernian School, which educates 400 children both Catholic and Protestant—a very admirable school—which is the means of effecting much good; the schools for girls and boys, in connection with the Liverpool Mechanics' Institution; and the Collegiate School, all of which are establishments of a very superior class, and not confined to the children of mechanics. Adding the whole of these together, and including day schools and Sunday schools in one total, the educational statistics of Liverpool, as accurately as I can make them, will be—

Established Sunday and Day Schools	14,090
Dissenters ditto	12,270
Roman Catholic Schools	3,070
Corporation Schools	1,200
Kirkdale ditto	1,150
Hibernian School	400
Schools omitted or not otherwise included—estimate	1,000
Total	33,180

To this total should be added the children of the rich, receiving their education either at home or in private seminaries. That there are more than five thousand of such children in the private boarding and day schools of the town is not probable. But taking them in round numbers at 5,000, and supposing, generally, that these figures are correct, and that the children "due to the school" in Liverpool, with a population of 350,000, is as one in six, it would follow that upwards of 20,000 children receive no education whatever. This calculation would also presume that the children attending these various schools were all above four years of age.

Had I space, however, to enter into the subject of the kind of education given at the greater portion of these schools, or to inquire how many of these children are infants under four, and how many are only Sunday scholars, and never receive instruction any other day of the week, it might appear that the results of this educational activity are not so favourable as they look. I must observe, however, in reference to the returns published of the thirty-four Sunday and day schools in connection with the Church of England, that they are calculated to mislead; inasmuch as many of the children who attend the day schools also attend the Sunday schools, and are thus entered twice over. Thus the total returns are swelled beyond the reality. The same explanation applies to the return published by the Dissenting bodies; so that the 14,090 scholars of the one, and the 12,277 scholars of the other, do not actually represent those numbers of children who are indebted to them for instruction. But even taking it for granted that the greater part of these children are really receiving a moral and religious, as well as general education—an education fitting them to become useful and virtuous members of society, and to be the worthy heirs of our civilization and our Christianity—the important inquiry remains, What number of children in the town is not reached by their efforts, and receives no education or schooling whatever? I have endeavoured to answer the question, but I do not pretend to have done so with strict accuracy, as I had no opportunity to enter thoroughly upon so large an investigation. The following facts—some of them the results of the careful inquiries of others, and some of them the results of equally careful inquiries of my own—will show that, however much may have been done in Liverpool, a great deal has been left undone, and that, notwithstanding all the efforts of the religious and the humane of every sect and denomination of Christians to teach the children of the poor, there remains an immense residuum of utter ignorance, which all existing means and all existing agencies have been unable to permeate, or even to reach. I shall also be enabled to show that this residuum of ignorance is the hot-bed of vice and crime; that out of its teeming numbers are recruited those regiments, or rather armies, of misery and wickedness which wage a daily warfare against the peace and the property of the better instructed and more prosperous classes; and that, to maintain itself on the defensive against these constantly-invading and rapacious hosts, society is obliged to keep up large and costly establishments of police, to build prison-palaces, and to set in operation a huge, cumbrous, and extravagant, but ineffective, machinery of repression and punishment.

The following statistics in reference to isolated streets and districts will give some idea of the subject. A house to house visitation of two streets in Liverpool, inhabited entirely by the poorer classes, was made for me, for the purposes of this inquiry, by the Rev. F. Bishop. The two streets were selected because they afforded a fair sample in all respects of the densely-crowded, unhealthy, immoral, poor, and ignorant districts of the town. In one of these streets, called Bird-street, the following is the result of the inquiry as regards population, religion, and education:—

<table>
<tr><td>Number of adults 384</td><td rowspan="2">Total, 820</td></tr>
<tr><td>Number of children 436</td></tr>
<tr><td>Protestants 103</td><td rowspan="2">Total, 820</td></tr>
<tr><td>Roman Catholics 717</td></tr>
<tr><td>Children attending a day or Sunday school 51</td><td rowspan="2">Total, 436</td></tr>
<tr><td>Children attending no school whatever 385</td></tr>
</table>

Closely adjoining Bird-street is a street of the same character, called Jordan-street, swarming with destitute or neglected children. In this street schools are established, with accommodation for 250 girls, 250 boys, and 200 infants. The number in ordinary attendance is 282 in all, according to Mr. Morell's Report on the British, Wesleyan, and other Denominational Schools, published in the Minutes of the Committee of Council on Education. It will be seen, therefore, that it is not entirely the want of school accommodation which keeps the children of this dense neighbourhood from school. What the real cause is will appear in a subsequent portion of this letter.

Crosbie-street, another street of the same character, and inhabited by a similar class of the poorest people, in the immediate neighbourhood of Brick-street and Jordan-street, yielded the following figures:—

<table>
<tr><td>Number of adults 413</td><td rowspan="2">Total, 897</td></tr>
<tr><td>Number of children 484</td></tr>
<tr><td>Protestants 37</td><td rowspan="2">Total, 897</td></tr>
<tr><td>Roman Catholics 860</td></tr>
<tr><td>Children attending a day school, Sunday school, or ragged school 47</td><td rowspan="2">Total, 484</td></tr>
<tr><td>Children attending no school whatever 437</td></tr>
</table>

In these numbers are of course included infants, and all children too young to attend school. Desirous of testing still further than Mr. Bishop had done the numbers of ignorant and neglected children in Liverpool—ignorant and neglected in spite of ample school accommodation—I caused a similar house to house visitation to be carefully made in three other streets—one in the same, and two at a different part of the town. These streets were Sawney Pope-street, Harrison-street, and New Bird-street. The following was the result:—

	Houses.	Population.	Adults.	Children under 14.	At Day or Sunday School.	At Ragged School.	At no School.
Sawney Pope-street ..	112	877	558	319	116	11	192
Harrison-street	36	340	212	128	26	..	102
New Bird-street	163	1301	789	512	144	22	346

Mr. Bishop's return may be in every respect depended upon, for frequent visits to the two streets, and a personal acquaintance with every family in them, enabled him to state with accuracy the exact numbers of the population. The second return, which tells a similar story, is possibly less accurate, for the following reason: the poor people are in general so afraid of being prosecuted for over-crowding their miserable cellars or rooms, or for contraventions of the Sanitary Act, that it is extremely difficult for a stranger to ascertain from them the real numbers of lodgers in each house, and the true numbers of each family. Hence the population of these three streets is probably understated. The whole three, Harrison-street more especially, are among the worst in Liverpool, not simply for over-crowding, but for the aggregation of physical and moral pollution contained within them. The next statement relates to a whole district of Liverpool, and comprises the statistics of the district of Vauxhall, drawn up by the Rev. Dr. Hume, and printed in the pamphlet already alluded to. "This table," says Dr. Hume, "was first published in January, 1848, and was a statement of results after a minute examination of all the people at their own residences. The streets and courts in the north end of the district were all examined by myself. The other streets and courts were examined partly by myself and by students at the Theological College, Birkenhead."

The table is so interesting, and is compiled with so much care, and corroborates so painfully, yet completely, the results of the minor investigations of the same kind instituted by Mr. Bishop and myself, with reference to other districts of the town, that I reproduce, without abridgment, all those parts of it which bear reference to the state of education:—

STATISTICS OF THE DISTRICT OF VAUXHALL.

	Dwellings.		Juvenile Education.			Country.			
	Houses.	Families.	Of proper ages: $3\frac{1}{2}$—12.	In actual attendance.	Receiving no education.	English.	Irish.	Scotch.	Welsh and Manx.
Carruthers-st.	10	13	13	8	5	50	—	4	—
5 courts	14	18	15	7	8	33	33	—	—
Chartres-street ..	33	35	42	18	24	41	109	—	—
14 courts	137	161	146	41	105	192	434	15	12
Chisenhale-st. ..	91	111	121	45	76	55	473	—	5
36 courts	161	221	324	50	274	167	796	26	17
Clement-street ..	55	68	90	42	48	152	157	16	—
9 courts	32	32	36	10	26	90	12	—	31
Cockspur-street .	28	43	68	8	60	112	65	—	—
3 courts	19	19	38	12	26	49	30	—	5
Dickson-street ..	6	6	8	8	—	27	10	—	—
Eaton-street	59	78	87	13	74	109	190	9	6
11 courts	49	62	66	14	52	136	123	4	—
Eccles-street	28	36	55	20	35	94	50	12	12
7 courts	28	30	26	17	9	61	47	4	5
Gascoyne-street .	68	86	120	46	74	292	92	5	29
16 courts	135	152	187	79	108	498	80	12	20
Highfield-street .	110	157	137	56	81	389	244	28	24
6 courts	33	34	29	19	10	55	65	6	10
Key-street	21	25	40	20	20	77	29	5	4
2 courts	9	9	19	10	9	9	39	—	—
Leeds-street	77	103	101	44	57	345	74	9	28
13 courts	91	99	95	38	57	352	56	—	17
Mᶜ Viccar-street .	2	2	3	1	2	10	4	—	—
2 courts	10	10	15	2	13	7	34	4	7
Milk-street	22	39	51	16	35	47	96	—	—
3 courts	19	19	33	5	28	26	55	—	—
Northampton-st.	33	37	39	19	20	88	48	11	15
10 courts	39	39	47	25	22	119	65	—	3
Pall-mall	58	81	85	41	44	214	118	11	22
14 courts	57	60	61	35	26	113	75	—	60
Plumbe-street ...	56	70	77	22	55	259	98	—	37
12 courts	47	49	72	25	47	142	77	6	33

STATISTICS OF THE DISTRICT OF VAUXHALL.

	Dwellings.		Juvenile Education.			Country.			
	Houses.	Families.	Of proper ages: $3\frac{1}{2}$—12.	In actual attendance.	Receiving no education.	English.	Irish.	Scotch.	Welsh and Manx.
Pownall-square ..	11	15	11	6	5	30	26	4	—
3 courts	20	21	25	4	21	—	95	—	—
Prussia-street ...	42	48	58	24	34	179	41	—	33
6 courts	50	52	35	14	21	179	15	6	29
Pump-fields	5	6	19	6	13	20	19	—	—
Ray-street	42	56	57	18	39	260	47	—	19
13 courts	100	100	115	25	90	341	109	23	68
Smithfield-street	66	82	120	37	83	98	281	—	6
12 courts	51	51	38	16	22	74	132	—	6
Tithebarn-street .	28	30	28	14	14	118	11	—	—
2 courts	14	16	33	13	20	16	59	—	—
Upper Milk-st. ...	39	63	47	19	28	124	168	—	7
8 courts	38	42	30	11	19	87	100	3	8
Vauxhall-road ...	54	54	48	34	14	148	77	13	11
3 courts	16	16	11	3	8	30	39	—	—
Westmorland-st.	50	99	78	16	62	174	236	—	10
11 courts	60	63	62	19	43	123	110	6	15
Wigan-street ...	9	12	11	4	7	8	34	9	—
2 courts	6	8	16	8	8	30	12	—	—
Worfield-street ..	27	42	30	21	9	101	46	2	18
3 courts	14	14	10	8	2	28	14	—	15
27 streets. 226 courts. 152 cellars.	2379	2894	3228	1136	2092	6578	5550	253	510
				3228		13028			

The above document shows that out of 3,228 children, no less than
2,092 had received and were receiving no education whatever. Most
readers will understand by this that they receive the education of vice
and crime—that they are tutored in the filthy language of the streets
and in the arts of mendicancy, and that they are systematically trained
to the trade of plunder. If such be the state of only one small district
of the town—a district to be paralleled, if not surpassed, by many
others still more dense and populous, for all the neglect, destitution,
ignorance, vice, and crime of which these appalling statistics suggest
the existence—what must be the moral state of Liverpool generally?
If one-half of the whole population are equally neglected—or equally
impervious to all the efforts made by the Church and by Dissent, and
by the various religious and philanthropic bodies who labour in the
cause of education—there must be between 20,000 and 30,000 children in Liverpool who live in a state of pagan darkness, and who

are training, by the efforts of those most pertinacious schoolmasters, poverty, ignorance, and bad example, to be the future scourges and pests, as well as the disgrace, of society. The whole extent of the evil is not, and probably never can be, known; but its magnitude, though unseen and undefinable, is felt. Nothing, however, has been done since this table was drawn up to remedy the enormous evils which it discloses, except to establish Ragged Schools in various parts of the town. It therefore remains to be seen to how great an extent the Ragged Schools have succeeded in diminishing the numbers of these "legions of ignorance."

The following is a complete list of the Ragged Schools in operation at the end of April last, when the fine weather, which always diminishes the Ragged School attendance, may be said to have begun. It will be seen that the total average attendance of boys was 1,151, and of girls 771, or of both sexes 1,922—a number far less than sufficient to meet the exigencies of the one district of Vauxhall:—

A LIST OF LIVERPOOL RAGGED SCHOOLS.	Numbers on the Books.		Average Atten-dance.		Open in the Week.
	Boys.	Girls.	Boys.	Girls.	
Mission House, Bed-ford-street	..	56	..	50	Open every night but Saturday and Sunday.*
Stanhope-street ...	86	..	70	..	
Lime-kiln-lane	..	230	..	75	One night only.
63, Gascoyne-street ..	..	..	30	..	Three nights and Sunday.
Naylor-street	..	..	120	110	Three nights and Sunday.
Campbell-street	..	..	100	..	Two nights and Sunday.
Wilde-street	..	..	74	..	Four nights.
Circus-street Ragg. Sunday School ..	90	110	75	95	Three times on Sunday only.
Barker-street, Windsor	60	..	35	..	Two nights.
Bedford-street Park ...	..	..	66	..	Three nights.
Harper-street	..	..	40	66	Every night except Saturday and Sunday.
Ashton-street	..	..	80	80	Two nights and Sunday.
Jordan-street	..	..	55	55	Four nights and Sunday.
Hodson-street	..	..	90	70	Every night but Sat. and Sunday.
Shaw's-alley	..	..	45†	..	
Cornwallis-st., about .	..	..	70	70	
Edgehill Church school	80	..	45	..	
Harrington School ...	75	85	60	70	Sunday night only.
Day School, Indus-trial, Soho-street	..	..	96	..	Every day, includ-ing Sunday.‡
Domestic Mission Sewing School ..	..	40	..	30	Every afternoon, except Saturday and Sunday.§
			1151	771	

* These are the schools of the "Liverpool Ragged School Society." They were the first established in Liverpool, and have been in operation for four years. A system of visitation to each school is kept up by the committee.

† This is the school established by the Roscoe Club, several members of which attend occasionally as voluntary teachers.

‡ In this school the boys have all their meals, and spend the whole of the day there, after the plan of the Juvenile Refuge in Pye-street, Westminster. As the name implies, boys are taught to work at various trades. The school was established on March 1.

§ The object of this school is to give domestic training to neglected girls, and especially to instruct them in plain needlework. Nearly all attend the evening school also of the Liverpool Ragged School Society. No food is given in the sewing school.

But these numbers, inconsiderable as they are, give only the *winter* view of the case. Within a week after this document was drawn up, I learned that the Roscoe Club Ragged School had been closed "for the season," partly because the attendance of scholars had grown thin, and partly because the young men who had volunteered their services as teachers had removed, or were about to remove, to summer quarters for the benefit of change of air or sea bathing. It is evident, therefore, that "Ragged Schools," excellent as they may be, do not effectually cope with the giant evil. They may rescue a few stragglers from destruction, but in Liverpool, whatever may be the case in other places, they leave the great multitude to perish.

The above statements will enable the reader to take a broad and general view both of what has been done and what has been left undone. The statistics of education, with the exception of the Ragged School returns and others which I caused to be made, are taken from the published statements of the parties engaged in the work, and which, if at all inaccurate, err on the side of exaggerating rather than that of understating the school attendance of the children.

The general statistics of ignorance have yet to be drawn up for Liverpool—unless the glimpses afforded by the zealous labours of Dr. Hume and Mr. Bishop, and the corroborations elicited by the minor inquiry which I instituted, be considered sufficient evidence of a social evil as mighty as it is deplorable. The following tables do not exhaust, but they throw a further light upon the subject, and prove that the utterly ignorant and uninstructed entail constant and most onerous burdens upon society for the prevention, repression, and punishment of crime. The partially and imperfectly instructed multitudes, even if they have mastered no more than the first elements, or tools of learning, give less trouble, and cost the State less money and care, than those who have received no instruction at all. Every figure in the following table is an argument for education:—

A RETURN, SHOWING THE NUMBER OF PRISONERS BROUGHT BEFORE THE MAGISTRATES
OF THE BOROUGH OF LIVERPOOL FOR FELONY FOR THE YEAR 1849:—

MONTHS.	Males.					Females.					Total of both Sexes.				
	Read and Write well.	Read and Write imperfectly.	Read.	Neither.	Total.	Read and Write well.	Read and Write imperfectly.	Read.	Neither.	Total.	Read and Write well.	Read and Write imperfectly.	Read.	Neither.	Total.
January	78	143	37	206	464	8	46	37	134	225	86	189	74	340	689
February ...	52	107	33	148	340	5	48	35	135	223	57	155	68	283	563
March	29	162	41	176	408	3	45	46	165	259	32	207	87	341	667
April	20	118	40	154	332	1	60	31	137	229	21	178	71	291	561
May	17	127	28	174	346	6	40	53	154	253	23	167	81	328	599
June	16	114	24	167	321	...	32	41	131	204	16	146	65	298	525
July	18	136	31	142	327	1	44	36	115	196	19	180	67	257	523
August	4	128	27	130	289	...	44	51	102	197	4	172	78	232	486
September .	2	131	28	131	292	...	43	36	117	196	2	174	64	248	488
October ...	6	122	26	142	296	...	45	43	156	244	6	167	69	298	540
November ..	1	149	38	139	327	...	41	39	148	228	1	190	77	287	555
December ..	4	124	31	152	311	...	44	28	123	195	4	168	59	275	506
Total	247	1,561	384	1,861	4,053	24	532	476	1,617	2,649	271	2,093	860	3,478	6,702

The following table shows the results of education and non-education in a new light, and if it do not prove that education necessarily makes women chaste, it seems to prove that, even among the unchaste, education so far improves the manners as to preserve the educated from being guilty of the grosser outrages and improprieties which distinguish the non-educated:—

A RETURN, SHOWING THE NUMBER OF PROSTITUTES BROUGHT BEFORE THE MAGISTRATES ON DISORDERLY CHARGES, DISTINGUISHING THEIR COUNTRIES AND DEGREE OF INSTRUCTION, FOR THE YEAR 1849.

MONTHS.	Degree of Instruction.					Countries.								How Disposed of.			
	Read and Write well.	Read and Write imperfectly.	Read.	Neither.	Total.	Liverpool.	English.	Irish.	Scotch.	Welsh.	Manx.	Foreign.	Total.	Committed.	Fined.	Discharged.	Total.
January	5	13	19	42	79	21	13	35	4	2	3	1	79	61	8	10	79
February ...	6	21	25	44	96	22	21	42	6	4	1	...	96	65	20	11	96
March	...	28	30	79	137	30	28	67	8	3	1	...	137	100	21	16	137
April	2	31	32	46	111	19	23	64	2	1	...	2	111	78	22	11	111
May	...	48	39	74	161	34	34	80	5	4	3	1	161	110	30	21	161
June	1	38	32	48	119	20	29	61	3	5	1	...	119	87	15	17	119
July	1	39	33	60	133	16	31	73	7	4	2	...	133	105	16	12	133
August	...	32	32	56	120	28	17	60	6	7	1	1	120	94	16	10	120
September .	...	41	23	60	124	26	28	58	4	5	3	...	124	94	16	14	124
October	1	39	30	66	136	31	19	70	6	5	2	3	136	108	15	13	136
November ..	...	45	35	66	146	36	27	69	6	5	3	...	146	114	22	10	146
December ..	...	31	26	47	104	28	18	51	3	3	...	1	104	78	20	6	104
Total	16	406	356	688	1,466	311	288	730	60	48	20	9	1,466	1,094	221	151	1,466

It appears from the above that out of 1,466 unfortunate and de-graded women brought before the magistrates in the year 1849, and charged with riotous and disorderly conduct, only 16 could read and write well; that 356 could read, without being able to write; that 406 could read and write imperfectly; and that 688 could neither read nor write at all. It further appears that as nearly as possible one-half of them were Irish.

I shall not enter upon the question of how far education might be the means of preserving the female children of the poor from this odious course of life; but having simply presented the document, as a somewhat remarkable illustration of the advantages of education in refining the manners of the morally depraved, even if it lead to no higher advantages, I proceed with the general subject of the efforts which have been made in Liverpool to prevent or diminish crime by extending education. It is necessary to recapitulate the ill-success which attended the most remarkable of these efforts, even although by so doing the ill-feeling, which has not totally subsided, may, to a certain extent, be re-excited.

Two "Corporation Free Schools"—one at the north, the other at the south end of the town—were opened in 1827. The land on which they are built was given by the corporation, and the expense of their erection, nearly £20,000, was borne by the corporate funds. After the passing of the Municipal Reform Bill, the system of instruction in these schools was placed on a similar footing to that of the national schools in Ireland. The children of Catholics and Protestants were taught together so far as general education is concerned, whilst facilities were afforded for direct religious and theological instruction, at the hands of the ministers of the communions to which the children severally belonged. This system was strongly opposed and vehemently denounced by a party in the town, who claimed to be the champions of Protestantism and the great upholders of the Bible. An outcry loud and long was raised against the reformed Town Council, who were charged with having insulted Protestants, because the Catholic clergy were allowed the same privileges with Catholic children as the clergy-man of the Established Church in the case of children of Protestant parents—and with having *excluded the Bible from the schools*, because the Douay version was used by the Catholic children, though the Protestants used only the authorized version, or the extracts from the Scriptures published under the sanction of the Archbishop of Dublin, Lord Stanley, and the Irish Board. An extensive machinery of agitation was put in motion. To the usual warmth of political contests was added the bitterness of theological strife. One well-known clergyman, a champion of ultra or Orange Protestantism, entered with impetuous zeal into the question, drawing a numerous train of followers after him. Meetings were held in the Amphitheatre; the cry of "No Popery" was revived with all the acrimony of days gone by; Protestant operative associations lived upon the all-absorbing "school question;" processions walked through the streets, headed by members bearing aloft a wooden Bible, to indicate at once their own reverence for the book, and the dishonour that was alleged to have been done to it in the Corporation Schools; and every kind of device was resorted to, to call forth theological and party prejudices against the town council, for having established, in schools maintained from funds derived from people of all sects, a system of education which excluded none, but included all. This agitation continued, more or less, for five or six years, until the municipal elections of 1841, when it was found to have done its work, and the extreme party gained a considerable ascendancy in the council. Accordingly, at a meeting of the town council on the 4th of January, 1842, it was resolved by a majority of 31 against 13:—

> "1. That the schools shall commence in the morning and close in the afternoon with singing and prayer. 2. That none but the authorised version of the Bible shall be used in the schools, and that the same shall be used without restriction or limit."

Other resolutions were passed at the same time, requiring all the children, except under formal protest, to learn the church catechism, and to go to church on Sundays.

The Catholic clergy of Liverpool, who had previously memorialized the council against the proposed changes, pointing out what would be their obvious and inevitable effect, met two days after the above decision was come to, and passed the following resolution and declarations:—

> "Resolved—That in consequence of the late alterations in the constitution of the corporation schools, the Catholic clergy of Liverpool can no longer conscientiously sanction the attendance of Catholic children in those schools.
>
> "By the new arrangement, the Catholic translation of the Scriptures has been excluded from the schools, so that all the children will

be required to use the Protestant Bible, which, for different reasons, the Catholic clergy cannot sanction. Another objection is, that, should any Catholic children attend, they will be required to join with the rest in a form of worship from which, both in practice and belief, they must conscientiously differ.

"There is too much reason to fear that these new arrangements have been entered into with a view of proselytizing and of seducing Catholic children from their religion; but whatever intentions the authors of these alterations may have had, the Catholic clergy feel it their duty, under present circumstances, to denounce those schools, and to tell Catholic parents they cannot conscientiously send their children to them."

The lamentable effect of all this agitation and of the changes it brought about was, that upwards of 900 children (there having been, according to the school returns dated January 4, 1842, 664 Catholics in the North School, and 272 in the South School), were virtually ejected from the schools, suddenly deprived of the benefits of education, and turned into the streets to beg or steal—a result the more to be deplored, as the Catholics are for the most part amongst the poorest of the population, and, therefore, most in need of such help in educating their children as the Corporation Schools were built to afford. This system is still continued, so that, from schools supported by the public funds for the benefit of all, the Catholic population—forming a fourth, or perhaps a third, of the gross population of the town, and much more than a third of the poorest of the population—are practically excluded.

I now turn to a brighter side of the question, and to a more recent effort to rescue the children of the poor from ignorance and misery. It is fortunate for the town of Liverpool, that the gentleman who exercises the onerous and highly responsible functions of stipendiary magistrate has directed the energies of his clear intellect and the sympathies of his warm heart to this deeply-important subject; and it is equally fortunate that the members of the town council have been induced to listen to the painful results of his experience, and that they have had the courage and good sense to co-operate with him in a well-considered project for checking the manufacture of young criminals, by the cheaper and more agreeable process of transforming them, by means of education, into self-respecting and industrious members of society. In the year 1846, a petition, signed by the magistrates of Liverpool, was presented to the House of Commons, praying the appointment of a committee "to inquire and to report on the state of the criminal population of these kingdoms, more particularly into the state of the juvenile part of that population, with a view to ascertain, after due and deliberate inquiry, the best means which can be devised for the reformation of both juvenile and adult criminals, and for their restoration to the ranks of the respectable portion of the people." That petition set forth the fact that in the previous seven years the magistrates of Liverpool had committed to trial, for offences within their jurisdiction, 51,434 persons, of whom 5,583 were under 17 years of age; and the petitioners alleged their belief, whatever differences of opinion might exist as to the practicability of reforming any considerable proportion of adult criminals, that a very considerable number of juvenile delinquents might be reformed; and that a still greater number of the same class might be prevented from becoming criminals, by giving them the advantages of an intellectual, moral, and industrial training. In order to enable the House to form a judgment of the cost of the actual system of neglecting these children, and afterwards punishing them for crime, they recorded the expense attending the prosecution of fourteen juvenile delinquents who had from time to time been inmates of the prisons of the borough. The cases referred to were stated to be fairly selected in 1842 from the mass of juvenile inmates of the prison. The following are the cases referred to, numbered from 1 to 14 for greater convenience of reference:—

"No. 1. Eighteen years old; can neither read nor write. First committed 8th January, 1835; last committed 22d February, 1841. Committed sixteen times; discharged six. Last sentence, twelve months' imprisonment.

"No. 2. Sixteen years old; can read imperfectly, cannot write. First committed 15th August, 1838; last committal 31st January, 1842. Committed twelve times; discharged once. Last sentence, ten years' transportation.

"No. 3. Twelve years old; can neither read nor write. First committed 3d June, 1837; last committal 13th January, 1842. Committed ten times; discharged ten. Last sentence, three months' imprisonment.

"No. 4. Twelve years old; can neither read nor write. First committed 26th September, 1838; last committal 31st January, 1842. Committed nine times; discharged seven. Last sentence, ten years' transportation.

"No. 5. Twelve years old; can neither read nor write. First committal 8th August, 1839; last committal 16th September, 1841. Committed eight times; discharged five. Last sentence, three months' imprisonment.

"No. 6. Ten years old; can neither read nor write. First committed 21st December, 1837; last committed 5th January, 1842. Committed eleven times; discharged three. Last sentence, seven years' transportation.

"No. 7. Fourteen years old; can neither read nor write. First committal 9th January, 1838; last committal 8th March, 1842. Committed nineteen times; discharged four. Last sentence, three months' imprisonment.

"No. 8. Thirteen years old; can neither read nor write. First committal 10th February, 1838; last committal 22d February, 1842. Committed sixteen times; discharged five. Last sentence, three months' imprisonment.

"No. 9. Fourteen years old; can neither read nor write. First committed 17th June, 1839; last committal 20th October, 1841. Committed seven times; discharged eight. Last sentence, three months' imprisonment.

"No. 10. Nine years old; can neither read nor write. First committed 30th September, 1839; last committal 25th October, 1841. Committed four times; discharged twelve. Last sentence, 25th October, 1841, seven years' transportation.

"No. 11. Twelve years old; can neither read nor write. First committed 16th October, 1838; last committal 18th August, 1841. Committed seven times; discharged four. Last sentence, fourteen days' imprisonment.

"No. 12. Twelve years old; can neither read nor write. First committal 2d January, 1840; last committal 17th December, 1841. Committed five times; discharged six. Last sentence, three months' imprisonment.

"No. 13. Thirteen years old; can neither read nor write. First committal 19th September, 1838; last committed 30th March, 1841. Committed three times; discharged five. Last sentence, three months' imprisonment.

"No. 14. Thirteen years old; can neither read nor write. First committal 30th August, 1839; last committal 2d February, 1842. Committed six times; discharged six. Last sentence, three months' imprisonment.

"The costs of apprehension, maintenance, prosecution, and punishment of No. 1 were, 129*l.* 5s. 6½d.; of No. 2, 71*l.* 2s. 10½d.; of No. 3, 74*l.* 1s. 10½d.; of No. 4, 71*l.* 13s. 1d.; of No. 5, 47*l.* 9s. 3d.; of No. 6, 64*l.* 6s. 6½d.; of No. 7, 99*l.* 2s. 5½d.; of No. 8, 72*l.* 1s. 4½d.; of No. 9, 52*l.* 9s. 7¼d.; of No. 10, 64*l.* 18s. 9¼d.; of No. 11, 28*l.* 10s. 4½d.; of No. 12, 39*l.* 8s. 10½d.; of No. 13, 26*l.* 10s. 10d.; of No. 14, 47*l.* 7s. 7½d. Thus these fourteen offenders cost the public the sum of 889*l.* 1s."

The petitioners added that, for the more full development of the moral and financial results of the present system of punishing juvenile offenders, they had traced, as far as it could be ascertained, the subsequent career of these fourteen prisoners. At the time of the return four of them, namely, numbers two, four, six, and ten, were under sentence of transportation; number one died in prison; number three, after being again once imprisoned, was transported; number five, after two several additional periods of imprisonment, was also transported; number seven, after six several additional periods of imprisonment, was also transported; number eight, after six several periods of imprisonment, was also transported; number nine, after one imprisonment, was also transported; number eleven, after sixteen several additional periods of imprisonment, was again in custody for trial; number twelve, a female, had been imprisoned seven times since the return, but was then out of gaol, a prostitute; number thirteen had not been heard of in Liverpool since the date of the last return; and number fourteen had been transported after an additional period of imprisonment.

Not one of these fourteen offenders could write, and only one of them could read, and that imperfectly.

The petitioners did not enter into a statement of their opinions as to the causes of crime, but simply observed that to want and ignorance much of it might be attributed. Upon that ground, as well as upon other considerations, they suggested that it was the duty of the Legislature to provide, "by a well-considered system of national education, for the redemption of a vast portion of the children of this country, particularly those in large towns, from ignorance, and its almost inseparable companion, vice."

Nothing further was done in the matter, except that well-meant endeavours continue to be made to combat the mighty evils of juvenile ignorance and depravity, by the establishment of Ragged Schools; and by extending as much as possible the benefits of the well-conducted Industrial Schools at Kirkdale. Mr. Rushton, who seems never to have omitted an opportunity of pointing out to the bench the cruelty, as well as impolicy, of suffering so many children to be trained in crime, and the folly of supposing that the evil was wholly irremediable, addressed, on the 28th of January last, an interesting letter upon the subject to the town council of Liverpool. After reciting the facts in the fourteen cases above-mentioned, Mr. Rushton presented some additional cases. He said:—

"At the October sessions, 1849, a man named ——, aged forty, was sent by me to trial. He was found guilty, and sentenced to three months' imprisonment. The man has three sons, and it is to the history of these children, in connection with the father, that I wish your particular attention. I begin with Patrick, *alias* Kelly, *alias* Nutter, *alias* O'Garr, *alias* Key, the eldest child, who is now fourteen years old. He was first brought before me on the 9th June, 1845, charged with stealing ropes. He was then about nine years old. I did not wish to send so young a child to gaol, so, as I usually do, I delivered him to his parents, with an admonition to them. On the 29th of September following he was again brought before me, and after a remand and a second admonition he was discharged. On the 25th of October, within a month, he was again before me, and sentenced, under the summary powers of the local act, to an imprisonment of one month. On the 15th of November, after being thirteen days out of prison, he was again accused and sentenced to two months' imprisonment. On the 16th of March, 1846, he was in custody on a charge not proved, and discharged. On the 25th of April he was imprisoned for stealing a small quantity of iron, and sent to gaol for a fortnight. On the 4th of June he was again imprisoned for a month. On his next appearance I thought it best, notwithstanding his tender years, to send the boy to trial, and at the Borough sessions, in September, he was tried and convicted for stealing a bag of currants from the dock-quays, and sentenced to be imprisoned for four months and to be twice whipped. In October, 1847, he was charged with stealing, and the case not being proved he was discharged. He was again in custody on the 30th of October, and imprisoned; also in November, 1847; in May, 1848; in March, 1849; in August, 1849; and on the 7th of January, 1850, he was again sent to gaol for three months, where he now remains. Thus, at fourteen years old, he has been seventeen times in custody. He has been five times discharged, twice imprisoned for fourteen days, once for one month, once for two months, six times for three months, and tried and convicted and sentenced to four months' imprisonment, and to be twice whipped.

"The second son of the same man was brought before me on the 2d March, 1849, and since that time up to the 2d of February last, he has been eight times charged with theft. He is now nine years old, and on Saturday last he was again brought before me for robbing a till, in company with three other lads about his own age, and he remains in custody.

"The third son, Thomas, was brought before me on the 8th of February, 1849, accused of theft, again in June, again in September, again in January, again on the 4th of February, and again on the 15th of February, and he also remains in custody. He is now eight years old.

"Both these last-mentioned prisoners are small of their age; when standing in the dock the lower parts of their faces are not visible. These lads have been trained by a vicious father to the work of plunder; he has taught them how to steal with dexterity, and he uses them as a means of supplying himself with a luxurious existence.

"Time after time I have remanded these infants, and after certain periods of delay I have sent them by night to places where they might have a chance of escape from the father, who is destroying them; but the father has always discovered them; and, having no power to detain the children, his demands have been obeyed, and here is the sad result. I shall now have to send both these wretched children to gaol. I cannot permit them to be any longer employed by their father as instruments of fraud; and I at the same time know that the children are not moral agents, that they know no distinctions of right or wrong; that all that is good in them has never been developed, or has been systematically destroyed; and no effectual means exist without your aid to rescue these children from worse than death."

Mr. Rushton proposed, instead of sending such unhappy children to gaol for a short or for a longer period, to be contaminated or hardened by the treatment they receive, and to be afterwards let loose upon society to run through a similar or a worse career, that they should be sent to school. His plan was as follows:—

"By the 3d and 4th Victoria, c. 90," said Mr. Rushton, "the Lord Chancellor of England may assign the persons of all children convicted of felony to the custody of any persons who are willing to take charge of them until they are 21 years of age. Now, if the select vestry of Liverpool will appropriate a department of the schools at Kirkdale to the reception of children of this description, and if the corporation will join in the plan, we shall take the first step in the right direction in dealing with crime. If this plan were adopted, I should send the children whose history I have detailed to you for trial. When the jury found them guilty, and the conviction was recorded, by the consent of the learned Recorder an application would be made to the Chancellor, and the children would be consigned to the care of the institution, and the vicious parents would be prevented from doing what the father of Patrick —— has done. I am convinced that the costs would not be more than those incurred by the repeated convictions and imprisonment of juvenile offenders. If this plan, to the consideration of which I invite your serious attention, were adopted, the children detained would, in the first instance, be separated from the children in the industrial schools, and only transferred thither when the chaplain should approve. If a premium were offered for good conduct, and a moral impulse given to the children, the work of reformation could soon begin; for it must not be forgotten that the children who are criminals are amongst the most intelligent. A stupid child has neither quickness nor dexterity sufficient to make a profitable thief. What I propose to you is, that the council and the select vestry should nominate a committee to confer with the magistrates on this subject, and that a report should be made to each of those bodies. I shall, of course, be happy to give all the information in my power, and I feel hopeful of the result if the Liverpool people will set about this work of mercy with a portion of that benevolent energy which they always show in the cause of humanity. If this plan should be adopted and extended to other places, we should, in my opinion, in time, abate the anxiety respecting the disposal of our convicts, for we should, I hope, decrease the number of adult criminals."

The town council received this letter with the attention due not only to the public usefulness and eminent attainments of Mr. Rushton, but to the high importance of the subject. A joint committee of eight members, appointed by the magistrates, the town council, and the select vestry, was authorized to consider the plan, who reported that for an outlay of £1,200 per annum, and an outfit of 500 guineas, the experiment could be tried, and strongly recommended the town council to act upon the suggestion. The Rev. Mr. Carter, the chaplain of the borough gaol, published a letter to the town council on the 25th of April, in support of the views of Mr. Rushton, in which he cited a number of cases within his own experience that fully corroborated the statements, and added force to the arguments, of that gentleman.

Shortly after the publication of these letters, I was shown over the borough gaol by the Rev. Mr. Carter, and saw the children referred to by Mr. Rushton, together with about sixty others, of ages varying from nine to sixteen. They were engaged with the schoolmaster of the prison. The general expression upon the countenances of these youthful criminals was that of extreme cunning. A few were peculiarly forbidding and sullen, and scowled upon me as I entered. Others grinned and leered from behind their books, while three or four showed a vacuity and stolidity of countenance which approached the idiotic. The schoolmaster said that some of the boys were very clever, and pointed out one in particular, "who could learn anything." The majority of them, he said, were very bad boys, and gave a great deal of trouble. I inquired for the youngest of the three boys alluded to in Mr. Rushton's letter, and he was brought from another room by a gaoler. He was an intelligent looking and very diminutive child. He said he was nine years of age. I asked the gaoler and the schoolmaster what sort of a boy he was? The reply was, "A very wicked boy indeed, and gives us more trouble than any other boy in the prison." I asked in what way, for I was rather surprised to hear such a character of a child, so pleasing and quiet in appearance, and who surveyed me with large eyes, full of curiosity, and with a subdued and sorrowful expression of countenance. The gaoler said that "He broke the prison regulations oftener than any other boy, and that he was incorrigibly wicked." "What has he done that is so wicked?" "He continually talks to the other boys in the school. We cannot keep him quiet." "Anything else?" "Yes, he nudges the other boys, pulls them about, and tries to play with them." Of course it will be alleged that it is necessary to maintain the regulations of a prison, and that such a place ought not to be made as comfortable as the workhouse or parochial schools, which are open for the reception of boys unconvicted of offences against the laws; but I would ask what good all the teaching in the world could effect upon the mind of a boy like this, when made to feel that his natural playfulness and exuberance of life and spirits were considered wickedness, and punished accordingly. The child, like any other young animal, requires to play, and to use its limbs; and if a child of average intelligence be told that life and motion are crimes, its notions of right and wrong cannot fail to be confounded. Such a course of punishment must very effectually educate a healthy boy into a hatred of the law under which he suffers such injustice. Reading and writing may no doubt be learned in a prison school, but that a boy can be educated in prison, I, for one, should feel inclined to deny, unless by education be meant a systematic deadening of the moral and a repression of the physical faculties.

A boy, who was represented to me as one of the cleverest and best-behaved in the gaol, but from whom this eulogium on his character was studiously concealed, was brought to me in an adjoining room from the workshop, where he was employed, as a tailor, in mending the clothes of the other prisoners. I was desirous to ascertain the extent of his general information. He gave the following answers in reply to my questions:—

"I am sixteen years of age. I have been twice in prison. The first time was for brass-candlesticks, which were missed out of Pedlar's-market. I am in this time for some tea. I went to Egremont with another boy to look for crabs on the shore. We had a handkerchief to put the crabs in. The other boy got into a shop at Egremont while I waited outside. He stole the tea, and gave it to me to put in the handkerchief. I was caught by a policeman, but the other boy ran away. I can read a little, but nothing to speak of. I can't write. I don't know the multiplication-table. I don't know what it means. I know that twice two are four. I can't tell how many eight times eight make. I learned my letters at a Sunday school. I never went to a day school. I was born in Liverpool. I believe Liverpool is in England. I am certain that it is not in Ireland, nor in Cheshire, nor in Lancashire, nor in any of those places. I don't know where London is, but I have heard of it. I don't know whether there is a King or a Queen in England. I never heard the name of Victoria. I think I have heard people speak of the Queen, but I don't know who she is. I never heard of Prince Albert, nor the Duke of Wellington. I know Mr. Rushton. He is the 'beak.' I have seen the ships leaving the docks. I believe a great many go to America. America is a kind of country, I think, but I don't know if it is as far off as Ireland. I don't know where Ireland is, but I have heard of it often. I never heard of France. I have heard the sailors talk of Botany Bay. I have been to church since I came to prison. I never went any other time. I heard of the Lord there. I heard that he was very good to us. He takes care of us, and gives us things to eat. He sends us cattle and beasts. I have heard of Jesus Christ. He was Eve's son. He died on the cross to save us. I don't know where he died; nor how long it was ago. I dare say it's about a hundred years ago. I can't tell. I never heard. I have learned the commandments. I know some of them. I know the eighth. I don't know the tenth. I know the fourth. I can say it. I don't know the fifth, nor the sixth, nor the seventh. I know the first. I don't know what I shall do when I get out of prison. I have no friends. I took a wrong name when I came to prison. I was put up to the dodge at Bridewell. I don't want to steal any more. I would rather work. I don't like prison."

Another boy, who said he was turned fifteen, did not know how many seasons there were in the year, nor which was the first month, nor the succession of the months. Had never heard the Queen's name. Did not know whether Liverpool was in England. Had heard people talk of Jesus Christ, but did not know who he was. Did not know who made the world. Had heard of God, but did not understand about him. Went to church and heard the chaplain preach, but it wasn't interesting. Could read a little, and would be very glad to read better. He had been four times in prison. He had tried to keep out, but he could do no work, except run errands, and nobody would take him into their shop. It was wrong to steal, but if he didn't steal he should starve. He didn't care so much about prison now as he used to do. His father couldn't keep him, and sent him out into the streets. He didn't know what his end would be. He should not be hanged, he knew that. They did not hang people for stealing now.

The facts and reasoning in the letters of Mr. Rushton and Mr. Carter—and of which I had full corroboration in my visit to the borough gaol—produced their due effect in the town council of Liverpool. The subject was fully debated at a numerous meeting of that body early in June last. A resolution was ultimately moved and seconded that Mr. Rushton's plan should be tried, and that the sum of £1,200 should be voted towards it. An amendment was moved, on the ground that the evil was too large for local agencies to grapple with, or local resources to afford a remedy for. The amendment, however, was not pressed, and the council resolved unanimously to try this great experiment. No doubt the result will be anxiously looked forward to, not only in Liverpool, but in every other part of the kingdom.

LABOUR AND THE POOR.

LIVERPOOL.

[FROM OUR SPECIAL CORRESPONDENT.]

THE MARITIME POPULATION.—THE SAILORS' HOME.

Letter XV.

As briefly stated in the third Letter of the series devoted to this town, the sailors in Liverpool, and indeed in every British port, may be divided into three classes—the crews of coasting vessels, British sailors engaged in the foreign and colonial trade, and the crews of foreign ships. The two first classes compose what is called the British merchant service. In Liverpool the men composing the third class, although called foreign sailors, and sailing under foreign protection, are to a great extent British born subjects. From the statement of a shipping master largely employed by the American liners to "ship" their crews, and who has been in the business for upwards of a quarter of a century, it would appear that upon the average of American crews shipped by him, not above six out of twenty-four are really American. Twelve or fourteen out of the twenty-four are Englishmen or Scotchmen, and the remainder are composed of Dutchmen, French, and Italians.

Liverpool swarms with sailors of these three classes. All these are victims more or less of the parasites and plunderers who consider mariners their lawful prey. The two last classes are most exposed to the knavery and temptation of the town; and the following statements will, therefore, relate more particularly to them. The crews of coasting vessels have not accumulations of wages to receive like sailors who return from long voyages; and being maintained at the expense of the owners while they are in port they are not thrown upon their own resources. Neither is the foreign sailor altogether at the mercy of those who plunder the maritime population, especially as regards lodging and boarding houses. It is the British sailor engaged in the foreign and colonial trade who is the most helpless, and who is too often robbed and defrauded, not only by one, but by every class of those who make it their business to live upon his necessities, his recklessness, and his vices.

Every large port has a considerable population of these false friends and real foes of the sailor. When a ship returns from a long voyage of eighteen or twenty months, or perhaps two years, with a crew of twenty or thirty men, each with an accumulation of wages to spend or waste, possibly each man with £40 or £50 in his pocket, she is (to use the phrase of a sailor who communicated some valuable information about his class) "a regular California," in which all the land-sharks of the port expect to get a "digging." These "land-sharks" of both sexes may be classed as follows:—First, the boarding and lodging house keepers of the disreputable class; second, the slop tailors and outfitters; and third, the abandoned women. All of these set to work to extract the hard-earned sovereigns from the pockets of the simple, extravagant, and licentious sailor. After long confinement on ship-board he is well inclined to amuse himself on shore, and will deny himself no gratification that money can procure. When these three have pretty well drained him dry he falls into the hands of a fourth variety of the tribe of plunderers, the crimps. In some instances the crimp's business is but a branch of that carried on by the boarding and lodging house keeper, and the sailor in this case may be said to be in the hands of the crimp from the moment he sets foot on shore. Three out of the four classes of plunderers thus play into each other's hands. The abandoned women alone carry on their own trade on their own separate account, although instances are known in which they are in the pay of the crimps and outfitters.

One instance, a specimen of hundreds of others that are of constant occurrence, will serve to explain the manner in which the sailors are defrauded. A ship lately entered the port of Liverpool, after a fifteen months' voyage to the coast of Africa. The crew of 18 men had in consequence fourteen months' wages to receive, or fifteen if they had not accepted advance notes before sailing. This made about £37 10s. per man, or £675 for the whole crew. A lodging-house keeper heard of the prize, and succeeded in inducing a portion of the crew to board and lodge with him. In less than five days some of these men expended with a Jew slop tailor, to whom they had been recommended by their complacent host, the sum of £104 and odd for clothes, or about £15 per man. The slop seller paid the lodging-house keeper £5 per man, or £35 in all, being at the rate of about 33 per cent., as compensation for the custom he had recommended. It must be confessed that sailors have themselves to blame in a great degree for the extortion of which they are the victims. With their pockets full of sovereigns, and being morally certain that they can get another ship when all their earnings are spent, they not only deliver themselves up to dissipation of every kind, but in very bravado play the most insane tricks with their money. It would be surprising, under the circumstances, if the needy and dishonest did not flock about them. When sailors intoxicate themselves night after night, and when they insist upon lighting their pipes with five or ten pound notes, in order to be enabled to boast of the achievement at a future time—a case of no unfrequent occurrence—it is no more to be wondered at that the "land-sharks" should gather about them, than that the kites and ravens should flock to the carcass of a dead sheep upon the mountains. One seaman, but a few weeks before my inquiries into this subject commenced, lit his pipe with a ten pound note, although the whole amount of wages he had received was only £17. The man was pointed out to me, and when I asked him why he had committed so foolish an act he said it was for a "lark;"—the money was his own, and he had a right to make use of it in that way if he pleased. Before proceeding further with the detail of the extortions systematically practised upon these extravagant and foolish, or simple and confiding sailors, it is right to state that some of the "shipping-masters," the name by which the "crimps" call themselves, are respectable men, and that many of the boarding and lodging houses of Liverpool, intended for the accommodation of sailors, are conducted upon honourable principles. Perhaps, also, some of the slop establishments in the neighbourhood of the docks may be fair and honourable in their dealings. It is, however, but too true, that the majority of people in this line make it their business to rob sailors in the manner of which the case above cited affords a specimen.

The sailors' lodging and boarding houses are situated in every part along the line of the docks, but the greater portion of them are to be found in the neighbourhood of the Prince's, the Waterloo, and the Clarence Docks. One street leading from the Waterloo-road, called Dennison-street, is wholly occupied with lodging and boarding houses and public-houses, with the exception of a huge pile of warehouses at the extremity. The stranger, on looking up the street, may see more public-houses at a glance than in any other street in Liverpool, or perhaps in the world. Out of less than forty houses he may reckon nearly twenty wine, beer, and spirit shops. Most, if not all of them, keep lodgings for sailors, while some of them combine the businesses of the crimp and the boarding-house keeper. The other houses in the street are chiefly, if not wholly, devoted to the boarding of foreign crews, this business being rendered necessary by the prohibition of fire and light in the docks. This street is frequented almost wholly by American sailors, who look upon it as so entirely their own, that they have established a rule forbidding a "darkey," or coloured man, to pass through it—a popular law, worthy of Charleston, or any other slave town in America. If a coloured man, unaware of the fact, should accidentally stray into this pro-slavery preserve, he would run the risk of being mobbed. Twelve o'clock is the general dinner-hour among sailors, at which time the whole female population of the neighbourhood seem to turn out to waylay the men as they pass to their boarding-houses. There comes a lull after this for twenty minutes or half an hour, during which the sailors are at dinner. After this they once more issue forth into the street, to be again waylaid by the women, and to be led from the streets to their lodgings, or into the public-houses, to pass the remainder of the hour allowed for dinner. The fights that take place keep the police continually on the alert, and help to maintain the old reputation of the street as one of the most turbulent, dissipated, and in every way disreputable, in the town. There are several other streets in this immediate vicinity, every one of which may share the bad character of Dennison-street.

The evils of the crimping system are perhaps still more notorious. The profits of the "crimp," if he do not keep a boarding and lodging house, are reducible into three kinds—the per centage he levies upon slopsellers and others for procuring them custom, the fee for "shipping," and the discount of advance notes. The business of the shipping master—acting as a middleman between the captain who wants a crew and the sailors who want a ship—might be, and sometimes is, very creditably conducted; but in general the "crimp" makes the sailor his victim, and extracts, without compunction, the last shilling that he can from the pockets of those whose prevalent fault is a disregard and ignorance of the value of money.

The sum paid to the crimp by the captain of a ship for "shipping" a crew is 2s. per man, and in some cases 3s. or 4s., according to previous arrangement. So far the business is fair and above-board. But the dishonest and greedy among the crimps, unfortunately the majority of that body, are not satisfied with this remuneration from the captain and owners. They require, and obtain, an additional reward from the sailor. The sum they ask is often as high as 20s. per man. To obtain this sum they resort to various manœuvres. The mates of ships are sometimes in collusion with the crimps, and especially with those crimps who keep boarding and lodging houses. The mate has generally the power to engage or reject the men that may offer; and between the mate and the crimp it occasionally happens that a ship is provided with a crew that do not know their business—that are not able seamen, and that in stormy weather may, by their ignorance and "lubberliness," endanger the safety of the ship. The crimp of the boarding and lodging house having picked up a set of destitute sailors, intermingled with "lubbers," for both of whom he keeps his emissaries on the watch, induces them to lodge at his house, and run up a bill. When they are firmly in his debt, he goes to the mate of a ship that may be in want of a crew, and represents that he has a lot of "able" seamen at his house, living upon his means, and running up long scores with him, whom he would be glad to get shipped. He promises the mate a pound per man if he will ship them. The mate agrees to the terms, and the men are shipped, inefficient as they may be. They ask for, and receive, the advance note of £2 5s., or £2 10s., the first month's wages, not above a few shillings of which sum are suffered to reach their hands. The note is received by the crimp, who gives the mate the promised pound, and keeps the greater portion of the remainder for his own trouble. He then induces his lodgers to sign an acknowledgment of the debt they may have contracted, every item of which is, in all probability, an extravagant overcharge, and trusts to his remedy against them when they return to port with the earnings of their voyage. Of course the operation of cashing an advance note is not unattended with risk. The sailor may desert before the ship sails, in which case the note becomes worthless.

In the year 1844, the attention of the principal merchants and shipowners having been repeatedly drawn to these and various other evils and extortions to which sailors were exposed, they resolved to establish an institution under the title of "The Sailors' Home." Among the promoters of this scheme the names of Mr. James Aikin, the chairman of the institution, and that of Mr. W. Brown, M.P. for South Lancashire, one of the most eminent merchants in the world, deserve especial mention for their zeal and liberality. The promoters declared the immediate objects of the institution to be, to provide for seamen frequenting the port of Liverpool board, lodging, and medical attendance at a moderate charge; to protect them from imposition and extortion, and to encourage them to husband their hard-earned wages; to promote their moral, intellectual, and professional improvement; and to afford them the opportunity of receiving religious instruction. It was also resolved to attach a reading-room, library, and savings bank to the institution; and with the view of securing to the able and well-conducted seaman a rate of wages proportionate to his merits, to keep a registry of character. Schools for sea apprentices and the sons of seamen, with special regard to the case of children who had lost one or both of their parents, were at the same time stated to be in contemplation. The first public meeting for the establishment of this institution was held on the 25th of October, 1844, and in the course of a few months the sum of £14,800 was subscribed towards the object in view. Temporary premises, for transacting all the business of the Home, with the exception of boarding and lodging the men, which could not be undertaken until the spacious building now in course of construction is completed, were opened in April, 1845, between which period and the end of the year 3,332 seamen were registered. The number of ships supplied with crews during the same period was 220, and of men shipped 2,412. The number of crews paid off in the institution was 231. A library and reading-room were opened for the sailors, at which the average attendance was about a hundred per day. From the opening of the institution until the close of the year 1849 the number of seamen shipped has been 29,975. This large number of sailors were not exposed to the extortion of the crimps, and had nothing to pay for being shipped. Formerly a shilling per man was the recognized charge made upon the sailor, but by an order of the Board of Trade, the officers of the Home were forbidden to levy this sum. This order has been considered injudicious. The shilling was but a small tax—which the sailor would have gladly continued to pay— and its abolition, while it has been attended with no good result to the sailor, has deprived the Home of a source of revenue which would have materially contributed to make it self-supporting. The society is yet deficient in funds to complete the building destined for the ac- commodation of the sailors; and had the abolition of this shilling fee not been resolved upon in London by men in authority, who did not know its working, the sum of £1,500 might have been raised in this manner from the 29,975 men shipped to the end of 1849, without the slightest hardship upon them.

A record kept at the "Sailors' Home" gives some authentic and curious information upon the general character of the sailors who are shipped by its agency. It will be seen from the following abstract of a tabular statement for the years 1848 and 1849 that the large majority of sailors are men who bear a good character from the captains with whom they sail, and that the utterly bad form but a very small minority. In the year 1848 the number of sailors registered at the Sailors' Home who obtained ships was 1,598. Their characters were thus stated by the captains with whom they sailed—

Very good	304
Good	906
Middling	101
Indifferent	71
Deserted	82
Bad	47
Not reported upon	87
Total	1,598

The number of sailors not previously registered at the office who obtained ships during the year was 1,041. Their characters were afterwards reported as follows:—

Very good	154
Good	575
Middling	61
Indifferent	33
Deserted	96
Bad	59
Not reported upon	63
Total	1,041

It thus appears that, of the registered seamen, five per cent. were noted as deserters, and three per cent. only as "bad." The good and very good amounted together to 77 per cent. of the whole number. The per centage of the various classes was slightly different among the non-registered seamen; the "good" and "very good" amounting to 70 per cent. of the whole—the deserters to 9 1-3 per cent.—and the "bad" to 5¾ per cent.

From a similar return for the year 1849, it appears that 3,329 sailors previously registered were shipped from the Home. Their characters were noted by the captains, in the books of the office, as follows:—

<pre>
Very good   875
Good   1,783
Middling   194
Indifferent   109
Bad   77
Deserted   147
Dead   50
Not reported upon   94
                                      ______
            Total 3,329
</pre>

The sailors not previously registered who obtained ships amounted to 2,342. Their characters were reported to be

<pre>
Very good   568
Good   1,231
Middling   136
Indifferent   74
Bad   57
Deserted   136
Dead   37
Not reported upon   103
                                      ______
            Total 2,342
</pre>

Calculating the per centage in the same way as before, it would result from these figures that among the registered seamen 80 per cent. were declared to be "good," or "very good," 4¼ per cent. deserters, and only 2¼ per cent. "*bad*." Among the non-registered seamen, the number of "good" and "very good" was 76 per cent., of deserters 5¾ per cent., and of "*bad*" 2½ per cent.

The ceremony of "shipping," as performed at the Sailors' Home, is very simple. By public notice affixed in the reading-room, the men are informed that a certain captain, trading to a certain port, is in want of a crew; that the wages are from £2 5s. to £3 per month, as the case may be; and that he will attend at a certain hour to make choice, among such as may be willing to sail with him. If the captain bear a bad character either for drunkenness or tyranny, or any other fault, it is generally well known to the sailors, and he finds a difficulty in getting good men to sail under him. But these are rare cases, the old race of intemperate and brutal commanders being very greatly diminished, and promising to become extinct. The captain or mate generally knows a good sailor at a glance. When he has made up his mind, and is disposed to "ship" a man, he inquires his name, and on reference to it in the books of the Home, sees a record of the voyages he has made, and the characters which the various captains have inscribed against his name. If he find the word "drunk," or "insubordinate," or worse than either, the fatal phrase "a sea-lawyer" against the name of a candidate, he makes choice of another man. The character of being a sea-lawyer, or argumentative, disputatious sailor, is the worst that can be given. No captain will knowingly have such a man on board of his ship. If, however, the inspection of the register be satisfactory, the man is told to step aside, and sign articles. When he has done this the bargain is concluded, and he can ask for his "advance note," or wages for the first month. The following is the form of "articles" to be signed by all the crew and the ship's officers.

"LIVERPOOL SAILORS' HOME, REGISTRY, AND SAVINGS BANK (in conformity with the Merchant Seamen's Act, 7 and 8 Vic., cap. 112, schedule A).

"Patron—Her Most Gracious Majesty the Queen.

"FORM OF AGREEMENT FOR FOREIGN OR COLONIAL VOYAGES.

"An agreement made pursuant to the directions of an Act of Parliament passed in the eighth year of the reign of Queen Victoria, between William Gibson, the master of the ship Crisis, of the port of Liverpool, and of the burden of 426 tons, and the several persons whose names are subscribed hereto. It is agreed by and on the part of the said persons, and they severally hereby engage to serve on board the said ship in the several capacities against their respective names expressed, on a voyage from the port of Liverpool to Hong Kong and Whampoa, from thence, if required, to any parts and places in the China or eastern seas, Indian, or Pacific Oceans, or where freight may offer, and back to a final port of discharge in the United Kingdom, or for a term not to exceed two years; and the said crew further engage to conduct themselves in an orderly, faithful, honest, careful, and sober manner, and to be at all times diligent to their respective duties and stations, and to be obedient to the lawful commands of the master in everything relating to the said ship, and the materials, stores, and cargo thereof, whether on board such ship, in boats, or on shore. No grog, no swearing, or profane language allowed, nor sheath knives, to be worn about the person; the crew to be on board on the day of sailing, sober, and two hours before the ship leaves the dock, haul the ship out of dock or forfeit such amount of wages as the Act of Parliament directs. In consideration of which services, to be duly, honestly, carefully, and faithfully performed, the said master doth hereby promise and agree to pay the said crew, by way of compensation or wages, the amount against their

names respectively expressed; and it is hereby agreed, that any embez-
zlement, or wilful or negligent loss or destruction, of any part of the
ship's cargo or stores, shall be made good to the owner out of the wages
(so far as they will extend) of the seamen guilty of the same; and if any
seaman shall have entered himself as qualified for a duty to which he
shall prove to be not competent, he shall be subject to a reduction of
the rate of wages hereby agreed for, in proportion to his incompetency.
In witness whereof the said parties have hereto subscribed their names
on the days against their respective signatures mentioned.

" WEEKLY SCALE OF VICTUALLING.

	Beef.	Pork.	Flour.	Peas.	Tea.	Sugar.	Water.
	lb.	lb.	lb.	Pint.	Oz.		
Sunday....	$1\frac{1}{2}$	—	$\frac{1}{2}$	—	$\frac{1}{4}$	1 lb. each weekly.	3 imp. qts. daily.
Monday...	—	$1\frac{1}{4}$	—	$\frac{1}{3}$	$\frac{1}{4}$		
Tuesday ...	$1\frac{1}{2}$	—	$\frac{1}{2}$	—	$\frac{1}{4}$		
Wednesday	—	$1\frac{1}{4}$	—	$\frac{1}{3}$	$\frac{1}{4}$		
Thursday ..	$1\frac{1}{2}$	—	$\frac{1}{2}$	—	$\frac{1}{4}$		
Friday	—	$1\frac{1}{4}$	—	$\frac{1}{3}$	$\frac{1}{4}$		
Saturday ..	$1\frac{1}{2}$	—	—	—	$\frac{1}{4}$		

"Beef or pork may be substituted for each other.

"Bread, as much as they can eat without waste, not to exceed 1 lb.
per day each.

"SUBSTITUTES.

"1 oz. of coffee, or cocoa, or chocolate, may be substituted for ¼ oz.
of tea.

"Molasses for sugar, the quantity to be one-half more.

"1 lb. of potatoes or yams, ½ lb. flour or rice, ⅓ pint of peas, or ¼
pint of barley, may be substituted for each other.

"When fresh meat be issued, the proportion to be 2 lbs. per man
per day, in lieu of salt meat, flour, rice, and peas.

"The allowance of small stores is considered as an equivalent for
spirits.

"Lime or lemon juice and sugar to be served out daily, and vinegar
weekly, to the crew, whenever they shall have been consuming salt provisions for ten days, and so long as the consumption of salt provisions
be continued (as per Act of Parliament).

———, master."

To this document, against each man's name, are appended the
number and date of the ship's register, the place and time of entry, the

age and place of birth of each sailor, his quality, whether an ordinary or able-bodied seaman, the amount of wages per calendar share or voyage, the amount of advance note (if any), the amount of monthly allotment he may wish paid to his wife and family when absent, the name of the ship in which he last served, the number of his registry or Government ticket, and his number in the books of the Home. The master and mate affix their names to the foot of the document, as a declaration of the truth of all the particulars set forth in the agreement, a copy of which is delivered to the collector or comptroller of customs of the port.

The advance notes to sailors are so frequent an occasion of mischief that a steady effort has been made to abolish them by the authorities of the Home, aided very generally by the captains and owners of vessels. Out of two crews that were shipped at the Home on the day I visited it, for the purpose of seeing the ceremony of "shipping," each man was offered 5s. a month extra wages if he would forgo the advance note. Of one crew of thirty men engaged for a large ship of 1,200 tons burden, sixteen accepted the higher rate of wages. In a smaller crew of only eight men, four accepted the terms. It is generally found to be well worth the extra expense to the owners to offer this inducement. Those who decline receiving the advance notes are generally careful men, who have saved money. Those who insist upon the advance note are very often men of dissipated habits, who require the money either to wipe off old scores incurred in extravagance, or to have a "spree" before leaving port. This class of men, having received the money, sometimes desert their ship, which is one of the most serious of the evils attendant upon the system. In some cases, however, the "advance note" is absolutely necessary. A man may need clothes for the voyage he is about to undertake, or he may have arrived utterly destitute in port after a shipwreck. It is for this reason that the Home does not absolutely set itself against advance notes, but endeavours to lessen the number of applicants by procuring a higher rate of wages for provident men, who are not reduced to the necessity of applying for them.

In the first year of the establishment of the Home, 1,308 advance notes, representing the sum of upwards of £3,000, were cashed at the institution. Great circumspection was used, and very few of the men who received this accommodation deserted their ships. In 1846, the second year of the institution, the amount of notes cashed was £2,248. The Home suffered no loss by desertion; and in consequence of the low rate of discount charged to deserving sailors, the crimps and lodging-house keepers, who make a great profit out of this business, sometimes charging £1 discount for a note of £2 10s., found it necessary to reduce their charges. Thus both a direct and an indirect benefit were afforded. In the year 1847, the amount of notes cashed was £3,150; in 1848, £2,449; and in 1849, not much above half that sum. During these three years very few desertions occurred on the part of men whose notes had been cashed by the institution.

In addition to this business, the Home manages a bank for savings and a bank for deposits; the first for the advantage of the careful and provident, and the second as a boon to the careless sailor, who will not be induced to save. The bank of deposit takes charge of his money, and allows him to draw it out without previous notice, and according to his wants, thus preserving it to some extent from the hands of thieves and prostitutes. The money deposited in the savings bank during the first year of the establishment of the Home amounted to about £1,000, but many of the sailors, according to the published report of the committee, notwithstanding all the advice and persuasion employed, instead of availing themselves of the bank even as a place of temporary security for their money, wasted it or lost it in the most reckless manner. Some few, who had left small sums in the bank for several months while they were absent on voyages, were quite astonished to find on their return that more money was due to them than they had put in. They were not aware of the reproductive power of capital. They did not know, in fact, that money increased by being left at interest. This ignorance, it may be observed, is not peculiar to sailors, but is shared by a large number of the working classes. The payments into the savings bank during the year 1848 were £1,505 0s. 10d., and the amount withdrawn was £1,509 10s. At the end of the year 1849, upwards of £1,000 belonging to sailors remained in the bank.

The foundation stone of the "Sailors' Home" was laid with the usual ceremonies by his Royal Highness Prince Albert, on the 31st of July, 1846, and the building is now advancing rapidly to completion. The architect is Mr. John Cunningham, on whose taste and ability it reflects high credit.

The site of this building is rather unfortunate, being upon a part of the lowest alluvial deposits from the river, and the building is shut out from a view of it by the Post-office, the Custom-house, and other buildings, which surround it on all sides. Hence a most important object to interest the inmates of the institution has been lost; but as the difficulties to secure a site for the institution were very great, the committee had no other alternative than to take the only available piece of land which the corporation had to dispose of. The form of the site is also very unfavourable for a public building of such a character, being triangular.

The style adopted for the building is that usually termed Elizabethan, and is well calculated to suit the purposes of the institution, admitting of great variety and extent of fenestration, and of outline and detail. The height of the walls from the surface of the street to the top of the ballustrade is 72 feet, and is divided by moulded string courses and bands of moulded and fielded panels between a moulded baseplinth and the main cornice into three horizontal spaces. An attic rises over the main cornice, and is surmounted at intervals with an open ballustrade.

The whole of the exterior mason work is of the red sandstone of the neighbourhood, which lends to the building rather a venerable appearance.

The interior of the building is laid out as follows, viz.: in the basement at the west end are the house stewards' room, with bread pantry, general store, bakery, flour store, beer cellar, milk house, general pantry, coals, &c.; hypocaust for heating the main building and offices above; kitchen, 43 feet by 21; scullery, 35 feet by 21; scullery and kitchen pantries, and larders between. Four large chest rooms, a steam storing room for the sailors' chests, when brought into the building, before they are allowed to be taken up to the cabins. A portion of each chest room is vaulted over, so as to render them partially fire proof.

The east end of the basement is occupied with cellarage for the shops and the superintendent's house.

On the ground floor, the main entrance is at the west end, rising by a flight of ten broad steps from the street to a porch 16 feet by 8 feet 10 inches. At the further end of the porch a wide double door opens upon the outer hall, 26 feet square, divided into two spaces, with Doric columns and pilasters. On the left are the Bank, 23 feet by 15 feet, containing an iron safe; a Registering-Room, 24 feet 6 inches by 17 feet 6 inches; and a Shipping-office, 16 feet 8 inches by 14 feet 6 inches. On the right are, a committee-room, 25 feet 9 inches by 19 feet 7 inches; and another Registering Room, 27 feet 6 inches by 19 feet 7 inches, with retiring room and water-closet.

On entering from the outer hall, through an ornamental glazed screen, the visitor passes into a triangular shaped general hall, 91 feet 10 inches long, 32 feet wide at the west end, and 9 feet 4 inches at the east, and 70 feet high. This hall is covered wholly over at the top with glass, which throws a flood of light into the interior. On two sides of the hall, at the height of fourteen feet from the floor, are three tiers of ornamental open cast-iron pilasters sixteen feet high each, with moulded cornices, brackets, &c., and four lines of galleries, with ornamental appropriate cast-iron railing, leading to the dormitories.

Upon the right of the general hall, on the same level as the outer, and running parallel with the south wall of the building, are, the mates' dining-room, 28 feet by 21; and the boys' dining-room, 56 feet 7 inches by 21; with a stair of cast-iron steps leading to the basement, and to the dormitories and other rooms above.

On the left are a school room, 41 feet 6 inches by 21 feet, and stair of cast-iron steps also leading to the basement and dormitories over; also three paying rooms and large waiting room, but entering from the north side of the building. All these rooms and offices are 13 feet high to the ceiling.

On the east end of the building are three shops, with stair to the superintendent's house and cellars. These are intended to be let to respectable slop tailors and other tenants, for the supply of clothing and other articles at a moderate price. On the second floor, or what is in London termed the first, are the offices; at the west end of the building is a general dining room 86 feet 10 inches by 40 feet, and 16 feet high, having a lift from the basement for the cooked viands to ascend by. Over this are a lecture room, 50 feet 10 inches, by 40 feet 6 inches; and a reading room, 40 feet by 35 feet 6 inches, both 16 feet high, and communicating with each other when required by a sliding door 20 feet wide.

On the south and north sides of the hall, up to the top, are six floors of dormitories, each containing 22 cabins, 8 feet by 5 feet, and 7 feet high. The cabins towards the streets have each an external light. Those next the hall have each an internal light. The cabins on these side galleries are in blocks of four, with a broad passage between, lighted by an external window in each passage, with two wash basins at the end of each.

The upper floors of the east and west ends, over the superintendent's house, and over the lecture and reading rooms, are filled up with cabins of a larger size, for the accommodation of ship's officers, all properly lighted and ventilated. The total number of sleeping cabins is 340.

Every floor is provided with five water-closets, and with thirty-two wash-basins. There are also two bath-rooms, provided with hot and cold and shower baths, the whole supplied with water from large cast-iron tanks placed one in each tower.

As no space could be obtained around the building for exercise, the roof of the Home has been adapted, and appropriated to that purpose, being covered with asphalte in a very superior manner. It will make a very good promenade, although it will not afford the sailors a view over the shipping and the Mersey.

The total cost of the building, with its internal fittings, is estimated at £25,000, of which about £20,000 has been already subscribed, including two munificent donations, one of £250 and the other of £1,000, from Mr. W. Brown, M.P.

Whatever may be the ultimate advantages of this institution as a sailors' club house when the full design of its founders shall have been carried out, there can be no question that by its present incomplete operations considerable good is effected. Not only is the sailor saved from extortion, but he is practically made to understand and feel the benefits of economy and forethought, the want of which is the greatest defect in his character. The whole tendency of the system pursued at the Home, in the shipping, registry, and banking departments is to elevate the condition of the maritime population. The only subject for regret in connection with the Home is, that the contributions of the wealthy and philanthropic should be necessary to maintain it. Such an institution should be in all respects self-supporting, that sailors, in availing themselves of its numerous benefits, might be enabled to cultivate the noble feeling of self-respect and self-reliance. So large and so well-paid a body of working men ought not to be under the necessity of receiving the pecuniary support of the benevolent; and it would be far better that sailors should pay a shipping fee to the Home than that the merchants and shipowners should contribute their annual and eleemosynary guineas to maintain it. Of course when the Home is opened for boarding and lodging the sailors, the rate of payment will be so regulated as to make the institution self-supporting in this respect; but to be as efficient as it ought to be, the whole of the working expenses should be borne by those for whose advantage it has been established. It is quite sufficient that funds for the building of the Home should be supplied by the merchants and shipowners, and

the general body of the wealthy and benevolent who take an interest in the social well-being and moral improvement of the sailor. The
sailors themselves must support the Home, without the charitable aid
of the public, or the institution will fail in one of the great objects for
which it was established.

LABOUR AND THE POOR.

LIVERPOOL.

[FROM OUR SPECIAL CORRESPONDENT.]

THE AMUSEMENTS AND LITERATURE OF THE PEOPLE.

Letter XVI.

The attention of the stranger who walks through the streets of Liverpool can scarcely fail to be directed to the great number of placards which invite the public to cheap or free concert-rooms. Of all shapes, sizes, and colours to attract the eye, they cover the walls of the town, and compete with one another in the inducements which they offer to the public to favour with its patronage the houses which they advertise. In some of these establishments a threepenny ticket of admission entitles the visitor to enjoy a musical entertainment, consisting of comic and sentimental songs by male and female singers, and to a glass of ale or porter besides. At other houses no charge is made for admission, the proprietors depending solely upon the sale of their liquors for the payment of their performers. One establishment, which is among the largest of the kind in Liverpool, depends upon the attractions of its *tableaux vivans* or *poses plastiques* for carrying away the greater portion of the public patronage. Another relies upon the vocal and mimetic powers of some popular favourite, whom the placards designate as "the laughter creating son of Momus." A third holds out the superior inducement of "real Ethiopians" and "unrivalled Bones;" a fourth vaunts possession of the services of the "world-renowned Swiss melodist and sentimental vocalist;" while a fifth proclaims that the establishment which issued it is alone enabled to offer, by "an unparalleled expenditure of capital, an unprecedented combination of the highest talent in Europe." These huge placards set forth in large and many-coloured letters the prices of the various liquors supplied, from a twopenny glass of ale or porter to a fourpenny or sixpenny glass of spirits and water. The rooms are situated in all parts of the town, but the greater portion are to be found along the line of the docks and the adjoining streets, and in the densely-peopled district around Williamson-square. This last-mentioned place is full of them. As a preliminary to a description of the entertainment they provide, the following authentic statement of their numbers will be found interesting. The number of public-houses in the town is no less than 1,480, and of beer-shops 700, or in all 2,180. Taking the population at 350,000, this would be one public-house or beer-shop to every 160 individuals—men, women, and children. Taking each family to amount to four persons—there would be one public-house or beer-shop to every forty adult males in Liverpool. But it is chiefly to the concerts held in public-houses that I wish at present to draw the reader's attention. A document, which was drawn up by the police, in August, 1849, and bearing the signature of the High Constable, has been obligingly communicated to me by the authorities of the town. It is entitled "A return of the number of public-houses and beer-houses within the borough of Liverpool in which there are musical entertainments either vocal or instrumental, and of the number of persons employed therein, distinguishing males from females, and of the salaries respectively received by the performers." The number of public-houses devoted to these purposes at that time was thirty-two, and of beer-shops five. The total number of performers employed nightly was 218, of whom 145, including about forty pianoforte players and violinists, were males, and 73 females. The lowest salary was 6s. a week, and the highest £2. Among the salaries were several at 9s., 12s., 15s., 18s., and £1 per week. The total amount paid was £218 2s. per week, making the average as nearly as possible £1 for each performer. The average number of performers at each concert-room was six, but some of the larger establishments employed ten or twelve, including a pianist and violin player. The same number of free concert-rooms exist in the town at the present time. All of them are open for six nights in the week—and a proportion of them are open for the sale of drink on the Sundays. The proprietor of one of the largest and best-frequented informed me that the love of music was so great among the sailors and others who patronized his room, that he found it necessary to give them music on the Sunday evening as well as the other six nights of the week. "I give them a touch of the organ," said he: "I bought an instrument on purpose, and paid 150 guineas for it. I allow nothing but sacred music on the Sunday evenings. We have the Evening Hymn, the National Anthem, the Old Hundredth, 'Guide me, O Thou Great Jehovah,' and other popular sacred pieces. The company are much pleased with these performances, and seem to enjoy them quite as much as they do the singing on other nights. Of course they drink, and smoke, otherwise it would not be worth my while to buy an organ for them." The annual sum in salaries paid by these 37 establishments is £11,341. The whole of this sum, and the additional profits of the various proprietors, are levied by an extra charge for the drink, amounting to at least 25 per cent. above the price charged at the bar.

These houses are for the most part conducted with the utmost possible regard to the peace of the neighbourhood. They are much too profitable for any gross acts of impropriety or disturbance of order to be tolerated. The proprietors rule with a despotic hand, and very summarily eject all visitors whose misconduct might be the means of calling in the police. The proprietor of one of them, a man who provides rather a superior entertainment of the kind, very willingly and politely gave me all the information I required, and he induced his performers to sing some songs that were not in the performance of the night, expressly that I might have a correct idea of the "treat" he provided for his guests. "That man," he said, "who is now singing is my best performer. He would do credit to any theatre in London. Mr. Lumley might be proud of him. I find it necessary to pay him a very high salary. Great talent always commands a great price." "Have you any objection to tell the amount of his salary?" "Why, it is very high. I can scarcely afford it; but then he is a valuable man, and there are plenty of concert-rooms in the town who would snap him up if I lost him. Talent is talent you know." "Well, what may his talent be worth?" "Oh, he is highly paid; he gets £2 a week, and he's well worth it." The liberal landlord who rewarded talent at this rate was somewhat lame at the time, and limped about the room, keeping order, and attending to his guests. He explained his lameness by stating that a few nights previously he had kicked a disorderly foreign sailor down stairs, and that he had in consequence sprained his foot. "It was a foolish thing of me to do," said he, "especially as I had only my slippers on at the time. The accident will be a warning to me. No man ought to kick another with his slippers on. It isn't safe. I shall never do so again without my heavy boots!" But incidents like the one recorded by this *naïf* landlord are of rare occurrence, and the assistance of the police is seldom required. These concerts are generally well attended by sailors, to whom every night in the week is the same, but on Saturday nights the attendance is more numerous. The mechanics in receipt of their week's wages then make their appearance in the streets, and swarm into the free concerts in all parts of the town. On two consecutive evenings, a Friday and a Saturday, I made a tour of inspection among them. The first I visited is one of the largest concert-rooms in Liverpool. The advertised charge for admission was threepence, but on my tendering that sum to the money-taker at the door, he refused it, and informed me that the charge was sixpence. An explanation was asked and given, from which it appeared that the money-taker decided from the dress of the visitor whether he should pay the greater or the smaller sum. Threepence, he said, was the price to sailors and the working classes only; and sixpence was always charged to gentlemen. "But then," he added, "it comes to the same thing, as the full value of the ticket is returned in drink; and the 'gent' who pays his sixpence has a glass of spirits and water, or a bottle of porter for it; while the working man has no more than a glass of beer for his threepence." The room was large and handsomely decorated. It was also fitted up with a stage at the further end, and with moveable scenery as at a theatre. There were about 400 people present. The audience were arranged on benches, in front of small tables, or rather ledges, with just sufficient room before each person to place a bottle and a glass. Men, women, and children were mingled together. A dense cloud of tobacco-smoke filled the room. The greater portion of the auditors were evidently mechanics and labourers, with their families; but there was a considerable number of sailors, British, American, and foreign. There was also a large number of young boys, of from fourteen to sixteen years of age, of whom there was scarcely one without a pipe or a cigar in his mouth. The presence of these boys was the most melancholy part of the whole exhibition. Their applause rang loudest throughout the room—their commands to the waiters for drink were more frequent, obstreperous, and rude, than those of other persons—and their whole behaviour was unbecoming and offensive. The performer in possession of the stage was a man dressed from chin to heel in flesh-coloured cotton, fitting tight to the form, to represent nudity. He played the part of Lady Godiva riding through Coventry. In front of him projected the pasteboard figure of a pony's head, and behind were seen the posterior quarters of the animal. A long drapery concealed his legs as he skipped about the stage, whilst a pair of stuffed legs, to represent the nude limbs of Lady Godiva, dangled over the saddle. He sang a comic song—a mixture of the old legend with modern allusions. The whole composition was not only vulgar and stupid, but indecent.

He was greeted with loud applause, and called upon for an *encore.* To him succeeded a genteel-looking young woman, who sang a sentimental song with considerable taste and feeling. The curtain then fell, and allowed a pause for a few minutes, during which the waiters zealously plied the guests to give their orders for liquor. An elderly woman seated on the bench before me called for ginger beer. She was very meanly dressed, and altogether unprepossessing; and when the waiter brought the liquor, in exchange for her threepenny ticket, he neglected to bring a glass for it. He was about to pour it into the glass of a previous visitor, in which were some remains of porter, when she held back his hand, and insisted upon a clean glass. The man told her that she was rather too particular, and that if she could not drink without a clean glass she might let it alone. She insisted that, having paid her money, she was as much entitled to a clean glass as any one else, although perhaps she was not quite so well dressed as some others in the room. The waiter insolently told her to "hold her jaw; glasses were scarce; and if she did not like the glass before her she could drink out of the bottle." The lowering of the gas-lights gave notice that the exhibition of the *poses plastiques* was about to commence. The room being reduced to semi-darkness, the curtain slowly rose, the whole blaze of the footlights was thrown upon the stage, and a *tableau vivant* was exhibited. The performers were three females and one male. The *tableau* represented a classical subject; and the criticism of the spectators, though somewhat freely expressed, and not of the most delicate kind, as regarded the development of the female forms exposed to their gaze, was in the highest degree approbatory of the exhibition. As the curtain began to fall, there was a loud clapping of hands and stamping of feet, a jingling of glasses and bottles, and a call for an *encore.* In the midst of the uproar of applause, and before the slowly descending curtain concealed the performers from sight, the elderly woman before mentioned directed my attention to the principal female figure in the group—a finely formed and handsome young woman. "The waiter treats me in this way," she said, "because I am old, and badly dressed; but I'll let him know that I am somebody, after all. That young woman, sir, is my daughter." I sympathised in her grievance respecting the waiter, upon which she became very communicative, and gave a detail of the professional life of her daughter. She was, she said, one of the first that ever exhibited in England in the *poses plastiques,* and learned the art under Madame Warton. Her salary was a pound a week, for which she performed four or five times every night. She had to provide her own flesh-coloured silks out of her earnings, and these articles were very expensive. Though the salary was not high, her daughter would have been contented with it; but the master of the establishment having determined to cut it down to 18s. a week, she had given him notice to quit, and the present was the last night of her performance in Liverpool. She had received another engagement in Manchester at 21s. a week, and was to leave on the following Monday to make her first appearance. "It is very hard work," said the old woman, "and is not sufficiently paid, considering the expense of the dress." A comic song from a young man dressed as a sailor interrupted her further confidences, and she soon afterwards left her seat, but not before bestowing a parting malediction upon the waiter. At the conclusion of the song, I left the place and visited another concert-room of the same kind. This establishment is divided into two separate rooms; the one entitled the "House of Commons," and the other the "House of Lords." The "House of Commons" is open to all comers, male and female; the "House of Lords," where the liquors are sold at a price somewhat in advance, is reserved exclusively for the male sex. The Hall of the "House of Commons" was a large room, in which about three hundred persons, sailors and their wives and sweethearts, mechanics with their wives and children, and a number of young lads and girls were assembled. The place was filled with tobacco smoke. The walls were adorned with gigantic full-length portraits of celebrated prizefighters, all in boxing attitude, and painted apparently in *fresco*. As at the previously visited establishment, there was a stage with moveable scenery at the extremity. A man in the traditional stage garb of a sailor sang a nautical song and danced a hornpipe. He was followed by a female performer in the sentimental line, who was twice encored. She was succeeded by a couple, representing a cobbler and his termagant wife. They performed a comic duet, abounding in *double entendres,* which elicited roars of laughter. The performances in the "House of Lords" were of a similar character, the principal difference being the exclusion of women and the superior attire of the guests, who seemed to be composed of clerks, shopmen, and tradesmen.

I also visited various other establishments of the kind. Their general characteristics were the same, except that the rooms were smaller, in some instances not being calculated for the accommodation of more than forty or fifty people. The performers were invariably on the best of terms with the company. The men smoked and drank with the auditory, and the women drank with all who invited them, until they were summoned by a little bell to appear on the stage, and sing the songs set down for them in the programme of the evening. This done, they returned to the body of the room without the least ceremony, and again mingled with the guests, the whole performance and arrangements being of the simplest and most primitive kind. I took an opportunity of asking one of these young women, whom I had seen drinking brandy and water, gin and water, and beer, with at least half a dozen people, whether she did not find it prejudicial to her health, to drink so many mixtures, and whether she drank as much every night? She replied that it sometimes made her very ill. "Ours is a very disagreeable life," she added. "We are obliged to drink with all sorts of people who ask us. It brings company to the house, and if we did not drink with the sailors and others who invite us, we should lose our situations. We are not told this, but we know what would happen if we did not. Singing in such houses is hard work, and altogether our kind of life is very disagreeable. I should be glad to exchange it for any other. But what can I do? I do not know a note of music. I sing altogether by ear, and if I left my present situation, I should either have to take in needlework, or go into the streets. At needlework I could not earn 5s. a week, and I gain 18s. a week at this. So you see it is good pay, and though disagreeable for some reasons, it is better than needlework, and more respectable than the streets." Though no positive coarseness of language was used in the songs and dialogues of the characters, the allusions were often broad and indecent enough, and were received with obstreperous merriment. The squabbles between husband and wife were frequently imitated, apparently to the immense delight of the company. The great majority of the auditors appeared in the garb of sailors, or mechanics; and as usual, the young boys, many of them prematurely old with dissipation, mustered in large numbers, and drank, smoked, and applauded with more vigour than the older portions of the company. It would be but a useless repetition to detail the various scenes of the kind of which I was a witness. The staple amusements were the same, except that the nearer the concert-room was to the docks, the larger the proportion of sailors that attended. In one or two instances families of Irish emigrants were among the auditors. In some of the houses, dancing was a portion of the entertainment, and included "nigger dances," the sailor's hornpipe, and the jig, and in one house a dance in pattens, by a woman with her face blackened, to personate a negress, and in another an imitation of Boz's Juba. In no instance did I observe any quarrelling or disturbance.

Such are the attractions offered in Liverpool to amuse the people in their hours of leisure. About six years ago this state of things, proving not only the popular love of music and singing, but the very inferior as well as immoral character of the entertainments, attracted the attention of some influential persons in the town. It suggested itself to the mind of Mr. Nathaniel Caine, a merchant of Liverpool, that it would be a philanthropic and humane act to provide for the people on Saturday evenings a musical entertainment of a superior and in every way unexceptionable character, at as cheap a rate, and without the accompaniments of drinking and smoking. Mr. Caine unfolded his views to other men of sentiments alike to his own; and ultimately a committee for conducting Saturday evening concerts for the people was organized and brought into operation. The project excited considerable opposition, not from the proprietors of the public-house concert-rooms, but from the respectable portion of the inhabitants. Some of them ridiculed the idea of engaging eminent singers to give concerts for the people, and others objected on religious grounds to the selection of Saturday evening, which they alleged would be more properly spent in preparation for the religious observances and duties of the succeeding day. But Mr. Caine and the gentlemen who supported him were not discouraged either by the ridicule of the one party, or by the solemn and more formidable opposition of the other. By arrangement with the Northern Mechanics' Institution of Liverpool, then in a languishing and decaying state, they engrafted the scheme of Saturday evening concerts upon that society, and commenced operations. They engaged the Concert-hall in Lord Nelson-street, a room capable of accommodating from 2,000 to 3,000 persons, and resolved to offer to the working classes the attraction of the most eminent vocal and instrumental performers, and to fix the price of admission at so low a rate that the humblest mechanic who could spare the money to go to one of the public-house concert-rooms, should have no excuse on the ground of expense for absenting himself from the superior entertainment provided for him. The prices of admission were fixed at 3d. for the body of the hall, 6d. for the gallery, and 1s. for the reserved seats. The result showed that Mr. Caine and his coadjutors had not miscalculated the taste, the temper, or the means of the people. The very highest talent available for the purpose was secured, as will be seen from the following list of vocalists and instrumentalists engaged from the commencement of the society, in 1844, until the present time.

Mr. John Parry, Mr. Henry Russell, Mr. Samuel Lover, the late John Wilson, Mr. Henry Phillips, Mr. John Templeton, Mr. Edney, Mr. E. Ransford, Mr. Blewitt, Mr. Syme Wilsone, Mr. Henry Smythe, Mr. James Rowlinson, Mr. John Hatton, Mr. Morley, Mr. Venables, Mr. Field, Mrs. F. Phillips, Miss Clara Seyton, the Ethiopian Serenaders, the Infant Sappho, Mr. Love, Mr. Sybald, Mr. Carpenter, Miss Witnall, Miss Maria B. Hawes, Mrs. Wood (formerly Miss Paton), Miss Birch and Miss E. Birch, Miss Rainforth, Mrs. Ransford, the Misses Smith, Mrs. Alexander Newton, Mrs. Sunderland, Mr. Lockey, Mr. Sims Reeves, Mr. Henry Phillips, Herr Staudigl, Herr Pischek, Herr Carl Formes, Mr. Braham, Mr. Charles Braham, Mr. Hamilton Braham, Mr. Cohen (pianist), the Distin Family, the Collins Family, the Tyler Family, the Hutchinson Family, and the Fraser Family.

The concerts have been invariably well attended—the average attendance has been 1,200, the lowest 500, and the highest 2,700 persons. They have been to the fullest extent self-supporting, although the expenses were necessarily very heavy. From the commencement, in 1844, to April, 1848, the expense of the concerts was £6,884, and for the year 1848-9, it was £1,802. Great interest is excited when any performer more than usually popular is advertised to make his appearance; and the working men and their families, long before the doors are opened, gather about in crowds, to secure the best places. The doors open at seven, and the performances commence at eight; and, to pass the intervening hour, many of them bring *Chambers' Journal, Eliza Cook's Journal,* the *Family Herald, Dickens's Household Words,* and other cheap publications for the current week—which they read until the performances begin, and in the intervals between the first and second parts. In order to make the attendance of married women with young children at the breast pleasant to themselves and not unpleasant to the audience, a box or pew close to the door has been set apart for them; and when the infants become troublesome, the mothers can retire without disturbing the audience or the performers, and re-enter when the child has been appeased.

The attendance of the police is not required at these performances. During the season of 1848 two policemen were engaged to keep order, but their services were not needed; and in the following season it was resolved that their attendance should be discontinued. Since 1844 only two occasions occurred for the interference of a police constable, and in both of these the disturbance was created by a drunken man.

In the season of 1848 a series of weekly lectures for Thursday evenings was added to the original design of music and singing, and proved equally successful. The charges for admission were fixed at a lower rate than to the Saturday evening concerts—at 1d. for the body of the hall, 3d. for the galleries, and 6d. for the side seats. At these the average attendance has been 450, the lowest 150, and the highest 1,500 persons. The lectures have comprised: three from Mr. George Dawson, on the Characteristics and Tendencies of the Present Age; three from Professor Greenbank, on English Poets and Prose Writers; one from Madame Steinberg, on Female Education; three from Mr. Frank Howard, on the Influence of the Fine Arts as a Medium of Education; two from Mr. Paxton Hood, on the Follies and Fallacies of the System and Spirit of Modern War; one from Madame Steinberg, on the Heroic Disinterestedness of Maternal Love; two from Elihu Burritt, on the Economic Bearings of an Armed Peace, and the Necessity of a General Disarmament, and on a Congress of Nations for a Settlement of International Disputes; two from Mr. Thomas Hogg, on the Education of the People; two from Dr. Owens, on the Revolutions of France, Austria, and Italy, and on the Mental Enfranchisement of the People; three from Dr. Nevins, on Domestic Chemistry; two from Mr. George Dawson, on Popular Proverbs; one from Mr. Catlin, on the North American Indians; two from Mr. John Smith, on the Pleasures to be Derived from the study of the Elementary Sciences; two from the Rev. Hugh Stowell Brown, on the Antediluvian World; and one from Mr. Guillaume Lea, on the Progress of Languages. Encouraged by this success the committee resolved, in September, 1848, to offer silver medals and premiums of the value of five, three, and two guineas for the three best essays, the maiden composition and production of working-men in Liverpool, on the Influence of Cheap Rational Amusements on the Working Classes. The essays were expected to embrace the subject in its religious, moral, domestic, social, intellectual, and political bearings upon the position and prospects of the working classes. Sixty-eight competitors appeared. The first prize was awarded to James Norris, a journeyman printer; the second to John Priest, a watchmaker; and the third to John Teare, a toolmaker. These successful essays were afterwards published, and dedicated by express permission to his Royal Highness

Prince Albert. At the distribution of the prizes it was announced that Mr. T. A. Curtis and Mr. William Rathbone, two gentlemen ever foremost in good works in the town of Liverpool, had jointly offered prizes for the ensuing year for the two best essays on the Influence of Temperance, Cleanliness, and Frugality on the working classes. For these prizes there were but eight competitors. The successful competitors were Mr. Woodward, an apprentice to a carver and gilder, and Mr. J. Carter, a journeyman printer. The prizes were a certain number of books, to be selected by the successful essayists. Mr. Woodward made the following selection:—The Family Bible, Chambers's Information for the People, 2 vols; Shakspeare, Smith's Wealth of Nations, Nicholas Nickleby, Rienzi, Milton's Paradise Lost, Crichton, Pursuit of Knowledge under Difficulties, two volumes of Chambers's Tracts, and Combe's Principles of Physiology. Mr. J. Carter selected Memoirs of a Working Man, 1 vol.; Lamb's Tales from Shakspeare, 2 vols; Pursuit of Knowledge under Difficulties, 3 vols.; Arabian Tales and Anecdotes, 4 vols.; British Museum, 2 vols.; Life of William Caxton, 1 vol.; Shakspeare's Works, and Maunder's Treasury of Knowledge. It appeared, however, to the adjudicators, that the best essay sent in was not the production of a working man resident in Liverpool, but of Mr. Syme, a journeyman stonemason resident at Woolton, in the immediate neighbourhood. But Mr. Syme was, in consequence of non-residence, declared to be disqualified. The circumstance being represented to Mr. Rathbone, that gentleman immediately offered an extra prize, which was adjudged to Mr. Syme. He chose the following works:—Nicholson's Carpenter's and Joiner's Companion, Liebig's Chemistry of Agriculture and Physiology, Smith's Wealth of Nations, Harris on Electricity, Epitome of Alison's History of Europe, Combe's Principles of Physiology, Combe's Moral Philosophy, Findlay's Modern Atlas, and Horne Tooke's Diversions of Purley.

The establishment in Lord Nelson-street at which the concerts and lectures are given combines the general advantages of a mechanics' institution, classes for English composition and the French language, and also a news-room and a library. Upon inquiry whether the middle classes did not to a great extent avail themselves of the privileges of the cheap concerts and of the other branches of the institution, it was stated by the secretary, that at the Saturday evening concerts the working men and their families averaged three out of every four of the visitors, and that at the Thursday evening lectures the attendance was almost exclusively confined to the labouring classes. It also appeared that the pupils of the grammar and composition classes were all mechanics and artizans; that about two-thirds of the pupils of the French class were mechanics, and the remainder clerks and waiters in hotels. The female French class was attended by young women engaged during the day as teachers. At the news-room, admission to which is 1d., two-thirds of the visitors belonged to the middle classes.

It must be recorded, however, that the gratifying success of the Saturday evening concerts has not diminished in any perceptible degree the attendance at the public-house concerts throughout the town, even upon the Saturday nights. It is doubtful whether the majority of those who attend the Saturday evening concerts ever attend at all at free concerts in public-houses, and whether they are not drawn from a class who, before the establishment of this superior kind of entertainment, were precluded by their habits of temperance, their sense of decency, and their moral and religious scruples, from seeking amusement in the only places in the town that provided it at a rate within the compass of their means. In addition to this, it should be remembered, that the fluctuating population of sailors, lodging in the vicinity of the docks and the river, require amusement every night in the week. They are not more at leisure or better provided with money on a Saturday than on any other night. Even supposing them to patronise the Saturday evening concerts, they require relaxation on the other five nights, and as they are resolved to have it, they flock to the only available places, the public-houses and free concert-rooms, in which drunkenness is not the only demoralizing influence to which they are exposed. There is also a large body of mechanics and labourers not yet educated into an appreciation of more elevating amusements than those afforded by the public-house, who, together with the sailors, form a class sufficiently numerous to support the thirty-seven concert-rooms of the town. It remains, therefore, a question for the serious consideration of all who desire to elevate the social and moral condition of the working-classes, whether the popular and daily increasing love of music might not be beneficially directed and developed by the establishment of cheap concerts every night in the week, at which the working man might hear music that would elevate and not degrade him, and at which he might procure relaxation without being compelled to drink and smoke, and listen to loose conversation. Hard working men, having a little money at command, will and must have amusement for their evenings, and if that which is good and ennobling be not provided, they will not merely tolerate, but they will encourage, that which is bad and demoralizing.

The directors of the Saturday evening concerts are steadily working in their philanthropic task of educating the adult population of Liverpool, and I shall rejoice if these few observations shall lead any among them to consider the possibility of extending their operations in the manner indicated. Already a committee of their body has made an attempt to wean the working classes from the public-house on Sunday evenings, by establishing what they call "The working men's Sabbath services." The free use of the Concert Hall has been granted to a committee of ministers of religion, and it is opened on one Sunday in every month for religious services. Too often the working man is deterred from going to church by his dislike to appear in dirty and ragged attire, and by the difficulty of obtaining a seat in a place where he is a stranger. At these services all the seats are free of charge, no objection is made to dress or appearance, and an efficient choir and organ accompaniment are provided. The hymns to be sung are printed and distributed gratuitously, and the following extract from the address of the committee to the working classes will show the kindly spirit that animates their proceedings:—

> "In studying the welfare of mankind, the first object to be considered is the elevation of the industrial classes. With this view, various institutions for social, moral, and intellectual improvement have been formed, and great has been the good effected. But there is still a higher and a better object to be attained—Man's spiritual advancement. With the desire to promote this most important end, those who now address you have established the Working Men's Sabbath Services, to be conducted by eminent ministers of various denominations from all parts of the United Kingdom; and as the highest talent has been engaged in furtherance of your social improvement, so is it the chief object of the committee to press into this service, able, earnest men—lovers of the people—men who, of all others, are best fitted to address you on subjects of such vital consequence.

> "Working men of Liverpool, accept this invitation; come to our meetings; crowd your Hall; bring with you your wives and children; all are welcome. Nothing need prevent you. Those who maintain a regard for proper attire do well, but let not the too common excuse of being without what are called Sunday clothes avail. In any garb, under any circumstances, we shall rejoice to meet you."

The Rev. Dr. Beaumont, of London, opened the services in January last, and was followed by the Rev. Mr. Dowson, of Bradford, the Rev. Dr. Stowell, of Rotherham, and the Rev. Mr. Baines, of Nottingham. Ministers of all Christian denominations have been invited to take part in the services. Doctrinal points of dispute are on all occasions avoided; and those great and vital principles and precepts in which all sects agree are inculcated. Though the idea originated with a dissenter, it is not a dissenting movement. It is not intended exclusively for any sect, denomination, or establishment, either for Churchmen, Dissenters, or for Roman Catholics, but is open to all. The attempt is to bring together the working classes, upon a broad basis, and to establish, if the expression may be used, a "Ragged Church," for the spiritual benefit of a class whose poverty and squalor, practically, though not theoretically, exclude them from the accommodation provided in existing churches and chapels. The attempt has been attended with moderate success.

The sale of cheap popular literature in Liverpool is large. The following account of his weekly business was furnished to me by Mr. Shepherd, by far the most extensive dealer in these publications in the town. His average sales per week of the penny publications were:—

	doz.		doz.
The Family Herald	145	The Town (Mr. Shepherd informed me that he never sold a copy of this publication in his shop, though often asked for it. He only sold it to the trade, which he was very sorry he was obliged to do)	10
London Journal	130		
Reynolds's Mysteries of the Court	50		
Reynolds's Miscellany	50		
Reynolds's Instructor	20		
Reynolds's Days of Hogarth	20		
The Reasoner (reduced from 2d. to 1d., and which at 2d. sold about 3 dozen)	12	Claude Duval	20
		Paul Jones	10
		Gretna Green	12
The Terrific Record	4	Horrors of Lindorf Castle	12
The Love Match	50	The Wife's Dream	12
Home Circle	20	The Working Man's Friend	50
Lloyd's Miscellany	20	Bastard of Mauleon	10
Penny Sunday Times	4	Mysteries of Paris	10
Gentleman Jack	18	Wandering Jew	10
The Brigand	16		

The sale of the three-halfpenny publications, including the monthly parts, averaged—

	doz.		doz.
Eliza Cook's Journal	50	People's and Howitt's Journal	8
Chambers' Papers for the People	25	Knight's Half-hours with the Best Authors	12
Chambers' Journal	20		

The twopenny publications averaged—

	doz.		doz.
Dickens's Household Words	30	The Family Friend (published once a fortnight)	150
Cottage Garden	6		

The sale of threepenny publications was—

	doz.		doz.
Punch	4	Ladies' Companion	2
Lloyd's Weekly Newspaper	12	Weekly Times	10
		News of the World	6

The sixpenny periodicals and newspapers supplied by Mr. Shepherd to his customers, and which are not, strictly speaking, to be ranked among the cheap publications, were—

	doz.		copies.
Illustrated London News	12	Examiner	4
Dispatch	7	Spectator	2
Bell's Life	4	Wesleyan Times	10
Sunday Times	1	Church and State Gazette	6
Era	1		
Lady's Newspaper	2	Banner	6
Leader	1	Watchman	6

Mr. Shepherd stated that there was a considerable demand for the indecent and scurrilous publications issued by the Holywell-street press in London, but that he invariably refused to supply them to individuals over the counter. As a wholesale agent, he was obliged to include them with others in executing the orders of the trade. He also stated that there was a growing demand for cheap political papers, and a still greater taste for cheap cookery books, and books of netting and crochet work. He thought the taste for the wild, the horrible, and the atrocious was somewhat on the decline, and that there was not such a run as there used to be for stories of thieves and highwaymen, such as Jack Sheppard, Claude Duval, and others. The statistics given by Mr. Shepherd are not to be taken as complete. They merely relate to his own business; but as his sales are greater than those of any other dealer in cheap publications in the town, they may be considered to represent with tolerable accuracy the prevalent tastes of the people.

While upon the subject of the amusements of the people of Liverpool, I cannot omit a description of a penny wax-work exhibition which I visited. The middle and upper classes of London have their shilling wax-work, where portraits of notorious criminals and murderers form the great attraction to the crowd of the well-dressed vulgar. The ill-dressed vulgar have their penny exhibition of a similar kind, and it is not at all surprising, considering the example set them, that they should encourage speculators of a still lower class than the renowned *entrepreneurs* in London, in providing them with waxen portraits of scoundrels and murderers. I never visited the fashionable "Chamber of Horrors" in London, and consequently cannot compare it with the penny wax-work of Liverpool, or state which is the worse and more demoralizing of the two; but as they appeal by similar agencies to the same classes of minds, I should imagine that there cannot be any very great difference in the results produced. Over the door of a wretched-looking house, in a dirty and narrow street leading from Whitechapel, was exhibited, on the day of my visit, a large and wretchedly executed painting of John Gleeson Wilson, leaving the house of Captain Henrichson, in Liverpool, after murdering Mrs. Henrichson, her servant, and her two children. It was set forth in a placard underneath, that the figure of this murderer had been recently added to the others in this "celebrated collection," and that the admission was only one penny. An Italian organ boy, hired for the purpose, and sole musician at this establishment, was stationed inside of the doorway, and was turning the handle of his organ very slowly, grinding most fitful music. I noticed that he was asleep over his work. His hand moved without being directed by his will. The money-taker, seeing me smile, looked at the boy, and discovering his condition, gave him a sudden and rather rough shaking, and swore if he caught him in that state again, "the idle, young wagabone," he would "sarve him out for it." I was ushered up stairs to a small room by a man who acted as guide to the exhibition, and who gave the following account of the various articles and portraits in the room, which I reproduce in his own words. There were about twenty other visitors at the same time, including some women of the labouring classes, and four boys, or lads, of fifteen or sixteen years of age. The remainder were mechanics, or labouring people, with the exception of one well-dressed man, a foreigner, and apparently either the captain or the mate of a ship. "These here chains," said the guide, "as you see against the wall, are the hidentical chains worn by John Gleeson Wilson, who committed the brutal and hawful murder of Mrs. Henrichson, her servant, and her two hinnocent children, and for which he was hung, as he properly desarved to be, and sarved him right, as every hindividual in this Christian country will acknowledge. This is the correct likeness of Mr. and Mrs. Manning, who was hexecuted for the murder of Mr. Patrick O'Connor. You will please to take notice of the beautiful long hair of Mrs. Manning, which everybody as knowed her did greatly admire. This is the true likeness of Reid, the Mirfield murderer. Everybody as sees it confesses it to be a fust-rate portrait. This," he said, pointing to the best executed figure in the room, "is a unfortunate sailor who went on shore from a ship in Greenland, and was left behind by the captain. He was found frozen to death nine years afterwards, sitting hexactly in the hattitude as he now appears in, with his back covered with snow, and his hands upon his knees, as if the hunfortunate hindividual was taking a nap. These two are the likenesses of Bishop and Williams, the Burkers, whose hawful and hodious performances are known to everybody as reads the newspapers. This is Guy Faux, as attempted to blow up the Houses of Parliament, and who was discovered in the coal cellar by the Dook of Wellington and other noblemen and gentlemen, and afterwards hanged at Newgate. This is the unfortunate Jane Shore, walking about the streets of London, with a white sheet, and a candle in her hand, because she was no better than she should be; and this is a unhappy baker, who was hanged and beheaded for giving her a halfpenny roll, when she was a dying of hunger in a ditch in Cheapside. This is John Gleeson Wilson, the most celebrated and notorious murderer as ever lived, who murdered four hinnocent people in the town of Liverpool, and was justly hung for the same. And this last is a correct portrait of John Gleeson Wilson's father." This last figure was in reality a full-length figure of Punch—the hook nose and the hump on the back being very marked and distinct. It had probably done duty as a sign for a coffee-shop or eating-house. This concluded the exhibition in the first room, and we were then ushered into a second, where the only figures were two groups, wretchedly executed in wax. The one represented a drunken family, and the other a sober family. In the first the husband was beating his wife about the head with an empty bottle, the idea being taken from George Cruikshank's well-known design. In the second, the husband with his wife and children were represented in a comfortable room enjoying their dinner. The faces of the children in both groups were black. Underneath was written *"Look upon this picture, and on that."* "You have now seen the whole of our hexhibition," said our guide; "but if any lady or gentleman wishes to see the Chamber of Horrors, which belongs to another proper-ietor, and not to the proper-ietor of these rooms, the charge is twopence hextra." I expressed my willingness to pay the twopence, and five or six more did the same. We stopped opposite a door where the words "Chamber of Horrors" were painted, our guide assuring us that it was altogether a distinct exhibition belonging to a different party, but which they had taken temporary charge of in the unavoidable absence of the real "proper-ietor." We were then ushered up another flight of stairs into a small room, across which a rope was drawn breast high, upon the outer side of which we took our places. The inner part was covered with an old and dirty carpet. A pair of moleskin trowsers hung against the wall, and a child's cot, a small wooden horse, a fender, with fire-irons, and a wash-hand stand and basin completed the list of articles in this room. "You will please look at those trowsers on the wall," said the guide. "They are the hidentical trowsers that John Gleeson Wilson had on when he murdered Mrs. Henrichson, her children, and her servant. You may see the spots of blood on them at this moment. They have the mark of Mr. Dowling, the commissioner of police, upon them, to prove that they are the hidentical trowsers of the hassassin, as anybody that doubts my word may find out to be correct by axin' of that gentleman. That fender is the werry fender which the unfortunate servant was cleaning, when John Gleeson Wilson came behind her and murdered her. You may also see the spots of blood upon it. That is the hidentical cot of one of the hinnocent little children, the werry cot it slept in before it was murdered. That ere horse is a toy as was bought for the other child by its unfortunate mother. You see the paper pinned on the carpet; pay particular attention to the blood all around it. On that werry spot Mrs. Henrichson was murdered by the bloody-minded willain; and at that werry washhand-stand, which you see standing under the window, and in that werry basin he washed his hands after committing his four murders. All these harticles cost the proper-ietor a great deal of money, and they are here exhibited at a werry low charge, for which I hope every lady and gentleman is satisfied." Such, without exaggeration, was the wax-work exhibition provided for the people in Liverpool. The guide discovered me making, on the back of a letter, a memorandum of what I saw, and exclaimed somewhat angrily, "What, you're a takin' on it down, are you? I s'pose you're a lobster or a hinformer; but this is a legal hexhibition, this is, and you can't stop it anyhow." I explained that I had nothing to do with the law or the police, and made my exit as expeditiously as I could, not without observing, however, that the organ boy was still in the doorway, grinding at his organ, and nodding over it in his sleep.

LABOUR AND THE POOR.

LIVERPOOL.

[FROM OUR SPECIAL CORRESPONDENT.]

SHIP-BUILDING AND REPAIRING.

LETTER XVII.

The Mersey, unlike the Tyne, the Clyde, and the Thames, is not noted for ship-building. Liverpool was never a great port for the construction of vessels, although during the last twenty or thirty years it has been one of the greatest ports in the world for their repair. A notion, however, has lately become prevalent in the town, not only that ship-building has been a great source of prosperity to it, but that the mismanagement of the Dock Trustees on the one hand, and the combination of the journeymen shipwrights on the other, have had the effect of driving away the trade, and inflicting serious injury upon various important interests. I made it my business to investigate this subject in all its bearings, as one which affected very large bodies of working men, as well as the general interests of the town and port, and I now proceed to detail the results of my inquiry. The following document, extracted from the annual circular of Messrs. Tonge, Curry, and Co., shows the state of the ship-building trade in the Mersey for the last thirty years—the present year included:—

Return of the total number and tonnage of vessels built at the Port of Liverpool, from 1821 to 1849, including those of iron:—

Year.	Number of Wood Vessels.	Tonnage.	Number of Iron Vessels.	Tonnage.
1821	14	2,175	...	...
1822	18	3,053	...	...
1823	17	3,517	...	...
1824	27	5,778	...	...
1825	18	3,957	...	...
1826	17	4,258	...	...
1827	9	1,933	...	...
1828	13	2,459	...	...
1829	16	4,251	...	...
1830	15	2,901	...	...
1831	14	2,511	...	...
1832	17	3,342	...	...
1833	12	2,445	...	...
1834	17	3,955	...	...
1835	20	5,759	...	...
1836	17	3,946	...	...
1837	8	1,042	...	...
1838	13	4,191	2	452
1839	14	3,293	1	280
1840	18	5,870	2	190
1841	12	3,729	3	639
1842	12	3,221	1	67
1843	14	3,509	...	...
1844	6	2,262	3	538
1845	8	3,286	4	1,294
1846	12	3,195	4	1,558
1847	14	3,365	3	471
1848	10	3,218	1	449
1849	7	2,229	1	70
On the Stocks.	8	2,800	computed at	

It will be seen from the foregoing table that the ship-building trade of Liverpool has never been very large. Twenty-seven vessels are the utmost that ever were built on the Mersey in one year, while in Sunderland the number of vessels at present on the stocks is ninety-three. The greatest tonnage ever launched in Liverpool in one year was 6,000; whilst in New York, the great port with which Liverpool trades, the tonnage now in course of construction is moderately computed at more than 50,000. It further appears that the increase in ship-building in Liverpool has not been progressive, and that it has by no means kept pace with the increase in the commerce and wealth of so great a port. In the year 1849 the total tonnage of the ships built was very little higher than in 1821, and much less than in 1822. The three best years were 1824, 1835, and 1840, and the three worst 1821, 1827, and 1837. Since 1840 the decline has been gradual until the close of 1845.

It has been asked why Liverpool, situated upon a noble tidal river, with a large labouring population, with an immense and increasing commerce, and possessing a timber trade as extensive as any port in the world, does not build a larger number of ships? The inquiry is not difficult to answer. In the first place, the Dock Estate contains ten public graving docks, where urgent repairs can be executed satisfactorily and without delay; and ship-repairing is a great deal more profitable than ship-building; and, in the second place, the few men of capital who have building yards and establishments upon the Mersey, cannot obtain leases, and enjoy no certainty of being allowed to carry on their business even in their present sites. The last cause is probably the most powerful. The Albert Dock stands upon the site of several building yards, which were removed to make room for it; and the new Northern Docks, now in course of construction, have swallowed up the sites of the very builders who removed from the Albert Dock to that distant location, with the hope of being no more disturbed by the Dock Trustees in their insatiable thirst for dock extension. By the combined operation of these two causes, ship-building has been discouraged in Liverpool. So difficult has it been to procure sites, that Mr. Thomas Wilson, the greatest ship-builder in the port, on being removed from the north end of the town, where he established himself after the construction of the Albert Dock, retired from the business. His new location, like his old one, was required for dock room, and he was compelled to quit it, after he had made all his arrangements for permanently pursuing his business. Lately he has obtained, on favourable terms, a lease for a building yard from the corporation, on the Cheshire side of the Mersey—between Monksferry and Birkenhead—and it is expected that by his efforts the building trade will be raised to a better position than it has held since 1840.

At present, as appears from the circular of Messrs. Tonge and Curry, there are but eight ships on the stocks at Liverpool, and these not of the higher class of vessels, the aggregate tonnage only amounting to 2,800, or 350 tons each. One of the eight is of 800 tons burden, which is of the largest size ever built in the port. The cost of a first class built ship, A 1, for twelve years, is generally reckoned at £14 per ton for the hull alone, and from £4 to £6 per ton for the fittings. At this calculation the sum of £39,200 will be expended this year among the ship-builders of Liverpool, and from £11,200 to £16,800 among ropemakers, sailmakers, and all the various trades concerned in the internal and external fittings of ships. These sums are of course exclusive of the large amount expended in repairs, which I shall consider in a subsequent portion of this letter.

The following is a complete list of the trades engaged in building and fitting a ship:—

1. The Shipwright.—In Liverpool the shipwright and the caulker are the same. It is only in the ports of London and Yarmouth that these two departments of the trade are kept distinct.

2. The Shipsmith, who performs all the iron-work of a ship, with the exception of the anchors and iron cables.

3. The Chain and Anchorsmith.

4. The Coppersmith.

5. The Brassfounder, or Brazier.

6. The Block and Spar-maker. [In London the block-maker and the spar or mast-maker are distinct branches; but in Liverpool they are generally united.]

7. The Carver, who makes the figure-head and stern ornaments.

8. The Ship-joiner who does generally all the internal wood-work. He planes the ship outside and in, moulds her, puts on the bulwarks, the head, stern, and quarter galleries; builds the galley or house on deck, fits up the cabins and the between-decks, and performs all the cabinet-work.

9. The Ship-scraper, an inferior kind of workman, who scrapes the pitch off after the shipwright has done his work, coats the bends with tar, and prepares the hull for the painter. Ship-scrapers are generally old sailors, or dock labourers. Two of them would perform in about four days all the scraping required on a 500 ton ship.

10. The Painter and Plumber and Pump-maker.

11. The Cooper.

12. The Upholsterer.

13. The Ropemaker.

14. The Sailmaker.

15. The Rigger.

The following has been published as an estimate of the average expenditure upon a 500 ton ship built in the port of Liverpool—an expenditure which to a large extent finds its way into the pockets of the several trades above enumerated:—

```
Cost of Timber (average)  .........  £3,500
     „     Labour  ................   3,500
     „     Sails  ...................    500
     „     Copper  .................     400
     „     Chandlery, paint, &c.  .....  500
     „     Furniture, &c.  ...........    500
     „     Ropes  .................      400
     „     Smiths' work  ...........      500
                                      ______
              Total  ...........  £9,800
```

If these figures be correct, or even if £18 per ton be taken as a fairer average than the £19 12s. per ton which they would amount to, it may be presumed that the dock trustees, in monopolizing the river frontage for the whole extent of the town, for a distance of four miles from the southern docks to the Bootle shore—and in otherwise preventing, by the measures which they have successively adopted, great master shipwrights from permanently establishing themselves within their jurisdiction—have been the means of causing a considerable expenditure of money to be carried elsewhere which would otherwise have taken place in Liverpool. Among the ninety-three ships that are now said to be on the stocks in the Tyne, there are some for Liverpool merchants, but I was unable to ascertain the number. But it is not only to Sunderland that the Liverpool Dock trustees have sent the favours of Liverpool shipowners. At the present time there are ships building for Liverpool merchants at Workington, Whitehaven, Chepstow, Pwllheli, Greenock, Montrose, and Aberdeen, and also in Jersey and the Isle of Man.

But to understand the whole question, and the manner in which it affects the prosperity of the town and port, and the condition of the large class of operative shipwrights, it is necessary to consider the amount of ship repairs done in the town, and the number of men employed in the two branches of building and repairing, and in the other trades dependent upon them. For this purpose a few words upon the public graving docks of Liverpool will be necessary, to show the class of employers who have been called into existence by them, and the manner in which these employers affect the character and interests of the working men. Taking one day with another, all the year round, the average number of ships in the Liverpool docks is never less than 700, and very seldom above 1,000. With such a large number of vessels frequenting the port—many of them first-class ships, and built in all the ship-building ports in Europe and America, and of all ages and degrees of service—ships which have been for a longer or shorter period subjected to all the risks of storm and accident—it must be obvious that a very great amount of repairing is daily required. It must be equally obvious, considering that ship-repairing is a far more urgent business than ship-building, that the Liverpool Dock trustees would greatly neglect their duty both to the commerce of the port and the general interests of the town if they did not provide proper facilities for speedy repairs. A merchant who wishes to have a vessel built may please himself as to the builder and the port on whom he will confer the favour of his custom. He may admire the science of the Clyde builders, or he may prefer the Tyne or the Thames, either for the cheapness or the excellence of the fabric. He may also suit himself as to time. But when the captain of a vessel arrives in Liverpool, and finds that his ship needs repair, the repair must be done on the spot. The captain has no choice. It is, therefore, a matter of absolute necessity that the dock trustees should, in the first instance, look to the convenience of their best customers—the ships frequenting the port; and that ship-building, however desirable to be encouraged, should rank after ship-repairing. The dock trustees seem to have been fully aware of their duty in this respect; and they have constructed some of the finest graving or dry docks in the world, where ships can be repaired with the utmost possible celerity. There are already ten of these establishments in full operation, each calculated to accommodate four vessels of the average size of the traders frequenting the Mersey. These docks are seldom or never empty for a single day, so that about forty ships may be always considered to be under repair in the port of Liverpool. Should the new northern docks be completed, six new graving docks, of superior magnitude, will be added to the list. Four or five days seem to be sufficient under ordinary circumstances for the repair of a ship; but if a week be allowed for the purpose, it would result that 2,080 ships annually pass into the graving docks of Liverpool. The sum of £100 goes but a short way in the repair of a ship; but in fixing that sum as the average at which a vessel can be placed under the hands of a master shipwright, it would follow that the annual expenditure of the trade of the port for ship-repairing would be no less than £208,000. Whether these figures be or be not strictly accurate, it is evident, if they be compared with the amount expended in ship-building at the time when ship-building was considered to be in its most flourishing state in Liverpool, viz., in 1840, that ship repairing is the business most profitable to the town; and that, unless means could be adopted to combine the two, it is for the true interest of the dock estate and the port to facilitate ship-repairing in the first instance. The tonnage built in the most prosperous year was 5,870, which, exclusive of two iron ships built by Mr. Laird, of Birkenhead, at £10 a ton, would amount to no more than £105,600; whereas the ship-repairing, which is continually on the increase, and not subject to fluctuation, amounts, at a low estimate, to nearly double that sum. Too exclusive attention, however, to ship-repairing has its disadvantages, which are fully conceded by all who have studied the subject, including the more intelligent among the working men; and hence it becomes a matter of great importance for all parties, from the dock trustees, shipown-ers, and merchants on the one hand, to the master shipwrights and their operatives on the other, to consider whether Liverpool might not continue to possess all her present facilities for expeditious ship-repairing, in conjunction with proper facilities for ship construction. What the advantages and disadvantages of the present system are in reference to all parties in the town, will to some extent appear from the evidence which I collected on the subject, both from the employ-ers and the employed, and which I shall proceed to detail, after a few preliminary remarks on the manner in which the public graving docks are regulated.

A small building at the side of the Canning Dock is set apart as a "Regulating-office." At this place the harbourmaster of the port at-tends every morning at nine o'clock to receive applications for ships that require to go into the docks for repair. The length of the ship and her draught of water are given to the harbourmaster, who then decides when and in what dock she can be accommodated, and what other ships can go in with her. The operative shipwrights usually gather about this place in large numbers to learn the name of the ship to be repaired, and of the master shipwright who has got the job, in order that they may apply to him or to his foreman for work. As the master shipwright has the use of a public dock for the repairs which he un-dertakes, it is not necessary that he should have a yard of his own, and thus it follows that many men of little or no capital call themselves master shipwrights. They have perhaps a small workshop or forge, where the petty iron work is done, and a place for the preparation of their pitch. They are commonly called by the men the "pitch-pot mas-ters." It is customary in Liverpool for the merchant or owner of the ship to pay every Saturday to the master shipwright the wages of the men employed in repairing his vessel, so that a very small capital indeed will enable a man to set up in this business. This is the first evil of the system. The men have no respect for nor confidence in such masters, and, finding that the tendency of the system was to reduce their wages, and that the pitch-pot masters endeavoured to introduce cheap and inefficient labour, and to employ apprentices almost exclusively, they entered into a union, which is the most powerful associated body of working men in the town of Liverpool. They hold their meetings, not in a public-house, as too many trade unions and friendly societies do, but in rooms of their own, at the north-western end of the town. The "Carpenters' Rooms," as they are called, or "Carpenters' Buildings," are well known to all the working classes. At one time the shipwrights of Liverpool, being freemen of the borough, were a political body of some importance, and before the Reform Act had increased the number of voters in the town, they traded upon the franchise to a very considerable extent. Their importance in this respect has almost entirely ceased, and rich merchants are not now observed at election times walking down the fashionable streets, arm in arm with the leaders of the operatives, as in the years prior to 1830. The shipwrights form at present a mere Trade union, whose objects are to prevent the employment of strangers; to keep up wages to the present standard of five shillings a-day; to maintain a sick and burial club for the benefit of the trade; and to pension superannuated members. Their numbers for the half year ending on the 24th of May were 1,592, and their expenditure for the purposes of the society or union during the same period was £877. They have hitherto been successful in their object. They have prevented the "pitch-pot masters," as well as other more respectable master ship-builders, from bringing in a glut of unskilled and juvenile labour into the market. They have regulated the employment of apprentices so as not to interfere injuriously with the work and wages of full-grown men, and they have maintained, though not without difficulty, the rate of wages at 5s. a day—which is about 2s. a day more than is paid for the services of competent shipwrights in the Clyde, and in the ship-building ports of Wales, Cumberland, and the Channel Islands. The following statement, which was made to me by a member of the union, throws a further light upon the subject:—

"The union or society of the shipwrights of Liverpool was formed for the purpose of protecting the labourer. We do not interfere with the apprentices of those who have ship-building yards of their own. The ship-builders keep as many apprentices as they like. Most of the ships built in Liverpool are built by apprentices. We reckon that there are about 600 apprentices in the town. There are also a few strangers, not members of our union. But while the trade allows a master to employ as many apprentices as he chooses in the building of vessels, it will not allow him in the graving docks to employ more than one apprentice to three men. In the graving docks the apprentices receive a man's wages, 5s. a day. That is the rule of the trade. The masters have agreed to it. There has been no strike for twenty-three years. Some of the smaller masters require to be sharply looked after to prevent them from infringing the rules. They often try to put lads on to caulking, to save the expense of employing men. They pay the lads 7s. or 8s. a week, and charge the merchant or captain 5s. a day, putting the difference in their own pockets. They will not give the men a chance if they can help it. The union has not been able to regulate the number of apprentices in the yards. In some of the yards there are as many as twelve apprentices to one man. The masters will not give in on this point; and it is not now contested. The shipwrights, as a body, although their wages are considered high, do not earn upon an average above 18s. or £1 a week. Very few men can say that they have four days' work in a week the year round. He is considered pretty fortunate who has three-and-a-half days' work in the week. We consider our trade a very healthy one. During the five years that the union has been established, the average age of the members who have died has been 47 years 11 months, a very high average—considering that the general average for the town of Liverpool is only 17. Some people consider that the smell of tar is wholesome, and that that is the reason why the shipwrights are so healthy. I consider it more likely that their working in the open air is the true cause. If you walk down to the graving docks you will see many old men of seventy working for their living. The society has a superannuation fund, and allow members over 60 years of age a pension of 3s. a week. There are twenty-five of them on the books at the present time. We allow the old men to pick up what jobs they can in addition. Open air work has its inconveniences, but, take it all in all, it is much more healthy than in-door work—such as the tailor's or shoemaker's, for instance. It is not so much in their health, as in their pockets, that the shipwrights suffer from out-door work. A day of hard and continued rain is a serious loss to our trade. If a man is obliged to leave his work on account of the weather he loses his time and wages. In winter this is often the case, and it is a great hardship, because on account of the darkness we can't work over-hours, as we can in summer, to make up for lost time. You may imagine, therefore, that a shipwright is not easily driven from his work by the weather. He can't afford it, and will continue at work long after his clothes are wet through. In caulking a man is compelled to leave off if it rains, because the wet spoils the oakum, which cannot in consequence be properly driven into the seam. Even if it could be driven in it would be of no use, because it would rot; and the foremen, for this reason, force all the caulkers to stop work as soon as rain begins. The loss of work occasioned by the weather is perhaps the greatest hardship of our trade. We have petitioned the Dock Committee to build sheds in all the graving docks to remedy this evil, so that we may, when it rains, retire under shelter, and occupy ourselves in dressing timber and other necessary work. The Dock Committee have granted the accommodation to some extent, but not to the extent they ought to have done, and might easily do, more especially at the Brunswick Dock. We are seriously affected by the weather in other ways than this. A long continuance of easterly winds keeps the ships out; and, in the winter time especially, it sometimes happens that for five or six weeks in succession scarcely a day's work is to be obtained. At such times the men are in great distress, and have no resource but the pawnshop. When the wind changes to the west all the ships come in together, and there have not been men enough in the town to do the work thus suddenly required. In these cases the rule of the society as regards apprentices is not enforced. When every man has got work the masters may put on as many apprentices as they please. The trade complain sometimes of the want of proper care and attention in the management of the graving docks, by which men are needlessly thrown out of work. For instance, I have known a large vessel, after being repaired, detained in the dock for three days for want of water to float her out. This has perhaps detained three other vessels in the dock, and kept four vessels outside waiting in vain for their turn to come in. This is a serious loss to the shipwrights, who are thus kept idle because a proper calculation of tide was not made when the large vessel was allowed to enter the dock. The harbour-master might, we think, very often prevent this by not giving such a vessel her turn until a high tide could be made available for floating her out as soon as her repairs were finished. The greater the regularity of the dock management the greater the gain to the dock trust, as well as to the shipwrights. Sometimes the evil is caused by putting cargo on board in the graving dock, which the shipwrights think ought not to be allowed unless a proper calculation of her draught of water has been made. Coals and ballast, and even bale goods, are frequently put on board in the graving dock, and I have known ships sunk a foot deeper in the water by this means, and so prevented from getting out for several days after their time."

The following additional particulars of the trade and of the ship-wrights' union were given by the foreman employed in a shipbuilder's yard, and who was not a member of the "society:"—"Fifteen or twenty years ago there was more ship-building in the port of Liverpool than there is now. The men had the same wages as at present, but the yard rents were lower, and yards were more easily to be procured, and there was a greater demand for ships. Many ships for Liverpool merchants are now built in the Clyde, the Tyne, and in the ports of Cumberland and Wales. Little else but repairing is now done in Liverpool, as both wages and yard rents are much lower elsewhere. In the Clyde the men get 3s. 6d. a day, regular work, all the year round, and are much better off than the shipwrights of Liverpool with 5s. a day, with uncertain employment. There are great numbers of 'pitch-pot masters' in Liverpool. They require no capital—or very little; as the merchants provide them with money every Saturday to pay the men's wages. All sorts of people set up in the pitch-pot line—people who know nothing whatever about ship-building, or even of ship repairs, but who trust all to the foreman, whom they pay well. The men are not allowed to work piece work. A master will take a job by the piece, but by the rules of the society he is not permitted to give it out by the piece to his men. He must pay them their regular day's wages. Formerly a master would call his men together—possibly there were eight or ten of them—and ask them what they would do certain job of repairs for. They named a sum, and worked away till the job was done, overhours or not, as the case might be, and divided the total amount between them. Sometimes each man by this system gained as much as £2 10s. in a week; but it was forbidden by the union, because it was thought unfair to the trade, and tended to keep other men out of work. No doubt it was good for the hard-working and industrious man, but it seemed to be considered unjust to the general body of workmen. The pitch-pot masters would squeeze extra profits out of the men's labour if they could. The society prevents the pitch-pot men from having their own way, and will not allow a stranger to work in the docks. Some small masters, however, manage to set the society at defiance in this respect, and employ none but strangers. I do not know the number of strangers in the town; but they cannot be very many. If a stranger were set to work to repair a ship, all the men would strike and refuse to work with him. The pitch-pot masters, I have no doubt, would employ none but strangers and apprentices, if they had their own way. They give an apprentice from 5s. to 8s. a week, not more. The society prevents the master from employing more than one apprentice to three men. Much harm has been done in Liverpool by the exclusive attention of so many people to the repairing, to the neglect of the building trade. I am certain that one-half of the shipwrights of Liverpool are not fit to be employed in a yard to build ships. They have no experience in shipbuilding; their whole time is passed in botching and repairing in the graving docks; and it is not possible for any except a few of the best men to have learned shipbuilding as a regular business. Vast numbers of them, although they may have served their apprenticeship, have gained no real knowledge of the trade, except in its inferior branch of repairing. Very few of them have even regular indentures, but have simply a note from their masters, stating the fact that they have served. This character does not, however, apply to the whole of the Liverpool shipwrights. I have been a shipwright in the Clyde and in the Thames, and know that in Liverpool there as good shipwrights as there are anywhere—good steady men that can do any work about a ship—but these are certainly not above one half, if so many. The system pursued at the graving docks, by calling into operation so many inferior masters, and by loosening the connection between master and man, has injured the trade and the men too. The journeyman often does not even know his employer by sight, and works for one man to-day and for another to-morrow. Sometimes he is employed at the south, and sometimes at the north of the town. The master shipwrights have their yards at the south. The great timber dock, the Brunswick, is at the south also, and if a job of repairs has to be done at the north the men have to travel about the whole line of dock at a great loss of time. The system is also bad in this respect, that it compels the men to hunt for work, and make application day after day to this foreman or to the other, instead of working for one employer from month to month and from year to year at regular wages, in a proper establishment, where ship-building and ship repairing might both be carried on, and where the superior as well as the inferior branch of the business might be learned. It would be a great advantage to the working men if sheds were erected in all the graving docks. The expense to the dock estate would be very trifling. The grievance complained of by some of the men, that they lose work in consequence of the impracticability of floating out at certain tides the large vessels whose repairs are finished, is, I think, confined to the Queen's Graving Docks, Nos. 1 and 2. In the other graving docks this delay does not occur, as sufficient water can always be let in to float any vessels that have been admitted. There is, however, another evil, which is a want of accommodation for the repair of large steamers—some of which have been compelled to wait as long as three weeks for a turn, before they could get into the dry dock. Upon the whole, I think the men in our trade have no great reason to complain. They are better off than most operatives, and steady and properly qualified men can always obtain good wages. I am not certain whether the 'Society' has done good or harm. Perhaps it has done good in preventing the 'pitch-pot masters' from lowering wages, and swamping the labour-market—but I doubt whether a union or society would be necessary, if great master shipwrights had their own yards and graving docks, in which they could both build and repair ships, and offer permanent employment to men who know the business in all its details."

The opinions expressed by this intelligent foreman, I found to be generally entertained by the ship-builders and ship-repairers, whom I consulted on the subject. Ship-builders, however, objected to the public graving docks, as calling into existence the class of pitch-pot masters—men for the most part as destitute of skill as of capital—and who stood between the operatives and the superior class of responsible employers, without the confidence or respect of either. The ship-builders seemed to consider that, if proper sites were granted on the shore of the Mersey, the trades of ship-building and ship-repairing would be combined—that there would be no necessity for public graving docks—that a superior business would be done in the private graving docks as cheaply, if not more cheaply, to the merchant—and that the town would have the advantage of a ship-building trade as extensive as that of any port in the kingdom, not even excepting London or Sunderland. They were also of opinion that this system would be as much to the advantage of the large body of operative shipwrights, as to that of the town and port—alleging that, under the control of responsible masters combining both businesses, they would be better instructed in their work, and would secure permanent instead of temporary and casual employment. Though nominally receiving a lower rate of wages—the rate probably of the Clyde ship-builders, 3s. 6d., or even 4s., a day—they would be better off from week to week and from year to year than under the present system of jobbing for "pitch-pot" and other small masters, by which, according to their own showing, they do not average four days' labour in the week. Another advantage would be that they would not be compelled, as they are at present, to depend upon the wind for employment. If a long prevalence of easterly gales kept out the shipping, and repairing work was at a standstill, they would find employment in building, and be spared the cruel necessity of resorting to the pawnshop in the long winter months. A second advantage would be, that in large building yards and private graving docks, whether employed in the construction or repair of ships, they would not lose time, and consequently wages, in rainy weather. The ship-builder would construct proper sheds, inasmuch as the highest classification of a ship at Lloyd's—A 1 for 13 years—is made A 1 for 14 years, if the ship be built under a shed; and it would, therefore, be quite as much for the interest of the great shipbuilders, as for that of their men, to have sheds under which the necessary work might be done in all weathers.

While agreeing in the main with these views, I found that the class of shipowners, and captains of vessels, were far from adverse to the system of public graving docks. They alleged that the trade of ship-repairing, so important in a large port like Liverpool, was free under the present system, and that ships, upon the whole, were as well and as cheaply repaired in Liverpool as in any other port in the world; and that, although perhaps the same result as regards the cheapness and excellence of the work might be attained in private graving docks, it was extremely doubtful whether the same celerity could be attained if the trade were left to be monopolized by a few great ship-builders.

In conclusion, it is only necessary to add that the attention of the dock trustees has been urgently directed to the error which they committed in dispossessing the principal ship-builders of their sites in order to make room for docks; and in re-dispossessing a few of them after they had established themselves at the extreme north, in the full reliance that they would be no more interfered with. A committee of the Town-council has sat to collect evidence upon this subject, and to discuss what facilities can still be granted within the limits of the town for the establishment of ship-yards. An excellent site, upon very favourable terms, has been granted to Mr. Wilson at Monks'-ferry, on the Birkenhead side, upon a plot of the corporation land—this gentleman having been twice dispossessed of his yards on the Liverpool side in order that docks might be constructed. In his new location he will be free from all further risk of the kind. It seems highly probable, considering the difficulty, if not impossibility, of obtaining proper sites in Liverpool, owing to the pre-occupation of the whole line of river by the dock trustees, that the ship-building trade will ultimately cross over into Cheshire. Even if sites were afforded in the new northern docks, towards Bootle, and vessels built were launched into the docks instead of into the river, the Birkenhead side of the Mersey would offer many advantages. Among the principal of these would be its proximity to the business portions of Liverpool. From the Exchange and the Custom-house of Liverpool to Birkenhead is a less distance than from either of those places to the Northern Docks now in construction on the Liverpool side of the Mersey. Liverpool, for this and other reasons, will remain in all probability the great port for the repair, and Birkenhead will become the great port for the construction of ships. There does not seem any chance of the proper combination of the two trades within the boundaries of Liverpool.

Since the above was written, the committee of the town council are understood to have recommended the following plan for the encouragement of ship-building in the port—namely, that yards be made immediately to the north of Sandon graving docks, and eastward of the new steam dock; that graving docks be attached to each yard; that there be sufficient water space to launch the vessels without risk; and that cranes and other necessary appliances be provided for the adjustment of boilers, masts, and heavy rigging. There is room in the port for fourteen large-sized building-yards; and it is further recommended that they run east and west, so that each would be a protection to the other from the winds. The sites thus recommended are at least double, if not treble, the distance of Birkenhead from the Exchange and Custom-house of Liverpool.

LABOUR AND THE POOR.

—◆—

LIVERPOOL.

[FROM OUR SPECIAL CORRESPONDENT.]

SHIP JOINERS AND HOUSE JOINERS.

LETTER XVIII.

Next to the shipwrights, or ship carpenters, the ship-joiners are the most numerous body of associated workmen in Liverpool. Their union for the protection of their trade was founded on the 10th of March, 1845, and they number at the present time about five hundred men. I could not ascertain positively, from any reliable source of information, the number of men not "in society," but I have reason to believe that they are but few, especially those who may be strictly called ship-joiners, and who do not mingle the businesses of ship and house joining. They are employed to a large extent in the repair of ships, and also the external and internal work of ship building after the labours of the shipwright are concluded. Their services are required both in wooden and iron vessels. The objects of their association are "to facilitate the means of obtaining and affording information relative to the employment of the members, and for upholding the rights, interests, and privileges of the trade." The entrance money is one guinea, and the subscription two pence per month. The association has fixed the hours of labour both in the winter and summer months, and the rate of wages for ordinary and for extra work. The hours of labour from the 1st of March to the 11th of October are from six in the morning to six in the afternoon, with the exception of Saturday, when work finishes at five. Half an hour is allowed for breakfast, and an hour and a half for dinner. From the 11th of October to the 1st of March, the hours of labour are from daylight to dark, with half an hour for breakfast, and one for dinner. The rate of wages, summer and winter, is fixed at 4s. 6d. a day. For working in cases of necessity, which constantly occur when a ship has to be repaired, and must sail at an early and fixed period, double wages must be paid for every Good Friday, Christmas Day, or Sunday, on which the men may be employed.

If, in similar necessity, the members are required to work all night, they receive a day-and-a-half's wages. For work performed on board of ships lying out in the river, the wages are 5s. 6d. a day; and for "currying" ships, that is planing the sides or decks, or any painted or "payed" work in any part of the ship, they receive an extra sixpence, or 5s. a day, "in order," as they allege, "to compensate for the destructive wear and tear of both tools and clothes which such work causes." Such work in building yards, when "unpayed," and performed for the ship-builder, is not charged extra. The members of the association, if they contract for work, are not allowed to work for less wages than if they were employed by the day; and no member working by contract is allowed to work overtime, if there be a single member out of work in the town. No person is eligible as a member of the association who has not served his apprenticeship; and any member who may be discharged by his master "for upholding the rules of the association," is entitled to receive 12s. a week until he shall again obtain employment. If such a member refuse work when it is offered or procured for him, he forfeits all claim upon the society. There are various fines for infraction of these and the minor rules. It appears that the master ship-joiners have acceded to all these terms, and that they and their workmen are on good terms with each other. I did not find the members of this trade very communicative. The union meets weekly at a public-house, and sits with closed doors, making a show of as much secrecy as an association of "Carbonari." One of their office bearers, to whom I explained my object, handed me a small book containing the rules of the association, and merely added that the trade generally was good, and that the masters and the men had nothing to complain of, either of the state of the trade at that time, or of the conduct of each to the other.

The house-joiners are far more numerous, but they form by no means so well organized or so compact a body. The ship-joiners, as they perform the same kind of work in ships that house-joiners perform in houses, use the same tools, and are in reality, if not in name, members of the same trade, allow any of the house-joiners to become members of their association on payment of the usual entrance fee and the monthly subscription. Very few of the house-joiners seem, however, to have availed themselves of the organization of their comrades. While the ship-joiners are united, and seem to be on very good terms with their masters, the house-joiners seem, on the contrary, to have become utterly disunited and disorganized, and to be, not only on the very worst of terms with their masters, but mistrustful of one another. At a preliminary meeting of the trade, held at the commencement of the present year, to devise means for the establishment of a "Progressive Society of Joiners," which was attended by eighty individuals, an attempt was made to ascertain the number of house-joiners in the town. Each person present stated the number of workmen employed in his shop, and a calculation was made, from which it resulted that the total number was upwards of 1,600. There have been several unions, or attempts at union, which have failed to answer their purpose of keeping up wages at a fixed standard, as among the shipwrights and the ship-joiners; and in preventing the introduction into the trade of cheap and unskilled workmen. There have also been constant disputes, and partial if not general strikes. The whole trade, throughout England, struck in 1833 on a question of time and wages. The strike lasted for twenty weeks, when the men were compelled to succumb to their masters. There has been no thorough organization of the trade in Liverpool since that time. The masters seem to have brought down wages by employing to the utmost possible extent both apprentices and men who had not served their time; and the men seem to have looked upon the masters, many of whom have sprung from their own ranks, as their worst enemies, and to have mistrusted them accordingly. Among the tailors and the porters of Liverpool, the great influx of Irish labour has the effect of reducing wages; and the chief complaint of the men is against the excessive competition of the unskilled labourers of that country. Among the house-joiners there is no competition of Irish. The Irish labourers are for the most part quite unable to obtain employment in a business requiring somewhat more training than the use of the needle does; and in which mere strength is not the sole requisite, as it is in the commonest descriptions of porters' work. The chief competitors in this trade seem to be Welshmen. I found the English and Scottish joiners by no means well disposed towards them. It was alleged that while an Englishman generally would not work under four shillings, and occasionally three shillings a day, a Welshman would take any sum that was offered, and that there were some Welshmen in the town in regular employ at ten shillings a week. "The Welsh," said one of my informants, "can live where other people would starve. If a Welshman earn only ten shillings a week, he will save five. A good many of the small masters in Liverpool are Welshmen, who have saved a little money while journeymen. They are sober men, but very hard upon their workpeople."

In fact, with the sole exception of the unhappy slop tailors, whose ill-will against the cheap show and slop shops was extreme, I met with no class of operatives who complained more bitterly of oppression than the house-joiners. They spoke especially of the unfair conduct of the slop-builders, and other small employers. Slop houses are, as far as I could gather, the causes of as much grinding of the faces of the poor as slop coats—and the slop system seems to be the prolific parent of demoralization and misery wherever it is introduced.

The following information upon the past and present state of the house-joiners' trade was derived from several intelligent workmen whom I questioned at various times and in various places, and was confirmed generally by other persons well acquainted both with the employers and the employed. In April, 1846, in consequence of the efforts of the operatives to form a society to keep up the rate of wages at four shillings a day, and to regulate the hours of work in summer and winter, some of the masters in the town drew up a paper, which they called upon all their workmen to sign. It was to the effect that no one of them would join or belong to any society or union of the trade. Some of the men signed the document, but numbers refused, and were immediately discharged. A meeting of the trade was held to debate on the course to be pursued, and a general strike was resolved upon. Upwards of five hundred men struck, and this strike became notorious under the name of the "document strike." The men, however, were not very closely united. There were considerable numbers of slop-journeymen in the trade, who were willing to work for 3s. or 2s. 6d. a day, or even for less, especially among the Welshmen. Many of them who had joined the strike gave in after a fortnight, and were re-admitted to their work upon the masters' terms. Another section held out for five weeks, when they also succumbed to the pressure of distress. There were not funds to maintain the men, and in less than two months the "document strike" was at an end. Neither masters nor men held together; and, said my informant, "this unhappy business utterly destroyed the confidence of the trade. Ever since that time the house joiners have been scattered and disunited. The 'Old Union' of the trade gradually decreased till it did not number twenty members; and two or three other clubs in connection with the trade fell off in a similar manner." Since that time there has been no general strike in the town, but two partial strikes have occurred—the one in November, 1849, and the other in June of the present year. The first was in a large establishment employing upwards of a hundred men, and arose on a question of time; the second was in a smaller establishment, and was neither a question of time nor wages, but one affecting the comforts of the men. It is the custom of the trade to allow the workpeople to take their breakfast and dinner in the workshop, and to provide them with hot water for the former meal. The employer in this case refused the men this privilege, on the plea that he could not trust them in his workshop at meal time, as he had been so often robbed. He alleged that some of them, unknown to him, had made boxes and other articles out of his materials, for their own profit, in the time between the conclusion of their meals and the recommencement of their work. He offered them the accommodation of hot water for their breakfasts as usual, but cleared his workshop both at breakfast and dinner time. The men were in consequence compelled to take shelter under a gateway in the street, where they were exposed to the weather and to the close proximity of a most offensive public watering-place. After repeated expostulation on the subject, they all struck work. This strike only lasted two days, when the employer thought it advisable to accede to the reasonable demands of his workpeople. Some of the master-builders of Liverpool received the highest character from the operatives for their honesty and plain dealing, and for their courteous and sympathetic regard for the interests of the persons in their employ; but the great majority of the smaller masters, and the "slop" or "jerry" builders, as they are called in Liverpool, were spoken of with an animosity which after inquiries showed me to be very natural, although very deplorable.

The following account of jerry building, and the mode in which it operates to defraud the public and to oppress the working man, by squeezing down his wages to a limit far below that which will afford a decent or adequate subsistence, was given by a very intelligent workman who knew the trade, both in London and in Liverpool, but who, in his statement to me, confined himself exclusively to Liverpool:—

"The jerry builders are the builders of slop or 'scamped' houses. They are the causes of much poverty among the workmen, and are greater defrauders of the public than even the slop tailors. Slop tailors put good work in their bad materials, but jerry builders never provide either good materials or good workmanship. It is a most immoral and unjust system; and I often wonder how people dare to call themselves Christians, or to appear in a court of justice to prosecute an unfortunate child for stealing a piece of timber. The plan pursued by the jerry builders is to lease a bit of land in the town or in the neighbourhood, wherever they can procure it, and run up a lot of small houses for poor people—what is called 'cottage property' in Liverpool. Some of these houses, which don't cost much above £100 or £120, let for £12 a year or more. The building is done in the most scandalous manner, and at the lowest rate. The joiners' work is of the worst description. They use inferior timber—wet, and by far too light for the weight it has to bear. Instead of pitch-pine, which ought to be used in a properly-constructed house, they use yellow pine. The joists, instead of being two inches thick, are only one inch and a quarter. In these cottages the whole of the joiner's work is often contracted for, to be done by the piece, at £7 per house. I have known a contract taken as low as £5 per house. The work includes the laying of three floors of joists, the roofing, the flooring, the plugging (that is driving plugs in the walls to fix the wood-work to), the stairs from bottom to top, window sashes and frames, the doors and casings or jambs, the architraves, skirtings, cupboards, and drawers, and sometimes Venetian shutters. This work, if properly done, would be honestly worth £15 for the labour alone. A man who contracts to do work at this rate cannot afford to pay proper workmen their wages. Apprentices and others learn their business in making slop houses, and 10s. a week is about the most that is paid. Sometimes a man or two will get 18s. for a week's work. This system brings inferior men and raw lads into the town, who work without a knowledge of the business, and 'scamp' their work in the most shameful manner. Any man who looks active, and consents to work for half the usual wages, as many do, is sure of employment; and the skilled and conscientious workman has no chance. Such a man offers himself, and the jerry builder, or his contractor, makes no scruple of engaging him. 'Never mind,' they say, 'though he doesn't know his trade, he's a strong fellow, and we'll knock a profit out of him somehow.' Not very long ago the building of a lot of offices near the Exchange, a large stack of houses, was put up for public competition. Several respectable builders sent in estimates—men who would have done the work con-scientiously, and employed skilled labour and good materials. The fair estimate was about £3,500. A jerry builder sent in his estimate, which was for £2,400 only, a difference of £1,100. He got the contract, al-though he had no capital to work upon. This man, having no ready money, could not, like the respectable builder, go to the Brunswick Dock, and purchase his timber at a discount. He was obliged to get his timber on credit, and give his bills for three months for it. Of course, he had to pay for the accommodation. There were thus but two ways in which he could make any profit out of the job—by scamping the material, and putting in inferior stuff, and by screwing down wages and employing apprentices. Such things are very common in Liverpool among the jerry builders. They are the worst enemies of our trade."

The statement of this working-man was confirmed by an architect. He said: "The jerry builders are principally Welshmen. I do not know the origin of the name. They employ as few grown men as possible, and prefer boys and young lads, whom they instruct in their work, giving them little or nothing beyond their food. They are men without capital, and very ignorant, but, being backed by attorneys who have land to dispose of, they manage to do a tolerably extensive though very often a ruinous business—ruinous to themselves, as well as to the working classes. They are the disgrace of the building trade. If one of them sees a piece of land to let or sell, he applies immediately to the attorney, who shows him the plan of the allotments. If the jerry builder will undertake to put materials and labour upon the land, the attorney will advance him money to set to work, taking his bills for the amount. The attorney drives a safe bargain, and makes his advances cautiously as the work proceeds, and never to anything like the value put upon the land. If the bills are unpaid when they arrive at maturity, the attorney, by a very summary process, can resume possession in three days. Even if this should be the result, as it often is, the jerry builder, who is a mere working man, has been no loser by the transaction. He has paid himself his own wages out of the advances made to him, and has screwed a profit out of the wages of every person he has employed. These houses, whether built for the working or the middle classes, are run up in the lightest manner. I have known small houses that did not cost above £80 or £100, to let for £12 or £15 a year. Not long ago, I made a valuation for a building society of five cottages, each consisting of two rooms and a kitchen. They were miserable places; the rooms were less than twelve feet square, with a staircase leading directly from the kitchen, or lower room, to the rooms above. They had no back windows. There was but one privy for the five cottages. The joiners' work was of the most inferior and rude kind; and the timber was of the worst and commonest sort. These houses and the land on which they stood cost £400, and each house let for £8 per annum—thus yielding an interest of 10 per cent. They were seldom or never unlet, and the rents were collected weekly. I have known instances—not two or three, but I may say scores of instances—in which £15 per cent. has been cleared for cottage property of this inferior class. Even if such houses drop to pieces in twenty years, it is a first-rate investment. It is the poor who pay the highest prices for everything—houses not excepted. Middle-class houses are scamped in the same way. The walls are so thin that you can hear in one house the conversation of people in the next. The joists are not sufficiently thick or strong—the wood is 'green,' and instead of sound Baltic, or red American pine, which ought to be employed for the bearing timber, the jerry builders invariably use the cheap, common yellow pine, which is not fit for the purpose. The workmanship is not quite so much 'scamped' as in the houses of the poorer classes; but is very far from being what it ought to be. These rows of nice new houses, and bran-new streets, may look pretty enough outside and in, but it is all show and no substance. Slop-work never lasts, and such houses will be old and rickety long before they have stood sixty years. To secure comfort in a house—to have a house honestly built—it ought to last for 200 years, with ordinary repairs from time to time. Very few such houses are built now for private occupation. Public buildings are necessarily stronger, and jerry builders do not get the chance of slopping them. The leasehold system is to some extent the cause of this evil; as when a man builds on a lease of seventy-five years, as leases run in this neighbourhood, he fancies he has done enough if he builds strong enough to last that time. But the principal source of the mischief is the dishonest competition of jerry builders, who are men without capital or character. They compete for contracts without the means of fulfilling them, and offer to construct private and public buildings upon estimates which are scandalously inadequate. The sums they name are sums for which the work cannot be honestly done. If they obtain a contract, and are compelled to put the good materials and the good workmanship which they bind themselves to provide, they cannot execute it, and must throw up the contract. They trust in most cases to the chapter of accidents and to 'extras' to repay themselves. The owner of the property and the competent working men are the main sufferers—the one from the bad material and bad workmanship, and the other from the number of boys, lads, and unskilful workpeople who must be employed to leave a margin of profit for the 'jerry.' It would take me a month to detail all the roguery of this trade, and the manner in which it affects the interests of all classes."

The corporation of Liverpool, which has done so much to improve the sanitary condition of the town, to sewer the streets, to prevent overcrowding, to remove nuisances, and to erect baths and washhouses, has never, as I have already observed in my report on the sanitary state of the town, turned its attention to the necessity of erecting dwellings for the labouring classes. Upwards of 25,000 persons have been ejected from underground cellars and unwholesome courts, but no means have been taken to provide them with better dwellings. They are still left to crowd together in larger tenements, or are left to occupy such expensive, flimsy, and inconvenient houses as the jerry builders can speculate in. The following comparative statement of the number of houses erected in Liverpool within each year from 1838 to 1849, both inclusive, will show the general extent of the building trade:—

1838	1,052
1839	997
1840	1,576
1841	1,761
1842	2,027
1843	1,390
1844	2,450
1845	3,728
1846	3,460
1847	1,220
1848	656
1849	446
Total	20,763

The number of the very lowest class of houses, or houses rented at less than £12 per annum, and built for the working classes, is very considerable, as the following returns for the years 1845, 1846, 1847, and 1848 will show:—

A statement of houses and their rentals, erected or in the course of erection in 1845.—Under £12 per annum, 1,212; from £12 to £25, 2,007; from £25 to £35, 332; from £35 upwards, 177. Total, 3,728. Warehouses, 86.

Ditto in 1846.—Under £12 per annum, 710; from £12 to £25, 2,328; from £25 to £35, 236; from £35 upwards, 186. Total, 3,460. Warehouses, 44.

Ditto in 1847.—Under £12 per annum, 59; from £12 to £25, 905; from £25 to £35, 167; from £35 upwards, 89. Total, 1,220. Warehouses, 3.

Ditto in 1848.—Under £12 per annum, 74; from £12 to £25, 506; from £25 to £35, 48; from £35 upwards, 28. Total, 656. Warehouses, 6.

In these four years there were thus erected no less than 2,055 houses of rentals under £12 per annum, destined for the working classes, and mostly built upon the "jerry," "scamp," or "slop" principle. The number of houses of a rental from £12 to £25, and, therefore, of a larger size and greater convenience, was 5,746. Of these, also, the large proportion were "jerry" houses.

Liverpool (and all other large towns) owes a duty to society and to itself in the proper control of building. It is not enough that it prevents overcrowding in existing tenements, but should with a due regard to the general health, and also to the pockets of the ratepayers, take care that no new buildings are erected that are frauds upon the people, and inconsistent with the general amenity of the town, and the well-being of all classes. Mr. Newlands, the borough engineer of Liverpool, in his excellent report to the Health Committee, published in 1848, directed their attention to this subject in the following terms:—

"It is," said he, "in the power of the council, on the extensive area of land belonging to the corporation, to develop correct sanitary principles in the laying out of streets, and in structural arrangements generally. Many intelligent and liberal co-operators will be found among the proprietors of land; and a good example set by them will be enforced on the unwilling by public opinion. But where neither a proper sense of duty, nor the influence of public opinion, can prevail, short-sighted views of present advantage must be compelled to give place to plans for the general good.

"In speaking of the difficulty in estimating the cost of the sewerage, I have already adverted to the necessity for the council having a servitude over land laid out for building purposes, so as to control the directions of the streets and their builded area, or, in other words, to limit the density of the population. It may be argued that such interference with the rights of property is unjust; but a little reflection will show that the real injustice is on the other side. The health of a community is public property, and from its deterioration the public suffer. From the over-crowding of the population, and the structural defects of our towns, the result of a sordid desire of the individual to benefit himself, at whatever risk, arise a high rate of mortality, unnecessary sickness, widowhood, and orphanage. From the same causes ensues the necessity for providing hospitals, dispensaries, workhouses, and the various other institutions for the relief of sickness and distress—and a worse necessity, the providing of prisons for the punishment of crime. The cost of these institutions to the country admits of precise calculation, and the amount is startling; but what arithmetic will enable us to compute the value of the lives which are daily lost, the anguish which the sufferers feel? 'Property,' it is well said, 'has its duties as well as its rights'—rights, unfortunately, too often sustained by the wrongs of the community; and although avarice must, for its own sake, provide checks to its rapacity, that it may not cease to have a victim, we yet daily see streets set out, and houses built with such disregard to human health, as to invite the approach of nature's avenging maladies. Surely, then, he who abuses his trust, by perpetuating this frightful evil, must be made by the strong hand of the law to understand that the right compels the duty."

Among the 2,055 jerry houses let under £12 per annum to the poor, the great majority were built in courts. Upon this part of the subject Mr. Newlands is equally emphatic:—

"Probably," said he, "there is no contrivance by which the health of the town is so much depreciated as by the structural monstrosities called courts. A court, in the proper meaning of the term, is a yard belonging to a house or houses; but the courts of Liverpool are passages, not yards. If such things are to be allowed at all, they should be subject to the same regulations as streets, with this difference, that as they have in general only one open end, the area to be allowed for every inhabitant should be doubled. A court, if constructed on proper principles, may be made conducive to a better state of things. Proper structural arrangements may render it healthy, by affording ample space for light and air, and the inhabitants may be made a co-operative society, by having a common kitchen, washing, and baking establishment. Such courts as these would be convenient, healthy, and economical. Economical in every respect, as regards construction, warming, lighting, and cleansing, and the saving of time to the inhabitants. A court, for example, in which the buildings form three sides of a square, of ample area, with the common kitchen and wash-house in the midst, would have space, and light, and air. The buildings might be lofty, having the houses in flats, entering directly from galleries running round. A large surface would thus be exposed to the action of the sun, and, becoming heated by it, would create motion in the air. Every house being furnished with a sink, and water-closet for its liquid and solid refuse, and a dust-shoot conducting to a common bin for ashes and vegetable refuse, of the construction described at page 115, the cost of collecting and carrying away that refuse would be reduced to a minimum. The third side of the court being enclosed by an open railing, the area would be free from the dangers of the streets, and children could be trusted to play in the open air without risk of accidents, to the great relief of their parents, and the advantage of their own health."

Liverpool has in reality done so much to retrieve its character, as the most unwholesome and overcrowded town in Great Britain—it has shown so much zeal and judgment in all sanitary questions, that it encourages the well-wishers of the labouring population to expect still more at its hands. To stop the building of "jerry" and slop houses is not impossible, although it may be so to stop the manufacture of slop trowsers or of slop cabinet work. Acts of Parliament have already regulated the thickness of walls in dwellings, and taken other similar matters under their protection. These acts are still deficient in attaining the end in view; but the principle of interference is already sanctioned, and must be carried still further, not with the object of protecting the labourer who builds the house, but with the object of protecting the health of the community. Mr. Newlands, in the following paragraph of his report, shows how the provisions of the Act of Parliament may be obeyed to the letter without attaining the object of the Legislature:—

"In the attempt," he says, "to improve the system of building cottage dwellings, a serious error has been committed by not doing enough. Back to back houses were certainly bad; but it is a question whether the substitution of back yards and narrow passages has not done more harm than good. A block of cottage dwellings, recently erected in Liverpool, in strict accordance with the requirements of the act, consists of a parallelogram, enclosed on its four sides by buildings. A passage, three feet wide, traverses the longest axis of the parallelogram; but in place of running through, to afford convenient access and ventilation, it turns outwards at right angles in opposite directions at each end. Each house is five yards wide, and seven yards and a half deep, and each has a back yard, of the same width and three yards deep, opening to the passage. Each yard contains a privy and a cesspool or ashpit. Here, then, we have an area enclosed on all sides, measuring 966 superficial yards, of which 97, or a tenth part, are occupied by the cesspools and privy, sending their reeking abominations into the stagnant atmosphere, from which the dwellings around are supplied with the breath of life. In a sanitary point of view, nothing could possibly be worse; and it is equally bad when we consider the subject economically in reference to the removal of the soil and ashes. In a passage, 169 feet long and three feet wide, there are 27 privies as ashpits, each containing on an average four cubic yards of refuse, all of which must be dug out in this contracted space, wheeled along in small handbarrows, the smallest with difficulty passing the right-angled turns, and emptied into the mud-cart. Notwithstanding the best endeavours of those employed in the removal of the contents of the ashpits, the contracted space causes much of the putrid matter to be spread about; and, as the ashpits are never all emptied together, there is a constant deposit of filth and a constant exhalation of deleterious gases."

These are the houses in which the class of "jerry" builders prefer to speculate. They are run up at the cheapest rate, and let to the poor at weekly rentals, averaging from 10 to 15 per cent. on the capital invested. These slop houses are far more demoralising in their effect than slop work of any other kind, for they demoralize not only the labourer employed in producing them, at wages insufficient for his proper maintenance, but the unhappy persons who are compelled by poverty to inhabit them. It is within the power of great municipalities such as Liverpool to remedy this evil, and by providing dwellings for the working classes built with a due regard to the health and comfort of the poor, as well as the general beauty and amenity of the town, to deprive the "jerry" builder of his occupation. Such undertakings would probably pay themselves as commercial investments, and would most certainly tend to elevate the position of all the various operatives employed in the construction of houses.

The operative house-joiners of Liverpool have recently formed an association for mutual aid and improvement, to which they have given the name of "The Progressive Society of Joiners."

A partial strike, which took place in November, 1849, led to several meetings of the trade, in which the present social position and future prospects of the members were anxiously debated. Ultimately, a suggestion that an attempt should be made to combine the members for mutual improvement and advantage was favourably received; and the "Progressive Society of Joiners" was instituted. Long after the strike had ended, a committee of joiners, who took charge of the infant society, continued to meet for the purpose of organising it; and on the 20th of May last a public meeting was held in the Concert Hall, which was attended by nearly 2,000 persons, of whom about nine-tenths were members of the trade. The Mayor of Liverpool presided, supported by Mr. William Rathbone, and other gentlemen of the town, known for their philanthropy, and for their sympathy with every effort at self-advancement made by the working classes. The objects of the meeting were declared to be—

1st. To establish an institution which shall afford facilities to the members meeting together for the transaction of business, the study of science, and for mutual improvement apart from the pernicious influences of the public-house.

2d. To establish a library of such works as treat on subjects relating to the trade, to assist in the formation of classes for their study, and to provide the institution with those current publications which may be considered most useful to its members.

3d. To make good any loss of tools by fire, theft, or accident, and to insure a sum of money at the death of any member or member's wife. The funds for such purpose to be raised by a separate contribution, and that it shall be optional to all members whether or no they join the last-named fund.

Several operative house-joiners addressed the assembly, and made very creditable speeches; and their institution was finally inaugurated with much enthusiasm, and with every promise of success and efficiency.

LABOUR AND THE POOR.

LIVERPOOL.

[FROM OUR SPECIAL CORRESPONDENT.]

BIRKENHEAD AND ITS DOCKS.

LETTER XIX.

The stranger to Birkenhead, in order to comprehend thoroughly the past and present condition and history of that town, should be informed of the mistakes committed by Liverpool, and of the numerous natural advantages possessed by the rising town on the opposite side of the Mersey. On comparing the relative position of the two places, he will see on the Liverpool side a thickly peopled town, built upon a low-lying alluvial flat. Upon the other he will see a high bank, sloping gently to the river, upon one part of which a handsome town has been recently erected, and along the whole line of which northwards, in proof of the attractiveness and beauty of the site, rise a succession of pleasant villages and villas—the retreats of the rich merchants of Liverpool. On the Liverpool side he will discover that the docks, instead of being carried inwards upon the low land, have been constructed along the line of the river, and that the distance between the docks at the extreme south and those at the extreme north is upwards of four miles. On the Birkenhead side, within three-quarters of a mile of the Liverpool Exchange and Custom-house, he will see a pool, or arm of the sea, which is left almost dry at low water, extending upwards of two miles into the land, and which seems to invite the enterprise of man to deepen it and convert it into a harbour. On inquiring further he will find that Liverpool once possessed a similar, though much smaller, pool, which her merchants and rulers in by-gone days, instead of widening and deepening, spent large sums of money in filling up and covering with houses. If he inquire still further into the subject, he will be informed that the authorities of Liverpool, in filling up this pool—their natural dock—and in constructing the twenty-two magnificent harbours which they possess along the bank of the river, have either spent, or rendered themselves liable for, the sum of upwards of £13,000,000 sterling. He will learn at the same time that the total superficies of these great works, when those now in course of erection shall be completed, will not amount to much more than 196 acres. Turning to the Birkenhead side, he will find that the superficies of Wallasey Pool, the great natural dock of the Mersey—after a considerable amount of "made land" shall have been taken from it—will be 197 acres, equal to that of all the Liverpool docks together, and that the sea has already done half, or more than half, the work of excavating it. He will furthermore ascertain, upon inquiry, that the total expense of deepening and walling this splendid dock, and constructing all the necessary works, was once estimated under half a million, but that more mature experience has proved that a million sterling will amply suffice for the purpose; or, in other words, that a thirteenth part of the sum expended for the accommodation of the trade of the Mersey by the dock trustees of Liverpool will provide for the accommodation of as large a trade on the Cheshire shore of the river. When Mr. Telford, the eminent engineer, was engaged with Messrs. Nimmo and Stevenson to drain Wallasey Pool, he was so struck with the superior advantages of that natural dock, and by the beauty of Birkenhead and Woodside, as he looked down upon them from the heights of Bidstone, that he exclaimed, "Liverpool has been built on the wrong side of the river." I propose to devote the concluding letters of this series to a detailed history of the efforts made by a few enterprising men to turn the dock advantages of Birkenhead to proper account; and also to build a town, upon a regular plan, with rectangular and wide streets, with squares, markets, and a public park, and with all the aid derivable from modern experience in drainage and sewerage, and other accessories to the health, comfort, and enjoyment of the people, which the old, closely-packed, and irregular towns of Great Britain so seldom possess. The history will be found full of instruction for all those who take an interest in the social comfort of the people and in the great question of "Labour and the Poor."

The name of Birkenhead is derived from Birchen-haven, or the "harbour of Birch-trees." It was a place of no importance until of late years, and long after the commencement of the present century it was chiefly noted as a resort for the merchants of Liverpool who desired a purer air than their own town affords. In 1815 it only contained a few scattered villas and cottages. In 1824 the late Mr. William Laird purchased several acres of land, on the south margin of Wallasey Pool, from Mr. T. R. Price, of Bryn-y-Pys, the lord of the manor, and established his ship-building yard upon the site. Mr. Laird saw the great capabilities of the place. Perhaps, also, he was aware of the mistake made by the Liverpool Dock Trustees in extending their docks on the banks of the river, instead of carrying them up into the very heart of the low-lying ground on the level of the ancient Liver or "Lyr" pool. However that may be, he made a still larger purchase of land in two years after his establishment at Birkenhead; and Sir John Tobin, a merchant of Liverpool, imitated his example. In consequence of the purchases of these two gentlemen, the services of Messrs. Telford, Nimmo, and Stevenson, the engineers, were engaged to report upon the capabilities of Wallasey Pool. Their report was so favourable that the corporation of Liverpool deemed it advisable to buy up all the land that was still to be sold on either side of the Pool. The reason of this purchase appears to have been, not to make use of Wallasey Pool, but to prevent its being constructed into a dock to the injury of Liverpool. It does not seem to have struck the leading men of Liverpool that Birkenhead and Wallasey Pool were in reality nearer to Liverpool than many portions of their own town; and that to all intents and purposes the two might have been as much identified as Southwark and London. Mr. Laird, who had paid £80 per statute acre for his land, disposed of it all within three years afterwards to the corporation, at the rate of £720 per acre. From this time the idea of converting Wallasey Pool into a dock was allowed to slumber. The corporation of Liverpool never entertained it at all; but the attention of Mr. Laird and his friends continued to be directed to it. Birkenhead, in the meantime, participated in the growing wealth and importance of Liverpool. The merchants gradually flocked in greater numbers to the Cheshire side of the river, for the better enjoyment of the sea breezes on the higher bank; and a small town was formed. In the year 1833 it had increased sufficiently to warrant an application to Parliament for powers for its local government and improvement. The Birkenhead Improvement and Township Commissioners were accordingly appointed, and exercised, though without the name of a municipality, such of the powers of a civic corporation as were necessary in such a place. They planned out the town, established a public market, suggested the purchase of land for a park, purchased the right of ferry to Liverpool from the lord of the manor, and laid the foundation of many future projects of usefulness. The Birkenhead Commissioners were composed of the mayor and bailiffs of the borough and town of Liverpool for the time being, and the four junior aldermen of that town, together with sixty other persons especially named, the design being to comprise the general owners of property and the principal ratepayers of the township. These sixty commissioners were appointed for life. After the passing of the Municipal Reform Act, a second act was obtained for the government of Birkenhead, by which the life appointment of the commissioners was annulled, and the government of the township entrusted to twenty-four commissioners—three of them to be chosen from the Town Council of Liverpool, and the other twenty-one to be elected by the general body of the ratepayers of Birkenhead. Two other acts of Parliament were successively passed, amending or extending the former acts—of which the more important received the royal assent on the 11th of April, 1843. This act, which contained 125 clauses, gave powers to purchase land for improvements, and for the formation of a park, and for the appropriation of land for public baths. It also provided for the appointment of a health committee, and regulated in various ways the width of streets, the building of houses, the prevention of over-crowding in cellars, and the removal of nuisances. An act supplementary to this was passed in the same year for establishing a public cemetery without the boundaries of the town.

During the spring and summer of 1843 there were great complaints in Liverpool of the want of dock accommodation; and the town council, the dock committee, and the local newspapers, severally discussed the question. On the 20th of October, the Liverpool Shipowners' Association was especially convened, to consider "the extreme and increasing inconvenience and loss sustained by the mercantile community from the great want of dock room." Each of the members present detailed facts coming within his own knowledge of the grievous delay and expense occasioned by vessels being compelled to anchor in the river; and a return was presented, drawn up from authentic sources, showing the number of days during a twelvemonth at which the flags had been kept flying at the twelve principal dock gates, to notify that the docks were full. From this return it appeared that for 175 days in the Victoria and Waterloo Docks, 235 days in the Prince's, 302 in the George's, 251 in the Brunswick, and for similar periods in the other docks, there was no possibility of entrance; and that the average delay in the whole of the docks was 146 days, or about twenty-one weeks in the year. The meeting unanimously declared its opinion that the dock committee should apply to Parliament for powers for the construction of new docks at the north and south ends of the town of Liverpool. Four days afterwards a similar resolution was passed by the North American Association; and on the ordinary meeting of the dock committee, on the 26th, these documents were laid before it, and duly considered. While the dock committee and others were thus debating, not alone the propriety, but the absolute necessity of extending the dock accommodation of the port, the town council of Liverpool, which had some years previously purchased all the available land on the borders of Wallasey Pool, began to consider the inexpediency of their continuing to hold it. No revenue was derived from it, and the land was all but waste. Whatever may have been their real motives for acting as they did at this time, the Birkenhead estates were put up for sale on seventy-five years' leases; and found ready purchasers at reasonable prices. Mr. William Laird did not live to see the realization of his great projects, but his son and successor, Mr. John Laird, entered into negotiations with the corporation in June or July, 1843, and purchased the lease of 50,000 square yards for £25,000. He declined to take the land unless permission were given "to make docks, slips, basins, and other works of a similar kind," without let or hindrance from the corporation. The terms were acceded to, and clauses to that effect inserted in all the leases granted to him. Mr. William Jackson next obtained 28,000 square yards for £14,000, on the same conditions. Messrs. Laird, Jackson, and Potter afterwards purchased 600,000 square yards—all that the corporation had to dispose of—upon similarly advantageous terms. The Birkenhead people were, to use a common phrase, "wide awake." Though the necessity for dock extension in the Mersey was so apparent as to be the general theme of conversation and debate, no one on the Liverpool side of the water ever suggested the idea of converting Wallasey Pool into a dock. Mr. Laird's idea, if ever mentioned at all, was treated as visionary and romantic, and all thoughts were directed to the extension of the docks northwards towards the Bootle-point, and to the purchase of the Harrington Dock and estate to the southward of the town.

During all this time the originators of the Birkenhead project kept their own counsel. They bought the land on Wallasey Pool, which the corporation of Liverpool put up for sale; they employed Mr. Rendel, the civil engineer, to draw up a plan for the embankment of the Pool, and its conversion into a dock. They obtained the favourable opinion of the Board of Admiralty for their project, and on the 7th of November—within less than a fortnight after the Liverpool Dock Committee had heard evidence on the necessity of extending their docks north and south, a general meeting of the commissioners of the township of Birkenhead was summoned to consider matters of urgent importance to the prosperity of the town. At this meeting Mr. Wm. Jackson, now M.P. for Newcastle-under-Lyme, introduced the subject of the Wallasey Pool. The following extract from his speech will show in what manner:—

"There are two subjects (said he) which I wish particularly to bring before you—one of which has been already before nearly every member of the board; and, perhaps, it is the most important measure ever brought forward, so far as regards Birkenhead. You are aware that our neighbours on the opposite side of the water, in the council and in the dock committee, have, for several months past, been discussing the propriety of dock extension, and I certainly have been surprised that in all the discussions they never alluded to the advantages of Wallasey Pool. But, however silent they may have been, I can assure you that we have not been idle; for you are all well aware, from what has passed in committee, that plans have been prepared, sections taken, borings made, levels obtained, notices prepared, and everything ready for your instructions this evening for our law clerk to go to Parliament, for the purpose of receiving powers to make the most capacious dock that ever was made in the kingdom of Great Britain and Ireland. We have obtained, as you are aware, the assent of the Admiralty to our enclosing the whole space from the bottom of the Woodside Ferry to Seacombe, an area of not less than 350 acres, with gates, and a tidal basin of 30 acres, or nearly three times the space of the Prince's-dock, which at all times of tide will never have less than 12 feet of water for vessels to float in; and by damming up at the narrowest point, we shall have dock space at Wallasey Pool to the extent of 120 acres. This may take the public by surprise, but I would only say that though the matter was under our consideration, prudence induced us to keep our own counsel until such times as our plans were ripe, and we had received the assent of the authorities. Such, gentlemen, is the subject upon which the committee have to report; and they now come before you for the purpose of obtaining the necessary sanction to proceed to Parliament. I may as well state, for the information of the members generally, that the principle upon which we proceed is this:—That we, as commissioners of Birkenhead, proceed to obtain powers for the necessary works in Wallasey Pool; that on its own merits we raise the money; that, while the commissioners of Birkenhead will be the commissioners of the dock estate, the rate-payers of the townships will not be taxed, directly or indirectly, for the undertaking. I may also state, that there are parties prepared to meet the necessary expenses, provided we are defeated in Parliament—a result which I cannot possibly anticipate—so that no reflection can be made on the commissioners that they are using the money of the township for this purpose. It is proposed that all the pecuniary advantages derived from the dock shall be appropriated to the measure itself; and if ever, from the sale of land, or otherwise, any other revenue from the dock shall arise, it is proposed that that also shall go in the reduction of the cost first of all, and then in the reduction of the dock rates; and I hope that the amount received in this manner will be sufficient to defray the cost of the construction of the whole."

Mr. Jackson concluded his very plain, business-like, and effective speech by proposing that the law clerk should have power to insert the necessary notices in the next *London Gazette*, and to take the proper steps to "obtain an act of Parliament to execute the works, and to borrow money on the credit thereof." This proceeding fairly startled the people of Liverpool. "Had a bomb-shell alighted among them from Birkenhead," said the *Liverpool Mercury*, "it could not have created a greater sensation." The local press, without a single exception, approved of the undertaking, and wished it success—and generally among the public there was but one feeling of commendation of the spirit and energy of the Birkenhead commissioners, and of regret at the mistake which the Liverpool authorities had committed in suffering such a prize to escape from their hands. No opposition to their bill was, at this early period, hinted at. "The Birkenhead Commissioners," said a letter signed Cosmopolite, "have every advantage on their side. They have no warehouse interest to contend with, and by introducing the London dock system they may lower the insurance to the metropolitan rates. They have always before their eyes the huge and ugly Custom-house, to remind them of the blunders made by the Liverpool dock makers—they have the flood-gate of commercial prosperity to start with; a cheap money market to borrow in; cheap materials to build with; all the Government departments to back them—the approval of the conservators of the Mersey—and the support of all the manufacturing and mining districts."

It was under these favourable auspices that the Birkenhead Docks were first brought under the notice of the world. The application to Parliament was successful, although it was vigorously opposed by Liverpool, and received the royal assent on the 19th July, 1844, exactly a year after the first determination to proceed to Parliament for powers to enclose Wallasey Pool had been privately made at the house of Mr. Laird. Money was for a while abundantly supplied; the construction of the docks was commenced; a dock and warehouse company was formed; and the Chester and Birkenhead Railway Company took the necessary powers to extend their rails to the dock side. By the 23d of October, sufficient progress having been made with the works, the foundation stone of the docks was laid with great ceremony, by Sir Philip de Malpas Grey Egerton, the member for South Cheshire. A great banquet afterwards took place in the large engine-room of the Chester and Birkenhead Railway Station. About 500 guests were present; Mr. John Laird filling the chair, and Mr. William Jackson the vice-chair of the assemblage. After the banquet there was a ball, at which about 800 of the nobility and gentry of Cheshire attended; and Mr. Jackson, at his own expense, gave another ball to the trades-people of the township. A general holiday was instituted, and all the working people received for the day their full day's wages, the amount necessary for the purpose having been raised by a general subscription. The sum collected was about £2,000, which was distributed, not only to those in the actual receipt of wages, but to all the poor of the town. Contracts were entered into for the supply of beef and bread to the necessitous, and for giving a holiday, and a repast of buns and fruit to all the children in the public schools of the town. At this time, and for months afterwards, all was *couleur de rose* at Birkenhead, and the town seemed destined not simply to rival in wealth but to surpass in beauty her older neighbour on the opposite shore of the Mersey.

The people of Birkenhead were, however, too sanguine, and had not sufficiently calculated the influence of the national fortunes upon all public and private schemes of any magnitude. The railway mania and the potato famine were destined, in conjunction with other more private and local matters, to nip in the bud many of their promising projects, to retard very seriously the great work of constructing the docks, to ruin the fortunes of some who had embarked their capital in one or other of these undertakings, and to inflict serious loss upon others. But before entering into any account of Birkenhead as a town— of the excellent sanitary measures adopted and planned—of the construction of sewers—of the laying out of the public park—of the erection of public dwellings for the labouring classes, upon a plan superior to any previously attempted—of the influx of labour into the town and neighbourhood—or generally detailing the present state and future prospects of Birkenhead, I will proceed with the history of the dock project. As soon as the act of Parliament was obtained, a company was formed to work the docks, under the title of "The Birkenhead Dock and Warehouse Company." This company obtained its act in 1845. At this time there were four public bodies, with separate jurisdictions, but all bound together, and feeling a general interest in the growth, good management, and prosperity of Birkenhead. The two first were strictly public bodies, without private interests, namely, the Commissioners of the township and the Dock Trustees. The other two bodies had personal and private interests to subserve, and their shareholders invested their capital with the hope of a profitable return. These were the Birkenhead Dock and Warehouse Company, and the Birkenhead, Lancashire, and Cheshire Junction Railway Company. All these public and private bodies were necessary to each other, and the scheme for the transformation of Birkenhead into a large and important town would have been incomplete without any one of them.

The fair sky and halcyon days of 1843 and 1844 were soon at an end. Clouds succeeded to the sunshine, and a period of storm and difficulty followed closely on the youthful days of the Birkenhead dock project. Difficulties arose with the Government, in consequence of the claims made by the Commissioners of Woods and Forests on behalf of the Crown. The railway mania also approached its termination; and the panic, of which the first premonitory symptoms occurred towards the end of 1845, cramped and crippled the operations of every public body which had occasion to make their appearance in the money market as extensive borrowers. The various projects for the embellishment of the rising town, and for the construction of the dock warehouses, also required large sums to carry them to completion; and these sums were not always available when they were wanted. Ultimately, it was admitted on all hands that the projectors of Birkenhead had not calculated upon these difficulties—that they had been going too fast—and that a crash would sooner or later take place. *Delenda est Carthago* was the cry of many persons in Liverpool, who entertained the notion that Birkenhead was not the ally but the rival of the old town, and that the prosperity of the one was inconsistent with the prosperity of the other. To a certain extent, these predictions of evil were verified, and the Birkenhead Dock Company, the Dock and Warehouse Company, and all persons interested in the town and port, had to pass through a long and trying ordeal, from which at the present moment they are but slowly emerging.

The first difficulty, which has been already alluded to, and which was altogether independent of the state of the money market, and in no degree attributable to the faults or mistakes of the originators of the Birkenhead projects, was created by the Crown. It arose, as appears from the statements submitted to Parliament in April and

May last, in the following manner:—The Birkenhead Dock scheme was originated on the principle that the amount required to complete it should be raised on the security of the works and lands reclaimed by them; that the rate of interest should be limited to 5 per cent., and that any advantages from surplus rates, or disposal of reclaimed lands, should go in reduction of the cost of works, or of rates, with the view to the dock being entirely free.

The office of Woods and Forests, however, claimed the foreshore on behalf of the Crown, and decided that it could not agree to this principle. It thereupon called upon two parties—Messrs. Hartley and Son, the engineers to the Liverpool Dock Trust, and on Mr. Cubitt, the consulting engineer of that body—to ascertain the value of the foreshore. At that time it was quite unproductive and valueless, and would have continued so to this day, had it not been for the Birkenhead Dock trustees. Messrs. Hartley valued the land when reclaimed at £798,600, but from this they admitted would have to be deducted the cost of the works and reclaiming the land, which they estimated at £300,000; Mr. Cubitt valued the Crown interest in the whole foreshore, including the Great Float, at £8,500, "under the circumstances of the same being under the management of commissioners for the use of the public, instead of a company or a corporate body for private gain."

This last-mentioned sum the Dock Trustees were willing to give; but the Woods and Forests did not come to any decision till the 21st of May, 1844, fifteen days after the bill went into committee, when they made the proposals embodied in the act, and to which the promoters assented, having no other alternative but to withdraw the bill. This act authorised the trustees to construct a low-water basin, dam, and other works, and by means thereof to convert Wallasey Pool into a floating dock, and to reclaim about 60 acres of foreshore for the Crown. It also authorized the raising of £400,000 on bonds, and contained a clause of forfeiture of the works to the Crown if not completed in 1854. The effect of this arrangement was to upset the original principle of making the land reclaimed contribute towards the cost of the works, and to create a valuable property for the Crown, at the expense of the bondholders in the Dock warehouses and of the trade of the Mersey.

A second act was passed in 1845, for walling and excavating the Great Float of 150 acres; authorizing the raising of £300,000 on bonds for that purpose. In consequence of the commercial panic that came to its climax in 1847, only £22,950 of this sum was ever obtained.

A third and a fourth act were passed in 1847, the first authorizing the raising of £400,000 on bonds, to pay for the extra cost of the outer works and graving docks; and the second, amending the act of 1845 for walling and excavating the Great Float.

The Commissioners of Woods and Forests agreed, in 1846, to grant land for the site of a temporary cut, called the Morpeth Dock, on condition that it should be "forthwith walled and converted into a dock for the purposes of trade." They also consented to co-operate in obtaining an act to carry out that arrangement; but during the progress of the bill through Parliament, they required the insertion of a clause making the same dock entrance illegal on the 22d of July, 1850.

A fifth act was passed in 1848, constituting a new trust, consisting of thirteen members, six being elected by the bondholders, and seven by the ratepayers of Birkenhead and of Wallasey, with power to raise £50,000 on preferential bonds towards the opening a portion of the Great Float in connection with the Morpeth and Egerton docks and entrance by Woodside Basin. Up to the spring of 1850 nearly £500,000 was expended on, or was due in respect of, the undertaking, including £50,000 raised on preferential bonds; and the trustees had parliamentary authority to raise £977,050 more. This power, in consequence of the state of the money market, remained quite inoperative. The Dock and Warehouse Company expended up to the same period about £600,000, in land, warehouses, buildings, and other accommodation for trade. The Railway Company expended upwards of a million in connecting the docks with Manchester and the manufacturing districts. Other parties expended large sums for bringing supplies of coal and other minerals down to the docks, and in building premises and stations; while the Chester and Shrewsbury, and Shrewsbury and Birmingham Railway Companies looked to Birkenhead as their outlet to the sea. A large portion of this outlay was made on the faith of these docks being permanently kept open, and eventually completed.

The trustees were in consequence compelled to apply to Parliament, and introduced a bill to remove the clauses of forfeiture of the works to the Crown in 1854, and the restrictions placed on their entrance by Woodside Basin. They stated that unless these objects were accomplished the efforts of the trustees to get trade or revenue would be impeded, and their power of proceeding with the outer works deferred to an indefinite period.

They urged that it was obvious that these penalties of forfeiture, and restrictions as to the use of the Woodside Basin entrance, were only admitted by Parliament as a supposed stimulus towards an early completion of the whole work, and that the effect of the forfeiture clause, if acted upon, would be a confiscation, to the land revenues of the Crown, of the funds embarked and the property created with the view of carrying out a great public work.

The trustees gave evidence on these and other points before a committee of the House, and stated that such clauses, so far from answering the desired end, only fettered and weakened their efforts, and that until withdrawn the public would feel no confidence in advancing money to forward the undertaking. The committee was favourably impressed with the general evidence, not only with reference to the trade of the Mersey, but with respect to the social and moral position of the maritime population. Some captains of American packet-ships attended in London, and stated their determination to make use of the Birkenhead Docks, where fire and light on board of their vessels would not be denied them, as in Liverpool; and detailed in what manner the regulations of the Liverpool Docks affected the health, morals, and efficiency of the sailors, besides inflicting a very heavy tax upon commerce. They also gave evidence of the practicability and desirability of establishing a large emigration depôt at Birkenhead. The committee of the house were so well satisfied that they unanimously passed the bill repealing the clause of which the dock trustees complained, and thus removed one great impediment to the success of Birkenhead. The next point was to obtain the consent of the Crown to the bill as approved by the committee, and for this purpose negotiations, which had long been fruitlessly pending with the Commissioners of Woods and Forests, were renewed, with a somewhat better prospect of success. After considerable delay and difficulty, a compromise satisfactory to all parties was agreed to. By this arrangement the Woods and Forests granted to the trustees "all her Majesty's interest in and over the foreshore at Birkenhead, commonly known as the south reserve, for the purpose of aiding the trustees in obtaining funds for the completion of the river wall in front of the said reserve, the wharf wall on the south side of the intended low-water basin, and the excavation of the said basin, the erection of the permanent dam, to form the main entrance into the Great Float, and the other works authorized by the acts of 1844 and the first act of 1847." The dock trustees undertook to apply all moneys raised from the sale of the south reserve to those purposes.

The Woods and Forests further granted to the trustees "all her Majesty's rights in and over the spaces of foreshore on each side of the Great Float, to be reclaimed by means of the wharf wall to be built under the several Walling Acts." It was stipulated that such spaces should be afterwards conveyed to the respective owners of the lands in front of which they were reclaimed, as soon as their respective wharf walls should have been built.

The dock trustees consented that the north reserve, and so much of the river wall as was then constructed, should be absolutely vested in the Crown. The Commissioners of the Woods and Forests, on their part, agreed to pay the sum of £22,000 for so much of the wall as was already built in front of the north reserve, stipulating that the money so paid should be expended in continuing and completing the river wall in front of the south reserve and other works.

The Crown agreed to continue the river wall of the north reserve round the north side of the Low Water Basin, and within twelve months after the permanent embankment across the Wallasey Pool should have been completed and open for traffic to make "a good and sufficient carriage-road, with a raised causeway on one side of it for foot passengers, such carriage-road and causeway to be maintained and repaired by the Wallasey Improvement Commissioners, and to be a public thoroughfare."

The Crown also agreed that the penalties of forfeiture imposed by the acts of 1844 and 1847 should be repealed; and the use of the Woodside Basin as an entrance into the Morpeth and Egerton Docks legalized as a permanent entrance. When the conditions of those articles shall have been performed, all connection between the dock trustees and the Commissioners of Woods, in respect of the land revenues of the Crown, will cease. The dock trustees are not to exercise control or jurisdiction over the north reserve, and the Commissioners of Woods, as far as regards the land revenues of the Crown, are not to interfere with the dock trustees in the execution of their trust, or in the management of any of their affairs or property, but each party is to be independent of the other.

As soon as these negotiations were concluded the construction of the dock walls and the excavation of the Pool were resumed with more vigour, and during the whole of the summer months nearly 1,800 workmen were daily employed. Passengers crossing in the ferry-boats from Liverpool to Woodside, although they can see Birkenhead at a glance, can form no conception of the magnitude of the works. It is necessary to descend into the area of the future dock before any one can realize to his mind the great extent of the operations which are in progress. At one part may be seen, rising under the labours of men, a line of gigantic walls of solid masonry, six feet thick and thirty feet high; at another, the splendid gates, through which a fleet of 120-gun ships, each with 1,000 men, and all her guns, munition, and sea stores, and drawing 27 feet of water, may hereafter pass in safety; while at a third portion of the Pool, a row of great steam hammers are driving a foundation of closely-wedged piles in to the soft bottom, the whole place swarming with busy and laborious men engaged in digging, wheeling, building, stone-cutting, and in all the multifarious operations of engineering work. On the particular day upon which my visit was made, the number of carpenters employed was 85; of sawyers, 32; of smiths and strikers, 38; of engine-drivers and firemen (on the temporary railway laid down in the bed of the Pool), 29; of masons, 220; of quarrymen, 197; and of labourers or excavators, 1,150; or, in all, 1,751 men. The wages of the carpenters were 27s. per week; of the sawyers, 24s.; of the smiths, 21s.; of the engine-drivers, 21s.; of the firemen, 17s.; of the masons, 24s.; of the quarrymen, 18s.; and of the excavators or "navvies," 15s., making an expenditure altogether of nearly £1,500 per week. How long this activity will continue it is impossible to say, as so much is dependent on the facilities with which money can be raised on the credit of the project; but sooner or later the temporary depression of Birkenhead will pass away, and the town will vie with and assist Liverpool, until both—not rivals and enemies, but friends and partners—will form a port or ports, superior even to London for the amount of wealth that shall pass through them. Already the tonnage of Liverpool is greater than that of London, although the actual number of ships entering and clearing from the Thames is greater than the number entering and clearing from the Mersey. But when the Birkenhead Docks shall be completed and opened it is likely that not only will the tonnage be still greater, but that the actual number of ships trading with the two ports of Liverpool and Birkenhead will exceed that of all the vessels trading with London.

Birkenhead will, in fact, possess many advantages which no other port in the kingdom possesses, and which Liverpool never can possess on her own side of the water. The immense extent to which the system of private warehousing has been carried in Liverpool is such as to preclude all hope of remedy; but in Birkenhead, this and all its concomitant evils of expensive cartage, high rate of insurance, and liability to plunder, will be avoided. The warehouses, of which a large and handsome pile has already been built, at an expense of £113,000, are all fireproof, of the best construction, and situated on the dock quays; so that cargoes can be lifted direct from the hold of the largest class of vessels, and either raised at once into the warehouses, or placed upon trucks, on the railway that runs along the quays, to be conveyed to any part of the kingdom. In consequence of the erroneous warehouse system of Liverpool, and the situation of the various warehouses in remote parts of the town, the merchant and importer has to pay for cartage, and in the case of bulky goods—such as cotton and timber—the tax is a very serious one. All this will be avoided at Birkenhead, and that town will not, like Liverpool, have to maintain three or four thousand horses, and as many drivers, at the expense of the commerce of England. Another evil consequent upon the warehouse system in Liverpool is, the increased rate of insurance demanded for goods lodged in places which are not under proper guardianship, and which may be situated next door to houses and buildings where no suitable precautions are taken against fire. At Birkenhead the insurance upon the warehouses and the produce in them is five shillings per cent., while in Liverpool the ordinary rates of insurance range from ten shillings to eighteen shillings per cent. for this reason alone.

The various advantages of Birkenhead have been classed as follows:—1. There are no dock dues payable on goods, whether imported or exported. 2. There is a considerable saving in the charges for cartage and porterage, in consequence of the Dock Company's warehouses being built close to the quay. By this means the warehousing and delivery of goods can be effected in the most expeditious manner, while a number of annoyances, such as the damage sustained by the frequent shifting of goods, petty robberies in the docks, &c., are avoided. 3. The rails of the Chester and Birkenhead Railway run along the quays and warehouses, forming a direct communication with the manufacturing districts of all the northern, midland, and western counties of England, so that the same waggons which receive the goods from the vessels or warehouses deliver them at Manchester, Birmingham, or London. 4. For the shipping interest the Birkenhead Dock offers great advantages, as vessels can enter in any weather, and lights and fires are allowed on board. The last-mentioned privilege is a great convenience and saving, especially to foreign vessels, whose crews remain with them while in port. Excellent steam coals are shipped at Birkenhead on the dock quays, and improvements are about to be carried out which will greatly facilitate this branch of trade. To these advantages must be added the concentration of business arising from the fact, that the foreign and coasting vessels, flats, &c., will be all in one dock, that there will be economy of time, labour, and expense, as well as security of property. Birkenhead will thus be found to possess facilities for business superior to any other port in the country. The small docks, the Morpeth and the Egerton, are now open at Birkenhead, where a considerable traffic is already carried on, especially in the shipment of coals and salt.

Efforts are being made to open the Great Float for the admission of vessels by the beginning or middle of October. It was at one time expected that a large timber trade would cross the Mersey from Liverpool, where it is insufficiently as well as expensively accommodated, as soon as the Birkenhead Dock was opened; but the Liverpool timber-merchants have otherwise decided for the present. A large portion of the mahogany trade has, however, already located itself at Birkenhead. The great mahogany shed on the quay is considered the finest in the world; and probably at some future day a portion of the timber trade will cross the Mersey.

The following extract from the circular of Messrs. Gibson, Andrew, and Co. shows the estimated saving of charges in certain cargoes of corn and grain consigned to Birkenhead, compared with the same consignments to Liverpool:—

1,000 QUARTERS WHEAT.

	Liverpool.				Birkenhead.		
Dock dues	£11	12	3		Nil.		
Cartage and porterage in and out	16	13	4		£4	3	4
Fire insurance, 2,200*l*., three months, at 7s. 6d.	8	5	0	2s. 9d.	3	0	6
	£36	0	7		£7	3	10
	7	3	10				
	£28	16	9	or nearly 7d. per qr.			

Calculating the price, free on board, at 35s. per quarter, the above shows a saving of about 1*l.* 13s. per cent. on the value.

1,000 QUARTERS BARLEY OR RYE.

	Liverpool.	Birkenhead.
Dock dues	£8 6 8	Nil.
Cartage in and out	16 13 4	£4 3 4
Fire insurance, 1,200*l*., three months, at 7s. 6d.	4 10 0	2s. 9d. 1 13 0
	£29 10 0	£5 16 4
	5 16 4	
	£23 13 8 or nearly 6d. per qr.	

Calculating the price, free on board, at 16s. per qr., this shows a saving of about 3 per cent. on the value.

1,000 QUARTERS PEAS, BEANS, OR INDIAN CORN.

	Liverpool.	Birkenhead.
Dock dues	£8 6 8	Nil.
Cartage and porterage in and out	16 13 4	£4 3 4
Fire insurance, 1,400*l*., three months, at 7s. 6d.	5 5 0	2s. 9d. 1 18 6
	£30 5 0	£6 1 10
	6 1 10	
	£24 3 2 or nearly 6d. per qr.	

Calculating the price, free on board, at 20s., thus showing a saving of nearly 2½ per cent. on the value.

1,000 QUARTERS OATS.

	Liverpool.	Birkenhead.
Dock dues	£5 11 2	Nil.
Cartage in and out	12 10 0	£4 3 4
Fire insurance, 800*l*., three months, at 7s. 6d.	3 0 0	2s. 9d. 1 2 0
	£21 1 2	£5 5 4
	5 5 4	
	£15 15 10 or about 3¾d. per qr.	

Calculating the price of oats at 12s. per qr. free on board, this shows a saving of about 2½ per cent. upon the value.

1,000 BARRELS FLOUR.

	Liverpool.	Birkenhead.
Dock dues	£7 5 10	Nil.
Cartage in and out	10 8 4	£2 1 8
Fire insurance, 1,200*l.*, three months, at 7s. 6d.	4 10 0	2s. 9d. 1 13 0
	£22 4 2	£3 14 8
	3 14 8	
	£18 9 6 or about 4½d. per brl.	

Calculating the price, free on board, at 18s. per barrel, this shows a saving of about 2 per cent. on the value.

1,000 SACKS FLOUR.

	Liverpool.	Birkenhead.
Dock dues	£10 8 4	Nil.
Cartage in and out	10 8 4	£2 1 8
Fire insurance, 1,700*l.*, three months, at 7s. 6d.	6 7 6	2s. 9d. 2 6 9
	£27 4 3	£4 8 5
	4 8 5	
	£22 15 9 or about 5½d. per sack.	

Calculating the price, free on board, at 26s. per sack, this shows a saving of about 1¾ per cent.

"It should be borne in mind," add Messrs. Gibson and Andrew, "that grain and flour are frequently sold ex ship, and that in such cases one-half of the saving in cartage would be annulled."

Many of the largest buyers from the country send their own flats alongside the vessels, so that in these cases no cartage is incurred in Liverpool, and the only advantage in Birkenhead then would be the absence of dock dues, which are very considerable.

The tonnage employed in importing timber from the Baltic and British America into Liverpool during the last three years was—

	Baltic.	British America.	Total.	
1847 ...	26,564	172,427	198,991	tons register.
1848 ...	26,606	190,186	216,792	„
1849 ...	14,141	225,783	239,924	„

IMPORTATIONS OF BREADSTUFFS INTO LIVERPOOL DURING THE
LAST THREE YEARS.

	Wheat.	Barley.	Malt.	Oats.	Rye.	Beans.	Peas.
1847 ...	694,590	89,650	70,330	178,780	3,990	146,510	31,340
1848 ...	453,140	35,420	76,660	208,040	1,080	121,840	28,550
1849 ...	552,545	62,982	69,567	213,627	10,913	142,991	33,943

	Indian Corn.	Corn Meal.	Oatmeal.	Flour.	
				Sacks.	Barrels.
1847 ...	1,196,860	496,150	106,960	60,320	2,281,850
1848 ...	685,420	96,390	207,430	183,060	751,520
1849 ...	851,597	43,867	254,141	162,495	725,178

It is assuming a very moderate calculation to estimate the tonnage employed in the above importations at:—

In 1847 ...... 600,000 tons register.
 „ 1848 ...... 330,000 „ „
 „ 1849 ...... 400,000 „ „

It is hoped by the people of Birkenhead that as soon as their dock is opened some portion of this tonnage, induced by the low charges, and the other advantages of their docks, their warehouses, and their railways, will cross to the other side of the Mersey.

With regard to the cotton trade, the same facilities and the same low charges will doubtless, in due time, create a trade for Birkenhead. The people of Manchester, Rochdale, Bury, and the manufacturing districts of Lancashire and Yorkshire generally, have no particular favour to show to Liverpool, and will encourage either side of the Mersey that shall offer the greatest advantages to the cotton trade.

The coal trade of the Mersey seems as yet in its infancy; the absence of proper facilities on the dock-quays, combined with other causes, having thrown almost the whole export and coasting trade in coals into the hands of the people of Northumberland and Durham. An interesting pamphlet upon this subject has just been published by Mr. Wm. Laird, of Birkenhead, pointing out in what manner Liverpool and Birkenhead have neglected their opportunities, and in what manner they can yet turn them to proper account for their mutual prosperity. The coal fields of Northumberland and Durham, according to Mr. Laird, cover an area of 780 square miles, while the coal-fields of Lancashire are not less than 550 miles. Mr. Laird's pamphlet shows that within the last 20 years the coal trade of the east coast has expanded prodigiously, while that of the west coast has made no progress. The total shipments of coal in the ports of Great Britain amounted in 1848 to 11,625,193 tons, of which 7,838,380 tons were for the ports of the east coast; and only 252,408 for the ports of Lancashire, or about one-thirtieth of the quantity exported from Northumberland and Durham. Mr. Laird is of opinion that the Lancashire coal-field is superior to that of Northumberland and Durham in point of position, in variety of its products, in the number and thickness of its seams, in the accessibility of its pits—in all, in fact, that nature has had to do for it; while, as regards capital invested, mechanical contrivances for shifts, and enterprise to conduct the trade, Lancashire has proved itself greatly inferior. Whatever steps Liverpool may be induced to take to repair her neglect cannot fail to turn in some respects to the advantage both of Liverpool and Birkenhead. Birkenhead, however, already possesses a small trade in coal, which only requires care and time to be fostered into a large one. The North Wales coal proprietors have long felt the want of an outlet for the produce of their magnificent field, which, till the opening of the Rhuabon branch of the Shrewsbury and Chester, and more recently of the Mold Railway, was quite shut out from all foreign markets, and confined to a very limited local supply. The opening of these lines has, however, changed the aspect of affairs, bringing the collieries of this district into direct communication with Birkenhead, where, owing to the immense import trade of Liverpool, freights can generally be had 25 per cent. below other ports.

The average distance of the mines from this, their port of shipment, is about the same as in South Wales—from 25 to 30 miles—and though not so well placed as those on the east coast, in this respect they are near enough to keep the price low, one of the great essentials in forming an export trade. From several trials made shortly after the opening of the Birkenhead Docks in steamers on the Mersey, the coal from this district was found to answer admirably for steam purposes, producing a hot, strong fire, and leaving little clinker, while the economy of the fuel in comparison with Lancashire coal was very apparent.

In the beginning of the present year, the opening of the Mold branch of the Chester and Holyhead Railway developed the mineral riches of that district, and the "Coed Talon" coal first made its appearance on the quays of the Birkenhead Docks. It is raised, as its name implies, at Coed Talon, about six miles from Mold.

There are now two collieries competing for trade, and the beneficial effect has been apparent in the exports of the last six months having risen to something like 17,000 tons against 6,000 for the six months previous. The trade has much increased during the last two months, and the quantity at present shipping is at the rate of 100,000 tons per annum.

The Brymbo, South Sea, and Avon are all from the same district beyond Wrexham, on the Shrewsbury and Chester line, and are a bright, strong, large coal, containing more bitumen than the "Coed Talon," though both are much alike in their immense size, some of the blocks weighing as much as 6 cwt. or 8 cwt. The Brymbo has been largely exported to the Mediterranean, and is spoken well of for steam purposes generally. One of its best markets is France, where its bright appearance and large size renders it very popular. It has also been sent out in considerable quantity to Spain.

Having now touched at greater or less length upon the dock question at Birkenhead, and all the great branches of trade which it either can at present or may in the future accommodate, it only remains to describe the state of Birkenhead as a town. In this last-mentioned respect it is still more interesting than as a port. I reserve the particulars for another and concluding Letter of the Liverpool series.

LABOUR AND THE POOR.

LIVERPOOL.

[FROM OUR SPECIAL CORRESPONDENT.]

PRESENT STATE AND PROSPECTS OF BIRKENHEAD.

LETTER XX.

The township of Birkenhead forms part of the parish of Bidston, a smaller township about two miles and a half distant. It is included in the poor-law union of Wirral. Its poor-rate for the present year is 1s. in the pound on a rental of £67,362. This rate is considered heavy by the inhabitants. The town, however, if compared with Liverpool and other places, cannot be considered very seriously burdened with pauperism. The aged and the impotent make the largest demands upon its funds, and it has little to pay for the support of vagrancy and able-bodied pauperism. That little might perhaps be less if it had not, in imitation of Liverpool, established a vagrant shed, or pauper hostelry, to accommodate tramps with a supper and a night's lodging. Upon inquiring of the relieving officer, the character of the tramps frequenting Birkenhead was found to be precisely similar to that of their compeers elsewhere. The professional vagrants formed the large majority of them, and among the numerous Irish applicants many were found to be in possession of concealed money. But two days before this inquiry was made an Irish tramp had appeared at the house of the relieving officer, telling a woful tale of destitution. He was clad in complete rags and covered with filth. He begged for a penny to carry him over the ferry to Liverpool. Suspicion being entertained, he was accommodated with a lodging in order that he might be searched. In a patch upon his filthy stockings were found a receipt for £13, which he had recently deposited in a savings bank, besides fifteen shillings in silver. Similar cases, I was informed, were not unfrequent.

In the year 1801 the population of Birkenhead amounted to no more than 110 souls. In 1821, it had reached only 200. In 1831, the population, including that of the adjoining township of Bidston, was

3,434. Ten years afterwards it had considerably more than doubled itself, and was ascertained by the census to amount to 8,277. In 1843, after the great scheme for the embankment of Wallasey Pool had arrived at maturity, people flocked into it from Liverpool, and all parts of the country, in search of work; and the population within three years appears to have trebled itself. It was estimated in 1843 and 1844 at little short of 25,000 souls. Birkenhead first became of importance at this period. Its name, formerly almost unknown to the world, was widely spread abroad. The originators of the great dock project were, in reality, the founders of the town. No one can walk through its streets at the present day without wonder at its growth, and without confessing that, whatever may have been the faults of these far-sighted and enterprising men, niggardliness was not of the number. If any blame is to be attached to them, it is that they attempted too much, and that they laid out a city rather than a town, and made provision for the prospective wants of at least 100,000 people, when provision for a quarter of the number would have been sufficient. The suspension of most of the great works in the Pool, consequent upon the panic of 1847, and the commercial depression of the succeeding year, caused a considerable diminution in the number of its inhabitants, which in 1848 did not exceed 13,800. The population is now estimated at from 18,000 to 20,000; but the smaller number is generally thought to be the more accurate. The number of inhabited houses in the township, which in 1848 was 2,300, is now 3,700; and in addition to these, there are upwards of 300 uncompleted, or uninhabited. Birkenhead is fast recovering from its depression, but gives palpable evidence of a great design unfulfilled. The portions which are completed are well-built, spacious, and elegant. Hamilton-square, with its handsome stone mansions, erected from the designs of Mr. Gillespie Graham of Edinburgh, rivals in architectural beauty the squares of the northern metropolis, and is far superior to most of the squares of London. Some of the principal streets are such as the metropolis might envy. Large gaps, however, occur to break the continuity of the principal lines, and rows of houses of imposing design, stand in melancholy nakedness, unlet, or half completed, to show how much was once attempted, and how much has yet to be done before Birkenhead can assume even the appearance of prosperity. To pass from Liverpool to Birkenhead is like passing from busy Cheapside and Cornhill to the solitary and rectilinear streets of some new or half finished extension of the metropolis. The eye may range for a mile, or a mile and a half, down excellently paved and perfectly straight roads, thoroughly sewered, and already called streets, although still without houses. Twenty-nine miles of streets have been laid out in the town, and twenty-six miles of them have been sewered. It was computed, in the summer of 1843, that in proportion to its size, and the wants of its population, Birkenhead had sixteen times as much sewerage as Liverpool, and that if it were admitted, for the sake of illustration, that the public wants of Liverpool were in this respect adequately supplied, the sewerage of Birkenhead would have sufficed for a population of 160,000 persons. But while the street sewerage is ample the house drainage is insufficient. Dr. Hunter Robertson, a resident medical practitioner, remarks, in his pamphlet on the sanitary condition of the town, "that through the absence of some compulsory power or obligation, the owners and builders of houses, both for the rich and the poor, pay no attention to the requirements of the people in this respect, and erect houses either insufficiently provided or wholly unprovided with drains connected with the sewers." It has been calculated that there are 700 houses in Birkenhead that have no connection with the sewers at all; and that there are at least 500 which are still capable of an improved drainage. A system is, however, in course of operation which will ensure a speedy completion of the drainage of all the property in the town, and 935 houses have had their drainage connected with the public sewers since October, 1848, at the instance of the Improvement Commissioners.

One of the first objects to which the attention of the founders of Birkenhead was directed, when they determined to make a "model town," was the ferry between Woodside and Liverpool. Frequent and cheap intercommunication with Liverpool was a matter of the most urgent importance and necessity. The most daring of engineers would not venture even to hint at the possibility of a bridge over such an arm of the sea as the Mersey is at this point. The only available means of communication was by steam-boat. At the commencement of the present century, sailing-boats proceeded morning and evening between the two places, and when the wind was unfavourable and the tides strong, these boats sometimes took a couple of hours to perform the distance. The first steam-boat between Liverpool and Birkenhead began to ply in 1820, and the fare each way was 6d. The ferry originally belonged to Mr. Price, of Bryn-y-Pys, the lord of the manor of Birkenhead; but the Improvement Commissioners of the township obtained an act of Parliament for its purchase in 1842. At this time the fare had been reduced to 3d. It was ascertained in 1843 that, upon an average, 5,500 persons each day, or 2,075,000 per annum, crossed and recrossed in ferry boats between the two towns, independently of the persons passing and repassing between Liverpool and the old Birkenhead-ferry, Monk's-ferry, Seacombe, and other places. The charge for a single passenger was then fixed at 2d. a journey, or 25s. per annum, and the boats at this time ran only twice an hour. This was the maximum fare fixed by the Act of Parliament which authorized the purchase of the ferry. The landing place, at St. George's Pier-head in Liverpool, was particularly incommodious, and even dangerous. In consequence of the efforts made by the people of the Cheshire shore, and of Birkenhead more particularly, and the urgent public necessity of better accommodation, the authorities of Liverpool constructed a magnificent landing stage at St. George's Pier-head, at an expense of upwards of £50,000. The fare was reduced to one penny, and boats were stationed to leave each side of the Mersey every ten minutes, from eight in the morning to seven in the evening in summer and winter.

In addition to these, night boats run regularly all the night through, at intervals of half an hour, for a fare of 6d. The fare was lowered from 2d. to 1d. on the 14th of June, 1848. The reduction of fares, as might be expected, had a great and immediate effect upon the traffic. From April, 1847, to April, 1848, when the fare was 2d., the number of passengers to and fro was 1,632,000. From April, 1849, to April, 1850, the numbers increased to 3,139,400. In this last number are not included contractors, or persons who subscribe for quarterly, half-yearly, or annual passages for themselves and families, and who are estimated to amount to more than 2,500 heads of families. About 2,000 of these pass daily through the contractor's gate. The number of people actually crossing and recrossing is continually on the increase, and during the present season averaged above 11,000 daily, or 4,015,000 per annum.

The boats kept at the Woodside and Monk's Ferries by the commissioners are superior in size, comfort, and accommodation to those of any other ferry; they are never taken off for towing or any casual work, and in foggy or very stormy weather they are sometimes the only boats that work. Passengers on such occasions come from all quarters of the Cheshire side in preference to going to their own ferries.

Holiday parties pass to and fro in crowds on Sundays and holidays to walk in the Birkenhead-park. From £70 to £80 in *penny fares* have been sometimes received on Sunday, and about £130 was received on Whit-Monday.

As the ferry belongs to the township, and is managed by the 21 commissioners, seven of whom are elected annually by the householders, any mismanagement is of easy rectification by the constituency at the annual elections. The cost of the right of ferry and the plant was nearly £90,000; and, at the present low fares, the annual return, after deduction of all expenses of working, wear and tear, &c., is about 7½ per cent.

The design of the Birkenhead Improvement Commissioners being to afford their new and rising town the advantage of all the sanitary measures of which the necessity was proved by the sad experience of other places, but which were difficult of establishment in them, on account of the value of existing property; their attention was directed to the prevention of those evils which were the subject of the greatest complaint in old and gradually formed towns. They therefore took powers in their act to prevent the building of narrow and crooked streets and courts, to compel sewerage, and to provide, under proper regulation, for the removal of nuisances and the prevention of overcrowding in the dwellings of the poor. Their attention to sewerage, and the compulsory widening of the streets, insured the blessing of fresh air to the inhabitants—although this blessing was to a considerable extent destroyed in some parts of the town by the neglect of house-drainage, to which allusion has already been made. Measures were also taken to provide an abundant supply of water, although the difficulty as regards the old parts of the town was such, that up to 1847, out of 2,845 inhabited houses 458 were supplied with water from private pumps, and 387 received no water supply at all. The number of inhabitants of these 387 houses was 2,437. The commissioners also obtained powers to purchase land for a handsome corn market, to establish a large public park for the recreation of the inhabitants, to erect slaughterhouses at a distance from the town, and to lay out a public cemetery upon the heights towards Bidston. They were aided in their public efforts by the private enterprize of some of the principal inhabitants, foremost among whom was the family of the Lairds. To Mr. Wm. Laird belongs the credit of erecting upon an extensive scale the first pile of buildings for dwellings for the working classes, and of setting an example, which has since been imitated in various parts of London and in other great towns and cities of the kingdom. A short description of these houses, now called Morpeth-buildings, and of the Dock-cottages, constructed upon a similar plan by the Birkenhead Dock and Warehouse Company for the accommodation of their workpeople, will prove of interest. It will show how greatly the efforts of those who wish to improve the condition of the labouring population are impeded by the Government.

The fact that nearly four hundred houses of the poorer classes of people were without a water supply, was of itself sufficient to suggest to the enterprising founders of Birkenhead the expediency of a better arrangement. These houses, in addition to the great evil of want of water, were densely overcrowded. Built in the older parts of the town, and upon the model of the fetid courts of Liverpool, they contained many cellars in which families were crowded together, without regard either to health or decency. But house property of this inferior description is unluckily very valuable—far too valuable to be bought up from the proprietors, and pulled down. At the same time it is exceedingly difficult to compel the owners to provide better accommodation for the poor people, and quite useless to talk to the people themselves of the state of filth and discomfort in which they live, unless better accommodation is put within the reach of their means. Mr. Laird therefore took the proper course, and erected within the limits of the township, and close to the Docks and all the scenes of the daily labour of the working classes, a pile of buildings for the proper accommodation of families. Morpeth-buildings, so named in honour of the present Earl of Carlisle, is a lofty row of houses, containing 64 separate dwellings. They are entered by eight stone staircases, each staircase being common to eight dwellings. The stairs are lighted with gas. Each dwelling contains a sitting room and two small bed rooms. From the sitting room or kitchen leads a scullery and a water-closet. Each house is abundantly supplied with water. From the scullery the dirty water is removed by the sink or the water-closet, and the mistress of the family is saved the labour of removing the dirt and ashes down stairs by the simple contrivance of a shaft, communicating from the scullery into a general receptacle, of which the periodical cleansing and emptying is provided for in the rent. The rooms are small, but the inestimable advantages of privacy and separate sleeping rooms, besides those of an abundant supply of water for all culinary and domestic purposes, without the labour of procuring it from a pump, are so highly appreciated by the wives and families of the labourers, that

Morpeth-buildings are always fully occupied. No sooner is a dwelling vacant, than an application is made for it. The rent, including water and all rates and taxes whatsoever, was originally fixed at 4s. 6d. per week. As it is not desirable that the labouring classes should be indebted to benevolence or charity for the houses in which they dwell, and as these model houses must answer as commercial speculations, and pay a fair rate of interest to the men who invest their capital in erecting them, if we are to expect them to supersede the old, inconvenient, and pestilential hovels in which they are too commonly crammed, it remains to be seen what the erection of these buildings cost Mr. Laird, and what return he received for his money. The following is a correct statement of both:—

COST OF ERECTING MORPETH-BUILDINGS, BIRKENHEAD.

The ground, 1,071$\frac{2}{3}$ yards of land, at 30s. ...	£1,607 0 0
The builders' contract	5,965 0 0
Extras—including the fitting of shelves, cupboards, &c.	192 0 0
Architects' commission	178 19 0
Total	£7,942 19 0

RENTAL OF MORPETH BUILDINGS.

Gross rental, or rents ranging between 3s. 6d. and 4s. 6d. per week, or averaging £9 15s. per annum		£624 0 0
Deductions, paid by the landlord.		
The window-tax ...	£127 0 0	
Township rates ...	96 0 0	
Water rates	19 4 0	
Insurance	15 15 0	— 257 19 0
Net rental		£366 1 0

The net rental therefore, leaving no margin for wear and tear, or for the occasional non-letting of any of the dwellings, was but 4½ per cent.—a return evidently insufficient to induce other men of capital to imitate the example and to enter into such undertakings as matters of business. It appears that at the present time a similar pile of buildings could be erected at 25 per cent. less cost. To this, however, it must be answered, that it has been found necessary to reduce the rental to a similar extent; so that the statement remains relatively exactly what it was. It is evident, however, that were it not for the window-tax the speculation would be remunerative. The necessity of building such houses in towns within a convenient proximity to the places where the men work, precludes the possibility of building them otherwise than upwards, one dwelling upon the top of another. Land is too expensive to admit of separate cottages being built—each dwelling upon the ground. But were land cheap enough to enable them to be so built, the government would have no claim to the window-tax, as no one house would contain the requisite number of windows to become liable. In Scotland, where it is customary to build houses for the middle classes upon the same principle—that of flats—or house upon house—each entered by a common stair—every separate tenement pays for its own windows. Were this principle adopted in England, Morpeth-buildings, and all similar piles of houses for the labouring people, would not be liable to the window-tax. The Government, however, will not relax its gripe, and insists that these sixty-four small houses shall rank to the window duties as one large house, and pay one and a half per cent. upon the whole cost of their construction and the land upon which they are built. It goes still further than this, and insists that if but one of these sixty-four dwellings be occupied, and the remaining sixty-three be unlet, the window duty shall be paid upon the whole. The Dock-cottages, built at the further extremity of the Pool, are a still more striking example than Morpeth-buildings of the injurious effect of this tax in deterring men of capital from investing their money in any attempt to improve the dwellings of the poor—and consequently to elevate the physical, social, and moral position of the people. The Dock-cottages were erected in the heyday of the prosperity of Birkenhead, at a time when hope was in the ascendant, and the enthusiasm of its leading men pictured a day, not far remote, when its inhabitants would number at least 100,000, and the riches of the world would be crowding into the port. The cottages stand far down the side of the Pool, isolated from all other buildings, and at least two miles from the heart of Birkenhead. They are a somewhat gloomy pile, and sadly deficient in light and air. The sunshine, I should imagine, never reaches the windows of the lower tenements, in consequence of the height of the buildings and the narrowness of the thoroughfare. They are planned to accommodate 350 families, with separate dwellings, such as are afforded in Morpeth-buildings, with the same number of rooms in each, the same accommodation of scullery, water-closet, and dust-shaft, and the same ample supply of water. They are fire-proof, and strongly built, and cost, for land and building, no less than £50,000. The window duty upon the pile is £600 per annum. These 350 houses are wholly unoccupied, and will continue to be so unless the owners can let the whole of them at once. If one single house be let for three or four shillings a week, the whole pile becomes liable for the whole window duty of £600 per annum! Surely such a state of the law—if it be the law—only requires to be known to be remedied. Sanitary questions are fashionable at the present time, and public men of all parties unite in their desire to improve the dwellings of the people. But improvement is evidently impossible while the window duty is allowed to fall with such crushing weight upon the only kind of houses that can be constructed for the poorer population in towns where land is dear. It is a mockery on the part of any Government to call itself a friend to sanitary improvement, when it allows such a state of things to continue. It appears that an attempt was made at Birkenhead to contest this point with the Commissioners of Assessed Taxes, and to assert that the practice in Scotland, of charging only each tenement or flat with its own windows, was the only legal one in England. The matter, however, was not pressed to an issue before the legal tribunals. Thus it appears that, as investments for money, the dwellings for the labouring classes in Birkenhead have proved failures, and solely on account of the injurious operation of the window duty, which spares the property of the selfish proprietors of filthy courts and alleys—in which no house contains so many as eight windows—but ruins the property of those who endeavour to combine philanthropy, and a regard for their fellow-creatures, with the ordinary and fair return for capital invested. The ownership of Morpeth-buildings has passed from the hands of Mr. William Laird, a gentleman who has suffered largely by the period of depression and probation through which Birkenhead has just passed; and it is possible, although I do not know it to be a fact, that the speculation may pay the present proprietors, even with the heavy weight of the window-tax upon it. But if the property have been sold at less than its cost, the case remains as originally stated. If such investments do not pay their original founders, they are not likely to be imitated; and plans for the elevation and improvement of the working classes, though much talked of, and patronised by platform orators, will remain plans, incapable of realization, except by the injudicious, if not mischievous, operation of charity—honourable it may be to him who bestows, but degrading to those who receive it.

One other fact in connection with Morpeth-buildings deserves to be stated. The wives of the labouring men who resided in them, in the prosperous days of Birkenhead, refused to leave them when work failed on that side of the Mersey, and preferred to remain, while their husbands sought and procured work in Liverpool. They felt the great convenience of separate sleeping rooms for their children, and the comfort of the abundant supply of water for all domestic and culinary purposes which was provided for them, as well as the great advantage to health (to say nothing of decency and convenience) of a private water closet, and naturally dreaded to return to the pestilential, filthy, and indecent courts and cellars of Liverpool. To accommodate these and other working people, arrangements were made to carry the men over to their work in Liverpool, and bring them back in the evening to Birkenhead for one fare, or a penny per day. The arrangement appears to have worked well, and to have been considered a great boon by the working-classes; but doubts having been started of its legality by the terms of the purchase of the ferry, the accommodation was discontinued. The revival of trade at Birkenhead, and the recommencement of the works at the docks, have since that period brought the work-people over more permanently, and there is no present necessity for the continuance of the boon.

The projectors and founders of Birkenhead were more fortunate in their effort to establish a public park for the people. By the act of 1843, by which the small township of Claughton-cum-Grange, and part of the township of Oxton, were included within the jurisdiction of the Birkenhead Improvement Commissioners, full powers were given to purchase land for a park. In conformity with this act, the commissioners secured one hundred and eighty-four acres of swampy land, within about a mile of the Woodside-ferry. The purchase money was £52,786. The first idea of a park appears to have originated with Mr. Holmes, one of the commissioners, and to have been afterwards taken up, and carried to a successful issue, by Mr. Jackson. The intention was to drain and plant the park, and lay out the interior of it in the most tasteful manner, and then let off or sell for the erection of villas a belt of about 70 acres, around the enclosure. It was anticipated that the purchase money to be derived from this belt would fully repay the original cost of the whole land, and all the improvements effected upon it; and that by this means, without the sacrifice of a shilling, the people of Birkenhead would possess the advantage of a free park for ever. Mr. Paxton, the eminent landscape gardener, was employed to lay out the ground. All his taste and skill were placed in requisition, and under his auspices the site was turned to the best advantage—

artificial lakes were formed, mounds were raised, light and elegant bridges were thrown over the water, handsome stone lodges or gates of imposing architecture were erected, walks and drives were formed, and the "swamp" became one of the most beautiful parks in England. The grand entrance is through an archway for carriages, with two minor arches for foot passengers. On each side is a lodge, two stories in height, built of the purest freestone. This gate is of the Ionic style of architecture, and forms a handsome object in the landscape, and one of the greatest ornaments of the town of Birkenhead. The proximity of Liverpool rendered this speculation as successful a one as its originator desired. The sanitary state of Liverpool, notwithstanding all the praiseworthy efforts of the Corporation to improve it, is not such as to induce any one to live permanently within its boundaries who can afford the luxury of a purer atmosphere; and Birkenhead, being conveniently situated, the wealthy were induced to make it their residence. The belt of land, extending all round the Birkenhead Park, offered, perhaps, the most agreeable sites for villa residences and gardens that the neighbourhood of Liverpool afforded; and the park was no sooner completed than purchasers for the villa lots eagerly presented themselves. The total cost of making the park within the railing, and in addition to the purchase-money of the land, and including draining, planting, decorating, railing, and building the lodges and entrance gates, was £74,989, or, in all, £127,765. Up to the time at which my inquiry was made during the present summer, out of the seventy acres reserved for the purpose there had been sold 300,000 square yards of land for the erection of ornamental villas. The sums received amounted to £105,119 1s. 8d. The minimum price of the land remaining unsold was £20,141 5s. For this land, amounting to 41,386 square yards, there were daily applications. It is possible that it may be all sold by the time this letter is in print; but if not, there can be no doubt that it will speedily be disposed of on advantageous terms. When all is sold there will, including the value of the lodges, be a balance to the credit of the Birkenhead Park of upwards of £1,500. Many of the villas have been erected, and add greatly to the beauty of the park. By this happy arrangement 114 acres of land have been presented to the public as a pleasure ground, free for ever. The advantages of the park are not confined to the Cheshire side of the river, but are as great to the opposite town of Liverpool as to Birkenhead itself. On Sundays and holidays the people of Liverpool flock over in large numbers by the penny ferry-boats to stroll in its serpentine walks and flowery avenues, and to enjoy a purer atmosphere than their own dense and unwholesome town affords. The maritime population of Liverpool seem especially to prize the boon; they cross over on Sundays in considerable numbers, attracted from the public-houses and spirit-shops, which were formerly, and are still, too often their Sunday resorts. The sailors, both American and English, seem to appreciate to the fullest extent the privilege of such a pleasure-ground—a rarity in seaport towns; and their behaviour on all occasions is represented as most orderly and becoming. Altogether, the founders and projectors of Birkenhead have every reason to be satisfied with the result of this experiment. The history of their project may perhaps point out the means to the leading men of other towns for securing a similar advantage to the people; without trusting to the chance benevolence of the wealthy on the one hand, and without burdening the public upon the other. If by skill and good management, aided by a little public spirit, Birkenhead has acquired a park in perpetuity, free of cost, it is possible that by corresponding means and corresponding energy the same boon might be secured to the public elsewhere. At all events, the history of Birkenhead Park deserves the study of sanitary reformers, and the earnest consideration of the municipalities and governing bodies of all the great towns of the kingdom that are yet unprovided with open spaces and pleasure-grounds for the health and recreation of the people.

The opening of the public park took place on the 6th of April, 1847, simultaneously with the opening of the Morpeth and Egerton Docks, and with the extension of the Birkenhead and Chester Junction Railway to the Dock Quay. The day was celebrated as a public holiday, and Lord Morpeth—after whom one of the Docks was named, as well as the stack of buildings erected by Mr. Laird for the dwellings of the workpeople—arrived from London to preside at the festival, accompanied by Lord Monteagle and the Earl of Lincoln. Shortly after noon on that day the Birkenhead Commissioners, with Lord Morpeth and the other guests, embarked at Monk's Ferry on board the Lord Warden, a handsome new iron steamer built by Mr. John Laird. Six pieces of artillery were posted along the quays; and the steamer, which was beautifully decorated, started amid music, the roar of cannon, and the cheers of the spectators. After steaming about a mile up the river, the boat returned, and, similarly saluted in its progress, slowly entered the Docks. The party then repaired to the Dock warehouses to partake of a banquet, at which 800 ladies and gentlemen sat down. The weather was fine; flags and streamers floated from every available spot, the ferry steamers were crowded, and Liverpool poured its throngs to the opposite bank. Four of the warehouse rooms, each 140 feet long and 50 feet wide, were tastefully fitted up for the festival with pink and white drapery. The reception-room was adorned with a magnificent cascade, which poured out a crystal jet amidst a profusion of choice plants and flowers. Joseph Bailey, jun., Esq., M.P., occupied the chair; and John Laird and William Potter, Esqrs., the vice-chairs.

The health of Lord Morpeth having been drunk, his lordship, in his usual ornate style, dwelt upon the splendours of the scene, and the future glories of Birkenhead:—

> "We often hear," said he, "of the old gala days of Venice, when the Doge went forth in his golden galley to plight his faith to the wave which bathed his palaces—but we have seen something this day beyond even the dreams of Venice. For instance, such an array of steamers as has to-day graced the Mersey, never could have been witnessed in Venice; and though perhaps a steamer, when viewed by itself, may not be so picturesque an object as a gondola, I may yet remind you that even in the palmiest days of her pomps and her argosies, Venice never could have sent forth a message which in ten days might reach those harbours and roadsteads of the new world where her flag never waved. My most recent occupation will not permit me to forget that this is one of the first places which has begun a systematic attention to the physical comforts of the vast numbers of workmen it calls together, and the important subject of public health. With this assurance about us and around us, I feel that the pageant of to-day, even when its gaieties shall have passed away and its shouts are silent, will still give us grounds for remembrance that it has not been a triumph which gathers its trophies from the strife of nations and the arts of destruction—that it has not been a mere unmeaning sacrifice to frivolity and dissipation, but that it has struck its roots deep in public usefulness, and will bear rich fruits of peace and progress through coming ages."

After the banquet Lord Morpeth and the distinguished company proceeded to open the park, which during the day was the scene of great festivity. In the evening there was a display of fireworks. The workmen at Birkenhead Docks, two thousand in number, each received a day's wages. Later in the evening a ball and supper took place in the dock warehouse, which had been appropriately fitted up for the occasion, at which were present the majority of the principal persons who had attended the previous proceedings.

Among the other public undertakings of the Birkenhead commissioners, either completed, in progress, or contemplated as soon as circumstances are favourable, three others deserve especial mention:— The establishment of a public market—of a cemetery—and of an emigration depôt. The market has been already completed, at a cost of £39,000, the price of the land included. It is 430 feet in length by 130 feet in breadth, and forms a spacious area, covered with wrought iron roofs of a light and elegant construction, divided into three bays, the outer of which is supported upon two rows of iron columns, connected by cast iron girders. The market hall is thus divided into three arcades, of which the centre is the smallest, being of 30 feet span, while the arcades on each side of it are of 50 feet span. The market has six entrances, and is far superior in convenience and beauty to any covered market in the metropolis.

The public cemetery has not yet been laid out, though powers were taken for its establishment in 1843. The recommencement of the works at the Docks, consequent upon the settlement of all matters in dispute with the Commissioners of Woods and Forests, will have the effect of expediting the establishment of the cemetery. The quarry at Claughton, from which the stone is taken for the erection of the dock walls, has been fixed upon for its site, and the cemetery will be laid out as soon as the requisite stone for the docks has been quarried out. The site will be picturesque, and the design is to make it one of the principal ornaments of the neighbourhood. There will be no interments within the boundaries of the town.

The next object contemplated at Birkenhead is one of great importance, the establishment of an emigration depôt. The want of such an establishment is severely felt at Liverpool, where the poorer classes of emigrants are exposed to the extortions of every species of robber and swindler, and huddled together in the filthiest and most unwholesome lodging-houses. The readers of this series will probably remember the bad practices of the "man-catchers," as detailed in those letters which related to the extent and character of the immense and growing Irish emigration, of which Liverpool is the outlet. The attention of the authorities of Liverpool has often been directed to the subject, but hitherto without result. As it is possible that hereafter the whole or a part of the American packet ships will put into Birkenhead instead of Liverpool, it has become a question with the Dock trustees of Birkenhead, the Dock and Warehouse Company, and the Birkenhead Improvement Commissioners, how the port may best accommodate the emigration trade. Among other subjects in connection with it, that of the establishment of a depôt under the surveillance of a Government officer, where the emigrant might be cheaply and comfortably lodged, and protected from the robbery of the man-catchers, has not escaped their notice. Mr. Arthur Holme, architect of Liverpool, has submitted to them a plan for this purpose, which has received the sanction of the Government, and only awaits the completion of the great dock, and the entry of a trade into the port to be carried into effect. It is proposed to erect the depôt on a site which commands a front to the Great Float, where emigrants may land or embark at any state of the tide, and whence a direct communication is already made from the street with the Chester and Birkenhead and other railways.

In the arrangement of the plans care has been taken that there shall be no restraint upon the emigrants beyond what is necessary for cleanliness, decency, and order. They will be allowed to purchase their own food, outfit, &c., either at the stores provided on the premises, or at any place they may think fit. They will also be provided with steam apparatus for cooking their own provisions and washing their own clothes, at a moderate rate.

The building, which is designed to accommodate 2,000 persons, will be divided into several departments:—

1. The Government offices, where the emigrants will be examined and receive the medical officer's certificate of health.

2. The main building, where the emigrants will be lodged, under the management of a general superintendent.

3. The stores and shops, where provisions, stores, and outfits will be sold, according to a fixed tariff of prices.

4. The luggage department, where there will be a disinfecting apparatus and stoves. In this department the property destined for the various emigrant ships will be properly classified.

5. The departure-office, under Government inspection.

The first, or Government department, it is proposed to erect in the centre fronting the main street. It will comprise a large hall or waiting-room, porters' room, the Government emigration-office in the centre, the medical officer's room, with dressing or examination rooms, ticket-office, yard, and plunge, hot and vapour baths. These offices will be all on the north side. A similar arrangement, with baths, female superintendent's room, dressing-rooms, &c., will be erected on the south.

As soon as the emigrants shall have procured the requisite tickets from the medical officer, they will be admitted to the general building, and their luggage will then be examined, and if need be disinfected, and placed in the stores, to await the appointed day for embarkation.

It is contemplated to have a small building in conjunction with this establishment, where emigrants may sleep and have their property taken care of, should they arrive at the depôt either before or after the hours appointed for the medical examination.

The second or main building will contain on the ground or principal floor a suite of kitchens where the emigrants may either cook for themselves or have their meat supplied at certain fixed rates. There will also be a scullery, washhouse, and drying closets, the whole being heated by steam, and open from morning till night.

The spacious dining, or day-room, may, in case it is thought desirable, be divided into sections to suit the various classes of emigrants.

It is proposed to reserve a floor immediately over the day-room for married couples and their children, the berths of which to be in two heights—the upper being used for the children. Space will be left at the head for adequate ventilation.

The upper floor in the centre will also be reserved for married couples; whilst one end wing will be set apart for unmarried females, and the other for unmarried males. There will be distinct staircases to these apartments from the corridor below.

The whole of the building will be of fire-proof construction, furnished with perforated pipes fixed to the ceilings, so that each floor may be thoroughly cleansed by flushing them with water.

The ventilation and warming to be similar to that employed in the prisons of modern construction, being heated by steam-pipes—the vitiated air being carried off by four large shafts over the staircases.

The gas for lighting is proposed to be fixed in the floor in cast-iron boxes, with strong glass on the lower side.

All the floors are proposed to be of the Staffordshire tiles.

Distinct airing yards will be arranged for males and females.

In the third division, spacious shops and other stores will be opened for the convenience of the emigrants. At these depôts will be provided and sold, at fixed rates, all that is really necessary for the present support or future wants of the emigrants. Printed lists to be furnished at the superintendent's office gratis, detailing what articles are absolutely necessary for any particular voyage.

In the fourth division there will be a department which will include a room for the reception of luggage, with disinfecting rooms and sectional stores. These last-mentioned will contain the property intended for each vessel, under charge of a proper officer, to admit the owners at stated times.

Fifth.—The departure is designed to be under the supervision of a Government officer, who will have an office on the quay, for examination and arranging all matters relating to the comforts of the emigrants on board ship.

By these arrangements the practice of stowing away would be prevented, and a systematic and orderly embarkation provided for.

Public gates and entrances are proposed under the care of the police (for whom lodges will be provided) to be open from morning to night, at regulated hours, for the free admission of the emigrants. Should a party of emigrants arrive after the hour of closing they would have access to the reception building proposed on the other side of the street.

The expense of the building, exclusive of the site, but including steam apparatus, baths, cooking and washing apparatus, gas fittings, beds, seats, tables, &c., has been found from actual estimate to be £24,700, affording accommodation for 2,000 emigrants at one time in the building.

It is believed that, under proper management, such an establishment as this would be self-supporting, and that it would not only confer a great advantage upon vast numbers of the poorer class of emigrants, hitherto the easy prey of the vilest class of the man-catching fraternity, but do honour to the philanthropy and public spirit of the town, and set an example worthy of imitation both in Liverpool and London.

Such is a brief history of Birkenhead in the past, and an anticipation of its future. No place in the world was ever planned with a greater regard for the comfort, health, welfare, and enjoyment of the labouring, and indeed all other classes of the people. It has passed through a trying ordeal, and there can be little doubt, to use the expression of its Liverpool friends, that "it will be a great place some day." At all events, it deserves to be so.

The Morning Chronicle, Saturday, October 12, 1850.

THE CONDITION OF LIVERPOOL.—The series of letters which have appeared in *The Morning Chronicle* on Liverpool has been brought to a close. The writer of these letters deserves the highest praise for the service which he has so well performed. He has investigated and accurately described the state and condition of the working classes, and has offered wise suggestions for the improvement of their morals and the increase of their physical comforts. He has, with elaborate care, shown the state of education in Liverpool; has written the history, boldly and truly, of the intolerant system pursued in our Corporate schools; has exposed to the world the triumph of local bigotry, and put us to shame among good men for our negligence and immorality. For it is negligent not to educate, and immoral to appropriate the funds of the whole municipality to the education of a portion of the people, leaving the most wretched without the blessings of instruction because they will not sacrifice what they believe to be true. Diving into the dark recesses where misery and crime strive to hide themselves, he has pourtrayed scenes of wretchedness which make the reader fear lest the moral and physical pestilence may have affected more than the places to which it is now confined. With care *The Chronicle* Commissioner has given all the details of our commercial affairs. Our docks, our warehouse system, the wonderful increase of our commerce, are all set forth. Praise is unsparingly given to good management, and censure is bestowed on defects. The writer has, on every subject affecting the morals and the prosperity of the people, given us a fearful, but a true picture of our actual state; one which our local rulers may study with advantage, and may not longer with impunity turn from, regardless of the evils it reveals. *The Morning Chronicle* has, by the labour of its Commissioner, directed public attention to the wants of the people; to their modes and habits of life; to the hard struggles of the labouring classes; and to the responsibility which is incurred by local governments, as well as by the general government, if they fail to remedy, as far as depends upon them—and that right speedily—the error and the wrong which have wrought so much suffering, sorrow, and crime. It is understood that the letters to which we refer are from the pen of Dr. Mackay, a writer not less distinguished for the possession of great talents than for the right use of them. We have often quoted his excellent poems in our columns, and it is with pleasure we now call attention to his works of another kind. We offer our humble tribute of praise to the spirit which has induced the editors (or proprietors) of *The Morning Chronicle* to set about so serious a labour as the examination and description of our great towns. They have done a great work for "those who labour," and rendered an eminent service to their country and to mankind. We trust other great towns will be submitted to the same fearless examination as that to which we have been subjected, and though the result may not be immediate, it must come, and must be beneficial to the people.—*Liverpool Mercury*.

Charles Mackay

Charles Mackay was born in Perth, Scotland, in 1814 and had a long and distinguished literary career. He maintained a lengthy association with newspapers, at one time holding the post of editor of *The Glasgow Argus*, and was employed by *The Morning Chronicle* for a number of years as sub-editor.

In his later Forty Years' Recollections he dedicates several interesting chapters to his work at *The Morning Chronicle*, including his "Labour and the Poor" assignments investigating the cities of Birmingham and Liverpool. He was a good friend of Angus B. Reach who also worked on the series and assisted Angus when he first moved to London to further his literary career.

He enjoyed considerable success with his book "Extraordinary Popular Delusions and the Madness of Crowds" but it was for his verse, particularly when put to music, that he became famous. He became known as "The People's Poet" and his songs were sung across the entire English-speaking world. Referring to his popular song "There's a good time coming, boys", *The Daily News* wrote in Charles Mackay's obituary in December 1889:—

> The verses were set to music by HENRY RUSSELL and sung everywhere. In the music halls, at concerts, at great public meetings, in private gatherings, and about the streets, the public were never tired of hearing and of singing of the good time coming. The original title of the song, as it was printed in our columns, was "Wait a little longer," and this was the refrain of every verse. From this country it spread to the United States and the colonies, and made its author's fame as widespread as the English tongue. Many of his other songs were set to music by the same composer, and enjoyed almost equal popularity. "Cheer boys, cheer" is still the song of the emigrant, and "Tubal Cain," which was perhaps the finest, was another of the most popular of his productions. These are the three pieces by which he will be chiefly remembered, though many other of his songs took the public fancy. From the publication of "There's a good time coming," down to the period of the American Civil War, Dr. MACKAY was justly regarded as the most eminent popular song writer of his time.

Shortly after his death, his friend Colin Rae Brown wrote the following article in *The Scots' Magazine*:—

The Scots' Magazine, Saturday, March 1, 1890.

CHARLES MACKAY.

BY COLIN RAE BROWN.

No one who conversed for any length of time with the late Dr. Mackay could remain long in ignorance of the poet's nationality. Not that it was observable in his accent, but because he never failed to introduce some reference to his fatherland into a conversation. Robert Browning said, that "Italy would be found graven on his heart:" in like manner, a similar remark might have been made regarding the subject of our sketch and "Scotland." Removed from Perth, his place of birth (in 1814), while yet an infant, and domiciled thereafter—till he entered on his thirtieth year—in England and Belgium, he did not again reside in Scotland till 1844; and then only for 3 years, during his editorship of the *Glasgow Argus* newspaper. While his education was being completed in Brussels, and even during the exciting period of the revolution in that country, the embryo-poet had begun to woo the Muse, who frequently led his young imagination over the moors, up the lone glens, and across the silvery lochs (only known to him through pen and pencil) of the ever-cherished mountain-land of his birth. Frequently he remarked to the writer, "the sight of a bit of wild continental heath would put my heart into a joyous, bounding flutter."

After terminating an engagement with an extensive commercial house in Brussels, during the continuance of which he had been more than a mere witness of the revolutionary struggles in Belgium, he came to London, and soon developed his latent literary instincts.

His first volume of verse, published in 1832, led to an engagement on the *Morning Chronicle*. While occupied in the sub-editorial department of that journal, he issued another poetical *brochure*, entitled "The Hope of the World." In 1844 he became (as before stated) editor of the *Glasgow Argus*, and was present at the Festival in honour of the "Sons of Burns" which took place during that year at the "Brig o' Doon." On this occasion he made the acquaintance of Professor Wilson and other eminent Scotsmen; but "Christopher North" seems to have overshadowed all the others, mentally as well as physically. He at once set the genial Professor down as "the noblest-looking and most Scottish of all the Scotsmen he had yet met!"—realising to the fullest extent two of the finest lines good old Andrew Park ever wrote. They were penned in reference to Fillan's marble bust of Wilson (which was produced for and placed in the Paisley Reading Room) and read as follows:—

> "How like a Lion in quiescent might
> The noble-souled old Christopher appears!"

The "leaders" in the *Argus* soon gave ample evidence of the writer's strong grasp of current politics. In them he developed a strong sympathy with the proposed Repeal of the Corn Laws, and advocated the endowment and the "broadening" of our Educational institutions. In conjunction with the tale of Mr. James McClelland, then a well-known public man of great energy, the new editor of the *Argus* held very advanced views in favour of the "Secular System." And though neither of them was destined to see their "views" carried out to the full extent of their fervid aspirations, their efforts greatly accelerated the early steps of the National Education Movement.

Leaving Glasgow in 1847, Mr. Mackay again repaired to London, and became connected with the *Illustrated News*. Ultimately, he took sole charge of the literary department of this important journal, and, while so engaged, his trenchant and incisive "leaders" on social and political topics arrested the attention of John Bright, Charles Gilpin, and other prominent Liberals. Through the connection thus formed, he eventually became a member of the Reform Club; and, till within a few years of his death, he was one of the most constant and familiar *habitués* of its precincts. He soon made his mark there—John Bright becoming not only his "fast friend," but also his colleague in several important movements. This alliance remained unbroken up to the breaking out of the great Civil War in the United States, when the subject of our sketch, after a lengthened consultation with the management of the *Times*, sailed for New York to become the representative of that Journal during the continuance of hostilities. Events moved very rapidly towards the close of this negotiation; so much so, that he had barely time to make the necessary domestic arrangements for a seemingly prolonged absence, and had to leave England without being able to pay farewell visits of any kind. Thus, while the "Man of letters" sailed for his distant post, there to espouse the cause of the South (if at all likely to prove the "winning horse"), the "Man of speech and action" remained at home to advocate (and that with no uncertain sound) the claim of the North for instant Abolition and an unbroken Union of all the States. And so their lives became divided ever after: they never exchanged words of speech again. This was Dr. Mackay's second trip across the Atlantic. During a part of 1857 and 1858, he had visited the United States and Canada in a two-fold capacity. First, as Mr. Sala and Sir Edwin Arnold have more recently done, to assist his paper with a series of bright, impressionable letters bearing on the aspects of the country and the people; and, in the second place, to deliver courses of lectures on "Poetry and Song." With the results of that visit he had been immensely pleased, and looked forward to the renewing of many pleasant friendships on the other side of the "herring-pond."

After the close of the American War, and a second tour through Canada, Dr. Mackay again returned to Great Britain—proceeding almost directly to the Scottish Highlands, with the view of some "recuperation" to his system, on which there had been a severe strain during the lengthened continuation of the fratricidal conflict in the States. Ultimately, he fixed on Oban for a stay of a few months. He and the members of his family were soon deeply enamoured of the "Key of the Highlands" and its surroundings. David Hutcheson, the never-to-be-forgotten pioneer of the Royal Route, became one of his most intimate associates, and they often "crooned" ancient and modern verse together, over a glass of steaming "toddy." (By the way, the enterprising owner of the famed "Iona" and "Columba" left some really excellent manuscript poetry behind him—What has come of it?)

One afternoon, while Dr. and Mrs. Mackay were taking a leisurely stroll to the west of the village, they observed a portly pedestrian approaching them. Without waiting for his coming up, and with no word of explanation to his companion, "the Doctor," as Mrs. Mackay afterwards remarked, "flew off like a rocket towards the stout gentleman." Being more than familiar with the *tout ensemble* and gait of his whilom friend, the poet had at once recognised, and hurried off to cordially greet—John Bright. But, alas! he met with a bitter and somewhat humiliating disappointment. To his cheery "Hallo! Bright! who'd have thought of meeting you in the heart of the Highlands?" the sturdy "pedestrian" not only turned a deaf ear, but also wheeled himself suddenly round, and so contemptuously ignored and rejected the proferred hand of his former friend. No feelings of "auld acquaintance" were allowed to step in before that which the stern "Tribune" deemed "principle." Dr. Mackay was cut to the quick. For many days he could not recover his equanimity or feel at ease. He wrote to a friend at the *Reform* in search of an explanation, and when the reply came his "wonderment" was soon at an end. Mr. Bright had not only denounced the *Times* openly enough during the continuance of the War, but had still more bitterly denounced what he termed the "hireling apostacy" of their "chief correspondent." The estrangement became permanent: they never exchanged words from that day forth;

and when they afterwards met in the celebrated Pall Mall Liberal haunt, it was always as "strangers."

Last year, when both had become confirmed invalids and developed strong Unionist principles, Dr. Mackay wrote to One Ash, pointing out that now at last, and on the brink of the grave, they had *one* bond in common regarding which there was *no misunderstanding*—"Could not they again shake hands, if only by letter?" The reply came by an early post. It was brief, emphatic, and wholly satisfactory. For both the sun of life was surely and swiftly setting—and it did not go down in wrath. The outcome of this correspondence proved a great consolation to Dr. Mackay, and up to the time of his death he frequently alluded to it in touching language.

The "misunderstanding" alluded to in Dr. Mackay's letter had reference to *his own* decided views on the Slavery question. He had always been an advocate of *gradual* Abolition. But neither in regard to this, or to Home politics, could he make up his mind to agree with radical or violent changes in the existing order of things.

Mr. Bright had been but one of a great many other friends of Dr. Mackay who gave him the credit of shaping the *Times* "policy" at the outset and throughout the course of the disastrous Civil War in America; but the following letter from the then manager of the *Times*, found amongst Dr. Mackay's papers, affords conclusive evidence of the strong position taken up at Printing House Square in favour of the South: more especially so in the concluding paragraph, which we have caused to be put in *italics*:—

"*Times* Office,
"September 22, 1862.

"My Dear Sir,—The only effect your slight illness seems to have had is to make your pen flow, if possible, more freely than ever; and a recumbent position appears to be favourable to vigorous writing. You are rightly informed that Mr. Lawley corresponds with us direct. There has been no stoppage of this letter hitherto, nor do I anticipate any; but he will not interfere with you, nor will the interest of his letters ever exceed that of yours. You must fall very far below your present mark before you cease to occupy the first place among our correspondents. Everyone expects to hear ere long that Baltimore is in the hands of the Confederates. The land communication thus cut off between New York and Washington, will the Government remain in the capital or seek refuge in New York? Our military men say that the Confederates will not attempt Washington, the policy being to keep a large force of the Federals idle around it. *All the little sympathy that once existed for the North has disappeared.*—

Very truly yours,
"MOWBRAY MORRIS.

"Charles Mackay, Esq., New York."

Returning once more to England, after a most enjoyable stay (if we except the "Bright episode") at Oban, to which he and his family bade adieu with great regret, Dr. Mackay took a lease of what he termed his "Poet's 'Pleasaunce'" at the foot of Boxhill, close to the village of Dorking in Surrey. George Meredith, the novelist, was his near neighbour, on the slope of the hill; and the celebrated hostelrie on the roadside to which Nelson and Lady Hamilton repaired on the eve of the hero's departure for his "last fight," was within a few minutes' walk of the poet's charmingly situated home.

But with all its beauteous surroundings, the "Pleasaunce" had to give way to the heart-cherished land of his infancy; and, year after year, up till about 1883, Dr. Mackay and his wife and daughter spent the greater part of summer and autumn at Oban. Here it was that he met and became intimately acquainted with Professor Blackie; and through lengthened conversations with him anent the "Gaelic," Dr. Mackay resolved to study and acquire a thorough knowledge of that intricate language. That he did so successfully is sufficiently well established by his "Gaelic Etymology of the English Language," a portly volume of over 600 double-column pages, published in 1877, and now equally scarce and valuable in the book-market. It is the versatile author's *magnum opus* in prose.

It is not our intention to enter into a detailed description of Dr. Mackay's prose works,—they are all equally able and recondite. His massive head was well stored with useful knowledge of every kind. Douglas Jerrold used to call it his "Lexicon." "Whenever," he said, "I am at a loss for the meaning or spelling of a word, or in search of a date, reference, or information regarding things terrestrial or celestial, I apply—if it be near me—to Mackay's 'Lexicon.'"

However, it is chiefly as a Poet, the designation he most coveted, and that which he has so nobly won, both on this and on the other side of the Atlantic, and in France and Germany (many of his poems having been translated in both countries and freely sold), that we now mean to briefly treat of Charles Mackay. He always laid it down as gospel, that a poet, to be truly such, should aim at more than merely "delighting" his readers. "The true poet," he affirmed, "must likewise be a Preacher of Natural Religion, and his utterances should have no uncertain sound."

The writer has frequently heard Thomas de Quincey speak highly of several of Dr. Mackay's poems—more especially of his social lyrics. He considered his "English" as amongst the "purest, most apt and direct" which was to be met with in modern poetry. And John Bright in one of his speeches (delivered at Bradford during Dr. Mackay's editorship of the *Illustrated London News*) described a certain "leader" as "a literary pearl beyond price." No other men of the time were better able to speak with authority on such a matter. The one as an essayist, and the other as an orator, occupied, and still occupy, the first rank as masters of pure, trenchant, and epigrammatic English. The joint verdict of these distinguished judges was but an act of simple justice. The force and directness of Charles Mackay's versified compositions are models of style and strength combined. In perusing his works— prose or verse, the latter more especially—the reader never comes in contact with weak or superfluous words. None are wasted; there is no "padding," no "filling out," but always the right word (with the weightiest meaning) in the right place. And yet this caused no restraint of the author's ever vivid and fruitful imagination.

The following extract from "The Dance of the Trees," furnishes us with an exquisite specimen of what the author termed "picturesque idealization":—

> " And thou, dear Hawthorn, sweetest sweet,
>   The beautiful, the tender,
>   Bright with the fondling of the sun,
>   And prankt in bridal splendour;
>   Come with thy sisters, full of bloom,
>   And all thy bridesmaids merry—
>   Acacia, Chestnut, Lilac fair,
>   The Apple, and the Cherry.
>
>   Strike up the music! Lo! it sounds!
>   The expectant woodlands listen:
>   They move their branches to the sky,
>   And all their dew-drops glisten.

> They move, they start, they thrill, they dance,
> They shake their boughs with pleasure;
> And flutter all their gay green leaves
> Obedient to the measure.
> They choose their partners—Oak and Beech
> Pair off, a stately couple,
> And Larch to Willow makes his bough,
> Th' unbending to the supple."

Some twenty joyous life and joy-giving verses such as these comprise the grand picturesque Rhapsody, making the old young, and the young younger.

There is no space at our command wherein to chronicle, however briefly, a thousandth part of the "gems" which go to make up the more than 600 closely-printed pages comprised in Messrs. Warne & Co's. latest cheap edition of Dr. Mackay's poetical works. But we cannot refrain from reminding the reader of the grand resonance and "ringing" power which, characteristically enough, are exhibited in his world-famed "Tubal Cain":—

> "Old Tubal Cain was a man of might
> In the days when earth was young,
> By the fierce red light of his furnace bright
> The strokes of his hammer rung.
> And he lifted high his brawny hand
> On the Iron glowing clear,
> Till the sparks rushed out in scarlet showers
> As he fashioned the Sword and Spear.
> And he sang:—'Hurrah for my handiwork!
> Hurrah for the Spear and Sword!
> Hurrah for the hand that shall wield them well,
> For he shall be King and Lord!'"

How the blood glows and tingles as we inwardly revel amongst the glorious "numbers" of this peerless lyric!

Who has not read, or heard sung, the soul-melting song of European celebrity entitled, "Oh! Ye Tears"? Yet thousands of those who are familiar with both words and music do not know that the author of the heart-thrilling verses was the aged poet we laid to rest at Kensal Green a few weeks ago. As a matter of fact, the composers of the music are better known (in the musical world especially) than the writer of the poetry. We give a stanza or two of this celebrated song, arranged by Sir Henry Bishop and Franz Abt:—

> " O! Ye tears! O! Ye tears! I am thankful that ye run,
>   Though ye trickle in the darkness, ye shall glitter in the sun:
>   The rainbow cannot shine if the rain refuse to fall,
>   And the eyes that cannot weep are the saddest eyes of all.
>
> O! Ye tears! O! Ye tears! till I felt you on my cheek,
>   I was selfish in my sorrow—I was stubborn, I was weak:
>   Ye have given me strength to conquer! and I stand erect and
>   free,
>   And know that I am human by the light of Sympathy."

Few social lyrics have ever commanded so much public interest and attention as our author's "Souls of the Children." It was put forth as "a plea for Free and Universal Education," and Prince Albert, at his own expense, ordered it to be sown "broadcast" over the Kingdom. If space permitted, never could space be better occupied than by its insertion as a whole. Failing that we give an example by quoting the 1st, 3rd, and 4th stanzas. It consists of 12 such:—

> " Who bids for the little children—
>   Body and soul and brain?
> Who bids for the little children—
>   Young, and without a stain?
> Will no one bid, said England,
>   For their souls so pure and white,
> And fit for all good or evil
>   The World on their page may write?"
>   * * * * * * *
> " I bid, said Beggary, howling,
>   I bid for them, one and all!
>   I'll teach them a thousand lessons—
>   To lie, to skulk, to crawl!
>   They shall sleep in my lair, like maggots,
>   They shall rot in the fair sunshine,
>   And if they serve my purpose
>   I hope they'll answer thine?

(This last line is an allusion to a previous "bid" by "Pest and Famine.")

" And I'll bid higher and higher,
  Said Crime with fiendish grin,
  For I love to lead the Children
  Through the pleasant paths of Sin!
  They shall swarm on the streets to pilfer,
  They shall plague the broad highway—
  Till they grow too old for Pity,
  And ripe for the Law to slay!"

Fletcher of Saltoun's doctrine, that the making of a Nation's songs was of more importance than the framing of its laws, found ready acceptance at the hands of Charles Mackay. "A Man's a Man for a' that," he remarked, not once, but a hundred times, "would of itself have entitled Burns to a place on the very pinnacle of Parnassus. I would rather be the author of that than of fifty learned volumes of mythical and transcendental verse—or worse." And he well endorsed this declaration by his still (and long-to-be) popular "Cheer Boys, Cheer!" and still more emphatically by his world-esteemed and world-sung "Psalm" (as he termed it), "There's a good Time Coming, Boys." These are the "silver songs" that go "down the ringing grooves of change" continually—and why? Because they find an echoing response in the big heart of our Common Humanity.

This estimate of the author's powers is more than endorsed by Charles Kingsley's opinion in "Alton Locke":—"Which," he says, "of Charles Mackay's lyrics can compare for a moment with the Æschylean grandeur, the terrible rhythmic lilt of his 'Cholera Chant'?"

"Dense on the stream the vapours lay,
  Thick as wool on the cold highway;
  Spungy and dim each lonely lamp
  Shone o'er the streets so dull and damp;
  The moonbeams could not pierce the cloud
  That swathed the city like a shroud;
  There stood three shapes on the bridge alone,
  Three figures by the coping-stone;
  Gaunt and tall and undefined,
  Spectres built of mist and wind.
       * * * * * *

I see his footmarks east and west—
I hear his tread in the silence fall—
He shall not sleep, he shall not rest—
He comes to aid us one and all.
Were men as wise as men might be,
They would not work for you, for me,
For him that cometh over the sea;
But they will not hear the warning voice:
The Cholera comes,—Rejoice! rejoice!
He shall be lord of the swarming town!
And mow them down, and mow them down!"

One more extract and we have done with such. It first appeared
in the author's "Interludes and Undertones" (1884), and exhibits a certain vein of atrabilarious humour which he credited Douglas Jerrold
with fostering. It is entitled "The Old Poet's last Resource":—

"Stand in the corner, thou sturdy old broomstick,
  Perhaps I shall need thee some cold winter day:
  Perhaps my support thou wilt be and my doom-stick
  When maimed and defeated in Life's cruel fray.
  My songs and my books may not yield me a penny,
  But while thou are mine, I've a prop and a trust:
  My humblest of friends, the survivor of many,
  I look to thee yet to procure me a crust!
       * * * * * *

This quaint effusion ends as follows:—

> " Sweeping pays better than wisdom or letters,
> 	So up with the Broomstick and down with the Song!"

Our author's poem, "At the Grave of Burns" has been so often read at Burns' Anniversary Gatherings at home and abroad, and so often quoted, that we need but to allude thereto *en passant,* and merely to introduce mention of his recently composed and as yet unpublished fancy, "At the Cradle of Burns." The writer had it read over to him by its author only a few weeks ago, and still retains much of the matter and measure in his memory. An angel at either side of the poet's "rocking-house," predicts, in turn, the ups and downs of the man-to-be, and the tempting subject is as exquisitely treated as it is sure to be highly appreciated.

The *very last* product of Dr. Mackay's brain and pen was a lyric after the manner of Burns' "My wife's a winsome wee thing," but is in no way indebted to that well-known ditty for its mode of treatment or subject. It was written on the evening of Sunday, the 22d December last, after his family had retired to rest. This touching Poem (printed in *Blackwood's Magazine* for February) was found on Monday morning (when he lay unconscious) between the leaves of a recently purchased copy of the works of Burns which Professor Wilson edited for Blackie & Son (1859), the concluding couplet reading as follows:—

> " And lead my happy soul to heav'n
> 	Rejoicing in her love."

Ere the shadows of Christmas Eve had fallen the Poet of the People had gone behind the Veil.

A portrait in oil by Sir Daniel Macnee, a marble bust by Patric Part, and a medallion in marble by Alexander Munro (all life-size) are amongst the few but choice "Art treasures" which the poet has bequeathed to his talented daughter, Miss Minnie Mackay, better known in the literary world as "Marie Corelli," and the authoress of "A Romance of Two Worlds," "Vendetta," &c. The venerable author also left behind him a considerable amount of valuable matter in prose and verse, which will in due time be given to the world.

As a Poet, he wrote mainly for the "crowd" and the "people," and in the hearts of the many—at home and abroad—the works and the name of Charles Mackay will long be heritages of which his countrymen (and "all men") may well be proud.

<h1 style="text-align:center">Index</h1>

Titles Available in the Series

LABOUR AND THE POOR

Volumes I to IV: **The Metropolitan Districts**
Henry Mayhew

ISBN 978-1-913515-11-9, 978-1-913515-12-6, 978-1-913515-13-3, 978-1-913515-14-0

Volume V: **The Manufacturing Districts**
Angus B. Reach

ISBN 978-1-913515-15-7

Volumes VI & VII: **The Rural Districts**
Alexander Mackay & Shirley Brooks

ISBN 978-1-913515-16-4, 978-1-913515-17-1

Volume VIII: **Wales**
Special Correspondent

ISBN 978-1-913515-18-8

Volume IX: **Birmingham**
Charles Mackay

ISBN 978-1-913515-19-5

Volume X: **Liverpool**
Charles Mackay

ISBN 978-1-913515-20-1

For information on these and other titles available please visit:

DittoBooks.co.uk